OXFORD WORLD'S CLASSICS · 32014

THE OXFORD SHAKESPEARE

General Editor · Stanley Wells

The Oxford Shakespeare offers new and authoritative editions of Shakespeare's plays in which the early printings have been scrupulously re-examined and interpreted. An introductory essay provides all relevant background information together with an appraisal of critical views and of the play's effects in performance. The detailed commentaries pay particular attention to language and staging. Reprints of sources, music for songs, genealogical tables, maps, etc. are included where necessary; many of the volumes are illustrated, and all contain an index.

MICHAEL TAYLOR, the editor of *Henry VI, Part One* in the Oxford Shakespeare, is former Professor of English at the University of New Brunswick.

THE OXFORD SHAKESPEARE

Currently available in paperback

The rest of the plays are forthcoming

OXFORD WORLD'S CLASSICS

WILLIAM SHAKESPEARE

Henry VI, Part One

Edited by
MICHAEL TAYLOR

OXFORD
UNIVERSITY PRESS

OXFORD
UNIVERSITY PRESS

Great Clarendon Street, Oxford OX2 6DP

Oxford University Press is a department of the University of Oxford.
It furthers the University's objective of excellence in research, scholarship,
and education by publishing worldwide in

Oxford New York

Auckland Bangkok Buenos Aires Cape Town Chennai
Dar es Salaam Delhi Hong Kong Istanbul Karachi Kolkata
Kuala Lumpur Madrid Melbourne Mexico City Mumbai Nairobi
São Paulo Shanghai Taipei Tokyo Toronto

Oxford is a registered trade mark of Oxford University Press
in the UK and in certain other countries

Published in the United States
by Oxford University Press Inc., New York

First published 2003
First published as an Oxford World's Classics paperback 2004

British Library Cataloguing in Publication Data

Data available

Library of Congress Cataloging in Publication Data

Data available

ISBN 0–19–818392–5 (hbk.)
ISBN 0–19–280471–5 (pbk.)

1 3 5 7 9 10 8 6 4 2

Typeset by SNP Best-set Typesetter Ltd., Hong Kong
Printed in Spain by
Book Print S.L., Barcelona

ACKNOWLEDGEMENTS

THE greatest boon to any editor of a work by Shakespeare is the lively if ghostly presence of his predecessors, and so I would like to acknowledge above all the stimulating company of previous editors of *1 Henry VI*, especially John Dover Wilson, Andrew S. Cairncross, Michael Hattaway, and Edward Burns. I'd like to thank Roger Warren for information about Edward Hall's production with the Propeller company at the Watermill Theatre, Newbury ('Rose Rage') and Stanley Wells for numerous benefits and kindnesses. At Oxford Frances Whistler was a pleasure to work with, and I owe a debt to Christine Buckley for saving me from many errors. Any that may remain are nothing if not my own.

MICHAEL TAYLOR

For
Stanley Wells

CONTENTS

LIST OF ILLUSTRATIONS

INTRODUCTION

1592

1592 begins the business of Shakespeare criticism. Anticipating centuries of polemic, this year records the opening salvoes from Shakespeare's denigrators and supporters, inspired, appropriately enough, by a series of plays that march to fife and kettledrum. The three parts of *Henry VI* exploited the Rose's wide and shallow stage for an often bewildering series of athletic battle sequences: the plays are full of alarums, excursions, hand-to-hand combat, and explosions, phenomena that later critics have castigated as fodder for the groundlings.[1] But for Shakespeare's first grateful acknowledger,[2] Thomas Nashe, the plays are inspiring, and his liberal praise of *1 Henry VI*, in particular, in his satirical pamphlet, *Piers Penniless his Supplication to the Devil*, entered in the Stationers' Register on 8 August 1592, constitutes the first glowing review of a Shakespeare production. For Nashe the clashes of arms that make up the action of so much of *1 Henry VI* (and even more of *The True Tragedy of Richard Duke of York* (*3 Henry VI*), though this play is not mentioned by him)[3] rekindle the glory of the heroic past to shame and discountenance the puerility of an insipid present. Like so many later critics, then, Nashe appropriates Shakespeare ideologically, using him in 1592 in his battle against what he conceives to

[1] In *The Elizabethan Stage*, E. K. Chambers notes that the company that presented *1 Henry VI* at the Rose in 1592, Lord Strange's Men, had a history of 'feats of activity and tumbling' (4 vols., 1965 Oxford, 1923; repr.; ii. 119). Some critics, such as Michael Goldman, find the athleticism clarifying: 'the sweep of athletic bodies across the stage is used in *1 Henry VI* not only to provide an exciting spectacle but to focus and clarify, to render dramatic, the entire unwieldy chronicle' (*The Energies of Drama* (Princeton, 1972), 161).

[2] Nashe does not, however, mention Shakespeare's name in his encomium, nor the name of any other author. Whoever wrote the play is subsidiary to character and actor, as far as Nashe is concerned, and this omission is piquant if we accept the likelihood of Nashe as one of Shakespeare's collaborators in this play (see p. 12 n. 1).

[3] The emphasis in this third play has, however, shifted considerably. Michael Hattaway in his Cambridge edition (1990) notes: 'In *Part III* we witness the final degradation of chivalry: this play contains some of the most horrific scenes in the canon as England's warlords sacrifice honour to a remorseless ethic of revenge' (p. ix).

be the Puritan obsession with gain-getting, the ambition of the 'clubfisted usurer' (i. 212). We can imagine how Hamlet (and Shakespeare) might have approved of Nashe's justification of the presentation of Shakespeare's early history plays on the stage as 'a rare exercise of virtue' providing a sharp reproof 'to these degenerate effeminate days of ours' (i. 212). Like Hamlet and most other defenders of stage plays at this time, Nashe is the supreme moralizer: plays, he argues, 'show the ill success of treason, the fall of hasty climbers, the wretched end of usurpers, the misery of civil dissension, and how just God is evermore in punishing of murder' (i. 213). Nashe praises the plays for the way that in them 'our forefathers' valiant acts (that have lain long buried in rusty brass and worm-eaten books) are revived' (i. 212). Although 'valiant acts' need not be restricted in meaning to moments of physical action, Nashe's contrast of them with their mere recording in 'worm-eaten books', and his later panegyric on the death of Talbot, establish him as one of the first writers on the theatre to respond enthusiastically to the power of physical representation on the stage. He is, then, in 1592, in his responses to the plays, both a proto-literary critic and a theatre critic.

The fact that Nashe must have had Shakespeare's plays largely in mind in his justification of plays in general as rare exercises of virtue is confirmed by his remarks on *I Henry VI*:

How would it have joyed brave Talbot (the terror of the French) to think that after he had lain two hundred years in his tomb, he should triumph again on the stage, and have his bones new embalmed with the tears of ten thousand spectators at least (at several times) who in the tragedian that represents his person, imagine they behold him fresh bleeding.[1]

Although some excessively cautious commentators have suggested that Nashe may be referring to some other unknown, non-Shakespearian play starring Talbot, it is not very likely. Nashe's emphasis on the popularity of the play in 1592 wherein Talbot's bones have been 'new embalmed with the tears of ten thousand spectators at least (at several times)' (i. 212) squares with the informa-

---

[1] In the theatre season that began on 19 February 1592 Nashe could have seen twenty-three plays at the Rose, among them Marlowe's *Jew of Malta*, Robert Greene's *Orlando Furioso* and *Friar Bacon and Friar Bungay*, Robert Greene and Thomas Lodge's *A Looking Glass for London*, and Thomas Kyd's *Spanish Tragedy*. None of these (nor any of the others) 'is borrowed out of our English Chronicles' (Nashe, i. 212) as is Shakespeare's first sequence of history plays.

tion we find in the account book, rather misleadingly called *Diary*, of the theatre manager Philip Henslowe.[1] On 3 March 1592 Henslowe recorded the box-office takings of 3 pounds 16 shillings and 8 pence for a performance at the Rose playhouse of 'harey the vj', a 'ne' (i.e. new) play as Henslowe notes in the margin, put on by Lord Strange's Men, a return that makes it almost as profitable as Henslowe's most profitable play, *The Wise Man of Westchester*.[2] The bare bones of Henslowe's cryptic entry have been gnawed on for centuries. Much debate has centered on the meaning of 'ne'. Does it mean an entirely new play written out of whole cloth? Or is it one that has been newly revived, perhaps, or one newly licensed by the Master of the Revels? Or even one that is new to London? Most commentators now take 'ne' at face value as meaning, simply, 'new'. Which of the *Henry VIs*, though, is new? Since 'harey the vj' is unqualified, is Henslowe referring to all three parts? If he is referring to only one of them, which one? Again, most commentators now accept the argument that Henslowe is referring to *Henry VI, Part One*.[3] So the consensus of critical opinion now accepts the proposition that Henslowe's '*harey the vj*' is Shakespeare's *Henry VI, Part One* and that by 'ne' Henslowe meant 'new'. (What we may mean by 'Shakespeare's' here is something I shall return to shortly.)

Thomas Nashe's positive review of one of Shakespeare's earliest plays[4] includes a celebration of the 'tragedian that represents' Talbot's person, namely the actor who played him. Nashe thus

---

[1] Nashe's account not only squares with information found in Henslowe's *Diary* about 1 *Henry VI* but the likelihood that he is referring to Shakespeare's play is supported by a number of expressions and images found in the text of another of his pamphlets, *The Terrors of the Night* (1593), which echo lines from the play (and may be, indirectly, an indication that he had a hand in the writing of Part One).

[2] Noted in Andrew Gurr's *Playgoing in Shakespeare's London* (Cambridge, 1987), 136. In his edition of 1 *Henry VI* (2000) Edward Burns tells us that the play outgrossed the other hits of the 1592 season, Robert Greene's *Friar Bacon and Friar Bungay*, Marlowe's *The Jew of Malta*, and Kyd's *The Spanish Tragedy*.

[3] In 'Shakespeare and Others: The Authorship of *Henry the Sixth, Part One*', *Medieval and Renaissance Drama in England*, 7 (1995), 145–205, Gary Taylor points out that Henslowe always identified a 'second part' but did not do so when dealing with a first, simply using the general title: thus 'Harey the vj could not be a *Part Two* or a *Part Three*, but could easily be a *Part One*' (152).

[4] The chronology of Shakespeare's early plays is smothered in surmise. Most commentators agree that Shakespeare's first plays were not seen on the stage until 1590–1 (though this is debatable). What he was doing between 1585 and 1590 has been the cause of much throwing about of brains.

inaugurates a line of theatre criticism in which the actor often bulks as large as, and in later times sometimes larger than, the character he or she is playing. We have here the beginnings of the worship of the celebrity actor that has been taken to such deplorable extremes in the twentieth century.[1] In 1592, although only 26, the actor most likely to have played Talbot was Edward Alleyn, who began his career with the Lord Admiral's Men in the 1580s and, when they disbanded in 1588, moved over to Lord Strange's Men. He continued to present himself as a 'servant to the Lord Admiral' perhaps expecting Lord Strange's Men to disband at some future time, which they obligingly did in 1594, allowing Alleyn to organize a new Admiral's Company which moved into the Rose again in May. A larger-than-life character—as Shakespearian actors so often are —he seems the ideal candidate for Nashe's admiration.[2] In the 1590s, besides Talbot, he made famous the roles of Orlando in Robert Greene's *Orlando Furioso*, Marlowe's Tamburlaine, Dr Faustus, and Barabas in *The Jew of Malta*, Muly Mahomet in George Peele's *The Battle of Alcazar*, and Tamar in the anonymous *Tamar Cham*. As S. P. Cerasano wryly observes, Alleyn 'was identified with egomaniacal fallen angels' (11), an identification that seems to have infected his own progress through life. Whether or not it is legitimate to think of Talbot in these terms is something to be taken up later. In 1592, after nine months at the Rose, Alleyn consolidated his position by marrying Henslowe's stepdaughter, but, according to Carol Chillington Rutter, 'perhaps stamped his personality too forcefully on Lord Strange's Men: to a man, the sharers named in the 1593 license abandoned him'.[3]

In 1592 another egomaniacal fallen angel, Robert Greene, writer of prose romances, pamphlets, and, among other plays, the romantic comedies *James IV* (*c*.1590–1), *Friar Bacon and Friar Bungay* (*c*.1589–92), and *Orlando Furioso* (1594), composed the first vituperative attack (and the last in Shakespeare's lifetime) on

[1] For a somewhat frenzied attack on this modern phenomenon, the reader should consult Martin Buzacott's *The Death of the Actor: Shakespeare on Page and Stage* (London and New York, 1991).

[2] A succinct account of his life can be found in S. P. Cerasano's 'Edward Alleyn: 1566–1626', in *Edward Alleyn. Elizabethan Actor, Jacobean Gentleman*, ed. Aileen Reid and Robert Maniura (1994), 11–31.

[3] Carol Chillington Rutter, ed., *Documents of the Rose Playhouse* (Manchester, 1984), 25.

Shakespeare as writer and actor.[1] This piece of invective, the dark obverse of Nashe's admiration, anticipates a still flourishing strain of carping dismissal in Shakespeare criticism that has sullied the reputations of critics such as John Dryden, Matthew Arnold, Shaw, and Tolstoy, all of them, like Robert Greene, writers themselves and hence candidates for the rancid mental disturbance we have come to know as the anxiety of influence.[2] In September 1592, shortly after his death, Robert Greene's pamphlet *Greene's Groatsworth of Wit . . . Written before his death and published at his dying request* was printed. In it appears his own rancid attack on Shakespeare, a bizarre and sour note on which to leave the world, in which he quotes from the third part of *Henry VI*:

trust them not; for there is an upstart Crow, beautified with our feathers, that with his *Tiger's heart wrapped in a Player's hide*, supposes he is as well able to bombast out a blank verse as the best of you: and being an absolute *Johannes fac totum* [Jack of all trades], is in his own conceit the only Shake-scene in a country. (45)[3]

The short shrift given to Alleyn by Lord Strange's Men in 1593 and Greene's volatility and instability displayed throughout his *Groatsworth of Wit* underscore the fragility, volatility, and instability of the theatrical enterprise itself in the London of the 1590s. Companies, theatres, and actors come and go with remarkable

[1] Ignoring Thomas Nashe's piece from the previous month, David Riggs argues that 'When Robert Greene warned his old acquaintances among the play-wrights to beware of an "upstart crow, beautified with our feathers," he launched the enterprise of Shakespeare criticism . . .' (*Shakespeare's Heroical Histories: Henry VI and Its Literary Tradition* (Cambridge, Mass., 1971), 1).

[2] Harold Bloom's phrase 'the anxiety of influence' has often been applied to the mutual stimulation, especially in Shakespeare's early career, of Marlowe and Shakespeare. See, for example, Charles R. Forker, 'Marlowe's *Edward II* and its Shakespearean Relatives: the Emergence of a Genre', in *Shakespeare's English Histories: a Quest for Form and Genre*, ed. John Velz (Binghamton, New York, 1996), 55–90; 61. Park Honan describes Greene's attack on Shakespeare as 'virtually a rape of Shakespeare, or an insinuating attack on not only his plays but his person, and had the force of seeming to be a candid statement by a dying man' (158–9).

[3] His '*Tiger's heart wrapped in a Player's hide*' is an adaptation of York's lines attacking Queen Margaret: 'O tiger's heart wrapped in a woman's hide!' (*True Tragedy* 1.4.138). Most commentators believe the '*Johannes fac totum*' to be Shakespeare, the only Shake-scene of a country. Greene's attack is violently self-flagellating: 'Black is the remembrance of my black works, blacker than night, blacker than death, blacker than hell' (41).

celerity.[1] The confused paucity of the facts lends itself to the hobgoblin of mercurial interpretation. Andrew Gurr makes his own contribution to scholarly evanescence in arguing against the up-to-then securely entrenched belief that in the early 1590s companies amalgamated, but he admits that

[s]orting out the evidence of playing companies and their memberships in the changeable years around 1591–2 is a tortuous exercise in what might be called the kaleidoscopic principle. Shake the fragments of evidence and you make one pattern, then shake them up again and you find a different one.[2]

Even the physical structures of the theatres themselves seem to be baseless fabrics subject to a variety of depredations—fire, government fiat, plague, riot. Or they might melt into thin air as the Theatre did in 1598, torn down by James Burbage's sons after disagreements with their landlord, Giles Allen, and spirited across the river to Bankside to be reconstituted as the great Globe itself, and soon to become the most famous playhouse in London.

More than any of the other years in the 1590s, 1592 and 1593 were brittle ones for the life of the theatre in London (not to mention the lives of London's citizens). By 1594 the theatrical scene had become more stable. In this year the Rose and the Theatre became the two allowed playhouses in London by order of the Privy Council, part of what Andrew Gurr calls the 'duopolizing deal' (*Playing Companies*, 66) which established the Admiral's and Lord Chamberlain's companies as the most privileged ones, so that between 1594 and 1600 no other company played at court. The violence endemic to the international scene not only found expression on the theatres' stages but in the throngs that attended on them. Scott McMillin picks out an important day in 1592:

A riot of apprentices actually broke out on June 11, and its assembly point was a play in Southwark. The immediate cause of the riot was offensive behaviour by the police—the Knight Marshall's men broke in upon the family of a feltmonger's servant with daggers drawn and carted

---

[1] A case in point is the comet-like career of Pembroke's Men which had come into existence probably in early 1592 (see Mary Edmond's 'Pembroke's Men', *Review of English Studies*, 25 (1974), 129–36) and had fizzled out by the following year.

[2] 'The Chimera of Amalgamation', *Theatre Research International*, 18 (1993), 85–93; 88. See also Gurr's *The Shakespearian Playing Companies* (Oxford, 1996).

him and some others to prison without charge—but the uprising had deeper roots, and it is the deeper roots that are revealed in [*Sir Thomas*] *More* (67–8).[1]

These deeper roots that the play reveals sound only too familiar to latter-day readers—fear and hatred of foreign craftsmen, aliens, streaming in from Europe in their flight from religious persecution on the continent. Later in the same month an outbreak of the plague closed the Rose (and all other London theatres) until December; and 1593 was even worse as the theatre for the same reason took in no customers for the ten months from February to December.[2] The actors—most of them at any rate—managed to maintain their livelihood by tramping across the countryside giving performances wherever they could find clean air. Given these times of crisis and flux, it is perhaps only appropriate that *1 Henry VI*, the Rose's great draw in the spring of 1592, should dramatize so kinetically the lives of soldiers, diplomats, kings, and insurrectionists, and that it should take as its argument the fractious instability of the court and nobility of fifteenth-century England and their squabbles with their French counterparts.

In so many ways, then, a year like 1592 seems made for a play like *1 Henry VI* and vice versa. Ever since E. H. Carr's famous little book *What Is History?* (first edition—of many since—in 1961) we have been obsessed with the notion that any work of history—especially any work of fiction with historical events forming the spine of its plot—cannot help but see its chosen historical period through the lens of its own times. For 1422 (the year of Henry V's death) or 1432 we may substitute 1592 with its continuing worries about the French, and the problems with Elizabeth's quarrelling courtiers, those 'greedy cormorants' as J. E. Neale calls them in his biography of Queen Elizabeth.[3] *Plus ça change.* Henry VI's own greedy cormorants—Winchester, Gloucester, Suffolk, Somerset, York and the houses and lineages they represent—can be matched several times over in 1592 by the likes of Elizabeth's Essex, Sussex,

---

[1] *The Elizabethan Theatre and The Book of Sir Thomas More* (Ithaca and London, 1987), 67–8.

[2] And so the decade goes. In 1595 the Rose was closed for two months in the summer, and for three months, from July to October in both 1596 and 1597. In 1599 the theatre shut its doors from June until October. In 1593 nearly eleven thousand Londoners died from the plague.

[3] *Queen Elizabeth I* (1934; repr. Oxford, 1961), 333.

the Cecils, Norfolk, Leicester, Walsingham.[1] Such internecine battles among the nobility were a European phenomenon. Perry Anderson writes: 'In England, the virulent Dudley/Seymour and Leicester/Cecil rivalries, in France the murderous three-cornered war betweeen the Guise, Montmorency and Bourbon lineages, in Spain the brutal backstairs struggle for power between the Alva and Eboli groups, were a keynote of the time'.[2] In France, faced by the Catholic League, Elizabeth, despite her policy of peace at almost any price, was forced to aid the Huguenot Henry of Navarre in his attempt to secure the French throne after the assassination of Henry III in 1589, sending armies over to Normandy, Brittany, and the Netherlands, and later in August 1591 an expedition under Essex to help Henry in the endless siege of Rouen (a prolongation, as it were, of the siege dramatized almost as endlessly in *1 Henry VI*). John Dover Wilson is one among many who believe that to understand Part One's extraordinary popularity in 1592 we must realize that any work celebrating the defeat of the French at that time would have given 'an outlet for the growing sense of exasperation, anger, and even despair which was felt in London at the impending failure of the invasion of France launched in the autumn of 1591' (p. xvi). (Indeed, Essex's expedition failed lamentably.) And, in this ongoing dialectical interpretative process, for 1422 or 1592 we might substitute 1922 or 1942. 'It is not difficult', writes Dover Wilson, 'for those who remember Gallipoli in 1915 or Norway and Dunkirk in 1940 to enter into the feelings of England at the beginning of 1592' (p. xvii).[3]

The general elusiveness of the comings and goings of actors, companies and playwrights in 1592 notoriously includes William Shakespeare and all three parts of *Henry VI*. In pursuit of them we

[1] Not too far back in English history for Shakespeare's original audiences—within in living memory—the minority of Edward VI resembled that of Henry VI. Like him, Edward had two feuding uncles, Somerset, the Protector, and Thomas Seymour, his brother, each in competition with the other for Edward's favour. Seymour was executed in March 1549 for treason.

[2] *Lineages of the Absolutist State* (1974), 49.

[3] This note continues to be struck. In *The Shakespearean Kings* (Boulder, Co., 1971) John Bromley notices how much we are at home now with 'the histories, a record of the fratricidal brawling conduct for nearly two centuries over a crown which in retrospect was not worth getting because not worth having' (2). For, after all, we live in a time of 'a dogma of futility, of limitations, of codified despair' (1).

have strayed into what Andrew Gurr calls 'a thicket of alternative interpretations' ('The Chimera of Amalgamation', 87). Hunting for Shakespeare in the famous 'lost years' from 1585 until 1594, when he surfaces with the Chamberlain's Men, joins with the search for the identity of the Dark Lady and her fair male counterpart of the Sonnets as famous black holes of investigation from which light is not able to escape. No one really knows where Shakespeare was during this time or what he was doing, but the most sensible hypotheses are those that link him with some theatrical company or other, as apprentice writer and actor, learning his trades. By 1592 Shakespeare was well enough established in the theatrical profession to have aroused Greene's ire and in this year we may see the three parts of *Henry VI* as among the first fruits and end products of what might have been a fairly extensive probationary period in the theatre. In one of the best known of the many forensic investigations into Shakespeare's boyhood and apprenticeship in the theatre, E. A. J. Honigmann believes him to have been with Lord Strange's Men for a number of years in the 1580s, the company that put on *1 Henry VI* in March 1592.[1] The latest edition of Honigmann's book in 1998 continues to propound what has become known as the 'early start' theory for Shakespeare as a writer and suggests dates for all the extant plays and poems up to 1600. According to this timetable, Shakespeare began his career in 1586 with *Titus Andronicus* followed by *The Two Gentlemen of Verona* in the next year. *1 Henry VI* and *The Taming of the Shrew* appeared in 1589, *The First Part of the Contention* (*2 Henry VI*) in 1590, and *The True Tragedy of Richard Duke of York* (*3 Henry VI*) and *Richard III* in 1591 (see p. xii). The three *Henry VI* plays appearing in sequence in consecutive years quite a time before their first recorded performances in 1592 regularizes in a reassuring timetable what many investigators now deem a much more complicated and devious chronology. We should contrast these dates with those that come from the 'late (or later) start' school with *1 Henry VI* as Shakespeare's 'prequel' to his 'two-part' play *The First Part of the*

---

[1] See *Shakespeare: The 'Lost Years'* (Manchester, 1985, rev. edn. 1998). It is pleasant to believe that Shakespeare belonged to Strange's Men when we consider that, as Andrew Gurr tells us in 'The Chimera of Amalgamation', 'There is no doubt that in the two seasons from late 1591 the Master of the Revels considered Strange's Men to be the strongest of the companies' (90).

Contention betwixt the Two Famous Houses of York and Lancaster (*2 Henry VI*) and *The True Tragedy of Richard, Duke of York* (*3 Henry VI*).[1]

The 'Henry VI' *Plays in 1592*

Who exactly do we mean by 'Shakespeare' in 1592, however? Not only are Shakespeare's whereabouts in this year uncertain but so too is his unitary existence as author (at least with regard to the Henry plays).[2] According to Gary Taylor in the *Textual Companion* only about 20 per cent of *1 Henry VI*, for example, can confidently be ascribed to Shakespeare (see p. 137) and Edward Burns in his edition of the play (2000) describes ' "Shakespeare's *Henry the Sixth, Part One*" as a necessary commercial fiction' (84)—a better title for the play, he believes, would be 'Harry the Sixth, as presented by Lord Strange's Men' or 'Harry the Sixth, by Shakespeare, Nashe and others' (84).[3] In 1592 the three history plays themselves—at least as physical entities—are in limbo (like their author(s)). *1 Henry VI*, indeed, does not take a printed form until its appearance some thirty years later in the 1623 Folio. Parts Two and Three take on curiously truncated printed forms in 1594 and 1595: Part Two as the 1594 quarto, *The First Part of the Contention Betwixt the Houses of York and Lancaster*, Part Three as the 1595 octavo, *The*

---

[1] A non-theatrical biography of Shakespeare during these years has the backing of many commentators including E. K. Chambers (*Elizabethan Stage*, ii. 130)—for instance Shakespeare as schoolmaster or as tourist—but to list these speculations here would be otiose. Recently, and more to the point, are discussions as to the likelihood or otherwise of the various companies other than Lord Strange's that Shakespeare might have been temporarily associated with before the certainty of his involvement with the Admiral's Men in 1594. Of the four companies touted—Strange's, Pembroke's, Queen's, Worcester's—Strange's and Queen's seem the most credible.

[2] And not just the Henry plays. *Timon of Athens* has come under suspicion as a collaborative enterprise, and so too have *The Taming of the Shrew* and *Titus Andronicus*, both coming from '[t]he very period of his career in which he [Shakespeare] is most likely to collaborate [which] is also the period for which Heminges and Condell must have had the least information and the dimmest memory' (*Textual Companion*, 73).

[3] Hardly anyone, interestingly enough, believed in the accuracy or desirability of the confident phrase 'Shakespeare's *Henry the Sixth, Part One*' until perhaps Peter Alexander's *Shakespeare's 'Henry VI' and 'Richard III'* (Cambridge, 1929) whose view that Shakespeare was the play's sole author was taken up by many others. Andrew S. Cairncross's Arden edition of the play in 1962 and Michael Hattaway's Cambridge edition in 1990—perhaps in despair—give the play entirely to Shakespeare. Before these scholars there were many doubters, stretching back into the eighteenth century.

True Tragedy of Richard Duke of York, both of them now deemed to be actors' memorial reconstructions, 'bad quartos' as they came to be known, of the longer versions of the plays that eventually found their ways into the 1623 Folio.[1] Neither *The Contention* nor *Richard Duke of York* mentions an author on its title-page, so neither Shakespeare nor anyone else is explicitly linked to these plays until 1623.[2] From Nashe's praise of *1 Henry VI* in August and Greene's quotation from *Richard Duke of York* (*3 Henry VI*) in September, we know that all three Henry plays must have been available in manuscript form in 1592 as the basis for theatrical productions, but there is no record of any such productions of these plays in 1592 or before except for the inference from the Henslowe entry for *1 Henry VI* and Nashe's remarks on the production he saw of it.

In every sense of the word, then, the 'whereabouts' of Shakespeare is a mystery in 1592. So elusive is he that one is tempted to adopt the annoying habit of some contemporary postmodernist critics and advertise his tenuous existence at this time by referring to him throughout this edition as 'Shakespeare' rather than Shakespeare.[3] Such a manoeuvre might be preferable, say, to appending 'and others' to his name's every appearance, but neither strategy seems necessary if we simply bear in mind that the word Shakespeare conceals problems and anomalies, not the least of which is the presence of other hands in the play's construction. If we cannot with absolute certainty give any of the play's scenes to anyone, even to Shakespeare, then we might as well defer to the decision by Heminges and Condell to include the play as Shakespeare's in the 1623 Folio and talk sanguinely of Shakespeare's

---

[1] See Madeleine Doran's *Henry VI Parts II and III: Their Relation to the Contention and the True Tragedy* (Iowa City, 1928) and Peter Alexander's *Shakespeare's 'Henry VI' and 'Richard III'*. Both these works independently came to the conclusion that *The Contention* and *The True Tragedy* were reported, pirated texts.

[2] This is not surprising; up until about 1597 the vast majority of plays presented on the public stage gave no indication of the authors' names on the title-page, just the name of the companies that owned them. In the case of the Henry plays, only *The True Tragedy* mentions an acting company, Pembroke's Men, and only the first quarto of *2 Henry IV* published in 1600 has Shakespeare's name on the title-page in minute italics below the advertising for the 'humours' of Falstaff and the 'swaggering' of Pistol.

[3] The postmodernist argument is that 'Shakespeare' is a more valid name than Shakespeare, however certain 'his' authorship of a play, as there are as many Shakespeares as there are reading and viewing cultures; there is no unmediated Shakespeare. Gary Taylor calls the punctuation round Shakespeare's name 'skeptical quotation marks' ('Shakespeare and Others', 168).

Henry the Sixth, Part One.[1] If the *who* of the problem can be dealt with in this summary manner, the *when* is both less and more difficult: less difficult in that it seems that we are dealing with a play that can be given the most precise of dates for its debut performance, 3 March 1592. (This is one of the very few plays by Shakespeare to have its opening performance so precisely dated.) But if the *when* of its first performance can be so accurately determined, the *when* of its construction is another matter.

The nub of this controversial issue is the order of composition of the three parts of *Henry VI*. It had long been assumed that *1 Henry VI* belied its Folio title and first appeared some time after *The Contention* (*2 Henry VI*) and *Richard Duke of York* (*3 Henry VI*). Between 1960 and 1990, however, opinion shifted to a date of composition corresponding to the play's place in the Folio. Many critics indeed had difficulty in believing that *1 Henry VI* was written by Shakespeare at all, so clumsy and pedestrian they thought its writing and construction. He can only be forgiven its manifest rankness, they argued, on the basis of its being his first tentative attempt at writing a chronicle history play. *The Contention* and *Richard Duke of York*, on the other hand, must have followed on from that first play because they display a far greater dramaturgical sophistication. In his edition in 1952, however, John Dover Wilson had revived the earlier hypothesis by arguing that certain oddities about this first play's relation to the two that 'follow' suggest that it may well have been written some time after Part Three, with which it has much in common, than before Part Two, with which it has much less in common.[2] It may in fact have been brought into being

---

[1] This is not to deny the salience of Gary Taylor's brilliant investigation of the different hands in 'Shakespeare's' *1 Henry VI* in 'Shakespeare and Others'. His article is particularly convincing in its argument that Act 1 was not written by Shakespeare, but by Thomas Nashe. Such an ascription, however, entails a remarkable reticence on Nashe's part when in *Piers Penniless* he praises the play for its presentation of Talbot's death but does not bother to mention that he himself was the author of its opening act, and some of its other parts.

[2] While it is true that *The Contention* (*2 Henry VI*) carries on the story of *1 Henry VI*, it does so without alluding to or taking up, or it unaccountably changes, many of the first play's significant incidents and characters. See Dover Wilson's edition, pp. xii–xiii. In 'Shakespeare and Others' Gary Taylor adds to this list of anomalies (see p. 150) and adverts us to the work of Eliot Slater who, on the basis of an analysis of the plays' vocabularies, links *1 Henry VI* with *Richard Duke of York* (*3 Henry VI*) rather than with *The Contention* (*2 Henry VI*): see *The Problem of 'The Reign of King Edward III': A Statistical Approach* (Cambridge, 1988). For an attempt to answer all of Dover Wilson's objections see Emrys Jones, 135–8.

as a 'prequel', a play constituted as an afterthought, one cashing in on the popularity of *The Contention* and *Richard Duke of York*, titles that in their indifference to the eponymous protagonist of the Folio plays offer the possibility that the titles *2 Henry VI* and *3 Henry VI* are themselves the afterthoughts of Heminges and Condell in 1623.[1] But if it was a prequel it was one with a difference. That is, unlike its successors, it was, as we have seen, written as much if not more by others than by Shakespeare; hence its manifest rankness can be blamed on whoever Shakespeare's collaborators were. And so the alleged turgidities of Act 1 can be laid at the door of Thomas Nashe, as they are in Gary Taylor's seminal article of 1995 refurbishing Dover Wilson, which is a somewhat dismal fate for someone like Nashe who has been described by Stanley Wells as 'one of the most brilliant stylists of the age'.[2] But better Nashe than Shakespeare, I suppose, if Act 1 is thought rebarbative.

The weight of evidence does in fact suggest that this first play was written after the other two. And so we have the odd situation where we have to imagine that Part Two and Part Three were plays written by Shakespeare alone (hence their superiority over Part One) and then, presumably, after having scored a theatrical success with them (why else write a 'prequel'?) Shakespeare, for some reason, decides to collaborate with others (hence the inferiority of *1 Henry VI*) to produce a play that acts as a prologue to the events described in *The Contention* and *Richard Duke of York*. We know so little of the dynamics of Elizabethan collaboration in the writing of plays that it is not difficult to construct an imaginary scenario that has, let us say, a harassed author calling on friends and colleagues to help him construct an unexpectedly commissioned piece in a hurry. Perhaps Shakespeare's dual career as playwright and actor at this time proved too burdensome for him; but it is nonetheless odd that, after writing two successful plays in his first venture into adapting chronicle history, apparently on his own,[3] he should write only 20 per cent of the third (if Taylor is correct in his

[1] Thus Edward Burns: 'With several other recent commentators, I take the view that the play is what in the Hollywood terms of the late twentieth century is known as a "prequel", a dramatic piece that returns for ironic and challenging effect to the narrative roots of an already familiar story' (4–5).

[2] *A Dictionary of Shakespeare* (Oxford, 1998), 125.

[3] Although this too has been questioned, beginning with Edmond Malone in 1790. Gary Taylor includes *The Contention* and *Richard Duke of York* in his list of suspected collaborative ventures in the *Textual Companion* on p. 73.

computation). If we suppose that *1 Henry VI* did not exist before *The Contention* and *Richard Duke of York* we can readily understand how an alert professional writer might look over his successful two-part play (if we can think of *The Contention* and *Richard Duke of York* in these terms) and see the possibilities for writing a prologue to it. He might have decided, for instance, as an imaginative and conscientious historian, that the full significance of *The Contention* and *Richard Duke of York* in their exclusive concern for the disintegration of England in the Wars of the Roses could only be brought out by seeing those civil wars in an international context which was their part-cause and parallel. This is the burden of Michael Hattaway's Introduction to his edition of Part One in 1990 (though he is not a proponent of a later writing for *1 Henry VI*) in which he urges us to contrast Shakespeare's later history plays, beginning with *Richard III*, where the emphasis is on the personality of the monarch, with the plays of the first tetralogy which together make up 'a complex essay on the *politics* of the mid-fifteenth century' (*1 Henry VI*, 1). (This does not mean to say that the later history plays are not also complex essays on fifteenth-century politics.) In his Introduction to *The Contention* (*2 Henry VI*) in 1991 Hattaway expands on this notion: '*1 Henry VI* may well have been written to show how the history of a nation is never to be understood in isolation' (6). Thus the play portrays 'the decline of England's empire over France and the accompanying decay of the ideals of feudalism that had sustained the order of the realm' (6). Of course, as Hattaway stoutly maintains, dramatizing such a decline could have been planned as part of the sweep of the trilogy from the beginning, but in its different emphasis and its move from England to France (twenty of the Folio play's twenty-seven scenes are set in France) Part One could also just as easily (if not more easily) be seen as the product of a process of sober, commercially driven second throughts.[1]

---

[1] Many commentators have pointed out the sheer unlikelihood of conceiving a play in three parts at this time. A two-part play, such as Marlowe's *Tamburlaine*, was itself a daring venture; a three-part play, so the argument runs, would have been inconceivable. (Although it is always dangerous to talk about the inconceivable when we are dealing with Shakespeare.)

Plays Popular

One of the few certainties, then, with regard to the theatrical state of affairs in the London of 1592 is the popularity of *1 Henry VI*. Exactly how many wrote the play, when they did so, how it was performed, who played what part, the nature of the manuscript behind the first performances—these all come with large questions attached to them. As does the play's relationship of course with its two extensions in historical time, if not in order of composition, *The First Part of the Contention of the Two Famous Houses of York and Lancaster* (*2 Henry VI*) and *The True Tragedy of Richard Duke of York* (*3 Henry VI*). But Nashe's praise of *1 Henry VI* and Henslowe's numbers tell us that Lord Strange's Men certainly had a hit on their hands in the spring of 1592. Despite the play's ventriloquial topicality, one might legitimately wonder why. After all, for centuries after this initial brief success the play has had the dubious distinction—with its other two parts—of being Shakespeare's least liked and least played.[1] And of the three plays *1 Henry VI* clearly is the least distinguished, though it is by no means as undistinguished as many commentators think. It only achieved a certain popularity in the theatre in the twentieth century as part of an abridged version of all three plays, often with additions and changes by its abridgers. These abridgements can come, however, with the force of revelation as we may see in Homer Swander's rapturous response to one of them in which the plays were least cut—the Royal Shakespeare Company's production in 1977–8 of what he calls *The Trilogy of King Henry VI*.[2] To be able to see these plays presented relatively uncut for the first time, he maintains, makes us realize that we are dealing with 'a work the vastness and complexity of which were utterly new in the world of the theatre' (162). For him this perfor-

---

[1] There was one garbled production in the eighteenth century at Covent Garden; in the nineteenth century, apart from performances in Germany and Austria, and three versions of a compacted amalgamation of all three parts in England, the only fully rigged production of Part One in England was at Stratford in 1889. The twentieth century saw more performances than in any other century, but they were in the main compressions of all three parts. Randall Martin's edition of *Henry VI, Part Three* (Oxford, 2001) and Roger Warren's of *Henry VI, Part Two* (Oxford, 2002) deal extensively with the plays in the theatre.

[2] See 'The Rediscovery of *Henry VI*', *SQ* 29 (1978), 146–63. About 7 per cent of *Henry VI, Part 1* was cut (mainly in the scenes set in France and in 2.5). Hands's production of the play was thus less mutilated than the previous abridgement.

mance of a streamlined set of three plays constitutes, as his article's title tells us, the rediscovery in the twentieth century of *Henry VI*: the RSC has enabled us, he says, to participate 'in the discovery of a work by Shakespeare that has been effectively lost for over 300 years' (147).[1]

You had to be there, I suppose, to understand the emotions of Londoners at those first performances of *1 Henry VI* in the spring of 1592. But the play's popularity at that time has to be seen today against the backdrop of an extraordinary efflorescence of interest in political history in the last two decades of the sixteenth century fed by self-conscious patriotic Protestantism's fascination with its own biography in history. (It is not for nothing that Part One is persistently anti-Catholic in a number of ways despite that fact that in the fifteenth century the entire population of England was nominally Catholic (though not of course in 1592)). In the play the French are presented as decadently Catholic, the English (with the exception of the Bishop of Winchester) as attractively proto-Protestant (at least). Hence the Mariolatry behind the presentation of Joan and her duplicitous, sinister, and farcical relationship with the miraculous. On the other hand, her chief antagonist, Talbot, comes across as a Protestant warrior. As Burns notices: 'Talbot's rhetoric is correspondingly Protestant. His biblical references are all from the Old Testament (a source less fully used by Catholics) and speak of stoicism and individual faith' (*1 Henry VI*, 47). Although an interest in English history stretches back to the invention of printing, David Scott Kastan tells us that history writing became 'spectacularly available'[2] to the Elizabethans in the massive folio volumes of John Foxe's *Acts and Monuments* (first published in 1563)—also known as *The Book of the Martyrs*. This often grisly account of Protestant martyrdom was so popular in the late sixteenth century that copies of it were chained, along with the Bible, to lecterns in cathedrals and many parish churches. In it Foxe recounts the history of Protestant and proto-Protestant suffering, the 'great persecutions and horrible troubles that have been

---

[1] Four years later in 1983 BBC TV enjoyed a quite astonishing success when Jane Howell presented the three Henry VI plays and *Richard III* on consecutive Sunday nights. An audience of 800,000 watched *1 Henry VI*. Remarkably only 5 per cent of the text was cut.

[2] 'Shakespeare and English History', in *The Cambridge Companion to Shakespeare*, ed. Margreta de Grazia and Stanley Wells (Cambridge, 2001), 167–82; 168.

wrought and practised by the Romish Prelates' in England and Scotland from the year 1,000 until the reign of Elizabeth. Where, one might think, Protestant suffering ends. But Foxe is interestingly equivocal—Shakespearianly so perhaps—in the manner of his compilation's conclusion: his wish is, he says,

that no more matter of such lamentable stories may ever be offered hereafter to write upon. But so it is, I cannot tell how, the elder the world waxes, the longer it continues, the nearer it hastens to its end, the more Satan rages; giving still new matter of writing books and volumes. (viii. 754)

Satan's rages are nothing, however, to the political ones described in those other popular sources of historical information for the Elizabethan reader, Robert Fabyan's *New Chronicles* (1516), Edward Hall's *The Union of the Two Noble and Illustre Families of Lancaster and York* (1548), Richard Grafton's *Chronicles* (1562–72), John Stow's *Chronicles* and *Annales* (dating from 1565), and Raphael Holinshed's *Chronicles of England, Scotland, and Ireland* (1577 and 1587; this incorporates work done by other Tudor historians for over seventy years). A measure of the popularity of these baggy monsters is the number of summaries that they spawned over the course of the century. For Shakespeare's history plays, of course, the most important chroniclers are Hall and Holinshed, and one of the ways to grasp Shakespeare's artistry is to monitor his dealings with them as he trims and embellishes the information they supply him.[1] Hall and the other chroniclers were popular with the Elizabethan reader precisely because they were the conduits for a historical investigation that eschewed the salvific trajectory of Foxe's work although the notion, especially with Hall, that the march of political events somehow manifests God's providential design for England subtends the whole work. Many books have been written on Shakespeare's creatively evasive relationship with this aspect of Tudor historiography.[2]

[1] As does W. G. Boswell-Stone, in his *Shakespeare's Holinshed*. Volume 3 of Geoffrey Bullough's edition of the *Narrative and Dramatic Sources of Shakespeare* lays out the relevant passages from Hall, Holinshed *et al.* that pertain to the history plays of the first tetralogy.

[2] Especially in the last half-century where the debate has raged as to Shakespeare's commitment or lack of it to Tudor determinism. In the Introduction to his edition of the play Edward Burns thinks of it as 'an ironic meditation on what history is, and as such it constantly exposes the gratuitousness of the signs and symbols which allow us to think we know history' (6).

It would be strange if Elizabethan drama before and contemporaneous with Shakespeare's early work had been uninfluenced by this intense national self-consciousness. In the past, however, critics have tended to deny the existence of a flourishing market for plays on themes derived from the Chronicles, partly because most of the plays that do so can be considered historical only in patches—a scene here or there—and partly because of the attractiveness of the myth that Shakespeare invented the English chronicle history play.[1] He certainly wrote more plays on English history than any of his fellow playwrights, ten in all, stretching in historical time from 1199, when King John was crowned, to the birth of Elizabeth in 1533. And more, somehow, means first, though the claim for Shakespeare's originality is often a self-conscious one as in F. P. Wilson's mock-humble tentativeness in the making of it: 'I am frightened at my own temerity in saying so'.[2] By 1623 all twenty-four kings from William the Conqueror to Elizabeth had been represented in a play. F. P. Wilson writes: 'For whatever reason, after the victory of the Armada, the dramatists took the risk, and were licensed to take the risk, of writing plays on English history, and for some ten years the plays were acted which have provided many an Englishman with his only knowledge of medieval history' (109).

Shakespeare was not, however, first in this field and the popularity of his early history plays owes much both to the popularity of the chroniclers of English history and to the plays their work at least in part provoked. Some thirty-nine history plays actually antedate the *Henry VI* plays of which sixteen are extant.[3] Not surprisingly, many of their writers were drawn to the great conflict between England and France over the French succession which

---

[1] Paola Pugliatti in *Shakespeare the Historian* (New York, 1996) claims that Shakespeare invented the historical genre in drama if we define it in restrictively sophisticated terms: 'he may not have been the first to bring English history before the audience of a public playhouse, but he was certainly the first to treat it in the manner of a mature historian rather than in the manner of a worshipper of historical, political and religious myths' (52).

[2] *Marlowe and the Early Shakespeare* (Oxford, 1953), 108.

[3] Among them are *1* and *2 Tamburlaine* (1587 and 1588); *Alphonsus, King of Aragon* (1587); *The Wars of Cyrus* (1588); *The Wounds of Civil War* (1588); *The Battle of Alcazar* (1589); *1 Selimus* (1592)—these are foreign histories. Among the English chronicle plays: *The Famous Victories of Henry V* (1586); *1 The Troublesome Reign of John, King of England* (1588); *Edward III* (1590); *Edmond Ironside* (1590); *Locrine* (1591); *Edward I* (1591); *The True Tragedy of Richard III* (1591). These are the plays that Shakespeare could turn to for models in and before 1592 (and one of which, *Edward III*, he may very well have written himself).

produced a series of wars that stretched for a hundred years (1337–1453); equally they were drawn to the monitory conflict between the Houses of York and Lancaster; and in *1 Henry VI* the two great themes converge. The play charts the disastrous breakdown of civility among the English nobility on the eve of the civil war—aggravated first by the minority and then by the pusillanimity of Henry VI—and the equally disastrous conduct of the coeval military campaigns against the French. All three of Shakespeare's early history plays can also be seen usefully as among a group of English history plays that constitutes a critical response to Marlowe's glorification of ruthless foreign individualism. Their anti-Marlovian thrust is captured baldly by 'To the Gentleman Readers' in the anonymous 1591 quarto of *1 The Troublesome Reign of John King of England*: [1]

> You that with friendly grace of smoothèd brow
> Have entertained the Scythian Tamburlaine,
> And given applause unto an Infidel:
> Vouchsafe to welcome (with like courtesy)
> A warlike Christian and your Countryman.
>
> (1–5)

The religio-patriotic note is firmly struck by this last line and can be applied, *mutatis mutandis*, to virtually all the English history plays including Shakespeare's two tetralogies. [2]

It can be applied particularly to *1 Henry VI* which, on one level at least, seems designed specifically as a hortatory piece of propaganda in the admonitory vein admired by Thomas Nashe. Its warlike Christian and fellow countryman manifests himself in the living body of Talbot (at least until his death in Act 4) and the dead one of Henry V, the paragon of English Christian kings. Their opponents on the international scene, the French, are the watered-down equivalent of the Scythian Tamburlaines. And so at a time of international tension in the fraught 1590s there is in this play a dominant, nostalgic, celebratory reminiscence of Henry V who lives on in the immortality of preternatural legend where '[h]is arms spread wider than a dragon's wings' (1.1.11) and the blaze of

---

[1] Ed. J. W. Sider (New York and London, 1979).

[2] This was particularly true of the Rose plays. Scott McMillin in *The Elizabethan Theatre* notes that 'The English gallimaufry at the Rose suggests that Londoners were attracted to the theatre by an awfully variegated nationalism' (67).

his 'sparkling eyes . . . dazzled and drove back his enemies' (1.1.12–13). His tragic surrogate in the play is Lord Talbot who takes on Henry's quasi-magical Tamburlaine-like military prowess as evidenced by the epic description of him in the play's first scene:

> Where valiant Talbot, above human thought,
> Enacted wonders with his sword and lance.
>
> (1.1.121–2)

For Emrys Jones 'He [Talbot] is a walking legend, whose famousness gives him a special kind of *mana*, as if he were surrounded by a golden light like a saint's aureole' (155).

Not only does the play suggest that such epic valour might be passed down the generations—hence the Bastard's praise of Talbot's son as the 'young whelp' who 'Did flesh his puny sword in Frenchmen's blood' (4.7.36)—but by some kind of battlefield osmosis it can at least occasionally, it seems, be spread among the ordinary soldiers. We can imagine perhaps how an English audience in the early 1590s would respond to the French description of the English in the play's second scene as all Olivers and Rolands, Samsons and Goliases, or to Charles's hyperbolic ruefulness as to the history of the English warrior character:

> Of old I know them; rather with their teeth
> The walls they'll tear down than forsake the siege
>
> (1.2.39–40)

backed up by Reignier's oddly comic variation:

> I think by some odd gimmers or device
> Their arms are set, like clocks, still to strike on,
> Else ne'er could they hold out so as they do.
>
> (1.2.41–3)

The play repeatedly titillates an atavistic xenophobia in its audiences. Talbot proclaims that

> For every drop of blood was drawn from him [Salisbury]
> There hath at least five Frenchmen died tonight.
>
> (2.2.8–9)

The English are always vastly outnumbered, beginning with the Third Messenger's ostentatiously precise enumeration of the difficulty facing Talbot outside Orléans who

> Having full [i.e. in full] scarce six thousand in his troop,
> By three-and-twenty thousand of the French
> Was round encompassèd and set upon
>
> (1.1.112–14)

(even so, the Messenger continues, Talbot would have prevailed, having personally dispatched 'hundreds' of the enemy to their deaths, had not Sir John Fastolf turned coward). And when Talbot recalls Fastolf's cowardice at the battle of Patay he notes that 'the French were almost ten to one' (4.1.21).

The ferocity of outnumbered English warriors is something Shakespeare returns to time and again in the history plays, most memorably in *Edward III* (if it is by Shakespeare) and *Henry V*. The English are, then, in this and other history plays, bulldog under-dogs: puny swords are celebrated, and so are hugely out-numbered troops, especially if they are in other ways physically inferior to the enemy—if they are, for instance, 'Lean raw-boned rascals' (1.2.35), famished, yet full of 'courage and audacity' (1.2.36). The hyperbolic apotheosis of this strain in the play occurs in the scene before Bordeaux where the French General assures Talbot that

> Ten thousand French have ta'en the sacrament
> To rive their dangerous artillery
> Upon no Christian soul but English Talbot.
>
> (4.2.28–30)

In the rough-and-tumble atmosphere of the public playhouse its undoubtedly patriotic audiences are often invited by the play, sometimes quite directly, to think of themselves as active par-ticipants in the play's battles as when Talbot, in all probability, addresses them at 4.2.54: 'And they shall find dear deer of us, my friends'. Talbot is 'the great Alcides of the field' (4.7.60), as Sir William Lucy calls him, the representative of a chivalry that was fast decaying in the real world but newly popular in the play world.[1] Of course, in 1592 Talbot may have well been considered by the intelligentsia in the audience as impossibly old-fashioned.

---

[1] It is this function of Talbot which gives pith and edge to his memorable encounter with the Countess of Auvergne, a scene in the play that many commen-tators inexplicably find extraneous and unnecessary and many productions cut. Yet there Talbot and the Countess, Talbot particularly, flesh out, away from the battle-field, chivalrous possibilities in the courtly exchanges between men and women of aristocratic rank. The scene looks forward to the chivalric community of the roman-tic comedies.

1. The 'great Alcides of the field' : Clive Morton as Talbot in *Henry VI*, the first part of John Barton's adapted Wars of the Roses cycle, directed by Peter Hall and John Barton at Stratford-upon-Avon in 1964.

After all, as David Riggs points out, 'Still disdainful of protective siege walls, horrified by the use of artillery, he epitomizes the feudal *noblesse d'épée*, envisioning every battle as a *beau geste* and a chance to fulfill a vow made on behalf of his fallen peers and his personal honor' (*Shakespeare's Heroical Histories*, 23). And this is how he is usually played in production. In a performance in the Royal Shakespeare Theatre in 1977, for instance, directed by Terry Hands, Talbot (David Swift) was 'an honest old English warrior in non-regulation battle-dress who has been left far behind in the new perfidious world of French villainy and up-to-date English politics'.[1]

And yet despite the prominence of Talbot the sense we get from this play—even when standing on its own let alone as part of an epically extended tetralogy—is that its real subject is no one individual but England itself. One of its frequent patriotic couplets—

> God and Saint George, Talbot and England's right,
> Prosper our colours in this dangerous fight
>
> (4.2.55–6)

—typically equates the epic hero with his defining purpose in defending England's right. And in the scene with the Countess of Auvergne, the play somewhat hamfistedly constructs a chivalric encounter between its representatives of the aristocratic sexes in order for Talbot to make the point that in his true essence he isn't an individual at all, not Lord Talbot, the grizzled old soldier, but rather a walking metonym for the English army and by extension the English people, not to say England itself. Talbot, the individual soldier, is a 'shadow', a primitive version of the cipher, the 'crooked figure [that] may | Attest in little place a million' about whose inadequacies the Chorus in *Henry V* is so apologetic (*Henry V*, Prologue, 15–16). And Talbot as sixteenth-century actor, as, in other words, the 'shadow' player Edward Alleyn, stands in for an England in 1592 under great duress. That is, as we have seen, the patriotic emotions to which this play shamelessly appeals resonate at an especially fragile time politically speaking. Frightening memories of the 1588 Spanish Armada, or of the Babington Plot of 1586 which led to the execution of Mary Queen of Scots; concern over a noticeably declining and still unmarried Elizabeth; worries over Catholic recusancy; fear of military involvement in Europe and, just as disquietingly, in Ireland, combine to make a patriotic response a matter of some urgency.[2]

---

[1] David Daniell, 'Opening up the Text: Shakespeare's *Henry VI* Plays in Performance', in *Themes in Drama*, 1 (1979), 247–77; 257.

[2] In *Shakespeare, Spenser, and the Crisis in Ireland* (Cambridge, 1997) Christopher Highley believes that Ireland overshadows Talbot's poignant words in *Henry VI* when he talks about his Englishness 'parked and bounded in a pale' (*1 Henry VI* 4.2.45): 'When Shakespeare surveyed the reign of Henry VI, he looked back to a moment that was widely considered to be the beginning of England's current and unresolved troubles in Ireland' (41).

There can be no doubt then that the play appeals to its sixteenth-century audience in the manner that Nashe describes: it is a bracing attempt to stiffen the sinews of the English in a time of danger and deceit. But what is most interesting about *1 Henry VI* is that the general tone of the play is hardly triumphal. Its popularity is based on something much more sophisticated—troublingly so perhaps—than mere appeal to gung-ho patriotic sentiment. Were Shakespeare truly intent on capturing a slice of the past as a means of fortifying men's spirits in the present, as Nashe believed, he might well have begun his story of the English past in better chronological fashion with the events of the last play of his second tetralogy which celebrates the successful Christian English machiavellianism of Henry V. Instead, Shakespeare begins his career as historian of the fifteenth century with the story of the weakling son, Henry VI,[1] of a revered strong father, Henry V, leaving the biography of the father to come as a kind of 'prequel' to the story of the son written five or six years earlier. It may be a symptom of patriotism to concern oneself with the history of England at all, but in this and the other plays the story of England is baleful and premonitory. Wilbur Sanders points out that

in choosing to treat this turbulent stretch of English history, Shakespeare has plunged into the very waters where the concept of kingship was fraught with the profoundest complexities. If he was planning to exemplify the simplified monarchic theory of Tudor propaganda, it was a singularly unhappy choice of subject.[2]

Ralph Berry calls the *Henry VI* sequence that 'unflinching account of class pride and class resistance'.[3] For any writer worth his salt, as Paola Pugliatti reminds us,

The choice of historical subjects…was neither neutral nor safe. Indeed, to go fishing for subjects in the established corpus of facts and political issues relating to national history was certainly a more demanding and more risky undertaking than simply ransacking the repertories of Italian novellas or even Plutarch's *Lives*. (*Shakespeare the Historian*, 36)

---

[1] Donald G. Watson writes in *Shakespeare's Early History Plays: Politics at Play on the Elizabethan Stage* (Athens, Georgia, 1990): 'the popularity of "Armada rhetoric" during the time of *1 Henry VI*'s composition would have seemed to ask for a play about Henry V not one which begins with his death and proceeds to dramatize English losses' (39).

[2] *The Dramatist and the Received Idea* (Cambridge, 1968), 76.

[3] *Shakespeare and Social Class* (Atlantic Highlands, NJ, 1988), 1.

Although the second tetralogy is infinitely superior in every way to the first—an indication if nothing else of the enormous strides a genius like Shakespeare makes in a few years—we can surely claim that Shakespeare's first tetralogy is superior, if not infinitely so, in its treatment of history to the history plays that came before. Despite the *sottises* of these early Shakespeare plays their general stance towards official history, unlike nearly all other history plays of the time, is a questioning, complicating one, critical, subversive, and ironic.[1]

This is hardly surprising. Throughout Europe the 'Elizabethan' age was characterized, so William J. Bouwsma argues, by a deep ambivalence towards its own time despite all the prevailing optimism and energy: it was 'both the best and the worst of times'; 'the mood of most people who contemplated the current scene was grim'.[2] Anxiety, dread, discontent, and a morbid fear of death that had intensified since the fourteenth century percolated darkly beneath the century's sparkling surface. And correspondingly in *1 Henry VI* there is an obsessive concern with death's 'insulting tyranny' (4.7.19). Eventually even Talbot, Nashe's terror of the French, wilts—and dies—before this 'world of odds' (4.4.25) as does his son in 'that sea of blood' (4.7.14). If we think back to Nashe's expression of gratification for the pungent example of Talbot's devotion to the English cause it is also something that has to be repeatedly mourned by the 'tears of ten thousand spectators at least' who 'imagined they behold him fresh bleeding' in his death agony. Talbot's bones are 'new embalmed' performance after performance in order for him to die and have us weep for him so that his bones may be newly embalmed all over again.[3] As the French General grimly predicts in Act 4, Scene 2, Talbot will shortly be seen as 'withered, bloody, pale, and dead' (4.2.38), but he doesn't predict Joan's mordant exultation over a putrefying corpse:

[1] For Paola Pugliatti, Shakespeare's 'Source manipulation and sheer invention may be read as a distinctly critical gesture, in that they show the need to question the official historiographical tradition' (*Shakespeare the Historian*, 54).

[2] *The Waning of the Renaissance 1550–1640* (New Haven and London, 2000), 113 and 112.

[3] In *Shakespeare: The Histories* (New York, 2000) Graham Holderness enlarges this theatrical moment: 'What gives history permanence is thus more than a rational process of patient reconstruction: it is rather a continually repeated sacrificial ritual, the rebirth and death of the hero' (45). As Michael Hattaway observes, *1 Henry VI* depicts 'the deaths of the titanic survivors of an *ancien régime*' (*2 Henry VI*, 17).

> Him that thou magnifiest with all these titles
> Stinking and flyblown lies here at our feet.
> (4.7.75–6)

The scene she describes has all the force of a medieval *memento mori*.[1]

Indeed history in this play, in Graham Holderness's words, takes the form of 'a manifestly contemporary exercise of lament and resurrection, nostalgic longing and sober reflection, vivid re-enactment and saddened resignation' (*Shakespeare: The Histories*, 110). And these responses combine to create a kind of grim satisfaction in the minds of the characters and perhaps in those of their audiences in the contemplation of the way death delivers them both from the miseries of their own lives and from their oppressors when they in their turn die. Part of this strange sense of satisfaction, of theatrical *schadenfreude*, is to see the medieval hero, always larger than life, often tyrannically so, succumb to that great leveller, death, as Henry V did. Talbot himself says:

> But kings and mightiest potentates must die,
> For that's the end of human misery.
> (3.2.134–5)

Even before the experience of death in the play, *1 Henry VI* insists that we see the once splendid and bedizened body of the erstwhile warrior in all the helplessness and futility of old age as in Mortimer's careful enumeration of his own decaying parts: eyes 'whose wasting oil is spent' (2.5.8), weak shoulders; pithless arms; numb, strengthless feet (2.5.10–14). And death is seen by him, as by so many of Shakespeare's characters in the history plays especially, as a 'comfort', a 'kind umpire of men's miseries' (2.5.29) bringing 'sweet enlargement' (2.5.30). 'O amiable, lovely Death!' as Constance declares in ecstatic agitation in *King John* (3.4.25). In the light of this predilection, there is something merely poignant in Talbot's fantastical 'triumph' over 'antic death' (4.7.18) when he contemplates an Elysian future for him and his son in which

---

[1] See Carol Chillington Rutter in *Enter the Body: Women and Representation on Shakespeare's Stage* (London and New York, 2001): 'I want to propose that, for spectators in Shakespeare's theatre, the actorly corpse reworked the *vanitas* tradition. . . . Cordelia at *Lear*'s end is there to be read as an anamorph, a *memento mori*' (10).

2. The dying Mortimer, represented in Bell's edition of Shakespeare
(1773–5).

> Coupled in bonds of perpetuity,
> Two Talbots, wingèd, through the lither sky
> In thy despite shall scape mortality.
>
> (4.7.20–2)

In a sensitive reading of this scene Alexander Leggatt notices that
in Talbot's speech the notion that he and his son have escaped
through death into freedom is countered almost immediately:
'Suddenly Talbot, like Lear with Cordelia, cannot accept his son's

death and asks him to speak. He cannot speak, but he can smile. His smile counters the grin of death, but it may also mirror it . . .'.[1] Leggatt believes that the history genre at this time was essentially a wavering one, intersecting confusingly with tragedy and comedy. He argues that the 1623 Folio presents the *Henry VI* trilogy as a series of individual tragedies: 'What we have in the *Henry VI* trilogy is an intersection of two forms, tragedy and history, each one shaping and affecting the other' (12). Hence the lingering over individual deaths, the Talbots in *1 Henry VI*, and the deaths of Gloucester and Suffolk in *2 Henry VI*. Leggatt imagines a title-page for a notional quarto for *1 Henry VI* in the early 1590s as *The Famous Life and Lamentable Death of Lord Talbot Earl of Shrewsbury*.

If death is the great leveller in such an acutely hierarchical society as the Elizabethan, we might argue that, in the land of the living, the theatre is its colourful counterpart. Merely to see impersonated figures of authority, dressed in their fraudulent finery,[2] exercising their fictional power in a public forum would have been enough to unnerve the real magistrates of the land. And when, as was the case with the characters in the chronicle history plays, those impersonated figures had descendants in the real world, and no doubt at times in the theatre's audiences, then actors and playwrights in the 1590s had to tread very warily to avoid the charge of sedition. F. P. Wilson is one of a number of commentators who have responded to this suggestive scenario: 'in Shakespeare's day as in Hall's the memory of the wars of Lancaster and York was still vivid in many an English family whose lineage had been "infected and plagued with this unnatural division"' (*Marlowe and the Early Shakespeare*, 128). We might in this context consider the club-like atmosphere to these international broils. Everyone knows everyone else—on both sides. More, everyone is related to nearly everyone else (at least on the English side). Hence insults like Gloucester's to Winchester, 'Thou bastard of my grandfather' (3.1.42). Some of the English are related to the

---

[1] 'The Death of John Talbot', in *Shakespeare's English Histories: A Quest for Form and Genre*, ed. J. W. L. Velz (Binghamton, NY, 1996), 11–30; 21.

[2] Donald G. Watson in *Shakespeare's Early History Plays* tells us that 'the players did consciously imitate their social betters in costuming, spending as much and more upon the finery of nobility as they did upon securing playscripts, and apparently this aspect of the spectacle comprised an important element of the theatre's ability to draw in the populace' (27).

French: Burgundy, for instance, is Henry's uncle, the Duke of Bedford having married Burgundy's sister, Anne. It seems undeniable at any rate that an Elizabethan audience would have taken much pleasure in being on such familiar terms with these past celebrities.[1] Despite Elizabeth's frequent flamboyantly exhibitionistic state processions there was nothing like the knowledge of the monarchy and the families of the influential nobility that our prying press gives us today—there were no tapped phone lines listening in to the private conversations of royal lovers. But here we have plays exposing, among other things, the graft and sexual low jinks of the exalted, the players protected by only a hundred years or so of history. What a stir it must have caused, and something very different, more intense perhaps, simply more immediate and topical, from the remoter grandiloquence of Marlowe's work, and, for that matter, from that educational aspect of the play praised by Thomas Nashe. How warmly a London audience would have responded to the fictional Lord Mayor of London's intimacy with them: '(*To the audience*) This Cardinal's more haughty than the devil' (1.3.82).

We might see *1 Henry VI*, then, advantageously if unusually, against a background of muckraking texts that expose, for instance, even the holy of holies, the angelic female monarch, to a sometimes caustic and scurrilous criticism. I'm thinking here of a fascinating collection of essays, edited by Julia M. Walker, which brings out from the shadows a 'contrasting rhetoric of dissent, criticism, and disrespect which permeated all aspects of Elizabeth's life, reign, and posthumous representation'.[2] Dissent, criticism and disrespect also permeate the *Henry VI* plays. In all of them the actors are asked to speak a rhetoric of vituperation or of passion brought about, as in our day, by the intrusion of the personal into

---

[1] A pleasure we now take for granted. As Patrick Balfour wrote sourly in 1933: 'The first duty of Society is to be a show for the masses, particularly during the three months of the London Season, when it has not a moment's rest . . . in fact to carry out each day is a spectacular programme quite beyond human powers' (*The Society Racket* (1933), 27).

[2] *Dissing Elizabeth: Negative Representations of Gloriana* (Durham and London, 1998), 1. Louis Montrose asks us to consider the connection between Shakespeare's portrait of Joan in *1 Henry VI* and Queen Elizabeth: 'As the Virgin Queen—and, by the 1590s, as an old, single woman—Elizabeth was, uniquely, a ruler whose political power, personal mythology, and physical condition bore a disquieting resemblance to those associated with Amazons, witches, and other unruly women' (*The Purpose of Playing: Shakespeare and the Cultural Politics of the Elizabethan Theatre* (Chicago and London, 1996), 167).

the political. Sometimes that intrusion is of a sexual nature as when personal sexual preference displaces the political considerations of a strategically arranged marriage. So in *1 Henry VI* the young and callow king is seduced by Suffolk's erotically freighted description of Margaret from pursuing Gloucester's far more suitable candidate for his wife, the Earl of Armagnac's daughter, who comes, unlike Margaret, with 'a large and sumptuous dowry' (5.1.20) and is moreover 'near knit' (5.1.17) to Charles, the king of France. The same thing happens, with even more dire consequences, in *Richard Duke of York* (*3 Henry VI*) when Warwick's candidate for marriage with King Edward, Lady Bona, the French King's sister, is abandoned in mid-negotiations by Edward for Lady Elizabeth Grey. Edward's defection produces Warwick's from Margaret (ironically when we consider that Margaret produced Henry's from the Earl of Armagnac's daughter). These histories make a mockery of Henry's claim in *1 Henry VI* to be well content with any marriage choice that 'Tends to God's glory and my country's weal' (5.1.27).

The play's muckraking tone can be experienced in its first scene. After due deference is given to the dead Henry V, we are immediately exposed to the private grudges of Winchester and Gloucester, the one accusing the other and his church of praying for Henry's death and of being a secret libertine, while Winchester accuses Gloucester of wanting to take over the kingdom and of being a slave to his wife's ambitions. This titillating glimpse into the lives of the mighty stretches back to Henry V's days when Gloucester later reminds his audience that Henry could never abide the pretensions of the Bishop (1.3.24). When Bedford hears of Talbot's capture in France he turns the rhetoric on himself:

> Is Talbot slain then? I will slay myself
> For living idly here [i.e. in England], in pomp and ease.
> (1.1.141–2)

One of the play's more memorable images has Joan describing glory's dispersal:

> Glory is like a circle in the water,
> Which never ceaseth to enlarge itself
> Till, by broad spreading, it disperse to naught.
> (1.2.133–5)

The image is more applicable in this play to the circles created by the 'private grudge' (4.1.109) as they spread broadly from the conflict between individuals—Gloucester and Winchester, York and Somerset—to their households, families, retinues, and followers, and ultimately to the whole of civil society itself. (As Somerset says: 'Your private grudge, my lord of York, will out, | Though ne'er so cunningly you smother it' (4.1.109–10).) Unrestrained private grudges lead to civil wars. And this is the point, I take it, of Shakespeare's invention of those circles of followers and servants—repeated in his other plays, most memorably in *Romeo and Juliet*—with whom the violence branches out in fatuous imitation of that between the principals. Hence Shakespeare's invention of Basset, Somerset's Lancastrian follower, who, with his counterpart Vernon, York's supporter, apes the style and tenor of their mentors' aggression in what Exeter describes as 'This factious bandying of their favourites' (4.1.190).

Shakespeare makes sure that we see this factious bandying as closely imitative of their superiors, and therefore at least as potentially comic. On the ship from England to France, Vernon, according to Basset, 'upbraids' Basset about the red rose he wears

> Saying the sanguine colour of the leaves
> Did represent my master's blushing cheeks,
> (4.1.92–3)

a version of Somerset's earlier jibe that York's cheeks 'Blush for pure shame to counterfeit our roses' (2.4.66). While Basset, according to Vernon, returns the insult by saying that the white of York's white rose 'Bewrayed the faintness of my master's heart' (4.1.107), itself a version of Richard Plantagenet's jibe against Somerset that

> your cheeks do counterfeit our roses,
> For pale they look with fear, as witnessing
> The truth on our side.
>
> (2.4.62–4)

These circles come full circle, comically so again, when Somerset and York then find themselves inspired by their followers' example to re-activate their quarrel, which incites Gloucester's exasperated accusation against them of taking 'occasion from their mouths | To raise a mutiny betwixt yourselves' (4.1.130–1). But everything that happens in all three Henry plays (not to mention *Richard III*) spills over from private grudges among the English nobility, reminding Shakespeare's audience at every turn of the dangers in their own time of those private grudges among Elizabeth's courtiers. It is no wonder that on many occasions Elizabeth, unlike Henry VI, adopted a competitive 'masculine' persona. And if we take Robert Greene's word for it, Shakespeare too felt constrained to assume an aggressive posture in a competitive world, the upstart crow, the only Shake-scene in a country.

Plays Unpopular

Despite Nashe's rhapsodic testimony as to their merit in 1592, commercially driven second thoughts consigned these early history plays to a theatrical limbo until, arguably, their rediscovery in the 1960s with Sir Peter Hall and John Barton's adaptation of them as *The Wars of the Roses*. This compilation set the stage for other cut-and-paste reconstructions of the three plays as one epic drama of Brechtian length (usually played in two parts on separate evenings). And, on each occasion, it was always Part One that was the most severely cut, its bastardized 'prequel' status making it the sacrificial goat for its two 'more Shakespearian' older brothers. The climax of this rather dismal treatment came in 2001 with Edward Hall and Roger Warren's exciting reconstitution of the three plays punningly entitled *Rose Rage* at the Watermill Theatre in Newbury, a 'desperately apt' title for Lyn Gardner in the *Guardian* (10 February 2001), because Hall's directorial approach concentrated on speed and violence. According to Sheridan Morley in *The Spectator*,

Hall's approach is that of a Hollywood action director; he goes for quick cuts (both to scenes and bodies) at literally breakneck speed, a murderous kind of satire and above all a determination that his audience will never get the time to reflect on what they have seen or let their attention wander even momentarily out of the frame. (24 February 2001)

In the words of Patrick Marmion in the *Evening Standard* (9 February 2001) what we get is 'High Church carnage in the style of a spaghetti western'. Squeezing the three plays into four hours' traffic on the stage in order to produce something 'pacy, gripping, imaginative, chilling and blessedly short' (Charles Spencer in the *Daily Telegraph*, 12 February 2001) meant the virtual disappearance of Part One and the absolute non-appearance of Joan.[1] Carnage indeed!

In the famous, trend-setting 1963 omnibus production by Barton and Hall the 12,350 lines of the original trilogy were reduced to some 6,000 lines of Shakespeare augmented by some 1,450 new lines by John Barton. Three plays for the price of two (the usual ratio for the recombinations) plus bits from elsewhere. According to G. K. Hunter, Barton and Hall were thus able to 'cut away the superfluous fat, tap out the unhealthy fluids, and rescue from the diffuse, stumbling, dropsical giant, a trim, lithe, and with-it figure sharp and resilient like Hall and Barton, and certainly sharing many of their current interests'.[2] One of those trim, lithe figures— inevitably—was Joan, who, in this production, 'shrinks to the wraithlike existence of a political tendency' (104). Something similar happens to Part One itself in the history of its theatrical amalgamations. In 1987–9 a second *Wars of the Roses* compendium, this time by Michael Bogdanov and Michael Pennington for the English Shakespeare Company, achieved a stark narrative clarity again largely at the expense of Part One. Joan's part, once again, was cut and rewritten. As a consequence she appeared as a prototype for Ophelia rather than Lady Macbeth, 'innocent and rather fey', according to Lois Potter,[3] without any hint of her troubling association with the powers of darkness, all-of-a-piece, in other words, unproblematic, and as a result not very interesting. She was more intriguingly represented in yet another two-for-three bargain in 1988–9, this time in a version by Charles Wood, *The Plantagenets*, directed by Adrian Noble for the Royal Shakespeare Company, which embraced what the English Shakespeare Company had shunned, namely the power of the irrational. But this production, like the others, cut heavily into Part One. In all of them, for instance, the Countess of Auvergne (a decent small part for an

---

[1] Alastair Macaulay in the *Financial Times* (13 February 2001) reckoned that about 90 per cent of Part One was sacrificed. Joan's final indignity at the hands of her English captors may be explained in part by the fact that Hall's is an all-male company, though it should be noted that Robert Hands was praised by reviewers for his intense portrayal of Margaret.

[2] 'The Royal Shakespeare Company Plays *Henry VI*', *Renaissance Drama*, 9 (1978), 91–108; 97. The text is available in *The Wars of the Roses*, ed. John Barton (1970).

[3] 'Recycling the Early Histories: "The Wars of the Roses" and "The Plantagenets"', *SS* 43 (1991), 171–81; 176.

actress) disappeared, and so that lively, rewarding scene between her and Talbot was sacrificed and with it a provocative insight that the 'riddling merchant' (2.3.56), as the Countess calls him, provides into the place of the individual in the larger scheme of things. (A Talbonite insight that the tetralogy as a whole may be said to counter rather than confirm.)

It may always have been thus. The disappearance of Part One as a theatrical entity is a touch surrealistic in Sir Barry Jackson's account of producing *Henry VI* at Birmingham Repertory Theatre in 1952, in performances directed by Douglas Seale ('On Producing *Henry VI*, SS 6 (1953), 49–52). The burden of Jackson's article is that '*Henry VI* is eminently actable' (50), a claim that probably needed stating in 1953, but although throughout Jackson talks of producing the 'trilogy' he never once mentions Part One, a surprising omission until we realize that Part One had not as yet appeared on the stage at the time of his writing the article. Its delayed appearance in itself suggests its wraithlike existence in the minds of theatrical impresarios. It was produced as last in the sequence and this series on 4 July 1953, so presumably Jackson's article was completed before the play went into rehearsal, perhaps before the final decision to stage it had been taken. According to David Daniell 'Part One was an after-thought' ('Opening Up the Text', 250) in the mind of its director, just as it had been in the minds of Shakespeare and his collaborators. And when Seale brought a streamlined version of this production to the Old Vic in 1957 it was unsurprisingly at the expense of Part One which, as in the case of its ghostly appearance in *Rose Rage*, all but disappeared a few scenes being tacked on to Part Two.[1] It did, however, make a number of more substantial appearances on the stage in modern times, when the three early history plays were given their due as separate, if connected, theatrical enterprises (though I haven't come across an important production of Part One without its having been chaperoned into existence each time by performances of the other two parts—a limitation that the first part of *Henry IV* has not had to put up with).

---

[1] Only the funeral of Henry V and the scene in the Temple Garden and some lines about Margaret were retained. In 1923 the Old Vic saw performances of yet another telescoped version of the three plays on two nights; directed by Robert Atkins they were part of the celebration to mark the tercentenary of the publication of the 1623 Folio.

The first unadapted, fully fledged production of *Henry VI, Part One* at Stratford-upon-Avon, since F. R. Benson's savagely cut version of all three parts in 1906, took place in 1977, directed by Terry Hands: this was the production that bowled over Homer Swander. Or at least what dazzled him, as we have seen, was not so much Part One itself as Part One as part of the vast and complex work 'utterly new in the world of the theatre' ('The Rediscovery of *Henry VI*', 162). In other words, even though Part One was presented as a play that could and did stand by itself it only took on the force of revelation for Swander as something that did not in fact stand by itself and perhaps, in his view, should not do so. And this subsidiary status, influenced by and borrowing from its compilational history, is confirmed, I would suggest, by Swander's praise for the fact that all the performances were directed by the same director, all designed by the same designer, and each character throughout the trilogy was played by the same actor.[1] 'Moreover', Swander continues breathlessly, 'once in Stratford, twice in Newcastle, and probably once or twice in London, all three parts will have been presented in the same day—morning, afternoon, and evening—about nine hours of actual playing time (with breaks for lunch and dinner)' (148). This is what he finds so marvellous: 'To see them all in one day intensifies the experience to a degree that I would never have thought possible, in itself demonstrating by its impact the force and clarity of the story and the subtlety and coherence of the artistic form' (160). At the same time, however, Swander does respond to Hands's treatment of Part One praising, for instance, the way in which it revealed the complexities of Talbot and Joan. Charlotte Cornwell's Joan in particular: 'Joan is a fascinating mixture of saint, witch, naive girl, clever woman, audacious warrior, and sensual tart' (158). And Swander goes on to give us an example of Hands's more 'complex' reading when, after the death of Talbot, Joan first 'slouches and sneers' (158), as is indicated in the text of the play, then, when alone on stage with his dead body, her scorn drops away, for, in Talbot's corpse 'she has seen her own death' (159).

---

[1] The desirability of this arrangement has aroused debate. Characters change so much from play to play, one argument runs, that having them played in each by the same actor is restrictive and unrewarding, though it would certainly tax the mettle of the imaginative actor having to appear as different people in the same person.

There is nothing wrong with any of this: neither with Swander's admiration, nor with Hands's interpretation of Joan's demeanour at this juncture in the play. But the subjective nature of the theatrical experience—and its evanescence—is usefully illustrated by both responses. There is nearly always some kind of healthy tension between what the text of the play clearly conveys—in this case Joan's slouching and sneering—and the untextual reaction Hands gives her when, alone on stage (not indicated by the Folio text), she gazes on Talbot's body, seeing it as a *memento mori*. It's certainly an interesting way of proceeding, but we might argue that, at this stage anyway, it is uncalled for. Again, there is certainly nothing wrong with Swander's ecstatic response to Stratford's presentation of these three early history plays in 1977. But its subjective nature, like Hands's, is starkly underlined by a response directly antithetical to it. For G. K. Hunter the 1977 Terry Hands production, while faithful to the text of the plays by and large, was 'diffuse and dull' (105). And even for Roger Warren, who responded more positively, the shapelessness of Part Two and Part Three in this production brought on nostalgic feelings for '*The Wars of the Roses* in 1963/4, which certainly *did* have a clear shape and a very powerful sense of purpose'.[1] A clear shape, we may recall, principally at the expense of *Henry VI, Part One*.

There was nothing diffuse or dull about Michael Boyd's production of the trilogy in all its epic glory at the Swan in Stratford-upon-Avon in 2000 (followed by *Richard III* in 2001). Epic for theatregoers too as the three Henries were performed on the same day on eight occasions, outlasting the Terry Hands 1977 marathon by over an hour. (Homer Swander would have been ecstatic.) All the plays,

---

[1] 'Comedies and Histories at Two Stratfords, 1977', *SS* 31 (1978), 141–53; 149. The 1963 *Wars of the Roses* was very popular with audiences, especially the performances of David Warner as Henry and Dame Peggy Ashcroft as Margaret. For Carole Woddis in the Glasgow *Herald* (19 December 2000) even Michael Boyd's well received production of the three plays in 2000 couldn't match Hall and Barton which 'remains still the benchmark in terms of political and psychological elucidation and drive'. For someone who saw the 1977 production through Swander's eyes see David Daniell's account. He thought it 'fine ensemble playing for the huge cast' ('Opening up the Text', 247), and was amazed by Peter McEnery's performance as Suffolk and Helen Mirren's as Margaret: 'The wooing scene . . . rises to greater heights than one would have thought possible' (257). Pictures of all the RSC productions can be viewed, at the time of writing, by searching the collection section of the company's website, www.rsc.org.uk.

including the 'much-disparaged part 1' emerged in performance, according to Michael Dobson, 'as compellingly vivid and engaging drama, and as possessed throughout their immense scope by a powerful argumentative logic',[1] an indication that Boyd, like many before him, sought to convey the teleological thrust of these plays as they culminate in *Richard III*. To this end, as has also frequently been the case, Boyd relied on the same actors throughout, and many reviewers were appreciative of the 'fierce and well drilled'[2] ensemble playing as a consequence. They responded too in Swander's manner to the sheer epic sweep of the trilogy: Michael Billington, indeed, in the *Guardian*, was convinced that 'If you are going to do the plays, you should also do them as a complete set finally incorporating *Richard III*' (16 December 2000). But this enabled him to pick and choose among the plays, designating Part Two 'as the trilogy's undisputed high point', with Part One and Part Three as also-rans (a familiar position for Part One). Although Boyd's production could never have been thought dull, it did induce nausea in some spectators, and also at one remove in some readers. Gore-Langton's *Daily Express* review, for example, began uncompromisingly: 'Blood from a severed arm sprayed over my lap. A human liver slopped to the floor by my feet. An eyeball scudded past, then a tongue.' If nothing else, Boyd's production raised the bar in the ongoing competition in the sensationalizing of Shakespeare by today's theatre productions, and it may be a mixed blessing if he ever decides to direct *Titus Andronicus*.

For anyone who does not think that *Henry VI, Part One* is eminently actable or cannot stand on its own five acts, there is a production of it permanently in the public domain that may—*may*, because of the hopelessly subjective nature of the viewing experience—give him or her pause. It seems to me that, despite some obvious vulgarities, the 1983 BBC television production of Part One, produced by Jonathan Miller and directed by Jane Howell,

---

[1] *SS* 54 (2002), 287. Reviewers by and large succumbed to the production's 'hurtling pace' (Nicholas de Jongh in the *Evening Standard*, 14 December 2000). 'Never', wrote Michael Coveney in the *Daily Mail* (15 December 2000) 'have these plays been done with such venom or athleticism'. Robert Gore-Langton in the *Daily Express* was overwhelmed by it all: 'This is a thundering, awesome, crimson piece of living theatre that thrillingly recounts a bloody episode in our island story'.

[2] Kate Bassett in *The Independent*, 15 December 2000. 'This was very much an ensemble piece throughout' is Michael Dobson's verdict (287).

gives permanent expression to the play's capacity to entertain and, taking a leaf out of Nashe's book, to instruct as well. Certainly this production, like many another in the modern era, exploits the possibilities for comic knockabout and sexual roguishness: there is no doubt, for example, that Joan and the Dauphin are sleeping together when the English surprise the French during the night in Orléans at the beginning of Act 2, just as there is no doubt where Talbot and the Countess of Auvergne are headed at the end of Act 2, Scene 3. In the Dauphin's sword fight with Joan the invitation to sexual horseplay is accepted with relish by this production. (At one point Joan breaks free from what has become an amorous entwining with a knee to the groin.[1])

In the scene between the Countess and Talbot, so frequently cut in production, there are a number of gratuitously comic moments: the Countess's Porter, for instance, is unaccountably crippled and hunchbacked (a comic prefiguration perhaps of *Richard III*, also directed for television by Jane Howell)—the Countess herself, played by Joanna McCallum, towers over Trevor Peacock's Talbot which gives resonance to her astonishment when she first meets him:

> Is this the Talbot, so much feared abroad
> That with his name the mothers still their babes?
>   (2.3.15–16)

A touch of pantomime in Act 1, Scene 3 has the Duke of Gloucester and the Bishop of Winchester cantering about on stage on hobby-horses as they and their followers brawl with each other, and in the same scene a pusillanimous Officer who delivers the Mayor's proclamation does so in a half-stooping position, sinking down as the speech progresses until he ends prostrate—an interpretation that hardly anticipates the stage direction that follows: '*The skirmishes cease*'. (Peter Benson's Henry VI, another pusillanimous officer, is the acme of effeminate, hand-wringing impotence.) These moments of comic, if enjoyable, vulgarity, are balanced by an overall seriousness of treatment; the verse is beautifully spoken

---

[1] Tame stuff, you might say, in comparison with what Michael Boyd's production did to Joan in Act 5, Scene 5, when York stabbed her between her legs with a dagger.

(despite Brenda Blethyn's somewhat rickety Lancashire accent as Joan); and the camera is both a discreet witness of events and useful confidant as Jane Howell often has the characters speaking directly into it. The scenes between the Talbots, limp couplets perhaps on the page, spring to life from the sheer force of the actors' conviction in their delivery of them. All in all, this production proves just how viable television can be as a medium for playing Shakespeare, and just how good *Henry VI, Part One* is as a theatrical entertainment, one that doesn't need its other parts to be a convincing whole.

Upstart Crows

1 Henry VI itself is full of upstart crows. The play's pedagogical impact is not restricted to Nashe's 'rare exercise of virtue'; there are other less virtuous exercises on display—in self-aggrandisement, machiavellian diplomacy, upward mobility. Shakespeare's original audiences may well have taken note not only of the satirical presentation of the country's elites but also of the less obvious opportunities the play offers as a handbook for a new kind of social behaviour (of insurrection even). Some members of the audience may have looked at Joan, or the Master Gunner's Boy, or the Master Gunner himself ('Something I must do to procure me grace', 1.4.7), or the dowerless Margaret, or the quarrelling lords, or the changeable Burgundy, and have seen the possibilities for themselves. Some of them, that is, may have identified themselves to some extent at least with this one or that one of the play's egomaniacal fallen angels, although these may not be the ones that Andrew Gurr has in mind in his fascinating discussion in *Playgoing in Shakespeare's London* of the growth of 'personation' in the 1590s 'signalling not only the concept of a player pretending to be a real human being (as distinct from Magnificence or a king like Cambyses) but the arrival of stage heroes with whom many of the spectators could identify themselves and their wants' (136). And we might note here in passing that many members of the audience would also have been well aware that what they were seeing was itself the result of the processes the play was in part dramatizing: many of the actors playing these and other parts had not always been actors but ordinary working-men like themselves—James

Burbage had been a joiner at one time, John Heminges a grocer, James Tunstall a saddler, Martin Slater an ironmonger.[1]

Despite itself, one might say, particularly in its schizophrenic presentation of Joan, Part One colludes with the forces it derides. So often in the play the tenets of chivalry are mocked by word and action. The play is full of moments of punctured aristocratic hauteur. Talbot is outraged, for instance, by the French refusal to play the aristocratic game of war by the outmoded rules of masculine chivalry. He and Burgundy are especially angered, and comically so, by Joan's ruse in 3.2 when she and some of her forces sneak into Rouen disguised as the 'vulgar sort of market men' (3.2.4) with sacks of corn for sale. (Talbot would have been even more affronted, one suspects, by the fact that she disguised herself as a market man rather than as a market woman.) Her French, female, and magical trickery—so he believes—makes him apoplectic when she refuses to come down from the walls of Rouen to meet the English in the field. We can imagine how well her eminently sensible

> Belike your lordship takes us then for fools,
> To try if that our own be ours or no
>
> (3.2.61–2)

would have gone down with a goodly fraction of Shakespeare's audience who may also have hooted at Talbot's impotent blustering:

> Base muleteers of France,
> Like peasant footboys do they keep the walls,
> And dare not take up arms like gentlemen.
>
> (3.2.66–7)

The puncturing of aristocratic hauteur turns literal when the Master Gunner's Boy kills Salisbury and Gargrave with a lucky shot, rather belying in its ordinariness Talbot's portentous 'Accursèd fatal hand | That hath contrived this woeful tragedy!' (1.5.54–5).

---

[1] For insurrectionary possibilities for the Elizabethan audience, see Phyllis Rackin in *Stages of History: Shakespeare's English Chronicles* (Ithaca, NY, 1990). Certainly, we are now invited to look farther down the social ladder to see the effects of play-acting on audiences in Shakespeare's time, as Robert Darnton argues in *The Kiss of Lamourette* (New York, 1990): '…the century's growing interest in individual identity may be found on levels lower than where we have been accustomed to look' (212; quoted in Jonathan Rose, *The Intellectual Life of the British Working Classes* (New Haven and London, 2001), 13).

These are moments of delightful nuance for an Elizabethan audience as is the whole scene of Talbot's encounter with the Countess of Auvergne, beginning with her feigned surprise at the discrepancy between report and real life conveyed in her disdainful use of an unmoored 'this' in relation to him:

> Is this the scourge of France?
> Is this the Talbot, so much feared abroad
> That with his name the mothers still their babes?
> (2.3.14–16)

Although the Countess may be feigning her surprise at Talbot's unprepossessing physique—this warrior is a 'writhled shrimp' (2.3.22) as she puts it—her apology only goes so far as to admit that he is what fame has bruited of him despite 'more than may be gathered by thy shape' (68). Throughout this scene there are intimations of the later sharp-edged dialogue between Shakespeare's men and women in his romantic comedies.[1]

Henry VI, Part One is not an isolated phenomenon in these respects. David Riggs writes:

Before a typical spectator went to the Fortune to see *Tamburlaine*, he was likely to have been conning such a work as William Baldwin's *A Treatise of Moral Philosophy, Containing the Sayings of the Wise* to learn how the achievement of fortitude and magnificence might help him to emulate an aristocratic style of life. (*Shakespeare's Heroical Histories*, 69)

But what he or she would have gleaned from *Tamburlaine* might have had the authorities worried, as E. Pearlman points out: 'Politically alert spectators at the Fortune would notice that the story of a shepherd who becomes rich enough to punish his royal rivals and marry a queen carries a potentially subversive message'.[2] Indeed the mere fact of attending a theatrical presentation could be interpreted as subversive. The theatre was frequently associated with the forbidden splendours of Catholic worship, its pageantry, colour and ritual; and this was especially true of the Rose, home to Lord Strange's company. Ferdinando Stanley, Lord Strange, was a Catholic based in Lancashire, 'a county which had a peculiarly

---

[1] Some commentators see more than nuance. Henry Kelly in *Divine Providence in the England of Shakespeare's Histories* (Cambridge, Mass., 1970) believes that compared to Joan Talbot 'is a blundering oaf, a railing *miles gloriosus*' (247).

[2] *William Shakespeare: the History Plays* (New York, 1992), 9.

intense record for pursuing recusants, and a lot of great-family recusants to pursue' (Andrew Gurr, *Playing Companies*, 34). At the same time, Strange's Men were known as a pugnacious, independently-minded company. E. K. Chambers records an incident in 1589 where the company refused to obey an injunction from the City Fathers prohibiting the playing of plays in London for a period of time. In a letter from the Lord Mayor of London, Sir John Harte, to Lord Burghley, written on 6 November 1589, the offence is duly noted: 'The L. Admiral's players very dutifully obeyed, but the others in very contemptuous manner departing from me, went to the Cross Keys and played that afternoon' (*Elizabethan Stage*, iv. 305–6).[1] Plays taken from the Chronicles had, arguably, potentially stronger, more immediately subversive messages than plays like *Tamburlaine* set in exotic climes. Other plays of the period, other history plays, certainly offered scandalous models of upstart ambition that crossed class and sexual lines. The most famous is Gaveston in Marlowe's *Edward II* who arouses contempt among Edward's courtiers not so much because he is Edward's 'minion' as because he is, in Mortimer's contemptuous phrase, 'so basely born' (1.4.401).

Would the women in Shakespeare's audience have seen the women in Shakespeare's early history plays as scandalous models of upstart ambition?[2] And if so, how would they have responded to them? If death and the theatre itself are the age's primary great levellers, can women be far behind? One of the fascinating differences between Shakespeare's two history tetralogies is the formidable presence of women characters in the first and the relative absence of them in the second. It is as though Gloucester's empty certainty in *2 Henry VI* that affairs of state 'are no women's matters' (1.3.120) were finally heeded by Shakespeare when he came to write of the events that led to the reign of Henry V—as though England's brief triumph in the Hundred Years War against France

---

[1] The company may have been pugnacious but it was so in a conservative, high-minded way. Scott McMillin in *The Elizabethan Theatre and The Book of Sir Thomas More* describes Strange's repertory of plays as by and large 'conservative in a stern, steel-ribbed, moralistic mode' (60).

[2] In 'Women in the Renaissance Theatre Audience', *SQ* 40 (1989), 165–74, Richard A. Levin maintains that women were an important constituency for dramatists and had to be catered to.

should not be sullied by the vagaries and conspiracies of women.[1] Especially French women. In the first tetralogy many of the major women characters are trickily French. As such they participate in the general scheme of things. Linda Woodbridge argues that in Shakespeare's history plays France is to England what in Edward Said's terms the Orient is to Europe: 'throughout the histories France is England's "cultural contestant", inferior of course, cowardly and cool, but great enough to be a worthy opponent.'[2] The French characters in these plays manifest 'lascivious sensuality, lying and untrustworthiness, lack of energy and initiative, cowardice, intrigue, cunning, cruelty to people and animals, and despotism' (112); but these dark French qualities are also English ones: 'France is England's dark double: many of its evil qualities have clearly being projected on it from what England fears in itself' (115).

But the women in these plays, as we have seen, also participate in the construction of a world of tempting possibilities, and not just sexual ones. As Alençon says of Joan in Part One: 'These women are shrewd tempters with their tongues' (1.2.123). Certainly, the men in all three of these early plays fear them and self-consciously parade an anxious contempt for women's agency, or a slavish dependence on it. Deborah Willis notices that 'In Shakespeare's first tetralogy, witches, wives, and mothers are endowed with similar nightmare powers; by both magical and nonmagical means they manipulate males and make them feel as if they have been turned back into dependent children.'[3] The play is pitted with anxious questions about their power. Suffolk's aside to himself— 'Wilt thou be daunted at a woman's sight?' (5.4.25)—is typical, for

[1] In their introduction to *True Rites and Maimed Rites: Ritual and Anti-Ritual in Shakespeare and His Age* (Urbana, 1992) Lynda Woodbridge and E. Berry note: 'The first tetralogy's dangerous women overcome, women largely disappear from history plays, which then explore a post-initiatory realm where power is male, the female ruthlessly suppressed' (25).

[2] *The Scythe of Saturn: Shakespeare and Magical Thinking* (Urbana and Chicago, 1994), 115.

[3] 'Shakespeare and the English witch-hunts: enclosing the maternal body', in *Enclosure Acts: Sexuality, Property, and Culture in Early Modern England*, ed. John Michael Archer and Richard Burt (Ithaca, NY, 1994), 96–120; 100. For Marilyn L. Williamson in ' "When Men Are Rul'd by Women": Shakespeare's First Tetralogy', *Shakespeare Studies*, 19 (1987), 41–60, 'The women are hated because they represent deep male fears: powerlessness and the rebellion of the traditionally weak' (42).

'beauty's princely majesty is such | Confounds the tongue, and makes the senses rough' (5.4.26–7). In the play's opening scene Gloucester appears briefly in the role of uxorious husband, and is criticized for it by Winchester:

> Thy wife is proud: she holdeth thee in awe
> More than God or religious churchmen may.
> (1.1.39–40)

And Part Two gives her her moment of defiance when she says that she 'will not be slack | To play [her] part in fortune's pageant' (1.2.66–7) though that part turns out to be a farcical one, leading to her banishment and the executions of her fellow conspirators. Despite banishments and executions the women in these early history plays personify the spirit of subversion that stalks the land: when one disappears, as Joan does in 5.5 of Part One, another takes her place, as Margaret does in 5.6.[1]

Of all the upstart crows in *1 Henry VI*, Joan of Arc is the most memorable, the most appealing, and the most fractured in characterization. For Harold Bloom she is the only thing in the play that makes it readable (or watchable): she is indeed for him an early Falstaff, 'quirkily memorable' with a 'rancid charm'.[2] Quirkiness is hardly an adequate explanation for the disconnected manner of her representation. No other character in Shakespeare comes to us so unapologetically discrepant. Despite desperate rebuttals from a number of critics to the contrary,[3] I agree with Edward Burns when he argues that 'She/he [Joan] cannot be read as a substantive realist character, a unified subject with a coherent single identity. If she establishes a subjectivity, it is as a performer, as a robustly

---

[1] Because the three women never appear on stage together, Part One offers the intriguing possibility that they could all be played by the same actor. Arguably, although he would be dressed very differently when playing Joan, the audience would recognize him on each appearance and respond to the implications of this. Michael Boyd seizes upon this possibility in his blood-spattered production of the Henries at the Swan in Stratford-upon-Avon in 2000. As Fiona Bell's Joan sinks from sight at her burning in Act 4, she rises a few minutes later, resurrected as Margaret. Most reviewers felt that her Joan was more convincing than her Margaret.

[2] *Shakespeare and the Invention of the Human* (New York, 1998), 45.

[3] Consider, for example, Michael Hattaway's suggestion in 1990 that Joan is the play's tragic figure, comparable with Faulconbridge in *King John*, especially 2.1.457–67. According to him, she turns to witchcraft only in despair. 'It cannot be taken as an unequivocal manifestation of the diabolic power of Joan' (24). He imagines her as a unified character.

comic presence, speaking out to the audience and undercutting the heroic identities conferred on her' (26–7). But she is even less coherent than he allows in that at the beginning of the play and, more joltingly, in her last appearances she sees herself as her awed supporters used to see her—as France's saviour, blessed by Heaven's hierarchy, the chosen one, with a lineage as noble as Talbot's. She is not in these final moments a robust comic presence; she possesses no charm, rancid or otherwise; at most she possesses the faint, perfidious allure of the victim.

Indeed the play really turns on Joan in 5.3 where the disjunctiveness in her presentation is at its most blatant and startling. Nothing has quite prepared us for the bald assertion of Joan's reliance on fiends and the abracadabra and hocus-pocus of those 'charming spells and periapts' (5.3.2), the 'choice spirits' (l. 3) and 'the lordly monarch of the north' (l. 6). Despite her recognition of their 'accustomed diligence' (l. 9), their 'wonted furtherance' (l. 21) to her, we have not been accustomed to them, for us they are unwonted (and unwanted), coming as an intrusive surprise. And the play moves into dispiriting farce in Joan's admission that she used to feed her fiends with her blood and now will offer them a 'member' 'In earnest of a further benefit' (l. 16) (presumably, in Faustian fashion, her immortal soul). A fiendish provenance replaces a divine one for her in this scene, a scene that reduces Joan to a comic, bathetic dependency on shifty representatives of the underworld:

> Help me this once, that France may get the field.
> O hold me not with silence overlong!
>
> (5.3.12–13)

Although they in fact say nothing their actions are indicated in a series of odd-sounding stage directions whereby they '*walk and speak not*', '*hang their heads*', '*shake their heads*' and '*depart*'. The idea of Fiends hanging their heads like chastened school-children belies the '*Thunder*' of the scene's stormy introduction of them. It's difficult to imagine Joan feeding these strangely bashful apparitions with her blood and offering to lop off one of her limbs 'In earnest of a further benefit' (5.3.16).

When Joan returns to the play in 5.5 it punishes her at first even more ferociously. As the climax to her perfidy she denies that she is the child of her shepherd father who, Lear-like, turns on her: 'O burn her, burn her! Hanging is too good' (5.5.33).¹ But 5.5 is a peculiar scene. Why does Shakespeare give Joan so much to say here in a play that doesn't give anyone very much to say at any one time? After our having experienced her at her most bathetic she is then given eighteen lines (36–53) of dignified self-justification, temperate and measured, which seem to have wandered in from an earlier scene, from another play even, as though her colloquy with the fiends in 5.3 and her contemptible repudiation of her father in the scene's early going had never occurred. For the moment Joan takes on Talbot's language, adopting, as it were, a silly stately style in contrast to the Joan-like honest kersey style of her shepherd father. After his use of the dialect word 'obstacle' and the affectionately colloquial 'collop', Joan repudiates him in language of a courtly sonority: 'You have suborned this man | Of purpose to obscure my noble birth' (5.5.21–2). 'First let me tell you whom you have condemned' (5.5.36) hardly seems in order when we know just how untrue what she then tells them is in the light of what we have just experienced. Here, at some length, in dignified language, she reverts to the play's original presentation of her as

> Virtuous and holy, chosen from above
> By inspiration of celestial grace
>
> (5.5.39–40)

But then the scene turns on her again, as she confesses her 'infirmity' (5.5.60), her fake (?) pregnancy, and trots out her farcical multiplication of likely inseminators.² Is Joan pregnant? Or is she simply lying in an attempt to save her own skin? We never find out and can hardly be satisfied with York's comment that 'This argues what her kind of life hath been —| Wicked and vile' (5.5.15–16), and we are even less satisfied with the play's last words on Joan (York's again): 'Thou foul accursèd minister of hell' (5.5.93).

The play begins with less outrageous variations of the same process. Joan first appears as Shaw's Joan, that is, in a state of beat-

---

¹ Leslie Fiedler points out in *The Stranger in Shakespeare* (1972) that 'Though the vilest of all Shakespeare's undutiful daughters, perhaps, Joan is by no means the last. Indeed, there is scarcely a play in the canon in which daughters do not betray or seem to betray their fathers' (79).

² We never see Joan again with any of her child's possible fathers. Not Charles, nor Alençon, nor Reignier. Later in 5.6 when we do see Charles, Alençon and Reignier again (negotiating with the English) there's no mention of Joan by anyone, let alone her three 'lovers'.

3. Joan warlike, even grand : Mrs Baddeley in the part, from Bell's edition
of Shakespeare (1773–5).

itude, patient, serene, the 'Divinest creature' (1.7.4) of Charles's
adoration, the object of the Virgin Mary's miraculous intercession,
chosen by her to rescue France, and so made beautiful, coura-
geous, and wise ('Ask me what question thou canst possible, | And
I will answer unpremeditated', 1.2.87–8). But almost immediately
the ethereal bubble is pricked by Joan herself in the bathos of her
description of the provenance of her epic 'keen-edged sword'
(1.2.98), the 'sword of Deborah' (1.2.105) as Charles calls it, which
she has picked up in Saint Katherine's churchyard 'Out of a great
deal of old iron' (1.2.101). Charles's own encomia of Joan
(1.2.140–5 and 1.7.4–7) play on her virtues in a disturbingly

47

4. Julia Ford's Joan (in part 1 of Adrian Noble's *Plantagenets*, Stratford-upon-Avon, 1988) was described by Irving Wardle as 'simultaneously vulnerable and invincible'. The production showed her burnt on stage.

disjunctive manner in their mingling of pagan and Christian icons: Mahomet, Helen, Saint Philip, Venus, Astraea, Saint Denis, Adonis. But, still, when the Messenger brings news of Joan's appearance to Talbot he calls her a 'holy prophetess' (1.5.80), despite his being an English messenger rather than a French one. On the other hand, and virtually at the same time, she's clearly an early combination of the demonic, the machiavellian, and the Marlovian, a 'virtual parody of the Marlovian prototype' as Riggs puts it (*Shakespeare's Heroical Histories*, p. 22), 'that railing Hecate' (3.2.63) according to Talbot, and a whore to boot according to Burgundy: 'Scoff on, vile fiend and shameless courtesan' (3.2.44).

I dwell on the disjunctiveness of Joan's representation because it may hold an insight into the queasy nature of the attractiveness that the play held for its original audiences, and perhaps also for Shakespeare. Of course the easiest way out of any dilemma that her contradictoriness provokes is to blame it, as has frequently been done, on the vicissitudes of collaboration, but it is difficult to imagine a change of collaborators within the space of a few lines as would have to be the case with 5.5. Some of the disjunctive elements can be partly accounted for by the obvious fact that they express the views of competing interests: the French regard her (while she is successful at least) as a saint, the English as demonic, an exponent of 'baleful sorcery' (2.1.15), a recipient of the 'help of hell' (2.1.18), and sexually rank, the Dauphin's 'trull' (2.2.28) according to Burgundy before he undergoes his conversion to her cause brought on by her 'haughty words' (3.3.78). 'One man's Sybil is another man's Hecate', as Gabriele Bernhard Jackson puts it.[1] In recent criticism Joan has been seen in the context of a renewed awareness of the instrumentality of Shakespeare's characterizations. A. R. Braunmuller, for instance, alerts us to the fact that 'Elizabethan playwrights will sacrifice virtually any inferred fictional character in order to get things said that need saying'.[2] When Joan says: 'Care is no cure, but rather corrosive, | For things that are not to be remedied' (3.3.3–4) the intention of this piece of sententiousness is to show up the French nobility's chronic susceptibility to internal dissension (like the English) rather than to highlight Joan's personal resoluteness (though it can't help but do that too). It's so like Shakespeare, Gabriele Jackson argues, 'to present unexplained and suggestive discontinuities' ('Topical Ideology', 43), to enmesh a character like Joan in 'a tangle of contradictory allusions' (48). Far from being a blight on the play, or a clumsiness in execution, Joan's successive discontinuities constitute Shakespeare's 'progressive exploitation of the varied ideological potential inherent in the topically relevant figure of the virago' (64–5). Or else, just as astutely on his part, they enable us to 'participate fully

---

[1] 'Topical Ideology: Witches, Amazons, and Shakespeare's Joan of Arc', *English Literary Renaissance*, 18 (1988), 40–65; 48.

[2] 'Characterization through language in the Early Plays of Shakespeare and His Contemporaries', in *Shakespeare: Man of the Theater*, edited by K. Muir, J. L. Halio and D. J. Palmer (Newark, Del., 1983), 128–47; 130.

in the unresolved contradictoriness of the historical legend' (Holderness, *Shakespeare: The Histories*, 126).

Maybe an Elizabethan audience would have been less conscious than we are of the jarring improbabilities in Joan's characterization. And it is certainly true that throughout his career as a dramatist Shakespeare at times sacrifices psychological consistency for some more important manipulation. In the history plays especially Shakespeare demands that his audience be trained in the art of shifting allegiances. In the Introduction to her edition of *Richard III* Janis Lull plots the play's trajectory:

In the first three acts of *Richard III*, Shakespeare almost seems to be on Richard's side, showing us the world of the play from Richard's point of view. Eventually, however, the play and presumably the audience withdraw their sympathy from Richard, turning instead to his victims, especially the relatively "flat" female characters.[1]

This, of course, is a controlled, gradual reversal of feeling; in Joan's case the reversals are multiple, precipitous, oxymoronic even. They resemble the spectacularly conventional conversion of Burgundy who succumbs immediately to Joan's (relatively undistinguished) speech of persuasion.[2] But Joan's angularities are much more insistent. They draw our attention to their unlikely contiguity in a manner that suggests something as deliberate as the emphasis in Shakespeare's last plays on their impossible artificiality. They bring to the surface the play's subterranean attachment to its promotion of lesemajesty. Turning hysterically on Joan, the play turns on its own half-hidden agenda, as though Shakespeare wanted to make it clear finally in the starkest of terms that in the last analysis Thomas Nashe was right in his original assessment of the play's pedagogical power, that Joan (and the other *arrivistes*) are in the pay of the devil.

[1] New Cambridge Shakespeare (Cambridge, 1999), 9.

[2] I am aware that what is being left out of account here is the power of the actors on the stage to make possible things impossible. The putative skill of the actors playing Burgundy and Joan may well be able to fly in the face of the text's impossible demands on them. In *The Plantagenets*, the 1988–9 Royal Shakespeare Company version of the three plays by Charles Wood, directed by Adrian Noble, Lois Potter recalls one such successful rendition: 'in the scene where Joan seduces Burgundy away from England, he was initially so revolted by her that he was on the point of running her through with his sword. She fearlessly urged him on, and then— desperately, as if bewitched—he threw it on the ground in front of her' ('Recycling the Early Histories', 176).

Design and Structure

The popularity of *1 Henry VI* did not depend solely on its ideology, either then in Shakespeare's time, or now in ours. Commentators have tended, however, to dismiss it as a largely infelicitous piece aesthetically speaking. They take their cue from Theobald in 1733 who believed that in all the *Henry VI* plays 'the diction . . . is more obsolete, and the numbers more mean and prosaical, than in the generality of his genuine compositions' (110). Part One has always been considered even meaner and more prosaical than its counter-parts of the first tetralogy, and for this reason, if for no other, it might be appropriate to linger a while on what felicities it has. Despite the committee-like status of its authorship, the play has come in for some discriminating praise for its architectonics. It may not have any decent poetry—its numbers are undeniably mean— but it does have design; there are thoughtful linkages, sometimes of an arrestingly ironic nature; there is a controlling idea. The most effusive commentator along these structural lines is Hereward T. Price who believes that Shakespeare was in this play 'daringly original . . . his mastery of design was just as superb as his mastery of language'.[1] (This last claim might be considered eccentric if Price intends it to refer to the language in Part One.) It is this conception of design that 'opens for modern times a new era in drama' (26).[2] Shakespeare might have agreed with this judgement. He is himself by far the most relaxed commentator on the status of the *Henry VI* plays. Looking back from the epilogue of *Henry V*, with the genius of the second tetralogy behind him, the Chorus, standing in for and written by Shakespeare, thinks highly enough of the first tetralogy to plead for *Henry V*'s 'acceptance' by its audience in 1599 with their memory of *Henry VI* as a benchmark:

---

[1] *Construction in Shakespeare* (East Lansing, Mich., 1951), 26.

[2] The more moderate, and more defensible, position along these lines can be represented by Geoffrey Bullough: 'Mastery of construction indeed seems to have preceded his mastery of a poetic imagery and texture; Shakespeare was a fine dramatist before he became a finished poet' (iii. 40). For Bullough, 'The play is quite cleverly built up as a series of see-saw movements in place and mood: from England to France and vice versa, between the French and English armies in France, between discord and harmony at home, between defeat and victory in France' (39).

> Henry the Sixth, in infant bands crowned king
> > Of France and England, did this king succeed,
> Whose state so many had the managing
> > That they lost France and made his England bleed,
> Which oft our stage hath shown—and, for their sake,
> In your fair minds let this acceptance take.
>
> > > > > > > > > (9–14)

Uncertain antecedents notwithstanding,[1] the 'their' in line 13 must refer to the plays that preceded *Richard II*, namely the *Henry VIs* and *Richard III*. So Shakespeare in 1599, like Nashe in 1592, responds unselfconsciously to their popularity, happy indeed to appeal to the fair minds of his audiences on the basis of their previous enjoyment of the prosaical plays that turned Henry V's triumph upside-down.[2]

The structure of *1 Henry VI*, we might say then, trumps its poetry. On numerous occasions, for instance, there is a sly irony in the order and placing of events. Consider, for example, the way in which Joan leaves the play and Margaret enters it. Both women are captured by the English forces near the play's end. In 5.3 York captures Joan, in 5.4 Suffolk Margaret. On the one hand, in Joan's case, the air is filled with curses, insults and sexual jibes; on the other, courtly delicacy prevails, Suffolk will touch Margaret 'but with reverent hands' (5.4.3). Nonetheless, as with Joan, there is enchantment involved in Suffolk's encounter with Margaret, but of the 'natural' kind, the sexual. Suffolk is bewitched by Margaret—'I have no power to let her pass' (5.4.16)—and his momentary paralysis is the courtly love equivalent of Talbot's loss of power in fighting Joan earlier in the play. The ironic parallel is made even more plain by Suffolk's remonstrating with himself over his 'cowardice': 'Wilt thou be daunted at a woman's sight?' (5.4.25) he asks himself. A similar tactical sense of ironic congruity fuels the ending of 2.2 and the opening of 2.3. Before Talbot goes off to spar with the Countess of Auvergne he whispers instructions to the Captain. Scene 3 begins with the Countess reminding her Porter of an off-stage direction from her:

---

[1] Who does the 'his' in line 12 belong to? Henry V or VI?

[2] If you were a reader of the 1623 Folio the connection between *Henry V* and *1 Henry VI* would be pronounced. The Epilogue to *Henry V* occurs on K2^r or p. 95; on K2^v or p. 96 are the opening exchanges of *1 Henry VI*.

5. Peggy Ashcroft as Margaret with William Squire as Suffolk in *Henry VI*,
Stratford-upon-Avon, 1964.

> Porter, remember what I gave in charge;
> And when you have done so, bring the keys to me.
>
> (2.3.1–2)

In neither case is the audience privy to the instructions, but soon
becomes enjoyably aware of how one slippery customer has out-
manoeuvred the other. Sometimes the reversals and counter-
reversals flash by. Consider, for instance, the shifting perspectives
achieved by the presence of the dying Bedford in the extended

second scene of Act 3 where his and the English army's helplessness are underscored by his being carried on to the stage in front of the jeering French and then, for the moment, imagining himself reviving 'the soldiers' hearts, | Because I ever found them as myself' (3.2.95–6). 'Then be it so' (3.2.98) says Talbot before this heroic function is dashed by Fastolf's cowardice. And yet a line or two later a number of excursions result in the flights of Joan, Alençon and Charles, enabling Bedford, who has witnessed these turns and counter-turns of Mars's 'moving', to expire with equanimity, 'For I have seen our enemies' overthrow' (3.2.109). 'Lost and recovered in a day again!' (3.2.113) exclaims Talbot voicing our own sense of the wonder of it all.[1]

Turns and counter-turns are matched by reinforcing repetitions. A. C. Hamilton notices how 'at the beginning of the play, Henry V's body is borne upon the stage; in the middle the aged Mortimer is brought in in a chair; and near the end Old Talbot is led by a servant',[2] each piece of stage business reinforcing our sense of a nation's decrepitude. A similar kind of reinforcement is achieved by following the rose-plucking scene with the scene of Mortimer's death, as also is the case with the repetition of the interrupted ceremony in 1.1, 3.1, and 4.1, an example of the 'repetition of likeness in difference which is the binding element of all design' (*Construction in Shakespeare*, 28). Henry's 'Be packing' (4.1.46) to the cowardly Fastolf is immediately followed by a reading of the letter of defection from Burgundy, as one brand of disloyalty replaces another. And in this context we should consider the force of the repetitive deaths of the two Talbots, father and son. Each of them is given his somewhat evasive military encounter with Joan and each also a kind of fugitive triumph over her. The father is given a draw in his encounter with her, and that draw, according to Talbot, only the result of a lassitude brought on him by her use of some kind of black art; the son refuses to fight her out of 'proud, majestical high scorn' (4.7.39) for a mere 'giglot wench' (4.7.41). Honour (of a

---

[1] Sometimes the irony does not rely on contiguity. Burgundy's opening words in the plays are about traitors: 'Traitors have never other company' (2.1.19). We discover later that he is himself a double traitor; first to France, then to England. On the other hand, the Bastard's line about Talbot, 'I think this Talbot be a fiend of hell' (2.1.47), occurs two lines before the entrance of Charles and Joan (for the English, the real fiend from hell). The Bastard then calls her holy Joan (2.1.50).

[2] *The Early Shakespeare* (San Marino, Cal., 1967), 23.

somewhat dubious kind) is therefore satisfied on all fronts. Sometimes repetition is more subtly interpenetrating. Not only are the white and red roses recurring props and tropes of some significance, but their redness and whiteness spread out into the play figuratively and literally as in the French General's anticipation of Talbot's death:

> These eyes that see thee now well colourèd
> Shall see thee withered, bloody, pale, and dead.
> (4.2.37–8)

On the other hand, Shakespeare quite cleverly exploits the technique of the reversal of expectations as described by Roger Warren in which the audience is entertainingly unsettled by 'the setting of one extreme against another, and especially of leading the audience to expect a particular consequence, and then reversing that expectation by presenting a quite different result, often the complete opposite of the one expected'.[1] He instances the play's second scene where the Dauphin vows not to retreat and then immediately does so:

The dramatic effect depends upon the fact that the Dauphin's extravagant vow that he will not fly and that his men can kill him if he does should be followed immediately by his ignominious retreat, and by his violent verbal attack on those men whom he said he would forgive for killing him if he did what he has in fact done. (76)

Fife and Drum

1 Henry VI is a colourful pageant—blue, tawny, black, crimson are specified colours—relying on the sights and sounds of international diplomacy and warfare. It is at times spectacular stuff. Alarums and excursions often come with the detailed stage directions that indicate the care that needs to be taken in physical representation, as in 4.6: '*Alarum, Excursions, wherein Lord Talbot's son John is hemmed about by French soldiers and Talbot rescues him*'. The play is full of martial sounds: the roar of cannon, swords clashing, drum beats (that 'heavy music' (4.2.40) as the French General calls it), thunder, trumpets, marching boots—little wonder perhaps that

---

[1] ' "Contrarieties Agree": an Aspect of Dramatic Technique in *Henry VI*', *SS* 37 (1984), 75–83; 75.

the play's words seem to play second fiddle to its percussion. Second fiddle too to the dumb significants (i.e. wordless symbols)—as Richard Plantagenet calls the roses in 2.4—that loom large in this play, often speaking louder than words, though their most theatrical moment comes at the beginning of *3 Henry VI* where Richard throws down the head of Somerset whom he has just killed in battle and says: 'Speak thou for me, and tell them what I did' (1.1.16). When in 4.1 of Part One Henry chooses foolishly to don a dumb significant, a red rose, his action negates the pretty oratory that Warwick praises him for; Richard, at all events, is not convinced: 'I like it not | In that he wears the badge of Somerset' (4.1.176–7). A gesture—especially such an ill-considered one—is worth and makes worthless a thousand pretty words (or perhaps a thousand of these pretty words) even when the words come with baleful consequences. All this can be summed up by Volumnia in *Coriolanus* who remarks that 'Action is eloquence, and the eyes of th'ignorant | More learnèd than the ears' (3.2.76–7). So too are the eyes of the learned (or at least the literate) in *1 Henry VI*: in 2.4 where the phrase first appears, Warwick cannot bring himself to say that he supports Richard Plantagenet in his 'case of truth', but he does manage to pick a white rose to indicate with a dumbly significant gesture whose side he is on.

We might consider action in this play as a species of dumb significant that has an emasculating effect on language. As Gloucester says, 'What should I say? His deeds exceed all speech' (1.1.15). When Bedford takes up this attitude—'O let no words, but deeds, revenge this treason' (3.2.48)—both words and action suffer as his urging comes from someone who is dying of grief, sickness, and old age, slumped in a chair before the walls of Rouen. The notion that in contrast with deeds words carry less conviction is a troubling thought for a poet, but it's one that Shakespeare returns to throughout his career with increasing concern. When Exeter says, 'We mourn in black; why mourn we not in blood?' (1.1.17), he might just as well have said 'we mourn in *words*, why mourn we not in blood?' It's futile, as he goes on to say, to curse 'the planets of mishap' (1.1.23), instead of righting mishap by force of arms. At times in the play the notion of silence conspires with the noises of the battlefield and the splendour of the pageantry to further undermine the adequacy of words. On the English side, Mortimer's advice to Richard Plantagenet is faithfully (and fruitfully) followed:

'With silence, nephew, be thou politic' (2.5.101). On the French, Joan's 'Be wary how you place your words' (3.2.3) has a comparable machiavellian application (though it is not so productively heeded). Both anticipate the doomed machiavellianism of Sir John Hume, a priest who dabbles in magic on behalf of the Duchess of Gloucester in Part Two, 'This business asketh silent secrecy' (1.2.90).[1] But, paradoxically enough, Shakespeare has yet to learn to trust—perhaps he never entirely learns to do so—the adequacy of visual representation (or of the unheard and unseen) so the play is filled with what we might now think to be unnecessary and supererogatory verbal descriptions of visual states of affairs that are as plain as the noses on the actors' faces. Hence, for instance, the lengthy self-descriptions of physical appearance that are superfluous if the actor looks the part, the most notable being Mortimer's description of his fading state, 2.5.4–12. We should bear in mind, however, the difficulty some spectators might have had in viewing the stage, especially if they were short-sighted, or were at a distance from the stage, or if pillars obscured the action.

Yet words and silence pale before Shakespeare's exuberant indulgence in martial violence—still a theatrical crowd-pleaser, arguably even more so in today's cinema and television. Part One gratifies the spectator with the 'rancorous spite', the 'furious raging broils' (4.1.185) of 'This jarring discord of nobility' (4.1.188), its 'worthless emulation' (4.4.21), its 'private discord' (4.4.22). Raging, jarring, and inevitably gruesome, as Talbot's lines indicate:

> Your hearts I'll stamp out with my horse's heels
> And make a quagmire of your mingled brains.
>
> (1.5.86–7)

The anticipated goriness of this threat is matched by what Shakespeare's audience may well have seen on stage, when, for instance, Talbot specifies the nature of Salisbury's injuries: 'One of thy eyes and thy cheek's side struck off?' (1.5.53). How would this have been

---

[1] A tactical acknowledgement of the use of silent secrecy in the *Henry VI* plays anticipates the more subtle and sophisticated enlargement of the significance of silence in Shakespeare's later plays. Frank Kermode notes in *Shakespeare's Language* (New York, 2000) that 'an increasing interest in silence might be thought to mark a general development away from rhetorical explicitness and towards a language that does not try to give everything away' (10).

played? Today no doubt with a macabre attention to authenticity and perhaps then also. The play's second scene quickly establishes the piece's athletic-warrior spirit in recording the first encounter between the English and French celebrated by the triumphal stage direction: '*They⌈ the French ⌉are beaten back by the English with great loss*' (1.2.21.1). Indeed there are as many as fourteen instances of stage combat in Part One; and on a number of occasions the sword fighters are principal characters, as Charles Edelman reminds us,[1] and Edward Burns makes much of the fact that the swords in Shakespeare's time would have been real ones and the fighting intense and athletic. Before Shakespeare only in Greene's *Alphonsus* (twice) and once in Peele's *The Battle of Alcazar* is it clear that important characters indulge in sword fighting.

There is, in fact, a hugely crowd-pleasing kineticism to all the history plays in both tetralogies, encouraged by the presence of so many people at different times on the stage. *1 Henry VI* has a cast of twenty-three and joins other history plays in being labour intensive.[2] These history plays were the late sixteenth-century equivalent of Hollywood's biblical epics of the 1930s and 1940s with their casts of thousands, and were at their most popular in the late 1580s dying out by 1594. *1 Henry VI* occasionally uses a full stage to richly comic effect as when the French soldiers '*half ready and half unready*' (2.1.39.3) leap over the walls of Orléans. And the cast comes on to the stage from every direction—the stage's three doors,[3] the gallery (and higher?), the trap-door for Joan's fiends, and often in today's performances the auditorium aisles. There are

---

[1] In *Brawl Ridiculous: Swordfighting in Shakespeare's Plays* (Manchester, 1992).

[2] Here is a partial list: *The Wounds of Civil War* (24 plus); *Edward I* (19 plus); *Edward II* (20); *Edward III* (20); *2 Seven Deadly Sins* (20 plus); *2 Henry VI* (23 or as *The Contention* 24 plus); *3 Henry VI* (17 or as *Richard Duke of York* 22); *Sir Thomas More* (20 plus). Of these Lord Strange's Men performed *1 Henry VI*, *2 Seven Deadly Sins*, and *Sir Thomas More*. We should, of course, keep in mind that the twenty-three named characters in *1 Henry VI* could, with the doubling of characters customary in Elizabethan stage production, be reduced quite significantly. In Burns's edition he constructs a casting chart that requires a cast of between fourteen and sixteen actors for the play. But he candidly admits that the chart is 'one of the ludic areas of an edition; its value is in suggesting possibilities, not in establishing historical "facts"' (301).

[3] It is generally agreed that Shakespeare's playhouses had three entry-ways in the tiring-house façade, i.e. two flanking doors and a central doorway or aperture (see Andrew Gurr and Mariko Ichikawa, *Staging in Shakespeare's Theatres* (Oxford, 2000), p. 96).

6. Alan Howard as the unworldly Henry VI in Terry Hands's production
at the Royal Shakespeare Theatre, 1977.

also individual moments of considerable theatrical power as when
the Master Gunner's Boy crosses the stage with his burning linstock, or when a triumphant Joan appears '*on the top, thrusting out
a torch*' (3.2.24.1).[1] And actors may well have relished (and no
doubt still do) the opportunities for a 'theatrical' death sequence
available to Mortimer, Salisbury, Gargrave, and the Talbots (as well
as a plenitude of extras).

What is violence without sex, its companion-in-arms? *1 Henry VI*
offers numerous opportunities for flirtation, bawdiness, erotic
exchanges, and other sexual shenanigans. What director, for
instance, could resist the invitation offered by Joan's bout with
Charles—'thou shalt buckle with me' (1.2.95), Charles says to
her—to embellish the encounter with titillating interpretations
of buckling in the physical action? (Modern productions find this

---

[1] According to Hereward Price: 'This torch must have "wowed" the audience'
(*Construction in Shakespeare*, 32).

invitation difficult to refuse.) In the case of the young Henry VI the play flirts with perversity in its insistence on his boyish, ultra-virginal attitude towards the courtship leading to marriage, which he calls 'wanton dalliance with a paramour' (5.1.23). (When we remind ourselves that the women's parts in this and all other Elizabethan plays were played by boys or young men the theatrical possibilities for polymorphous perversity don't need the sexual hesitancies of the young king.) Clearly, Henry's ultra-virginity is, however, not immune to erotic titillation, as the play's final scene makes clear. Suffolk's vocabulary of praise—'enticing', 'ravish', 'all delights'—works against the case he's making for Margaret's 'humble lowliness of mind' (5.6.18).[1] Coupled with his emphasis on her (erotic) submissiveness—a quality that would particularly appeal to a young king beset by fractious lords—the case is made convincingly. Not much sign as yet in Henry of the Protestant notion of companionate marriage. He gets an appropriate epitaph in Lady Anne's 'obsequious lament' over his corpse in *Richard III*:

> Poor key-cold figure of a holy king,
> Pale ashes of the house of Lancaster,
> Thou bloodless remnant of that royal blood.
>
> (1.2.5–7)

Grown-up sex rears its head in the play with Suffolk's predatory courtship of Margaret ostensibly on behalf of Henry, but really—with a cheeky lack of indirection—on his own behalf.

Key-cold figures in *1 Henry VI* rely more on words than on action. Henry VI himself, the eponymous (and anonymous) hero of the play, is clearly a youth of words not action in a play that prizes action. Henry is neither an active warrior nor a wooer. He woos and is wooed by proxy—the intermediaries are Gloucester and Suffolk—and is talked into contracts first with the Earl of Armagnac's daughter and then with Margaret. In a play that isn't terribly impressive rhetorically it amounts to something that Shakespeare chooses to give Henry lengthy speeches when judging between

---

[1] As does the way she is interpreted in most modern productions. Carol Chillington Rutter notes that in the Terry Hands production at Stratford for the Royal Shakespeare Company, Queen Margaret's costume changes across the *Henry VI* trilogy (designed by Farrah) 'mapped the personal, and political, metamorphosis from lissom girl, in figure-hugging velvet, stepping fastidiously through smoke and battlefield carnage, to harridan hag, her body made over in chain mail molded to her curves and monstering her sexuality' (*Enter the Body*, 107).

Vernon and Basset, Somerset and York, speeches that do sound prettily (in Warwick's words), and their judicious tone seems to come from someone who is more than just a stripling. Henry speaks the longest speech in the play in 4.1 where he at first sounds older than his years in his measured, steely rebuke to Somerset and York (the tenor of which is echoed by Othello in admonishing Cassio and Montano in Cyprus (*Othello* 2.3.197–210)). We might well agree with him that he should be 'umpire in this doubtful strife' (4.1.151) but the action that follows these lines, as we have seen— the donning of a red rose—is an indication of Henry's tactical naivete.[1] In a play that makes so much of 'dumb significants', Henry's action is much more important than the words he speaks, contradicting their symbolic potency. Exeter's judgement on Henry's action ends the scene and carries his usual choric authority: ''Tis much when sceptres are in children's hands' (4.1.192) especially 'when envy breeds unkind division' (4.1.193).

Despite all the colour, flair, and kineticism of this chronicle history play, what's conspicuously missing in it—conspicuous for those of us (that's probably most of us) brought up on the second tetralogy rather than on the first—is virtually any injection of vitality from 'the lower orders'. No tavern or brothel scenes, or scenes involving the lower ranks of the army. What we miss, according to Paola Pugliatti, is 'that part of Shakespeare's historical imagination [that] was devoted to admitting into the body of greater events the residues and scraps of history, what the chroniclers considered as background or "noise" in the stories of kings and dynasties and to admit them as fully respectable parts of the picture' (*Shakespeare the Historian*, 182). In *Henry VI, Part One* Shakespeare, so Park Honan believes, 'writes as if he could hardly see below the heads of nobles; his social contexts are surprisingly weak, vague, or thin' (146). What enlivens the theatrical experience of Part Two, on the other hand, is the presence of the 'hedge-born swain' (Part One, 4.1.43), Jack Cade, and Peter Levi's

---

[1] Some historians assess the character of the historical Henry VI far more harshly, as K. B. McFarlane does in *England in the Fifteenth Century* (Oxford, 1981) when he describes the crown as having descended 'upon the head of a baby who grew up an imbecile' (42). There are other views—at least of Shakespeare's king; according to D. L. Frey, in the *Henry VI* plays Henry 'becomes the one clear voice crying in the human jungle of England during the Wars of the Roses' (*The First Tetralogy: Shakespeare's Scrutiny of the Tudor Myth: A Dramatic Exploration of Divine Providence* (The Hague, 1976), 11).

response to the Cade scenes in *2 Henry VI* is not uncommon: 'For me at least, Cade's rebellion is the most surprising feature of the entire play, and no one but Shakespeare could have carried it off. It is a minor theme that insists on behaving like a major one.'[1] Cade's comic cruelty anticipates the superbly balanced tavern scenes in the two parts of *Henry IV* where the comedy only thinly camouflages a sinister nihilism. In *Henry VI, Part One* the energetic commons are heard in only the occasional scene of tumult from an undifferentiated crowd—and in the caricatured complaints of Joan's shepherd father (as well as perhaps of Joan herself)—so the one or two moments in the play when we hear voices from the scraps and residues of history have a curious force and eloquence. One such moment belongs to Gloucester's Third Servingman:

> My lord, we know your grace to be a man
> Just and upright and, for your royal birth
> Inferior to none but to his majesty;
> And ere that we will suffer such a prince,
> So kind a father of the commonweal,
> To be disgracèd by an inkhorn mate,
> We and our wives and children all will fight
> And have our bodies slaughtered by thy foes.
>
> (3.1.95–102)

But this in its own way supports Phyllis Rackin's contention in *Stages of History* that 'Shakespeare's representations of plebeian characters in the first tetralogy tend, in the last analysis, to reproduce the aristocratic bias he found in historical source and dramatic convention alike' (218). More genuinely anticipatory of more disturbing things to come later in Shakespeare's career is the unnamed sentinel's brief lament at the beginning of Act 2:

> Thus are poor servitors,
> When others sleep upon their quiet beds,
> Constrained to watch in darkness, rain, and cold.
>
> (2.1.5–7)[2]

---

[1] *The Life and Times of William Shakespeare* (1988), 72.

[2] In *1 Henry VI* we miss too the presence of an aristocratic *miles gloriosus* especially as the hauntingly named Fastolf anticipates his great successor in (mis)name only. Missing also is an embryonic extreme villain—an early Richard III say. We might have expected one of the Roses' belligerents to have been more devilish—perhaps Richard III's father.

Language Matters

There are few silk purses, linguistically speaking, in *1 Henry VI*, but there are phrases and words of a juicy Latinate sonority, that no doubt actors found attractive to declaim: 'intermissive miseries' (1.1.88); 'contumeliously' (1.3.58); 'pursuivants of death' (2.5.5); 'this loathsome sequestration' (2.5.25); the 'arbitrator of despairs' (2.5.28); 'disanimates his enemies' (3.1.184); 'this churlish super-scription' (4.1.53); 'Sleeping neglection' (4.3.49); 'wonted further-ance' (5.3.21). These are examples of the 'foot-and-half-foot words' that met with Jonson's disapproval in the 1605 Prologue to *Every Man In His Humour*, words that helped the writer, Jonson declares, to 'Fight over York and Lancaster's long jars' (*Prologue* 10–11), long words for long jars. S. S. Hussey responds to the originality dis-played by Shakespeare's appropriation of these terms in all the plays of the first tetralogy but especially in Part One: 'What is note-worthy in these plays, and especially in *1 Henry VI*, are the uncom-mon Latinate words, as if Shakespeare, like his contemporaries, was savouring the ability of Elizabethan English to borrow such terms'.[1] The Dauphin himself is 'astonished' by Joan's 'high terms' (1.2.93); while her 'sugared words' (3.3.18) seduce Burgundy. We may not agree with either of these conventional judgements of Joan's oratorical powers, but we have to grant the justice of Peter Levi's judgement that in the opening scenes of Part One the 'strong sinews of [Shakespeare's] poetry are already apparent' (*The Life and Times*, 67). From later in the play he equally justly instances lines like 'Here dies the dusky torch of Mortimer' (2.5.122), 'This quar-rel will drink blood another day' (2.4.134) and 'As festered mem-bers rot but by degree' (3.1.193) as '[b]are-looking lines that are wonderfully ominous' (68).

Even barer looking lines signal Shakespeare's early mastery of the plangent monosyllables that ring out so memorably later in his career, often from thickets of much more tangled locutions. When Talbot contemplates his son's dead body his words knell the young man's epitaph:

> Poor boy, he smiles, methinks, as who should say
> 'Had death been French, then death had died today'
> (4.7.27–8)

---

[1] *The Literary Language of Shakespeare* (London and New York, 1982), 42.

and he is equally affecting in the simplicity of his earlier encouragement of his men before battle:

> Sell every man his life as dear as mine
> And they shall find dear deer of us, my friends.
>
> (4.2.53–4)

Talbot's bewildered 'I know not where I am nor what I do' (1.6.20) matches Joan's impudent 'We came but to tell you | That we are here' (3.2.71–2) but his monosyllables speak for and from his stupefaction while hers have all the insouciance of their simple self-assurance. In all these cases the monosyllable is being used with purpose and conviction on the writer's part. Matching the simplicity and directness of these lines is the welcome infusion now and then of the homely and colloquial breaking up a style that most of the time seems cut out from monumental alabaster. Clearly speaking with the larger theatre audience in mind, the Mayor of London slices through the nobles' high-toned rhetoric with good-humoured self-deprecation:

> See the coast cleared, and then we will depart.
> Good God, these nobles should such stomachs bear!
> I myself fight not once in forty year.
>
> (1.3.86–8)

And of course Joan provides us with numerous examples of a colloquial language full of sardonic vigour of the kind introduced into the play by the Countess of Auvergne: 'This is a riddling merchant for the nonce' (2.3.56). But we could do with more in the play of the *vox populi*, the 'audacious prate' (4.1.124) that Gloucester accuses Vernon and Basset of using.

At times Part One sounds (and reads) like an exercise in rhetorical composition of the kind that Shakespeare might well have been obliged to endure when a pupil in Stratford Grammar School (only there he would be dealing with Latin not English). The play is full of exploding pieces of alliteration, for instance, sometimes used to great effect, as in Gloucester's contempt for Winchester:

> Thy lewd, pestiferous, and dissentious pranks,
> As very infants prattle of thy pride.
>
> (3.1.15–16)

(Consider the equally effective use of assonance as in Joan's 'One drop of blood drawn from thy country's bosom | Should grieve thee more than streams of foreign gore' (3.3.54–5).)

Frequently, as one might expect from a newly minted writer, the operation seems merely formulaic, as though the words were there simply because they happened to begin with the same consonant: 'Suffolk doth not flatter, face, or feign' (5.4.98). (Warwick's repeated use of anaphora at 2.4.11–16 gives the same impression of spinning wheels.) Sometimes alliteration combines with other figures of speech as in this use of anadiplosis, 'Strike those that hurt, and hurt not those that help' (3.3.53), and there are all kinds of scales practised on parallel correspondences as in Richard's:

> He dies, we lose; I break my warlike word;
> We mourn, France smiles; we lose, they daily get.
> (4.3.31–2)

Personified abstractions stalk the play, sometimes with considerable effect as in Talbot's apostrophe to his three attendants, 'Lean famine, quartering steel, and climbing fire' (4.2.11). Vacuous moments, however, are common as in Lucy's bout of orotund title-reciting in 4.7.60–71. Among others, we are told, Talbot is

> Great Earl of Wexford, Waterford, and Valence,
> Lord Talbot of Goodrich and Archenfield,
> Lord Strange of Blackmere, Lord Verdun of Alton,
> Lord Cromwell of Wingfield, Lord Furnival of Sheffield,
> The thrice victorious Lord of Falconbridge.
> (4.7.63–7)

And the roll-call continues for another four enervating lines.

Something needs to be said about Shakespeare's use of verse and rhyme at this early stage in his career. He never relinquishes entirely his use of the conventional scene-ending couplet or the one that signals a break in the action, and these are commonplace usages in the Henry plays. Another rule of thumb for the use of rhyme in these early plays is that the more solemn the occasion becomes, and the more dire the immediate prospects, the more likely we are to come across an extended passage of rhyme. When York and Lucy, for example, contemplate the imminent demise of the Talbots, its prospect induces York's not unaffecting passage in rhyme at 4.3.39–46. But the most extended exercise in rhyming the heartfelt occurs in the prolonged leave-taking of the Talbots that stretches across three scenes, 4.5, 6 and 7, and has provoked dismay from commentators.[1] It is the only occasion in Shakespeare where a tragic sequence—arguably the tragic climax to this play—comes hampered by the form Shakespeare chooses for it (so the argument runs). We may have been conditioned to see things this way by the later Shakespeare's own implicit rejection of rhyme as a vehicle for tragedy, keeping it in reserve for those passages of ritual badinage in the war between the sexes that enliven the romantic comedies. (For example, the competition between Luciana and Adriana in the opening scene of Act 2 in *The Comedy of Errors*.) Here, in *1 Henry VI* the rhyming dialogue between the Talbots—often stichomythic—shapes a kind of noble flyting match, a competition as to who can out-*oblige* the other, as each attempts to persuade the other to flee from certain death, neither of course able to accept the other's self-sacrifice. Its effectiveness may well vary from reader to reader (or spectator to spectator). Alexander Leggatt is one of the few critics to find the metronomic beat of the couplets psychologically and aesthetically satisfying: 'The relentless click-click of the rhymes reinforces the point that for John Talbot all arguments are arguments for death; as every other line ending is countered by a rhyme, so every argument Talbot gives John to flee becomes an argument for staying' ('The Death of John Talbot', 18).[2]

One of the noticeable linguistic features of the play is its early demonstration of Shakespeare's lifelong love affair with the pun. But we have to be careful, especially in editing the play, not to replace Shakespeare's ingenuity as a wordsmith with our own. Puns in *1 Henry VI* may come in different shapes and sizes but they all tend to announce themselves with the self-advertising tren-

---

[1] Shakespeare's use of the couplet throughout his career has attracted at best a grudging sympathy. Marco Mincoff is more forthright in his disapproval: 'It may seem heresy to say so, but Shakespeare never really mastered the couplet form; the fact that, outside the comedies, the rhyming passages in Shakespeare's plays down to *Macbeth* and *Cymbeline* are so frequently rejected as spurious should give one pause' ('The Composition of *Henry VI, Part 1*', *SQ* 16 (1965), 199–207; 203). The couplets that close out the sonnets have also come in for adverse criticism.

[2] Peter Holland defends one of the rhyming exchanges in *A Midsummer Night's Dream* with a similar argument: 'It seems at times as if they [the lovers] are turned into puppets by their couplets, made to speak in particularly limited ways by the style imposed upon them' (*A Midsummer Night's Dream* (Oxford, 1994), 64)—the point being that Shakespeare wants us to see them as puppets in the grip of irrational feelings.

chancy of Gloucester's 'Roam thither then' (3.1.51), his homo-phonic punning response to Winchester's 'Rome shall remedy this'. The same can be said of Shakespeare's attraction to all those combinations of puns on 'will' that crop up everywhere in his work, presaged here in *1 Henry VI* when Suffolk talks about his lack of prowess as a student of the law,

> And never yet could frame my will to it,
> And therefore frame the law unto my will.
> (2.4.8–9)

The fact that there are puns in this play—of an awkwardly trans-parent kind—combines with our knowledge of the extraordinary density of Shakespeare's poetry later in his career to tempt us to discover in kindergarten Shakespeare adult complexities both lin-guistic and psychological. Wordplay then becomes the beneficiary of a misplaced ingenuity which finds extensions of meaning that are by and large chimerical. Much of this misplaced ingenuity attempts to eroticize meaning, as though *1 Henry VI* were written in the spirit of the Sonnets or the problem comedies, or as though the commentator felt obliged to compete with the madcap inventive-ness of works like Frankie Rubinstein's *A Dictionary of Shake-speare's Sexual Puns and their Significance* (1984; reps. 1989). But for a simple illustration of what I mean, and one that can stand in for many others, we might look at the 'pun' that Edward Burns finds in Talbot's description of his effect on the French enemy: 'My grisly countenance made others fly' (1.5.25). According to Burns 'grisly' also comes 'with a sense of "grizzly", grey, ageing, grey-haired' (*1 Henry VI*, 152). But why should this be? There is no reason to sup-pose that an ageing warrior would make any of his opponents 'fly'; 'grizzly' was certainly available in the sixteenth century as a word in its own right but its availability then (or at any other time) does not mean that it was being punned upon, no matter how 'grizzly' the actor playing Talbot actually was.[1] See also Dover Wilson's mistaken contention that Henry is quibbling on medical terminol-ogy at 4.1.140–2. The same argument is even truer in some ways of more complex Shakespeare plays and is the burden of David Simp-son's criticism of Stephen Greenblatt's over-ingenuity in his

---

[1] *Grizzly* meaning grey-haired may have only recently become available. *OED* has 1594 as the date of its first citation with this meaning, but lists *grizzly* as a variant of *grisly* (see under *grisly a.*)

remarks on *Othello* in *Renaissance Self-Fashioning*. Simpson writes in terms of 'the ear perhaps over-developed, for ambiguities, the bold connections, the intense adjectives, the air of over-interpretation'.[1] An air of over-interpretation suffuses a number of recent editions of *1 Henry VI*, this one perhaps at times not excepted.

Memory and Legacy

It may seem only appropriate that a play that comes, so to speak, both before and after its successor should be obsessed with its place in history. *1 Henry VI* dwells almost as much in and on the past and future as it does in and on the present, and it makes the point constantly that what is remembered in the present is the legacy of the past. No wonder then that an obsession of the play's noble characters is with how they will be remembered. They do not need a poet to remind them, as the fair young man seems to do in the Sonnets, of the danger 'That thou no form of thee hast left behind' (Sonnet 9.6). They are obsessed with the form of what they leave behind, and Talbot speaks for many of the play's characters in his proprietorial concern for Salisbury's proper place in history:

> And that hereafter ages may behold
> What ruin happened in revenge of him,
> Within their chiefest temple I'll erect
> A tomb wherein his corpse shall be interred,
> Upon the which, that everyone may read,
> Shall be engraved the sack of Orléans,
> The treacherous manner of his mournful death,
> And what a terror he had been to France.
>
> (2.2.10–17)

Salisbury's legacy is a written one etched into the marble of his tomb, telling the story of his valiant life and death, not omitting the treachery and sorrow involved in it. *1 Henry VI* is also the written legacy of its characters' valiant lives and deaths (or of some of them anyway), and it too is at pains to leave a full record of the

---

[1] 'Remember Me', *London Review of Books*, 24 May 2001, 23; Greenblatt, *Renaissance Self-Fashioning: From More to Shakespeare* (Chicago, Ill., and London, 1980). A recent example of a work that bases its often fascinating judgements on a reckless over-inventiveness is Philippa Berry's *Shakespeare's Feminine Endings: Disfiguring Death in the Tragedies* (London and New York, 1999).

often shameful manner in which they were abandoned and traduced. In this respect individual and familial honour is more important than national, and is clearly a feudal inheritance.[1] Salisbury's immortality is to come via the siege of Orléans but it will not match Joan's, according to Reignier, for she will 'Drive them [the English] from Orléans and be immortalized' (1.2.148).

One might say that the history plays are at the mercy of history. The tragic climax to *Henry VI, Part One* rests in the extended rhetorical duel between Talbot father and son as to how posterity will judge their final actions. (As with Salisbury and Joan.) Each tries to save the life of the other without losing honour for himself, and each inevitably fails. The future has to be propitiated; what they leave to posterity must be their triumphant good name. The son begins as an apprentice to his father as Talbot's first words make clear: 'I did send for thee | To tutor thee in stratagems of war' (4.5.1–2). But this tutoring is with an eye on the father's reputation, 'That Talbot's name might be in thee revived' (4.5.3), as in the Sonnets: 'His tender heir might bear his memory' (1.4).[2] And it is with an eye to posterity that Talbot begs his son to fly from the battle and certain death: 'Part of thy father may be saved in thee' (4.5.38). So it's not merely a disinterested concern for the life of his son that motivates Talbot. And Talbot's son, who sees the tyrannical workings of posterity with perhaps a keener eye than his father, uses the same argument as his father in insisting on his own death: 'your renowned name—shall flight abuse it?' (4.5.41). In the context of this feudal high-mindedness, Norman Holland's Freudian reading of these scenes seems woefully anachronistic.[3] What Holland hears 'at a very deep level' (74) in this play is the son as the

---

[1] As Susan Brigden writes: 'In the restricted society of the nobility and gentry of England, the sense of lineage was vital to its members' self-conception. Seeing themselves as part of a line, with a future and a past, they recognized a compelling duty to the family that came before and would come after, and to the land which was the source of the family's wealth and power' (*New Worlds, Lost Worlds: The Rule of the Tudors 1485–1603* (2000), 70).

[2] The relationship between the Master Gunner of Orléans and his apprentice son is similar to the Talbots, though spiced comically with a competitive element, as each has his eye on his own reputation, the son's at the expense of the father's. 'I'll never trouble you, if I may spy them' (1.4.21) says the Boy, wishing to garner all the glory of killing some of the English nobility for himself.

[3] 'Sons and Substitutions: Shakespeare's Phallic Fantasy', in *Shakespeare's Personality*, ed. Norman N. Holland, Sidney Homan and Bernard J. Paris (Berkeley, 1989), 66–85.

father's phallus: 'Talbot wants his son to escape so that the Talbot line will survive; that is, for generative ends' (74). Fiedler, in *The Stranger in Shakespeare*, sounds uncertain of the value of his thesis, but his justification of it, swimming against the critical tide, is interesting in terms of the play's subservience to history:

I hesitate to offer so crudely Freudian a reading, but it does enable me to guess why the Lovejoy–Tillyard–Spencer version of Elizabethan hierarchy occupies so central a place in the psychology of Shakespeare's plays and poems. To question the great chain of being is to threaten castration. To restore it is to restore virility itself. (74–5)

In the context of the play's obsession with the purity of lineage, we might consider its concomitant fascination with bastardy. The Bastard lives up to his name—prefiguring his role in other Shakespeare plays—with the line, 'Hew them to pieces, hack their bones asunder' (4.7.47) directed at the harmless dead bodies of the Talbots. This command is flanked by Charles's plangent rebuke:

> O no, forbear; for that which we have fled
> During the life, let us not wrong it dead
> (4.7.49–50)

and by Burgundy's temperate, 'Doubtless he would have made a noble knight' (4.7.44). Bastards in Shakespeare are not usually chivalrous, despite Edmund's belated volte-face at the end of *King Lear*. Talbot, the high-minded feudal lord in *1 Henry VI*, contemplates his wounding of the Bastard as an appropriate medicinal blood-letting:

> Contaminated, base,
> And misbegotten blood I spill of thine;
> Mean and right poor, for that pure blood of mine
> Which thou didst force from Talbot, my brave boy.
> (4.6.21–4)

Alexander Leggatt remarks:

The Talbots dwell so much on John's legitimacy, and on the bond of father and son, that it seems appropriate his first encounter should be with a bastard, as though John, like a Spenserian knight, is testing himself against an allegorical opponent who represents the vice most opposed to his virtue. (p. 18)

In the feudal ethos the uncontaminated lineage is precious—but, *pace* Holland and Leggatt, there is also something attractive about bastardy that draws Shakespeare to it. It has to do with the attractiveness of characters conceived in 'the lusty stealth of nature' (*King Lear* 1.2.11) as opposed to the boredom of the marriage bed. And this excited view of bastardy is something that history plays before Shakespeare's exploited—and after for that matter—as in the case of the Bastard in *The Troublesome Reign of John, King of England* who declares insouciantly:

> Let land and living go, 'tis honour's fire
> That makes me swear King Richard was my Sire.
>   (ll. 277–8)

His proud declaration of his illegitimacy combined with his contempt for worldly pelf goes down well with King John who immediately knights him.

It is possible to see the characters in Shakespeare's history plays as locked into their roles in their own version of the great chain of being. But we now tend to see this restrictive construction not in terms of the feudal obligations of their own evaluation, nor of Hall's providential design for the history of the Tudors, but more pessimistically as a kind of machiavellian determinism, the opposite of providential. Graham Holderness explains: 'In Marlowe's *Edward II*, Shakespeare's *Richard II* and *Henry VI*, images of flight and recapture symbolize the helplessness of the individual confronted by the ineluctable tyranny of history, the inescapable determination of the unalterable past'.[1] Our postmodern consciousness finds this ineluctability curiously engaging even though we are accustomed to sneer at Hall's providential version of it. It sits comfortably with the New Historicists' grim reading of the futility of individual agency famously expressed in Stephen Greenblatt's essay 'Invisible Bullets: Renaissance Authority and its Subversion, *Henry IV* and *Henry V*'. According to Greenblatt, 'the subversive voices [in the history plays] are produced by the affirmation of order, and they are powerfully registered, but they do not undermine that order'.[2] Not

---

[1] *Shakespeare Recycled: The Making of Historical Drama* (Hemel Hempstead, 1992), 15.
[2] In *Political Shakespeare: New Essays in Cultural Materialism*, ed. Jonathan Dollimore and Alan Sinfield (Manchester and Ithaca, NY, 1985); reprinted in *New Historicism and Renaissance Drama*, 83–108; 102.

even in *2 Henry IV*, where the lies and the self-serving sentiments are utterly inescapable, where the illegitimacy of legitimate authority is repeatedly demonstrated, where the whole state seems—to adapt More's phrase—a conspiracy of the great to enrich and protect their interests under the name of commonwealth, even here the audience does not leave the theatre in a rebellious mood. (105)

For Frank Lentricchia it's a brand of determinism that makes the New Historicists what they are, 'the typically anxious expression of post-Watergate American humanist intellectuals'.[1] Hence 'the Renaissance is *our* culture because it is the origin of our disciplinary society' (97). None of this, however, actually approaches the radicalism of Emrys Jones's suggestion back in 1977 that there was perhaps, some kind of 'governmental impulse' (120) in the writing of Shakespeare's early history plays, making them agents of government propaganda.

Appropriately enough for a work so victimized by history, *1 Henry VI* is an immensely nostalgic play, hence its frequent emphasis on the lost golden time of Henry V and on an earlier, vaguer time when the spirit of a romantic chivalry was thought to inspire the actions of an uncorrupted aristocracy. Although the laws of chivalry are at best moot in Part One, they do operate intermittently in a bizarrely anachronistic way, especially in the presentation of the Talbots. Hence Talbot's high-minded, snobbish version of the operations of medieval ransom. Essentially, the realpolitik of ransom was as a kind of tax on military failure. You ransom off your captives—important ones like Talbot at least—who then return to waste your country and slay your citizens. Northrop Frye notes that 'medieval warfare was in large part a ransom racket: you took noblemen prisoner in battle, and then their tenants had to put up enough money to buy them back'.[2] A higher-minded ransoming practice was to exchange one noble prisoner for his social equivalent from the other side, so a subtle form of disparagement—continuing the struggle between the two sides on the level of symbol and gesture—involved a deliberate (and foolish) refusal to recognize the true value of the prisoner. Hence Talbot's outrage at the notion of being ransomed for a French prisoner of lower rank

---

[1] *Ariel and the Police: Michel Foucault, William James, Wallace Stevens* (Madison, Wis., 1988), 93.

[2] *Northrop Frye on Shakespeare*, ed. Robert Sandler (Markham, Ont., 1986), 70.

or caste than him. He 'cravèd death' rather than be so 'vile-esteemed' (1.5.10–11). It is of course an absurdity. If the French had any sense: (a) they wouldn't have ransomed Talbot in the first place or (at least) (b) they would have insisted on getting one of their top-flight warriors back in exchange for him. After all Talbot is, as the French admit themselves, the 'terror of the French' (1.5.20). There is of course no question of ransoming Joan. The laws of chivalry unchivalrously do not apply to her. Talbot, however, is no 'Fell banning hag' (5.3.42); and nor is Margaret whose ransom status goes without saying. One of Joan's telling arguments in persuading Burgundy to rejoin the French is to remind him that when the English captured the Duke of Orléans and heard he was Burgundy's enemy, they let him go without demanding a ransom. Even more tellingly it isn't historically true. Perhaps the most powerful indictment of the out-of-date tenets of a self-regarding chivalry is in the absurd adherence to protocol that is demonstrated by Somerset in his refusal to send the cavalry he had promised York because York had failed to ask for it specifically—perhaps because Henry had already commanded Somerset to do so. Somerset says:

> He might have sent and had the horse.
> I owe him little duty and less love,
> And take foul scorn to fawn on him by sending.
> (4.4.33–5)

Nostalgia in *1 Henry VI* also manifests itself in a ponderous recrudescence of the significance of the Order of the Garter as Talbot both unceremoniously and ceremoniously tears off the garter from Fastolf's thigh in 4.1. Fastolf 'usurp[s] the sacred name of knight' (4.1.40), but his de-gartering offers the opportunity for Talbot to reminisce about a long-lost time when knights were knights and ladies like Joan of Arc existed only in mythology. Unlike in the slipshod present, Talbot argues,

> When first this order was ordained, my lords,
> Knights of the Garter were of noble birth,
> Valiant and virtuous, full of haughty courage...
> (4.1.33–5)

According to Holinshed this Order was devised, in 1344, by Edward III, who found a garter of the queen, or of some other noble-woman, somewhere in his court, and whimsically established its

Order. So the Order began not inappropriately in an atmosphere of erotic chivalry, its romantic inception defended by Holinshed:

> Though some may think, that so noble an order had but a mean beginning, if this tale be true, yet many honorable degrees of estates have had their beginnings of more base and mean things, than of love, which being orderly used, is most noble and commendable, sith nobility itself is covered under love…(ii. 628–9)

This affectionate, nostalgic remembrance of things past helps to explain perhaps why the notorious genealogies of the history plays are often confused and inaccurate. Indulging in them seems to be a rhetorical necessity, a sonorous evocation of a distinguished past—getting them precisely right is less compelling.[1]

Memories in this play, whether or not nostalgic, are often more immediate and urgent. Richard, like Somerset, is obsessed with the 'trespass' of his father, the Earl of Cambridge, and embodies the process of selective remembering when he says to Somerset:

> I'll note you in my book of memory,
> To scourge you for this apprehension.
> (2.4.101–2)

'Of old I know them' (1.2.39) is Charles's rueful memory of previous encounters with the English army. The phenomenon most often noted nostalgically in the book of memory in *1 Henry VI* is the exemplary Henry V whose name is on everyone's lips, even on those of the French, as a kind of *deus absconditus*, belying Exeter's lament that 'Henry is dead and never shall revive' (1.1.18). It is his ghost that Bedford invocates—unavailingly—to 'Prosper this realm, keep it from civil broils' (1.1.53). 'O think upon the conquest of my father' (4.1.148) urges Henry VI when he wants his subjects to do his bidding. Henry V positively invades the present of this play, and is the object of attention particularly in the first scene but also throughout as 'our scarce-cold conqueror, | That ever-living

---

[1] Living the chivalric ideal continued to attract the English crown and nobility. Susan Brigden notes the ambition of Henry VII: 'At home, he aspired to lead a noble order of chivalry; abroad, to pursue honor. Reading chivalric romance, especially Thomas Malory's *Le Morte d'Arthur*, Henry saw his court as a chivalric fellowship united in a quest for honor and loyal service to their prince' (*New Worlds, Lost Worlds*, 104). He named his first son Arthur.

man of memory' (4.3.50–1). His actual words are quoted by Exeter in a salient aside, giving him a kind of ghostly presence as a character in the play:

> Then, I perceive, that will be verified
> Henry the Fifth did sometime prophesy:
> 'If once he come to be a cardinal,
> He'll make his cap co-equal with the crown.'
>
> (5.1.30–3)

Phyllis Rackin argues that '[t]he entire play [*1 Henry VI*] can be seen as a series of attempts on the part of the English to write a history that will preserve Henry's fame'.[1] But the events of this history play and those in the ones immediately following it undermine such an ambition. And so Shakespeare reopens negotiations with history by writing the (ambiguously) triumphant 'prequel' to this first set of history plays culminating in 1599 in the 'literal' return of that ever-living man of memory in Shakespeare's greatest history play, *The Life of Henry V*.

The Text

1 Henry VI first appeared in the posthumous 1623 Folio edition of Shakespeare's works. It follows *The Life of Henry V* and comes before *The Second Part of Henry VI* giving the misleading impression of a trouble-free chronology in the writing and publication. Clearly Heminges and Condell were only too happy—once the play's manuscript was in their hands—to insert it into its chronological place in the Folio whatever they may or may not have known about its enigmatic provenance. A hint as to its uncertain textual history can be deduced from the way it is mentioned in the Stationers' Register as part of the Folio registration: 'Mr William Shakespeare's Comedies Histories, and Tragedies so many of the said Copies as are not formerly entered to other men. viz . . . The

---

[1] *Stages of History: Shakespeare's English Chronicles* (Ithaca, NY, 1990), 150. Even more immediately the play's audience too is asked to exercise its memory in holding together the complications of a busy plot, which helps us in how to read Joan. J. P. Brockbank notes: 'The barbs of Joan's searching indictment of English hypocrisy cannot be removed by the spectacle of her converse with evil spirits', 'The Frame of Disorder—*Henry VI*', in *Early Shakespeare*, ed. John Russell Brown and Bernard Harris (1961), 73–99; 80.

third part of Henry the Sixth . . .' (quoted in Cairncross, p. xiii).[1] Presumably Isaac Jaggard and Edward Blount, two of the Folio's compilers, call *1 Henry VI* the third part of *Henry VI* because of the previous quarto publication of *The First Part of the Contention betwixt the Two Famous Houses of Yorke and Lancaster* (*2 Henry VI*) in 1594 and the octavo publication in 1595 of *The True Tragedy of Richard Duke of York* (*3 Henry VI*). Inadvertently, by labelling the play the third part of *Henry VI*, they call attention to the order in which the history plays may well have been written.

Loose ends, inconsistencies, contradictions, misplaced stage directions, changeable speech prefixes combine, with other irregularities in the Folio text, to make it very unlikely that the manuscript came from the playhouse.[2] On the other hand, some of the stage directions, in their indulgence of information unnecessary and superfluous for the book-keeper, suggest the authors' hand. Indeed, for John Dover Wilson in his edition of the play 'everything about the text leads me to believe that it was printed from the actual draft supplied by the authors for its performance at the Rose on 3 March 1592' (102). Dover Wilson's precise wording here suggests that there was no other intermediary activity—that the text was, in Hattaway's words, 'set up from holographic fair copy' (*1 Henry*

---

[1] The Stationers' Register entry for the First Folio (8 November 1623, Register D) is reproduced in the *Textual Companion*, p. 32. The *Companion*'s General Introduction usefully deals with matters germane to the Folio's publication.

[2] A list and analysis of F's oddities can be found in the *Textual Companion*, 217–19. Among them are inconsistencies in the speech prefixes for Charles who is sometimes Dauphin—Pucelle, Joan—Richard—York, Cardinal—Winchester, Pole—Suffolk, General—Captain. There are omitted entrances for characters: the Captain at 2.2.0.1 (he speaks one line at 2.2.60: 'I do, my lord, and mean accordingly'); the Porter at 2.3.0.1; Vernon and a Lawyer (in F = '*and others*') at 2.4.0.2; Burgundy at 3.3.36.1; Vernon and Basset at 3.4.0.4 and 0.5; a Captain at 4.4.0.1; Lucy at 4.4.9.1; a French herald at 4.7.50.1. Two of the most significant omissions are for Reignier at 3.2.16.1—significant because Reignier plays a large part in this scene— and Alençon at 3.2.39.4 as Talbot picks him out when he addresses the French: 'I speak not to that railing Hecate, | But unto thee, Alençon, and the rest' (3.2.63–4). Missing too are important stage properties: a rose-bush (2.4.0.1); roses for characters to wear (3.1.0.1–4, 3.4.0.1–5, 4.1.0.1–4); paper (5.2.0.1). A typically muddled stage direction follows 1.6.39 in the Folio: '*Exit Talbot.* | *Alarm, Retreat, Flourish*' where it is clear the soldiers exeunt before Talbot does, and the '*Flourish*' should announce the entrance of Joan, the Dauphin and the French nobility that begins Scene 7 (in this edition). And there are a number of minor discrepancies duly noted by the *Textual Companion*. Most instances of the Folio's anomalies are discussed more thoroughly in the Commentary as they occur.

VI, 190).[1] It is difficult to imagine, however, a fair copy that contains so many irregularities coming from a single author.[2] But when we think of the manuscript as coming from several hands, the strangenesses and anomalies in the Folio text are much more understandable. The last word on this issue should be given to the *Textual Companion*: 'all the features of the Folio text are most economically explained by the hypothesis that the copy was collaborative foul papers, containing last-minute adjustments; there is no need to suspect intervention by scribe or book-keeper' (218).

[1] W. W. Greg is one of a number of commentators who dispute the pristine nature of the copy implied by 'holograph'. He argues that 'the marking of the acts must point to prompt copy of some sort' (*The Editorial Problem in Shakespeare: A Survey of the Foundations of the Text* (Oxford, 1951), 139. In *The Shakespeare First Folio: Its Bibliographical and Textual History* (Oxford, 1955) Greg argues that the manuscript had been annotated by the book-keeper and used by the prompter (187).

[2] A list and analysis of these can be found most accessibly in Cairncross (pp. xiii–xxvii) and in *A Textual Companion*.

EDITORIAL PROCEDURES

No early edition of *Henry VI, Part One* exists before the one that appears in the Folio of 1623, so it carries most authority and has been used as the control text. Deviations from it have been recorded as scrupulously as possible. The Folio text is punctuated rhetorically. Wherever possible I have chosen to punctuate more lightly, following the rhythm of the speaking voice rather than the abstraction of rhetorical pattern. However, the play's verse is often declamatory, exclamatory and in the imperative mood, and the punctuation at times should reflect this. Hence I have for instance inserted exclamation marks in Bedford's grandiose command that opens the play: 'Hung be the heavens with black! Yield day to night!' In many instances F's heavy use of the colon has been replaced by lighter punctuation—a dash occasionally, more frequently a semicolon. Replacing colons with semicolons can stand as the abstract of a more general procedure whereby F's lines are given more room to breathe. Along similar lines, the F text frequently invites enjambement or the abandonment of phrasal or clausal commas. Where possible I've accepted the invitation and allowed the speaking voice a more natural, unconstrained expression as in 1.2.20–1: 'Him I forgive my death that killeth me | When he sees me go back one foot or flee'. In F a comma conventionally follows 'death', 'me' and 'foot'. On the other hand, where the text offers the choice of a period or a colon I have often preferred the stronger stop.

A minor question of punctuation occurs at the end of lines where the next line begins with an 'And', as in 'The Earl of Salisbury craveth supply, | And hardly keeps his men from mutiny' (1.1.159–60). It's tempting here to strike out the Folio comma following 'supply' (as Edward Burns does in his Arden edition of the play), but it seems to me more appropriate to keep the comma in this and many other similar constructions as it reflects the natural pause the actor's voice makes in linking the clauses. On the other hand, an 'And' linkage such as the following, 'Ordainèd is to raise this tedious siege | And drive the English forth the bounds of France' (1.2.53–4), where the first clause drives so vigorously into the second, clearly benefits from the absence of the slight pause the comma demands. And the comma is obviously anathema in coupled phrasal units such as 'for his grim aspect | And large proportion of his strong-knit limbs' (2.3.19–20).

Of all the other collated editions of the play the one appearing in the Oxford Complete Works (first published in 1988) has been accorded a particularly careful reading as it established and manifests the principles on which this series has been based. I have, however, not been shy to veer away from it on occasion, especially in the matter of naming names and constructing scenes. In the case of naming names I have been somewhat eclectic, sometimes favouring the form of the names found in the Chronicle sources, sometimes the different form adopted by the 1623 Folio. In the case of minor figures (e.g. Glasdale) I have used his historical name (in the Folio he is called Glansdale). In the case of more important figures (e.g. Reignier) I have—as have most other editors—stuck with one of the Folio's preferences (his historical name is René, which the Oxford Complete Works adopts). (Not unexpectedly the Folio itself is cavalier about spelling names with any degree of consistency.) Fastolf is of particular interest and the form of his name is discussed thoroughly in the Commentary, as are any others that are problematic. The general principles followed in this edition in these and other matters have been succinctly laid out by Gary Taylor in his edition of *Henry V* (Oxford, 1982), while the treatment of Shakespeare's spelling and verse indentation and other procedural matters can be gleaned from Stanley Wells and Gary Taylor's *Modernizing Shakespeare's Spelling, with Three Studies in the Text of 'Henry V'* (Oxford, 1979). I have to record also a debt to *William Shakespeare: A Textual Companion* (Oxford, 1987 repr. 1997) by Stanley Wells, Gary Taylor, John Jowett and William Montgomery.

As with the other plays in this series I have used broken brackets to signify debatable stage directions—debatable as to their placement or their form or whether they should exist at all. Sometimes I have moved exits and entrances to what I perceive to be more compatible locations in the text; in the Folio they sometimes appear wherever there is space for them in the margin. I have on occasion refrained from specifying in the frequently expanded stage directions exactly how a particular piece of stage business is transacted on the basis that the edition should give some indication of the flexibility involved in any individual production of the play. I have not, however, been averse to introducing a specifically precise stage direction that may fly in the face of tradition (e.g. the suggestion at 4.1.120 that a rose be used as the 'pledge' for the duel between York and Somerset).

Quotations from other early texts are usually silently modernized, as is the form of the words in the collations (except for quotations from the 1623 Folio) unless there is some point in retaining the old form of the spelling. Punctuation changes have not been collated unless they materially affect the sense. References to other editions are printed in capitals in the collations, except where they are conjectural as in 5.4.148 WILSON (*conj.* Perring) which indicates that Wilson has incorporated the suggestion of Perring in his edition of the play. All '*asides*' and '*to . . .*' directions are editorial and have not been reproduced in the collations. I have followed Oxford's expansion of names in the stage directions, for example '*the Duke of Gloucester*' for F's *Gloucester* and '*the Bishop of Winchester*' for F's *Winchester*. In the collations I have recorded only the first time these occur. References to Shakespeare's other works are from *The Complete Works*, ed. Stanley Wells, Gary Taylor *et al.* (Oxford, 1986). I've frequently quoted admiringly from other editions of *Part One* in the Commentary as the wording of other editors often bears repeating such is the felicity of their phrasing or the astuteness of their insight.

Abbreviations and References

Unless otherwise indicated, the place of publication is London. Only the editions of Shakespeare found in the Collation and Commentary are listed.

EDITIONS OF SHAKESPEARE

F, F1	The First Folio, 1623
F2	The Second Folio, 1632
F3	The Third Folio, 1663
F4	The Fourth Folio, 1685
Alexander	Peter Alexander, *Complete Works* (1951)
Burns	Edward Burns, *King Henry VI, Part 1*, The Arden Shakespeare (2000)

Cairncross	Andrew S. Cairncross, *The First Part of King Henry VI*, The Arden Shakespeare (1962)
Capell	Edward Capell, *Comedies, Histories, and Tragedies*, 10 vols. (1767–8)
Collier	John Payne Collier, *Works*, 8 vols. (1842–4)
Collier 1858	John Payne Collier, *Works*, 6 vols. (1858)
Contention	*The First Part of the Contention betwixt the Two Famous Houses of York and Lancaster* (the 1595 quarto) [*2 Henry VI*]
Dyce	Alexander Dyce, *Works*, 6 vols. (1857)
Dyce 1864–7	Alexander Dyce, *Works*, 9 vols. (1864–7)
Globe	W. G. Clark and W. A. Wright, *Works* (1864)
Halliwell	James O. Halliwell [-Phillipps], *Works*, 16 vols. (1853–65)
Hanmer	Thomas Hanmer, *Works*, 6 vols. (1743–4)
Hart	H. C. Hart, *King Henry VI, Part 1*, The Arden Shakespeare (1909)
Hattaway	Michael Hattaway, *The First Part of King Henry VI*, The New Cambridge Shakespeare (Cambridge, 1990)
Hudson	Henry N. Hudson, *Works*, 20 vols. (Boston, 1886)
Johnson	Samuel Johnson, *Plays*, 8 vols. (1765)
Keightley	Thomas Keightley, *Plays*, 6 vols. (1864)
Kittredge	George Lyman Kittredge, *Works* (1936)
Malone	Edmond Malone, *Plays and Poems*, 10 vols. (1790)
Marshall	Henry Irving and F. A. Marshall, *Works*, 8 vols. (1887–90)
Montgomery	William Montgomery, *Henry VI, Part 1*, The Pelican Shakespeare (2000)
Munro	F. J. Furnivall and John Munro, *Works*, 40 vols. (1908)
Neilson	William Alan Neilson, *Works* (1906)
Oxford	Stanley Wells and Gary Taylor, *The Complete Works* (Oxford, 1986; Compact Edition, 1988)
Pope	Alexander Pope, *Works*, 6 vols. (1723–5)
Riverside	G. Blakemore Evans and J. J. M. Tobin, *The Riverside Shakespeare*, 2nd end. (Boston, 1997)
Rowe	Nicholas Rowe, *Works*, 6 vols. (1709)
Rowe 1714	Nicholas Rowe, *Works*, 8 vols. (1714)
Sanders	Norman Sanders, *Henry VI, Part One*, The New Penguin Shakespeare (Harmondsworth, 1981)
Singer	Samuel Weller Singer, *Works*, 10 vols. (1856)

Sisson	C. J. Sisson, *Works* (1954)
Staunton	Howard Staunton, *Plays*, 3 vols. (1858–60)
Steevens	Samuel Johnson and George Steevens, *Works*, 10 vols. (1773)
Theobald	Lewis Theobald, *Works*, 7 vols. (1733)
Theobald 1757	Lewis Theobald, *Works*, 7 vols. (1757)
Tucker Brooke	C. F. Tucker Brooke, *1 Henry VI*, The Yale Shakespeare (New Haven, 1918)
Warburton	William Warburton, *Works*, 8 vols. (1747)
Wilson	John Dover Wilson, *The First Part of King Henry VI*, The New Shakespeare (Cambridge, 1952)
Wright	W. A. Wright, *Works*, The Cambridge Shakespeare, 9 vols. (Cambridge, 1891–3)

OTHER ABBREVIATIONS

Abbott	E. A. Abbott, *A Shakespearian Grammar: An Attempt to Illustrate some of the Differences between Elizabethan and Modern English*, 2nd edn. (1870; repr. New York, 1972)
Bible	*The Geneva Bible*, 1560, ed. Lloyd E. Berry (Madison, 1969)
Boswell-Stone	W. G. Boswell-Stone, *Shakespeare's Holinshed: The Chronicle and the Historical Plays Compared* (1896; repr. New York, 1966)
Bullough	Geoffrey Bullough, ed., *Narrative and Dramatic Sources of Shakespeare*, 8 vols. (1957–75), vol. iii (London and New York, 1960)
Coulson	John Coulson, *The Saints: A Concise Biographical Dictionary* (New York, 1958)
Dent	R. W. Dent, *Shakespeare's Proverbial Language: An Index* (Berkeley and Los Angeles, 1981)
Eccles	Christine Eccles, *The Rose Theatre* (1990)
Edelman	Charles Edelman, *Brawl Ridiculous: Swordfighting in Shakespeare's Plays* (Manchester, 1992)
Fabyan	Robert Fabyan, *The New Chronicles of England and France* (1516; repr. 1811)
Fox-Davies	Arthur Charles Fox-Davies, *A Complete Guide to Heraldry* (1925)
Greene	*The Life and Works of Robert Greene M. A.*, ed. Alexander B. Grosart, 15 vols. (New York, 1964)

Hall	Edward Hall, *The Union of the Two Noble and Illustre Families of Lancastre and York* (1548–50; repr. 1809)
Herodotus	Herodotus, *The Histories*, trans. Robin Waterfield (Oxford, 1998)
Holinshed	Raphael Holinshed, *Holinshed's Chronicles of England, Scotland, and Ireland*, 2nd edn., 6 vols.: vol. iii (1587; repr. New York, 1965)
Honan	Park Honan, *Shakespeare: A Life* (Oxford, 1998)
Jones	Emrys Jones, *The Origins of Shakespeare* (Oxford, 1977)
Kökeritz	Helge Kökeritz, *Shakespeare's Pronunciation* (New Haven, 1953)
Leggatt	Alexander Leggatt, 'The Death of John Talbot', in *Shakespeare's English Histories: A Quest for Form and Genre*, ed. J. W. L. Velz (Binghampton, NY, 1996), 11–30
Nashe	*The Works of Thomas Nashe*, ed. R. B. McKerrow, 5 vols. (Oxford, 1904–10)
OED	*Oxford English Dictionary*, 2nd edn. (Oxford, 1989)
Ovid	Ovid, *Metamorphoses*, Loeb edn., trans. Frank Justus Miller, 2 vols., (1916; repr. Cambridge, Mass., 1946)
Partridge	Eric Partridge, *Shakespeare's Bawdy* (1947; repr. 1968)
Pliny	Pliny, *Naturalis Historia*, Loeb edn., trans. H. Rackham and others, 10 vols. (1938–62)
Price	Hereward T. Price, *Construction in Shakespeare* (East Lansing, Michigan, 1951)
Prockter and Taylor	Adrian Prockter and Robert Taylor, *The A to Z of Elizabethan London*, London Topographical Society Publications No. 122 (1979)
Ringrose	Hyacinthe Ringrose, *The Inns of Court: An Historical Description of the Inns of Court and Chancery of England* (1909; repr. Littleton, Colo., 1983)
Rutter	Carol Chillington Rutter, ed., *Documents of the Rose Playhouse* (Manchester, 1984)
Shaheen	Naseeb Shaheen, *Biblical References in Shakespeare's History Plays* (Newark, NJ, 1989)
Southworth	John Southworth, *Shakespeare the Player: A Life in the Theatre* (Sparkford, 2000)
SQ	*Shakespeare Quarterly*
SS	*Shakespeare Survey*
Stow	John Stow, *The Survey of London* (1598), ed. C. L. Kingsford, 2 vols. (Oxford, 1908)

Textual Companion	Stanley Wells and Gary Taylor with John Jowett and William Montgomery, *William Shakespeare: A Textual Companion* (Oxford, 1987; repr. 1997)
Tilley	M. P. Tilley, *A Dictionary of the Proverbs in England in the Sixteenth and Seventeenth Centuries* (Ann Arbor, 1950)
True Tragedy	*The True Tragedy of Richard Duke of York* (the 1594 quarto) [*3 Henry VI*]
Vaughan	Henry H. Vaughan, *New Readings and Renderings of Shakespeare's Tragedies* (1886)
Walker	W. S. Walker, *A Critical Examination of the Text of Shakespeare, with remarks on his Language and that of his Contemporaries, together with notes on his Plays and Poems*, ed. with a preface, W. N. Lettsom, 3 vols. (1860)
Warner	Marina Warner, *Joan of Arc: The Image of Female Heroism* (New York, 1981)

Henry VI, Part One

THE PERSONS OF THE PLAY

The English

KING HENRY VI

Duke of BEDFORD, John of Lancaster, Regent of France, Henry IV's third son, the King's uncle

Duke of GLOUCESTER, Humphrey of Lancaster, Henry IV's fourth son, Lord Protector of England, the King's uncle

Duke of EXETER, Thomas Beaufort, Henry IV's brother, the King's great-uncle

Bishop of WINCHESTER (later Cardinal), Henry Beaufort, Exeter's younger brother, the King's great-uncle

Duke of SOMERSET, Edmund Beaufort, Exeter's nephew

RICHARD PLANTAGENET, son of Richard, late Earl of Cambridge, later DUKE OF YORK, and Regent of France

Earl of WARWICK, Richard de Beauchamp

Earl of SALISBURY, Thomas de Montague

Earl of SUFFOLK, William de la Pole

Lord TALBOT, later Earl of Shrewsbury

Young JOHN Talbot, his son

Edmund MORTIMER, Earl of March

Sir John FASTOLF

Sir William GLASDALE

Sir Thomas GARGRAVE

Sir William LUCY

Richard WOODVILLE, Lieutenant of the Tower of London

MAYOR of London

VERNON of the Yorkist (White Rose) faction

BASSET of the Lancastrian (Red Rose) faction

A LAWYER of the Temple

A Papal LEGATE

MESSENGERS; WARDERS and KEEPERS of the Tower of London, SERVING-MEN, OFFICERS, CAPTAINS, soldiers, heralds, watch

The French

CHARLES, Dauphin of France (later King)

REIGNIER, Duke of Anjou, titular King of Naples

MARGARET, his daughter

Duke of ALENÇON

BASTARD of Orléans

Duke of BURGUNDY, Henry VI's uncle

GENERAL of the French garrison at Bordeaux

COUNTESS of Auvergne

MASTER GUNNER of Orléans

A BOY, his son

JOAN la Pucelle, also called Joan of Arc

A SHEPHERD, Joan's father

PORTER, SERGEANT, SENTINELS, ambassador, scout, heralds, the Governor of Paris, fiends, and SOLDIERS

KING HENRY VI (1421–71) Shakespeare introduces his eponymous hero late in the play—at the beginning of Act 3—thus underlining his insignificance as king and character (though Shakespeare can delay the introduction of his protagonist with a quite opposite effect, as in *Hamlet* and *Othello*). An alternative view, argued by D. L. Frey (see p. 61 n. 1), sees that delay as lessening 'the possibility that Henry himself may be blamed for the results of his reign' (11). Hattaway suggests that Henry's tender years would allow him to be played by a boy-player, but not in Act 5, Scene 6 where he has grown to marriageable age, and not of course in *The First Part of the Contention* (*2 Henry VI*) and *Richard Duke of York* (*3 Henry VI*). In these last two plays Henry continues his unhappy pilgrimage through life, fitfully regal, religious, at times lyrically poignant, but usually ineffectual, unable e.g. in *The First Part of the Contention* to aid Gloucester except '[w]ith sad unhelpful tears' (*The First Part of the Contention* 3.1.218), and in *Richard Duke of York* tragically pusillanimous in his dealings with York. He dies a prisoner in the Tower of London in the last scene of *Richard Duke of York*, at the hands of Richard of Gloucester, York's youngest surviving son and the future Richard III, but not before prophesying in lyrical and ringing terms the

waste land that will be created by Richard (*Richard Duke of York* 5.6.35–56). Typically, his last words are saintly: 'O, God forgive my sins, and pardon thee' (5.6.60). This emphasis on his character stretches into *Richard III* where Lady Anne comments on his corpse: 'Poor keycold figure of a holy king, | Pale ashes of the house of Lancaster, | Thou bloodless remnant of that royal blood' (1.2.5–7).

Duke of BEDFORD John of Lancaster (1389–1435), third son of Henry IV, and the younger brother of Henry V, dramatized in the first and second parts of *Henry IV* as a 'young sober-blooded boy' (*2 Henry IV* 4.2.84–5) and a machiavellian diplomat. A more one-dimensional presence in this play, he, as England's governor in France, represents, in Talbot's words, an 'Undaunted spirit in a dying breast' (3.2.97), dying of grief for the lapsed honour of England.

Duke of GLOUCESTER Humphrey of Lancaster (1391–1447), youngest son of Henry IV. Protector of the realm during the King's minority, his story runs through this play and into Part Two where he dies a martyr's death. In *1 Henry VI* Shakespeare's presentation of him is characterized by his undignified squabbles with his uncle, the Bishop of Winchester (later Cardinal). Hattaway describes their struggle as 'naked and graceless rivalry between two political worldlings' (14). S. M. Pratt's article, however, 'Shakespeare and Humphrey Duke of Gloucester: A Study in Myth', *SQ* 16 (1965), 201–16, explores the myth-making propensity of Shakespeare's presentation in *The First Part of the Contention* (*2 Henry VI*) of a man who was 'at once the pillar of the law and the selfless man who could give up anything, including wife, high office, and even life itself, if England would benefit thereby' (205). Nonetheless in Part Two he and Winchester continue their 'ancient bickerings' (*The First Part of the Contention* 1.1.141). It is notable that in *1 Henry VI* he has a better sense of decorum than Winchester—e.g. his willingness to back down to keep the peace, 'Compassion on the King commands me stoop' (3.1.120). He has the most minor of minor roles in *Henry V*.

Duke of EXETER Thomas Beaufort (d. 1427), Henry VI's great-uncle and co-guardian—'his special governor' (1.1.171)—with the Bishop of Winchester. Like the Bishop, one of John of Gaunt's illegitimate sons, but their propinquity doesn't make him the Bishop's natural (or unnatural) ally. The Beauforts were legitimated after John of Gaunt married Catherine Swynford; a legal clause was supposed to bar their claim to the throne, however. Both in this play and in *Henry V* Exeter plays a subdued role as the worried quasi-choric observer of unfolding events and in *1 Henry VI* performs the added function of nostalgic memorialist of Henry V's time (see his soliloquy—one of the few in this play—at 3.1.188–202). (He may have been played by Shakespeare himself according to Honan, 205.) He speaks two undistinguished lines in the last scene of the play and then disappears. There is no Exeter in *The First Part of the Contention* (*2 Henry VI*), but there is a later one in *Richard Duke of York* (*3 Henry VI*).

Bishop of WINCHESTER John of Gaunt's second illegitimate child, Henry Beaufort (d. 1447), and Henry VI's great-uncle and guardian. He is the type of unscrupulous, ambitious Roman Catholic prelate whom sixteenth-century Protestant audiences in the London theatres loved to hate. (The fact that everybody in the play on both sides was historically Catholic did not prevent a later audience from identifying the Bishop and the French as Catholic and the rest of the English as somehow not.) His bishopric was the wealthiest in England,

and his power therefore immense. Besides his church role, Henry Beaufort served as Chancellor under both Henry V and Henry VI. Winchester's feud with Gloucester is an important element of the scenes set in England in this play. In *The First Part of the Contention* (*2 Henry VI*) the feud between them intensifies, climaxing in Gloucester's murder by Winchester's and Suffolk's henchmen followed by Winchester's own death '*in his bed raving and staring as if he were mad*' (*The First Part of the Contention* 3.3.0.3–4).

Duke of SOMERSET 'Shakespeare, like the chroniclers, conflated two historical personages. John Beaufort, first Duke of Somerset (1403–44) . . . [and] . . . Edmund Beaufort, second Duke of Somerset (1406–55) . . . John Beaufort's younger brother' (Hattaway). Both were of the second Beaufort generation, nephews of Exeter and Winchester. In *1 Henry VI* he is the chief antagonist of Richard Plantagenet in a quarrel over an unexplained, presumably arcane, point of law (perhaps about Richard's succession). The Wars of the Roses stem from this altercation—Richard choosing the white rose, Somerset the red. In the last act of *The First Part of the Contention* Richard's son, the future Richard III, kills Somerset in battle 'underneath an alehouse' paltry sign' (5.2.2).

RICHARD PLANTAGENET (1411–60) Richard comes into the play in Act 2, Scene 4 with a heavy burden of inheritance (explained in fine detail by Mortimer in the next scene). His royal roots go back to his grandfather, Edmund Langley, fifth son of Edward III. His father, the Earl of Cambridge, was sentenced to death by Henry V in 1415 for attempting to install Edmund Mortimer, Richard's uncle, on the throne. (Cambridge's arrest is dramatized in *Henry V* 2.2.) In his monograph *Duke Richard of York 1411–1460* (Oxford, 1988), P. A. Johnson examines the reasons for Henry's 'deep-seated fear' (p. 78) that Richard, the wealthiest of England's peers, might well claim the throne through his Mortimer lineage. In *1 Henry VI* Richard is restored to the dukedom of York in 3.1, and as Duke of York he goes on to play a major role in *The First Part of the Contention* and *Richard Duke of York*. He is stabbed to death by Clifford and Margaret in *Richard Duke of York* after a battle in which the 'army of the Queen hath got the field' (1.4.1). For ease of reference I have adopted Oxford's policy of giving

Richard the speech prefix Richard Plantagenet before 3.1 and Richard Duke of York
thereafter. Richard's appropriation of
'Plantagenet' as part of his linguistic
identity is an attempt to give himself an
aura of royal legitimacy: it was used by
the English royal dynasty from the acces-
sion of Henry II in 1154 until the death of
Richard III in 1485.

Earl of WARWICK Richard de Beauchamp
(1382–1439), father-in-law of Richard
Neville, Earl of Warwick (1428–71), who
has a significant role in *The First Part of
the Contention* and *Richard Duke of York*. In
1 Henry VI the father-in-law attempts to
act as a mediator between the various
warring factions in England (though he
plucks a white rose in support of Richard
Plantagenet). Historically, Richard
Beauchamp was in charge of Henry VI's
education, and began as a Lancastrian.
Burns notes that Barton and Hall's adaptation of the three *Henry VI* plays as *The
Wars of the Roses* conflates the two War-
wicks into a single puzzling figure, though
this conflation has the merit of cutting
through the confusion to prepare us for
the character Warwick's later support of
York. Neither he nor Somerset speaks in
the play's first scene. They are there presumably to stress the importance of the
occasion—one that brings the English
nobility together for a brief moment
of unity. No doubt their faces would be
remembered by the audience on their
reappearance.

Earl of SALISBURY Thomas de Montague or
Montacute (1388–1428) was, with
Talbot, the greatest of the English soldiers
fighting in France: 'mad-brained' (= hot-
headed) (1.2.15) according to Reignier
and a 'desperate homicide' (1.2.25). His
and Talbot's deaths—his by a lucky shot
from the French gunner's son later in the
opening act, Talbot's through English
incompetence and hubris in the fourth—
emphasize the decline of the English after
the death of Henry V. Historically, Salisbury's death occurred in 1428 before the
coming of Joan or Talbot's capture.

Earl of SUFFOLK William de la Pole
(1396–1450), Earl of Suffolk, fought in
the French wars with Henry V, married
the widowed Countess of Salisbury, and
in this play falls in love with Margaret of
Anjou whom he successfully woos on
behalf of Henry VI. In *The First Part of the
Contention* as Margaret's self-serving,
not-so-secret paramour, and murderer of
Gloucester, he is banished by the king and

killed by Walter Whitmore. F's direction
at 2.4.0 calls him 'Poole', a variation of
his family name, 'de la Pole'. Burns
adopts 'Poole' and 'de la Poole' for his
edition as 'a deliberately contemptuous
choice of the English form of his family
name' by the other nobles. However, he
changes Somerset's use to 'Pole' at 2.4.80
because Somerset is a supporter of Suffolk, and therefore not contemptuous of
him. In F, however, Somerset like the
others addresses him as 'Poole'. It would
seem to be advisable to stick with one or
the other, 'Pole' or 'Poole', given F's
apparent indifference to semantic
niceties. In *The First Part of the Contention*
(*2 Henry VI*) Pole as Poole is given its
scornful apotheosis in the Lieutenant's
contempt for his prisoner, Suffolk: 'Poole!
Sir Poole! Lord! | Ay, kennel, puddle,
sink, whose filth and dirt | Troubles the
silver spring where England drinks'
(4.1.70–2). (The quotation is from
Sanders's edition; the Oxford has 'Pole'.)

Lord TALBOT If the play could be said to have a
hero it would be John, first Earl of Shrewsbury (1388?–1453), the greatest English
soldier of his time, whose death proved to
be the play's great sentimental attraction
for audiences in the 1590s. (See Introduction, pp. ••–••). Shakespeare manipulates
space and time to focus on Talbot and
Joan as antagonists, with Talbot as the
last link to England's heroic past. He has
more lines to speak than any other character and his name is mentioned in every
Act, over 70 times in all. Interestingly
enough, he is not mentioned in the second and third parts of *Henry VI*.

Young JOHN Talbot (d. 1453), as Hall and
Holinshed tell us, died with his father at
the Battle of Castillon. So too did Talbot's
bastard son, Henry, who is not mentioned
in the play. This John Talbot was Lord
Lisle, a title that distinguishes him from
his half-brother John, Talbot's eldest son
of his first marriage (who became the second Earl of Shrewsbury and died in the
Battle of Northampton, 1460).

Edmund MORTIMER (1391–1425) Despite Mortimer's convoluted explanation of his
pedigree in Act 2, Scene 5, he, like the
Duke of Somerset, is a composite character, the conflation of at least two and
possibly three historical characters. One
of them, Edmund Mortimer, fifth Earl of
March, uncle to Richard Plantagenet,
was declared heir presumptive to Richard
II in 1398, and Shakespeare revisits this
character (or one very like him) princip-

ally in *1 Henry IV* where he and his cause become a mantra ('revolted Mortimer!') for Hotspur and the rebels. Shakespeare's confusion of the Mortimers has its source in the Chronicles. Jailed, lame, old, and dying, Mortimer in this play joins Bedford, Salisbury, and Talbot as a representative of a disappearing heroic past.

Sir John FASTOLF (*c*.1378–1459) A Norfolk landowner, served in France under Bedford and became governor of Anjou and Maine in 1423. Shakespeare's play follows the chroniclers in maligning him as a coward. The four Folios—followed by Rowe (1709 and 1714) and Pope (1723–5)—give this character the name Falstaff (or Falstaffe). In the Chronicles his name is Sir John Fastolf (or Fastolfe/ Fastolffe). Should an editor give him his historical or his Folio name? G. Walton Williams, in 'Fastolf or Falstaff', *English Literary Renaissance*, 5 (1975), 308–12, speculated that the consistency of the spelling Falstaffe in the Folio in a text noted for its inconsistent spelling can be ascribed to a zealous reviser cashing in on the popularity of the character Falstaff in the two parts of *Henry IV* and *The Merry Wives of Windsor*, written in the late 1590s. So more than likely, he argues, Shakespeare wrote Fastolf (or a version thereof) in his manuscript. Prompted by Norman Davis in 'Falstaff's Name', *SQ* 28 (1977), 513–15, however, Williams later acknowledged that Falstaff(e) may well be a variant of Fastolf(fe) in 'Second Thoughts on Falstaff's Name', *SQ* 30 (1979), 82–4. Either way it seems preferable to choose the spelling, Fastolf(fe), found consistently in Hall and Holinshed, if only to distinguish him from the later and greater comic creation, Falstaff, with whom he has nothing in common, and to avoid succumbing to the 'tyranny of the copy text' (*ELR*, 309) as Williams puts it.

Sir William GLASDALE F has Glansdale which is historically inaccurate. In the play Glasdale's fate is even less significant than Sir Thomas Gargrave's in that he appears to be unhurt by the Boy's shot in Act 1, Scene 5. This would allow him to help with the removal of either Gargrave's body or Salisbury's at the end of the scene.

Sir Thomas GARGRAVE His death is mentioned in the Chronicles. Suitably for an attendant lord (and for his name), he dies immediately after being hit in Act 1, Scene 5, allowing the audience's attention to focus on the lingering death of his superior officer, the Earl of Salisbury. (In Holinshed Gargrave takes two days to die.)

Sir William LUCY He was the Sheriff of Warwickshire in Henry VI's reign, and an ancestor of Sir Thomas Lucy (1532–1600), a landowner of Charlecote, near Stratford-upon-Avon. He is not mentioned in the Chronicles as being in France at this time.

Richard WOODVILLE In charge of the Tower of London, historically Richard Woodville (d. *c*.1441) was Lieutenant of Calais, a Lancastrian, and a supporter of Winchester. Although his appearance in the play is fleeting his descendants—as Burns outlines—surface in history and in later Shakespeare (in *Richard Duke of York* (3 *Henry VI*) and *Richard III*).

CHARLES, Dauphin of France (1403–61) Eldest son of the French king, Charles VI (who died two months after Henry V, on 21 October 1422) and heir to the throne. Burns departs from recent editorial practice in retaining throughout his edition the Folio spelling, Dolphin. As a consequence of this refusal to modernize the word (which differs from his general treatment of words other than proper names in the rest of his edition) actors are not allowed the opportunity orthographically of pronouncing the name Dawfin (an acceptable pronunciation of Dolphin in Shakespeare's time). As the General Editors themselves in Burns's edition point out, this is a restrictive prescription and fails to do justice to what amounts to Talbot's uniquely contemptuous pun on the Dauphin's name at 1.5.85 when the pronunciation Dolphin is clearly intended.

REIGNIER René, Duke of Anjou and Lorraine, titular king of Naples and Jerusalem (1409–80). (Reignier is the anglicized version of the name used in F.) The last two royal positions—even if they were not merely titular—had no economic clout, making a mockery of Suffolk's claim for Reignier as an appropriately 'royal' father for Margaret, Suffolk's successful candidate for Henry's wife. In *Richard Duke of York* (3 *Henry VI*) York describes him as being 'not so wealthy as an English yeoman' (1.4.124).

MARGARET Margaret of Anjou (1430–82), daughter of Reignier, Duke of Anjou and Lorraine, married Henry VI in 1445. In this play she does so at the eloquent instigation of Suffolk who persuades Henry that Margaret is superior in every way (but especially sexually) to the woman to whom he is already betrothed, the Earl of Armagnac's daughter (see 5.1). As Joan's star wanes, Margaret's waxes, and she goes on to play a major role in *The First Part of the Contention* and *Richard Duke of York*. In these last two plays, especially *Richard Duke of York*, Margaret, 'stern, obdurate, flinty, rough, remorseless' (*Richard Duke of York* 1.4.143) according to York, takes on ogreish dimensions: she has, famously, a 'tiger's heart wrapped in a woman's hide!' (1.4.138). Unhistorically, she returns in *Richard III* to pepper Richard with the invective he had questioned so querulously at the end of *Richard Duke of York*: 'Why should she live to fill the world with words?' (5.5.43).

Duke of **ALENÇON** Jean, fifth Duke of Alençon (1409–76), and, rather like Exeter in the English camp, a choric responder to events. He has a brief moment of individuation in Act 2, Scene 1, where Charles accuses him of slacking on guard duty, allowing the English a momentary triumph outside Orléans.

BASTARD of **Orléans** Jean, Count of Dunois (1403?–68), illegitimate son of Charles, Duke of Orléans, first cousin to Charles VII. Like Talbot he was one of the finest soldiers of his time. He introduces the 'holy maid' (1.2.51), Joan, to the Dauphin's court: illegitimacy introducing a specious holiness. The honorific remains firmly French in this play; we have to wait until Faulconbridge in *King John* for his English counterpart, although Shakespeare could have included Talbot's bastard son, who in history died at the Battle of Castillon with his father and brother (Castillon becomes Bordeaux in *1 Henry VI*). (There could very well be honour in the honorific at this time; i.e. to be known as a bastard or to be titled Bastard was not necessarily opprobrious.)

Duke of **BURGUNDY** Inflamed by the murder of his father in 1419 by the Dauphin's men, Philip the Good, Duke of Burgundy (1396–1467), became an ally of the English at the Treaty of Troyes (1420) and for his reward Henry V named him co-regent of France with Bedford. In history he transferred his allegiance to Charles VII in 1435 but not at the suasion of Joan as in this play. His abrupt surrender to Joan's blandishments in the third act is made pointedly outrageous in that, until then, he and Talbot share a vituperative vocabulary at Joan's expense. (E. F. Jacob points out that although the agreements at Arras in 1435 amounted to 'a decisive blow . . . at the old co-operation' between England and Burgundy they 'did not mean the end of Anglo-Burgundian relations' (*Oxford History of England: The Fifteenth Century, 1399–1485*, p. 263).)

COUNTESS of **Auvergne** is an invented character in an invented episode. Wilson suggests, however, that Talbot's 'encounter' with her was based on 'similar visits of young English officers to ladies in neighbouring castles when . . . fighting was not the order of the day' (pp. xix–xx).

JOAN la Pucelle (1412–31) The story of Joan of Arc is well known through fiction, drama, and numerous biographies. After various military successes against the English, she was captured by them at the defence of Compiègne, tried as a heretic and a witch and burnt at the stake by the Inquisition at Rouen on 30 May 1431. In 1920 she was canonized. Her name assumes various guises in the Folio, none of them precisely her historical name, Pucelle. (We might note that the French spelling of Joan's name was no more fixed at this time than the English.) However, the most frequent form in F is a variation on Pucell (Puzel occurs mainly in the first Act). Most editors plump for Pucelle (or la Pucelle) rather than any of the play's other variants. A notable exception is Edward Burns who chooses Puzel, a form of the name with an exclusively derogatory meaning, thus leaving the French with no respectful term for her. How unnecessary Burns's change is can be judged by the fact that in English 'pucelle' meant both drab/slut and girl/maid (*OED* 1 and 2). In French 'pucelle' = virgin, 'but in a special way, with distinct shades connoting youth, innocence and, paradoxically, nubility' (Warner, 22). Warner also notes: 'As well as forming part of the language of the courtly romances, *Pucelle* was a country word and survived, for instance, in a local children's game, Le Jeu de la Pucelle, recorded by Retif de la Bretonne at the end of the 18th century' (23).

The First Part of Henry the Sixth

1.1   *Dead March. Enter the funeral of King Henry the Fifth,*
attended on by the Duke of Bedford, Regent of France;
the Duke of Gloucester, Protector; the Duke of Exeter;
the Earl of Warwick; the Bishop of Winchester; and the
Duke of Somerset; ⌈*Heralds*⌉

BEDFORD

Hung be the heavens with black! Yield day to night!
Comets, importing change of times and states,
Brandish your crystal tresses in the sky,

Title *The First Part of Henry the Sixth*] F (*The first Part of Henry the Sixt.* (*title-page and running titles*))
1.1] F (*Actus Primus. Scoena Prima.*)   0.4 *the Earl of*] HART (*so throughout play*); *not in* F
0.5 *Heralds*] MALONE (*subs.*); *not in* F   3 crystal] F; crested WARBURTON *conj.*

1.1.0.1 *Dead March* Funeral march, played
most likely on a muffled drum.

0.1 *funeral* i.e. the coffin and its bearers.
Edward Burns notes that the latter could
be the nobles themselves—effective the-
atrically—or, more accurate historically,
six extras, hooded, and dressed in black.
Edward Hall describes Henry V's historical 'charet' (the coffin) as 'richly apparelled with cloth of gold' (113) and this
resplendent container of England's past
glory would be in vivid and symbolic
contrast with the stage hung in black
and the bearers and mourners in their
black 'wailing robes' (1.1.86). (But see
note on l. 19.) The funeral takes place in
Westminster Abbey.

0.1 *Henry the Fifth* (1387–1422) Henry VI's
illustrious father, the paragon of English
kings, conqueror of France, and hugely
intimidating role model for his son, celebrated later in Shakespeare's *The Life of
Henry the Fifth* (1599). He broods over
the events of this play as the 'ever-living
man of memory' (4.3.51). See note to
4.3.51.

1 **Hung . . . night** Southworth suggests this
line echoes 'Black is the beauty of the
brightest day . . . Ready to darken earth

with endless night' from Marlowe's *2
Tamburlaine* (2.4.1, 7).

1 **Hung . . . black!** There are no exclamation marks in the play's opening line in F.
It's possible to read this first half as a
statement of fact, especially as 'heavens'
was a familiar term for the canopy above
the stage, customarily draped in black
cloth for tragedies. But Bedford's opening
speech hinges on a series of sonorous
imperatives so that 'hung be' = 'let [the
heavens] be hung' and 'yield day' = 'let
day give way'.

2 **Comets** Conventionally thought to
presage dire events for nations and the
deaths of great men, though here Bedford
seems to want to use them as weapons
in some kind of galactic conflagration
brought on by the cosmic disturbance of
Henry V's death.
importing signifying
states (a) conditions (b) countries

3 **Brandish . . . sky** A somewhat strained
image: Bedford imagines the distinctive
tails (tresses) of the comets as threaten-
ing, transparent whips. In *William
Shakespeare: the History Plays* (New York,
1992) E. Pearlman notes: 'None of [Bed-
ford's] injunctive verbs ('yield,' 'brandish,'

And with them scourge the bad revolting stars
That have consented unto Henry's death—   5
King Henry the Fifth, too famous to live long.
England ne'er lost a king of so much worth.

GLOUCESTER

England ne'er had a king until his time.
Virtue he had, deserving to command;
His brandished sword did blind men with his beams,   10
His arms spread wider than a dragon's wings,
His sparkling eyes, replete with wrathful fire,
More dazzled and drove back his enemies
Than midday sun fierce bent against their faces.
What should I say? His deeds exceed all speech;   15
He ne'er lift up his hand but conquerèd.

EXETER

We mourn in black; why mourn we not in blood?
Henry is dead and never shall revive;
Upon a wooden coffin we attend,

---

6 King Henry] F; Henry POPE

'scourge') quite hits the mark' (23).

3 **crystal** transparent
tresses ' "Comet" derives from a Greek word meaning "long-haired star" ' (Hattaway).

4 **scourge** Although *OED* gives this example as the figurative use of 'scourge', the context here tends to make the meaning more literal: the tresses of the previous line have now become whips.
revolting (a) rebellious (b) unfavourable (*OED, revolt, v.* 5a)

5 **consented unto** acted together to cause

6 **too . . . long** Proverbial: 'Those that God loves do not live long' (Dent G251).

7 **ne'er** never

9 **Virtue** vertu, the power to command (cf. charismata: a divinely conferred power or talent)

10–14 **His . . . faces** Henry V is conceived here in terms of a mythical force (preternatural and supernatural) that is also a force of nature (the midday sun).

10 **his** its

12 **replete with** full of

14 **bent** turned

15 **What . . . say** words fail me
exceed exceeded (Abbott §342)

16 **lift** lifted

16 **his hand** The hand that would have held 'his brandished sword' (1.1.10).

17 **We . . . blood** In *Richard Duke of York* [3 *Henry VI*] Clifford expresses a similar sentiment: 'The hope thereof [of revenge] makes Clifford mourn in steel' (1.1.58).
blood i.e. of the rebellious French

18–19 **Henry . . . attend** The hyperbolic nostalgia indulged in by Bedford and Gloucester in the play's opening speeches contrasts with Exeter's plain-speaking here. This is the first of a number of occasions in this play (and in many of Shakespeare's later ones) where the language of excess is followed by its counterweight in bluntness. (The most notable in *1 Henry VI* is Joan's derisive response to Lucy's encomium of Talbot, 'Here's a silly stately style indeed' (4.7.72).)

19 **wooden** The same pun on 'wooden' as 'drab', 'dull', 'unfeeling', occurs in *The Tempest* when Ferdinand, the 'patient log-man', complains to Miranda about his 'wooden slavery' (3.1.67, 62). It also subtends an exchange between Suffolk and Margaret at 5.4.45–6. In the 1983 BBC production the coffin is uncovered, clearly made of wood, with a skeleton crudely chalked on its lid.

And death's dishonourable victory   20
We with our stately presence glorify,
Like captives bound to a triumphant car.
What? Shall we curse the planets of mishap
That plotted thus our glory's overthrow?
Or shall we think the subtle-witted French   · 25
Conjurers and sorcerers, that, afraid of him,
By magic verses have contrived his end?

WINCHESTER

He was a king blest of the King of kings.
Unto the French the dreadful judgement day
So dreadful will not be as was his sight.   30
The battles of the Lord of Hosts he fought;
The church's prayers made him so prosperous.

GLOUCESTER

The church? Where is it? Had not churchmen prayed,
His thread of life had not so soon decayed.

33 The . . . prayed] POPE; The . . . it? | Had . . . pray'd F   34 not] F; but VAUGHAN *conj.*

21 **stately** noble
   presence ceremonial attendance (*OED* 2b)
22 **car** chariot. The Roman custom of dis-
   playing the human trophies of their
   military victories in their triumphant
   re-entries into Rome was popular on
   the Elizabethan stage. Marlowe's *2 Tamburlaine*, in the most famous of these
   representations, has the captured
   nobility—the pampered jades of Asia—
   actually pull the chariot in which he is
   riding on to the stage. But Tamburlaine
   was a Mongol not a Roman.
23–7 **What . . . end** Both these rhetorical
   questions are intended sardonically;
   Henry V died in his bed of a sickness.
   However, he did die in France, in
   Vincennes, so there is some justification
   for the direction of Exeter's second
   question.
23 **planets of mishap** planets that regulate
   misfortune
25 **subtle-witted** deviously inventive
26 **Conjurers** magicians who deal with
   spirits, exorcists. Joan is one such as we
   see in Act 5.
27 **magic verses** rhymed spells
28 **King of kings** See 1 Timothy 6: 15 followed there (and frequently in later times)
   by 'Lord of lords'.
29 **judgement day** The time of God's last
   judgement, the day the world will end,

described (with its attendant horrors) in
Revelation 6 and 20.
30 **his sight** the sight of him (i.e. Henry V)
31 **battles . . . fought** Henry is compared here
   to the Christian warrior-king David, 1
   Samuel 25: 28.
   Lord of Hosts Another well-known
   biblical phrase, appearing frequently in
   the Old Testament. In *Henry V* Henry's
   Christian piety is frequently emphasized,
   perhaps to counterbalance the fragility of
   his claim to the French throne.
32 **prosperous** successful
33 **Where is it** i.e. where is its allegiance
   directed
33–4 **Had . . . decayed** 'Winchester is being
   accused of "praying against" Henry as a
   "foe" and hence of having "contriv'd to
   murder" him' (Cairncross). Although the
   'not' before 'churchmen' is clear in F, the
   accusation struck Vaughan as sufficiently
   extreme for him to suggest 'but' as a
   conjectural emendation. The rhyme
   prayed/decayed is probably deliberate and
   is the first of many occasions where
   rhyme is used for special emphasis. See
   also ll. 87–8, 143–4, and 155–6.
33 **prayed** With a pun on 'preyed'.
34 **thread of life** In classical mythology a
   man's thread of life was spun, measured,
   and cut by the three Fates, the sisters—
   and harsh spinners, as they were

None do you like but an effeminate prince   35
Whom like a schoolboy you may overawe.

WINCHESTER

Gloucester, whate'er we like, thou art Protector,
And lookest to command the prince and realm.
Thy wife is proud: she holdeth thee in awe
More than God or religious churchmen may.   40

GLOUCESTER

Name not religion, for thou lov'st the flesh,
And ne'er throughout the year to church thou go'st,
Except it be to pray against thy foes.

BEDFORD

Cease, cease these jars and rest your minds in peace;
Let's to the altar. Heralds, wait on us.   45

45 Heralds,] POPE; ~∧ F us.] F; us. *Exit Funeral* CAIRNCROSS; us. *Exeunt Warwick, Somerset,
and heralds with coffin* OXFORD

known—Clotho (the spinner), Lachesis
(the measurer), and Atropos (the
cutter).

34 **decayed** Although the word implies a
gradual process, *so soon* suggests a
reliance on *decay* as 'ruin', 'destruction'
(*OED sb.* 1b).

35-6 **None . . . overawe** Gloucester means
that Winchester can only like a king who
is callowly dependent on him, not one,
like Henry V, who has a mind of his own.

35 **effeminate** Did not necessarily imply
unmanliness (*OED adj.* 1c), but the play
goes on to present Henry VI as feeble, self-
indulgent, and unbecomingly delicate—
all characteristics of 'effeminate' in the
pejorative sense (*OED adj.* 1a). See also
5.5.107.

37 **whate'er we like** i.e. whether we like it or
not. It is notable even in this early play
how successfully the sense of an ongoing
conversation is conveyed by the way characters echo their interlocutors' words and
phrases. (See 'None do you like' in l. 35
and 'overawe' and 'awe' in ll. 36 and
39.)
   Protector regent during the king's
minority

38 **And lookest . . . realm** As does Suffolk in
the play's ominous final line: 'But I will
rule both her, the King, and realm'
(5.6.108).
   lookest aspire
   prince ruler

39-40 **she . . . may** you are more in awe of
her than you are of God or your colleagues in the church. (Perhaps there is a
particular emphasis on 'religious' to
distinguish them from Winchester.) This
proves not to be true in *The First Part of the
Contention* [*2 Henry VI*] as Gloucester
repudiates his wife's treasonable supernatural solicitings on his behalf. The
matter is complicated, however, as Burns
points out, in that Gloucester was in real
life married twice. It's just possible (but
not likely) that the reference here is to
Gloucester's first wife, not to Eleanor
Cobham, his second, so named in
Contention.

43 **Except** unless
   foes One of them being Henry V, according to Gloucester.

44 **jars** discords

45 **Heralds, . . . us** F is unhelpful. There is
neither a comma after 'Heralds', which
would suggest that the half-line is a command, nor any clarifying stage direction.
Burns follows F arguing that Bedford may
be asking the others to go to the altar
because the Heralds are waiting for them.
It hardly seems likely that Bedford would
concern himself with the impatience of
subordinates. But, if the line is a command, where do the Heralds wait on them
? Some editions, e.g. Oxford, take this
opportunity to rid the stage of the coffin,
the heralds, and the mute Warwick and
Somerset. But this convenient exeunt

Instead of gold we'll offer up our arms,
Since arms avail not now that Henry's dead.
Posterity, await for wretched years
When, at their mothers' moistened eyes, babes shall
    suck,
Our isle be made a marish of salt tears,   50
And none but women left to wail the dead.
Henry the Fifth, thy ghost I invoke:
Prosper this realm, keep it from civil broils,
Combat with adverse planets in the heavens.
A far more glorious star thy soul will make   55
Than Julius Caesar or bright—
    Enter a Messenger

47 not . . . dead.] BURNS; not, now . . . dead, F; not, now . . . dead. CAPELL; not; now . . . dead, CAIRNCROSS   48 for] F; fond CAIRNCROSS *conj.*   49 moistened] FI (moistned); moist F2   50 marish] POPE; Nourish F

means that the silent reminder of past glories, Henry V's coffin, is no longer an ironic presence during the Messengers' dispatches from the crumbling French front. Its absence also makes a near nonsense of Bedford's command to the first Messenger to speak softly '[b]efore dead Henry's corpse' (1.1.62). Perhaps Bedford is simply asking the heralds to move ahead or to one side while the nobles regroup around the altar. (In the Terry Hands production of the play in 1977, the coffin remains on stage, and at one point Winchester pounds on it in anger.)

46 **arms** weapons
48 **await** watch
49 **When . . . suck** Another strained conceit in an unmetrical line. The sense seems to be that the mothers will only be able to feed their children with their tears, so overwhelming will be the wretchedness of the times. See Joan's appeal to Burgundy at 3.3.45–6. In *The Early Shakespeare* (San Marino, Cal., 1967) A. C. Hamilton notes that Bedford's prophecy 'awaits complete fulfillment until *Richard III*, where the weeping women—Margaret, the Duchess of York, Elizabeth, and Anne—gather to lament their dead husbands and sons' (31).
50 **marish** marsh. Editions seem more or less evenly divided between adopting Pope's emendation or staying with F's 'Nourish' (= nurse). Pope's emendation is justifiable

both on compositorial grounds—it is easy to confuse the minims—and stylistic.
51 **And . . . dead** This plangent line (and the ones preceding it) anticipate in cruder terms Northumberland's 'strained passion' in *2 Henry IV* which ends 'And darkness be the burier of the dead!' (1.1.160).
52 **ghost** spirit
52 **invocate** call upon in prayer. Hattaway suggests that at this point Bedford may turn to pray at the altar.
53 **Prosper** make prosperous
   broils disturbances, wars
55 **glorious star** Julius Caesar's soul, says Ovid at the end of the *Metamorphoses*, was translated into a star at his death. Shakespeare has Pericles and Juliet call for the same glorious fate for Thaisa's father and Romeo. In *Julius Caesar*, Caesar says: 'But I am constant as the Northern Star, | Of whose true fixed and resting quality | There is no fellow in the firmament' (3.1.60–2),
56 **bright**—Commentators have speculated on a number of three-syllabled candidates to accompany Julius Caesar here: among them, Charlemagne, Constantine, Hercules, Augustus, Berenice, Orion. (We might note that Hercules and Orion are constellations.) But Shakespeare may have had none of these (or anyone else) in mind as the Messenger's interruption of Bedford's encomium is dramatically effective.
56.1 ***Enter a Messenger*** Who, in his derisive manner, is one of a line of individualized

MESSENGER

My honourable lords, health to you all.
Sad tidings bring I to you out of France,
Of loss, of slaughter, and discomfiture:
Guyenne, Compiègne, Rheims, Rouen, Orléans,   60
Paris, Gisors, Poitiers, are all quite lost.

BEDFORD

What say'st thou, man, before dead Henry's corpse?
Speak softly, or the loss of those great towns
Will make him burst his lead and rise from death.

GLOUCESTER

Is Paris lost? Is Rouen yielded up?   65
If Henry were recalled to life again
These news would cause him once more yield the ghost.

EXETER

How were they lost? What treachery was used?

MESSENGER

No treachery, but want of men and money.
Amongst the soldiers this is mutterèd: 70
That here you maintain several factions,
And, whilst a field should be dispatched and fought,

---

60 Compiègne] OXFORD; Champaigne F   Rouen,] CAPELL; *not in* F   62 What . . . corpse?] F
(*subs.*); What . . . man! Before . . . corse STAUNTON   corpse] F (Coarse)   65 Rouen] F (Roan)

---

minor, socially obscure characters in
Shakespeare bearing unpalatable truths.
In *Shakespeare the Historian* (New York,
1996) Paola Pugliatti suggests that the
Messenger's scornful tone perhaps
indicates that he fought with Henry at
Agincourt. At all events, he and the two
others who follow 'seem to have acquired
a sharper consciousness of the common
good than those who ruled them, and
have taken upon themselves heavier
responsibilities than their function
entails' (207). See Sir William Lucy's
trenchant criticism, 4.4.13–28.

59 **discomfiture** utter defeat
60–1 **Guyenne . . . lost** Lost they all were—
except for Orléans and Poitiers which
were never won—but not all at one time.
Shakespeare telescopes nearly twenty-five
years of warfare in two lines.
60 **Rouen** As Gloucester specifically mentions Rouen ('Roan' in F) at l. 65, Capell's
emendation is compelling. The omission

in F was probably caused by eyeskip from
one 'R' to another.
64 **lead** The inner lining of Henry's wooden
coffin would have been made of
lead.
69 **want . . . money** A kind of treachery, one
would think.
want lack
71 **maintain several factions** Cairncross helpfully suggests that this phrase refers to the
maintenance of bodies of retainers by
the English nobility, a divisive and costly
business (in illuminating contrast to the
failure to provide moneys for the army in
France). But 'maintain' might = 'keep
up', 'cause to continue' (*OED v.* 4) and
'factions' = 'quarrel' or 'intrigue' (*OED
sb.* 4b). The phrase would then = 'perpet-
uate factious disputes'.
several separate, divisive
72 **field** (a) army (*OED sb.* 8b) (subject of 'dispatched') (b) battle (*OED sb.* 8a) (subject
of 'fought')
dispatched settled urgently

You are disputing of your generals.
One would have ling'ring wars with little cost;
Another would fly swift, but wanteth wings;   75
A third thinks, without expense at all,
By guileful words fair peace may be obtained.
Awake, awake, English nobility!
Let not sloth dim your honours new begot.
Cropped are the flower-de-luces in your arms;   80
Of England's coat one half is cut away.   ⌈*Exit*⌉
EXETER
Were our tears wanting to this funeral,
These tidings would call forth her flowing tides.

76 third] F1; ~ man F2; ~ one WALKER *conj.*   thinks] F; ~ that KEIGHTLEY *conj.*   77 words
fair peace] This edition; faire words, Peace F   78 Awake, awake] F1; ~, away F2   81 *Exit*]
WILSON; *not in* F   83 her] F; their THEOBALD; his WALKER *conj.*

73 **of** about (Abbott §174)
generals Burns notes that the word makes
little sense in this context as the rank of
an army officer; i.e. that the English high
command is engaged in internal bickering
to the neglect of the war in France. Burns
points out in an Appendix that an army at
this time would have only one general. He
suggests instead that the word = 'general
principles' (*OED* B *sb.* 2a). Perhaps
'tactics' would be the closest modern
equivalent in view of the Messenger's
itemization of the points of dispute.

74 **ling'ring . . . cost** The wars would be lingering because there would be no money
available for a decisive victory. We might
note just how lingering the real wars were
between England and France at this time.
The encounters dramatized in this play
were part of the Hundred Years War
which was in fact a series of wars between
the two countries stretching from 1337 to
1453. The claim to the French throne was
only finally abandoned by the English in
1801.

75 **Another . . . wings** Proverbial: 'He would
fain fly but he wants feathers' (Dent
F164).
wings i.e. the material and men (and the
money) needed for a quick and favourable
outcome.

76 **A third . . . all** An unmetrical line which

F2 corrects by inserting 'man'. But the
collocation 'One', 'another', 'A third',
contributes to the Messenger's terse
delivery.

77 **guileful words fair** *OED* gives F's word-
order ('guileful fair words') as the only
one where 'guileful' qualifies another
adjective. The transposition would have
been easy to make in the printing-house.

79 **new begot** recently acquired (under
Henry V)

80 **Cropped** plucked
flower-de-luces The complicated gene-
alogy of the French *fleur-de-lis*, the iris
(Fox-Davies, 273–4), the heraldic symbol
of the French monarchy, should not
obscure the essential fact that the English
appropriated it for the English royal coat
of arms as a cultural symbol of Edward
III's claim to the sovereignty of France.
(Cf. the appropriation of the German song
'Lili Marlene' by British troops during the
First World War.)
arms coat of arms

81 **coat** i.e. of arms
one half i.e. the French half
Exit The first messenger has to make way
for the second at some time before l. 89
and this seems an appropriate moment,
leaving Exeter and Bedford to respond to
his last ringing lines.

83 **her** England's

BEDFORD

    Me they concern; regent I am of France.

    Give me my steelèd coat, I'll fight for France.   85

    Away with these disgraceful wailing robes.

      ⌈*He removes his mourning cloak*⌉

    Wounds will I lend the French, instead of eyes,

    To weep their intermissive miseries.

      Enter to them another Messenger

SECOND MESSENGER

    Lords, view these letters, full of bad mischance.

    France is revolted from the English quite,   90

    Except some petty towns of no import;

    The Dauphin Charles is crownèd king in Rheims;

    The Bastard of Orléans with him is joined;

    Reignier, Duke of Anjou, doth take his part;

    The Duke of Alençon flieth to his side.   *Exit*   95

EXETER

    The Dauphin crownèd king? All fly to him?

    O whither shall we fly from this reproach?

GLOUCESTER

    We will not fly but to our enemies' throats.

    Bedford, if thou be slack, I'll fight it out.

86.1 *He . . . cloak*] OXFORD (*subs.*); *not in* F
92 Dauphin] F (Dolphin) (*so throughout play*)
(*so throughout play*); *Reynold* F; *René* OXFORD
F1; *on* F3

89 SECOND MESSENGER] ROWE (*subs.*); *Mess.* F
crownèd] F (crown'd) 94 Reignier] ROWE
doth take] F1; *doth* F2; *takes* HANMER 95 to]

84 **they** the tidings
   regent i.e. in the king's absence
85 **steelèd** made of steel
   for i.e. to win
86.1 **He . . . cloak** Burns disputes the appropriateness of Oxford's stage direction
   here, arguing that such an action focuses
   too much on a single figure (unless all the
   others follow suit). But Bedford's vehe-
   ment expression of disgust with his 'wailing robes' in the previous line invites an
   action, especially as it is action that he is
   calling for. If all the lords follow Bedford's
   example they immediately become distin-
   guishable on the stage as individuals for
   the quarrelling that ensues.
87–8 **Wounds . . . miseries** So the French will
   weep blood. 'Eyes' (pronounced 'ees')
   rhymes with 'miseries' (Kökeritz, 437).
   See note to 1.1.33–4.

87 **lend** give
88 **intermissive** coming at intervals. Referring to the sporadic nature of the conflict.
90 **quite** completely
91 **petty** small
92 **Rheims** Charles VII was crowned seven
   years later at Rheims in 1429 though he
   had also been crowned king at Poitiers in
   1422. The English do not acknowledge
   Charles as king until (perhaps) 5.5.123.
   (See note there.) The French also
   continue to refer to him as 'the Prince
   Dauphin' (1.2.46), as does Charles
   himself (1.2.112).
96 **fly** flock
97 **we** The actor may wish to stress this word
   after 'All fly to him'.
   reproach disgrace. (Because Henry VI is
   supposed to be King of France.)

BEDFORD

Gloucester, why doubt'st thou of my forwardness?   100
An army have I mustered in my thoughts,
Wherewith already France is overrun.
    Enter another Messenger

THIRD MESSENGER

My gracious lords, to add to your laments
Wherewith you now bedew King Henry's hearse,
I must inform you of a dismal fight   105
Betwixt the stout Lord Talbot and the French.

WINCHESTER

What? Wherein Talbot overcame—is't so?

THIRD MESSENGER

O no, wherein Lord Talbot was o'erthrown;
The circumstance I'll tell you more at large.
The tenth of August last, this dreadful lord,   110
Retiring from the siege of Orléans,
Having full scarce six thousand in his troop,
By three-and-twenty thousand of the French
Was round encompassèd and set upon:
No leisure had he to enrank his men.   115
He wanted pikes to set before his archers;

103 THIRD MESSENGER] ROWE (*subs.*); *Mes.* F   109 more at large] F; at more large BURNS
112 full scarce] F; scarce full ROWE   114 encompassèd] F (incompassed)

105 **dismal fight** The Battle of Patay (1429)
   which occurred about six weeks after the
   siege at Orléans but is moved here to an
   earlier time by Shakespeare for dramatic
   purposes.
   dismal with an unhappy outcome (for the
   English); though Winchester doesn't
   seem to pick up on this meaning (or its
   direction) in his query that follows.
106 **stout** valiant
107 **is't so** isn't that the case
109 **circumstance** details (*OED sb.* 9)
   at large in full. Full indeed: the Messenger's subsequent description of Talbot's
   capture constitutes what may be a first
   attempt by Shakespeare at a full-blooded
   epic description of battle brought to glorious fruition in the Captain's speeches in
   the first scene of *Macbeth*. Burns—puz-
   zlingly—has 'at more large' which he
   glosses as 'at greater length'.
110 **tenth of August** In reality, 18 June 1429.
   Hattaway reminds us that in history this

would have been about six weeks after
the siege of Orléans which makes up the
matter of the next two scenes.
   dreadful inspiring dread
112–13 **Having . . . French**   Shakespeare's
history plays make much of the valour of
outnumbered English armies fighting on
French soil. At this time France's population was four or five times that of
England. For the significance of this
see Perry Anderson's *Lineages of the
Absolutist State* (1974), pp. 122 ff.
112 **full** in full
114 **round encompassèd** surrounded
115 **enrank** place in military formation
116 **wanted** lacked
   pikes Six-foot (two-metre) stakes, bound
with a sharpened iron point at both ends,
and stuck in the ground to protect
the archers by impeding and injuring
the opposing cavalry and foot-soldiers.
Hattaway suggests 'pikemen' but 'stakes'
in the next line precludes this meaning. In

Instead whereof sharp stakes plucked out of hedges
They pitchèd in the ground confusedly
To keep the horsemen off from breaking in.
More than three hours the fight continuèd,   120
Where valiant Talbot, above human thought,
Enacted wonders with his sword and lance.
Hundreds he sent to hell, and none durst stand him;
Here, there, and everywhere, enraged he slew.
The French exclaimed the devil was in arms: 125
All the whole army stood agazed on him.
His soldiers, spying his undaunted spirit,
'À Talbot! À Talbot!' cried out amain,
And rushed into the bowels of the battle.
Here had the conquest fully been sealed up   130
If Sir John Fastolf had not played the coward.
He, being in the vanguard placed behind,
With purpose to relieve and follow them,
Cowardly fled, not having struck one stroke.
Hence grew the general wrack and massacre;   135
Enclosèd were they with their enemies.
A base Walloon, to win the Dauphin's grace,
Thrust Talbot with a spear into the back—

124 slew] F; flew ROWE 1714   126 the] F; their CAPELL *conj.*   131 Fastolf] THEOBALD (*subs.*);
Falstaffe F (*so throughout play*)   132 vanguard] F (Vauward); rereward HANMER (*conj.*
Theobald)   135 wrack] F; wreck STEEVENS   137 Walloon] F (Wallon); villain BURNS

Henry V Shakespeare doesn't mention
the English use of stakes at the historical
Battle of Agincourt in order to stress
the miraculousness of the English
victory.

118 **confusedly** in a random manner
119 **off** 'Inserted for metrical purposes'
    (Cairncross).
123 **stand** challenge, face
125 **The . . . arms** The first of a number of
    occasions when the French describe
    Talbot as a satanic force.
126 **whole army** i.e. the French army
    agazed on amazed by, astounded at
127 **spying** seeing, perceiving
128 **À Talbot** i.e. to Talbot (the soldiers' rally-
    ing cry). When the commons change
    sides in *The First Part of the Contention*
    [*2 Henry VI*] they shout 'À Clifford! À
    Clifford!' (4.7.208).
    amain with all their might

129 **bowels** centre (*OED sb.* 4)
130 **sealed up** 'concluded, like a document
    closed over, and authorized, by a seal of
    wax' (Burns).
132 **vanguard placed behind** the forefront of
    the support troops
135 **wrack** (a) disaster (b) destruction
136 **Enclosèd** surrounded
    with by
137 **Walloon** Burns objects to Folio's
    'Wallon' on the grounds that at this time
    the Walloons (the inhabitants of the area,
    now in south Belgium, still known as the
    Pays Wallon) were allies of Burgundy and
    hence of the English also. (The Chronicles
    don't mention the Walloons at all in this
    incident.) But allegiances at this time
    were notoriously unstable (as Burgundy
    himself proves later in the play) and such
    a treacherous action as this by a putative
    ally would certainly earn the term 'base',
    as Burns acknowledges.

Whom all France, with their chief assemble⟨
Durst not presume to look once in the face.

BEDFORD

Is Talbot slain then? I will slay myself
For living idly here, in pomp and ease,
Whilst such a worthy leader, wanting aid,
Unto his dastard foemen is betrayed.

THIRD MESSENGER

O no, he lives, but is took prisoner,   145
And Lord Scales with him, and Lord Hungerford;
Most of the rest slaughtered or took likewise.

BEDFORD

His ransom there is none but I shall pay.
I'll hale the Dauphin headlong from his throne;
His crown shall be the ransom of my friend.   150
Four of their lords I'll change for one of ours.
Farewell, my masters; to my task will I.
Bonfires in France forthwith I am to make,
To keep our great Saint George's feast withal.
Ten thousand soldiers with me I will take,   155
Whose bloody deeds shall make all Europe quake.

---

139 their chief] F1; their F3   141 slain then?] F; slain? Then THEOBALD 1757

139 **chief** finest
   strength army
146 **Lord Scales** (1399?–1460) Thomas de
   Scales served under Bedford in the French
   wars. He died in 1460 at the hands of the
   Yorkists. In *The First Part of the Contention*
   [*2 Henry VI*] he has the briefest of speaking parts urging the Lancastrians to
   '[f]light for your king, your country,
   and your lives!' (4.5.12) in successfully
   defending the Tower of London against
   the rebel, Jack Cade.
   Lord Hungerford (d. 1449) Sir Walter was
   a Lancastrian who fought at Agincourt
   and Rouen, and was an executor of
   Henry V's will. He is mentioned briefly in
   Richard Duke of York [*3 Henry VI*] but not
   at all in *Henry V* where he might have
   been expected to play a larger role.
148 **His . . . pay** Editors have been tempted to
   see the following lines as the only ransom
   Bedford will pay for Talbot, namely to hale
   the Dauphin from his throne, etc. They
   consequently end the line with a colon.

But the fact that Talbot mentions that
his ransom was paid by Lord Bedford
in exchanging him for Lord Poton de
Saintrailles (1.5.6) suggests that the line
should be end-stopped with what follows
as a separate if connected thought. By
itself the line is ambiguous: (a) 'I will pay
any ransom for him no matter what it is'
(b) 'I alone will pay his ransom'.
149 **hale** drag
151 **change** exchange, i.e. kill
153 **Bonfires** i.e. of celebration (for a victory)
   and conflagration
154 **Saint George's feast** On St George's Day
   (23 April). But it would be usual for the
   victorious English to light bonfires on
   any day of victory over the enemy. Saint
   George is the patron saint of England and
   the Order of the Garter and the rallying
   cry for patriotic English warriors in
   Shakespeare's Histories (e.g. Talbot's cry
   at 4.2.55–6 and 4.6.1).
   withal therewith

MESSENGER

So you had need; for Orléans is besieged.
The English army is grown weak and faint,
The Earl of Salisbury craveth supply,
And hardly keeps his men from mutiny,   160
Since they, so few, watch such a multitude.   ⌈*Exit*⌉

EXETER

Remember, lords, your oaths to Henry sworn:
Either to quell the Dauphin utterly,
Or bring him in obedience to your yoke.

BEDFORD

I do remember it, and here take my leave   165
To go about my preparation.   *Exit*

GLOUCESTER

I'll to the Tower with all the haste I can,
To view th'artillery and munition,
And then I will proclaim young Henry king.   *Exit*

EXETER

To Eltham will I, where the young king is,   170

---

157 for ... besieged] F (*subs.*); 'fore Orléans besieg'd HANMER   161 *Exit*] WILSON; *not in* F
165 my leave] F1; leave F2   166 *Exit*] F (*Exit Bedford.*)   169 *Exit*] F (*Exit Gloster.*)

157 **for ... besieged** Who is besieging whom here? The English are besieging Orléans and so Hanmer amends the lines to ''fore Orléans besieged | The English'. But likely the Messenger means that the besiegers have become the besieged, as they clearly are in the second scene of the play by an army led by the Dauphin, Alençon, and Reignier.
  Orléans is The retention of F's 'is' requires 'Orléans' to be pronounced as two syllables, without an accent on the 'e', an available alternative at the time.
159 **supply** reinforcements
160 **hardly** with difficulty
161 **watch** keep under surveillance
162 **your ... sworn** On his deathbed, Holinshed reports, Henry V urged Bedford, Gloucester, Salisbury and Warwick never to surrender any part of France to the Dauphin; instead they should 'persecute Charles ... either to bring him to reason and obeisance, or to drive and expel him out of the realm of France' (Bullough, 44). This reminder comes appropriately

enough from Exeter; see note in 'Persons of the Play'.
163 **quell** destroy
166 **go about** set about
  preparation Pronounced as five syllables. *Exit* Bedford, Gloucester and Exeter exeunt in the order in which they spoke at the beginning of the scene.
167 **Tower** i.e. of London. This venerable building, Burns reminds us, was the repository of the royal armoury. 'As Protector Gloucester is trying to secure the young King's position against possible opposition' (Burns), although he may be simply reviewing what was available for the upcoming conflict with France. Shakespeare alludes more often to this building in his works than to any other in London. 'Penetrating the Tower's romance, he would see it as a gateway to England's real history—and as one enticing, blood-ridden and tragic locale of events' (Honan, 98).
170 **Eltham** A royal residence, situated in Kent on the road to Canterbury about nine miles from London.

Being ordained his special governor,
And for his safety there I'll best devise.   *Exit*
WINCHESTER
Each hath his place and function to attend;
I am left out; for me nothing remains;
But long I will not be Jack-out-of-office.   175
The King from Eltham I intend to steal,
And sit at chiefest stern of public weal.
      Exit ⌈*Winchester at one door. Exeunt*
      funeral cortège, Warwick and Somerset at another⌉

I.2   *Sound a flourish. Enter Charles the Dauphin, the Duke*
      of Alençon, and Reignier Duke of Anjou, marching
      with drum and soldiers

CHARLES
Mars his true moving—even as in the heavens
So in the earth—to this day is not known.

170, 176 Eltham] F (Eltam)   176 steal] SINGER (*conj.* Mason); send F   177. 1–2 *Winchester*
. . . *another*] BURNS (*subs.*); *not in* F

   I.2] CAPELL; *not in* F   0.1 *the Dauphin*] OXFORD (*so throughout play*); *not in* F   *the Duke of*]
OXFORD (*so throughout play*); *not in* F   0.2 *Reignier*] F4 (*subs.*); *Reigneir* F1 (*so throughout scene*)
Duke of Anjou] OXFORD (*so throughout play*); *not in* F

---

171 **special governor** Exeter held joint
guardianship of the King with Winchester, but he clearly has the King's interests
more at heart than does the self-serving
bishop.

173–5 **Each . . . office** One of many occasions
in Shakespeare where the ambitious
malcontent takes the audience into his
confidence. How uncomfortable such a
complicity may become can be experienced best in the later tragedies where
malcontents like Iago and Edmund appal
and entertain in equal proportions their
eavesdropping audiences. Hereward Price
notes: 'It is part of Shakespeare's construction to lead along to the last speech
and make that sum up the scene and fix
the impression he wants to leave in our
minds' (27).

175 **Jack . . . office** Proverbial (Tilley J23).
Boswell-Stone (209) reminds us, following Holinshed, that, in fact, Winchester
was not a Jack-out-of-office but had
been made co-guardian with Exeter of
Henry.

176 **steal** F reads 'send' which is inadequate
on all grounds. Previous editors point to
'intend' as the likely culprit for the compositor's mistake.

177 **sit . . . weal** be the most important
helmsman of the state. Burns suggests
that '[s]it makes him sound almost comically complacent, and *chiefest* is a self-
aggrandizing tautology'.

I.2 With this scene Shakespeare begins a
(loose) pattern of alternation that runs
throughout the play as we move between
the French and English camps. (For its
masterful exploitation see *Henry V.*) It is
the first expression in Shakespeare of a
frequently followed structural principle—
e.g. the alternation of court and country in the second historical tetralogy,
Belmont and Venice in *The Merchant of
Venice*, Egypt and Rome in *Antony and
Cleopatra*, and so on. Historically, neither
Charles VII nor Reignier was at the siege
of Orléans.

0.1 *flourish* Fanfare of trumpets at the
approach of a dignitary.

Late did he shine upon the English side;
Now we are victors: upon us he smiles.
What towns of any moment but we have?   5
At pleasure here we lie near Orléans:
Otherwhiles the famished English, like pale ghosts,
Faintly besiege us one hour in a month.

ALENÇON

They want their porridge and their fat bull beeves.
Either they must be dieted like mules,   10
And have their provender tied to their mouths,
Or piteous they will look, like drownèd mice.

---

7 Otherwhiles] F; The whiles CAPELL

0.3 **Drum** drummer. 'Presumably the lively
march of the French would provide a dramatic contrast with the dead march of the
play's opening scene' (Hattaway).

1–2 **Mars . . . known** Many commentators
have disparaged the cryptic lameness of
these lines, but they serve at least to introduce the French in terms of a supersti-
tious ignorance. (In the previous scene
the English knew only too well why they
lost the battle. See 1.1.130–4.) Tucker
Brooke thinks there is here a strikingly
similar allusion in Thomas Nashe's
preface to *Have With You to Saffron Walden*
(1596): 'you are as ignorant . . . as the
astronomers are in the true movings of
Mars, which to this day they could never
attain to' (Nashe, iii. 20).

1 **Mars his** Mars's (the old form of the
genitive)
Mars (a) the Roman god of war (b) the
planet. 'Not until Kepler published his *De
Motibus Stellae Martis* in 1609 could the
eccentricity of the orbit of Mars be understood' (Hattaway).

1–2 **even . . . earth** i.e. the waywardness of
the god of war's favours matches the
eccentricity of the planet's orbit

3 **Late** recently

5 **moment** importance

6 **At pleasure** without fear of attack
lie are encamped
near How near exactly? Hattaway suggests—without acting on it—that an
emendation to 'in' might be appropriate.
It's more likely, as Burns argues, that the
French army under Charles has arrived

on the English flank to relieve the pressure
on the besieged French behind the walls of
Orléans. The 'faint' besieging—one hour
in a month—in l. 8 would then describe
the occasional foray by the English
against both the French in Orléans itself
and the French force camped like the
English outside its walls. (Chambers notes
that *1 Henry VI* makes the fullest use of
walls of any sixteenth-century play (*The
Elizabethan Stage*, 4 vols. (Oxford, 1923;
repr. 1965), iii. 55)).

7 **Otherwhiles** while occasionally

8 **one . . . month**   (a   contemptuous
exaggeration)

9 **want** lack
porridge Unlike our watered-down break-
fast version, porridge in Shakespeare's
day was a hearty meal consisting of
stewed meat, vegetables, and herbs,
thickened with barley. The English had a
reputation in Europe for gluttony.
bull beeves i.e. bull beef. Burns notes that
then as now beef, especially roast beef,
was the food of demarcation between the
French and the English. The French used
the term 'Bull-beef' opprobriously in relation to the English (*OED, bull, sb.*[1] 11), but
acknowledged the justice of the English
claim that it was the diet of assertive
masculinity and courage. Dent records
the proverbial saying, 'He looks as big as if
he had eaten Bull Beef' (B719).

10 **dieted** fed

11 **have . . . mouths** i.e. wear nosebags with
hay in them

12 **like drownèd mice** Proverbial (Tilley
M1237).

REIGNIER

Let's raise the siege. Why live we idly here?
Talbot is taken, whom we wont to fear.
Remaineth none but mad-brained Salisbury,   15
And he may well in fretting spend his gall;
Nor men nor money hath he to make war.

CHARLES

Sound, sound, alarum! We will rush on them.
Now for the honour of the forlorn French;
Him I forgive my death that killeth me   20
When he sees me go back one foot or flee.   *Exeunt*
            Here alarum. They ⌈the French⌉ are beaten back by the
            English with great loss.
            Enter Charles the Dauphin, the Duke of Alençon and
            Reignier Duke of Anjou

CHARLES

Who ever saw the like? What men have I?
Dogs, cowards, dastards! I would ne'er have fled,
But that they left me 'midst my enemies.

REIGNIER

Salisbury is a desperate homicide;   25
He fighteth as one weary of his life.
The other lords, like lions wanting food,
Do rush upon us as their hungry prey.

---

13 live] F; lie HUDSON   21 flee] F (flye)   21.1] *scene-break* OXFORD (1.3); *not in* F   the French]
OXFORD; *not in* F   28 hungry] F; hungred JOHNSON *conj.*

13 **raise the siege** expel the English forces
  besieging Orléans
  live dwell
14 **wont** were accustomed
15 **mad-brained** hot-headed
16 **fretting** ill-temper, peevishness
  spend his gall use up his bitterness of
  spirit. The gall-bladder was thought to
  control the flow of the humour 'choler',
  and hence considered the seat of anger.
  Reignier hopes the flow will be mis-
  directed, self-consuming.
18 **alarum** call to arms (on a trumpet)
19 **forlorn** desperate
21.1 Oxford begins a new scene here, but this
  adherence to the letter of the dramatic
  law—an unwritten one—that a new
  scene begins each time the stage is cleared
  seems pedantic in this case.

21.1 ***alarum*** 'In this instance, it could
  include drums, trumpets, and most significantly, the sound of cannon—in an
  enclosed theatre, even one with no roof,
  explosives make a frightening amount of
  noise, and can establish the convention of
  a pitched battle with considerable force'
  (Edelman, 52).
23 **I . . . fled** In contrast with Talbot in the
  preceding scene.
25 **homicide** murderer
26 **weary . . . life** Shaheen suggests that
  Shakespeare may have had Scripture in
  mind in using this expression (29).
28 **their hungry prey** A transferred epithet: it
  is the English, the lions, who are hungry
  not the French, the prey.

ALENÇON

    Froissart, a countryman of ours, records
    England all Olivers and Rolands bred   30
    During the time Edward the Third did reign.
    More truly now may this be verified,
    For none but Samsons and Goliases
    It sendeth forth to skirmish. One to ten?
    Lean raw-boned rascals—who would e'er suppose   35
    They had such courage and audacity?

CHARLES

    Let's leave this town, for they are hare-brained slaves,
    And hunger will enforce them to be more eager.
    Of old I know them; rather with their teeth
    The walls they'll tear down than forsake the siege.   40

REIGNIER

    I think by some odd gimmers or device
    Their arms are set, like clocks, still to strike on,
    Else ne'er could they hold out so as they do.
    By my consent we'll even let them alone.

ALENÇON Be it so.   45

    Enter the Bastard of Orléans

29 Froissart] F (*Froysard*)   30 bred] ROWE; breed F   37 Let's . . . slaves] POPE; Let's . . .
Towne | For . . . Slaues F   hare-brained] F (hayre-brayn'd)   38 to be] F; be POPE   41 gim-
mers] F1 (Gimmors); Gimmalls F2

29 **Froissart** Jean Froissart (*c*.1338–*c*.1410),
the French counterpart of Hall and
Holinshed (and a poet also), wrote in
Volume 2 of his *Chronicle,* translated by
Lord Berners (1523–5), that in the victory
of the English over the French in 1367
every English soldier fought like a Roland
or an Oliver, the most famous of
Charlemagne's knights.

30 **Olivers and Rolands** Oliver and Roland
are in *La Chanson de Roland* (*c*.1150)
thought to be written by the Norman
poet, Turold, whose name is introduced in
the last line of the poem. Oliver and
Roland became the byword for heroic
friendship in the Renaissance.

31 **Edward the Third** (1312–77) Infamous for
beginning the Hundred Years War against
France by claiming the French throne in
right of his mother in 1337.

33 **Samsons and Goliases** Old Testament
strong men (a giant in the case of Goliath)
who, as Burns points out, were most
famous in defeat. The story of Samson

can be found in Judges 14–16; Goliath in
1 Samuel 17: 4–54. Shaheen notes that
the form Goliases is odd considering that
all 16th-century Bibles spell the name
Goliath, and may indicate Nashe's hand
in the scene (30).

34 **It** i.e. England
   skirmish do battle
   One to ten i.e. one English soldier to every
ten French.

35 **raw-boned** like a skeleton
   rascals (a) rogues (b) lean inferior deer

37 **hare-brained** mad as hares

38 **eager** (a) fierce (*OED a.* 5) (b) hungry
(*OED a.* 7)

41 **gimmers** A corruption of gimmals, the
connecting parts in a machine, especially
in the transmission of motion (*OED, gim-
mal, sb.* 2).

42 **still** continually

44 **By my consent** I agree (i.e. with Charles's
'Let's leave this town')
   even definitely

BASTARD
    Where's the Prince Dauphin? I have news for him.
CHARLES
    Bastard of Orléans, thrice welcome to us.
BASTARD
    Methinks your looks are sad, your cheer appalled.
    Hath the late overthrow wrought this offence?
    Be not dismayed, for succour is at hand.   50
    A holy maid hither with me I bring,
    Which, by a vision sent to her from heaven,
    Ordainèd is to raise this tedious siege
    And drive the English forth the bounds of France.
    The spirit of deep prophecy she hath,   55
    Exceeding the nine sibyls of old Rome.
    What's past and what's to come she can descry.
    Speak: shall I call her in? Believe my words,
    For they are certain and unfallible.
CHARLES
    Go call her in.   *Exit Bastard*
                    But first, to try her skill,   60
    Reignier stand thou as Dauphin in my place;
    Question her proudly; let thy looks be stern.
    By this means shall we sound what skill she hath.
        Enter ⌈the Bastard of Orléans with⌉ Joan la Pucelle
REIGNIER
    Fair maid, is't thou wilt do these wondrous feats?

47 CHARLES] ROWE; *Dolph⟨in⟩.* F   58 my] F; her JOHNSON *conj.*   60 *Exit Bastard*] CAPELL; *not
in* F   63.1 *Enter . . . Pucelle*] DYCE; *Enter . . . armed* OXFORD; *Enter Ioane Puzel* F

48 **Methinks** it seems to me
    your cheer appalled disheartened
49 **late overthrow** recent defeat
    offence harm, injury
51 **holy maid** Joan la Pucelle is here intro-
    duced to the French by her original cham-
    pion, the Bastard, thereby tainting her
    holiness with illegitimacy as far as an
    English theatre audience was concerned.
    (In Holinshed she is introduced to Charles
    by one Peter Badricourt (163).)
54 **forth** out of
    bounds boundaries
56 **nine . . . Rome** Sibyl was a name for any
    ancient Greek or Roman prophetess. The

number usually associated with them was
ten or four rather than nine. Burns suggests that reducing the number by one
intimates that the play wants us to think
of Joan as the tenth. More likely, as
Sanders argues, the number comes from a
confusion with the nine books of the
Sibyl of Cumae (or even with the Nine
Worthies).
58–9 **Believe . . . unfallible** Something of
    Joan's religious certainty seems to have
    infected the Bastard's phrasing.
59 **unfallible** Obsolete form of infallible.
60 **try** test
63 **sound** measure

ier, is't thou that thinkest to beguile me? 65
:e is the Dauphin? (*To Charles*) Come, come from
   hind.
I know thee well, though never seen before.
Be not amazed. There's nothing hid from me.
In private will I talk with thee apart.
Stand back you lords, and give us leave awhile. 70
   Reignier, Alençon ⌈and Bastard⌉ stand apart
REIGNIER ⌈*to Alençon and Bastard*⌉
She takes upon her bravely at first dash.
JOAN
Dauphin, I am by birth a shepherd's daughter,
My wit untrained in any kind of art.
Heaven and Our Lady gracious hath it pleased
To shine on my contemptible estate. 75
Lo, whilst I waited on my tender lambs,
And to sun's parching heat displayed my cheeks,
God's mother deignèd to appear to me,
And, in a vision full of majesty,
Willed me to leave my base vocation 80
And free my country from calamity.
Her aid she promised and assured success.
In complete glory she revealed herself.

---

65 JOAN] OXFORD; *Puzel* F   70.1 *Reignier . . . apart*] OXFORD (*subs.*); *not in* F   76 whilst] F
(whilest)

65 **beguile** deceive
67 **thee** 'Joan significantly addresses the
Dolphin without ascribing to him any
royal title' (Burns). Equally significant is
her use of the familiar 'thee' instead of
the more formal 'you' which she has
picked up from Reignier's address to her.
68 **There's . . . me** Joan's unerring eye for the
real Dauphin was of pivotal significance
at her trial in proving her to be in the grip
of the supernatural. Marina Warner
writes: 'Joan herself told her judges . . .
that she recognised Charles because her
voices had guided her' (60), and Bernard
Shaw makes much of this moment in his
play, *Saint Joan* (1924).
71 **She . . . dash** The bawdy colloquialism 'at
first dash' undermines the line's ostensibly respectable meaning: that she begins
marvellously well. Any miraculous aura

produced by Joan's recognition of Charles
is nicely undercut here by the French lords'
casual, patronizing, and sexist responses.
takes upon her plays her part
72 **Dauphin . . . daughter** This she denies in
no uncertain terms in 5.5 when the
English produce her shepherd father:
'Decrepit miser, base ignoble wretch, | I
am descended of a gentler blood'
(5.5.7–8).
Dauphin Joan's blunt mode of address
resembles Reignier's to her at l. 147.
73 **wit** mind
   art skill
74 **Our Lady** i.e. the Virgin Mary
75 **estate** condition of life
80 **base** low
   vocation Pronounced as four syllables.
83 **complete** The accent is on the first
syllable.

And whereas I was black and swart before,
With those clear rays which she infused on me   85
That beauty am I blest with, which you may see.
Ask me what question thou canst possible,
And I will answer unpremeditated.
My courage try by combat, if thou dar'st,
And thou shalt find that I exceed my sex.   90
Resolve on this: thou shalt be fortunate
If thou receive me for thy warlike mate.

CHARLES

Thou hast astonished me with thy high terms.
Only this proof I'll of thy valour make:
In single combat thou shalt buckle with me.   95
And if thou vanquishest, thy words are true;
Otherwise I renounce all confidence.

JOAN

I am prepared. Here is my keen-edged sword,
Decked with fine flower-de-luces on each side—

---

86 which you may] F1; which you F2; you may CAIRNCROSS *conj.*   99 fine] F; five STEEVENS

84 **black and swart** dark-skinned and swarthy. Some editors have suggested that black here refers to hair colour so that the intervention of the Virgin Mary has miraculously turned Joan into a blonde (the boy playing her part could wear a blonde wig). More likely both adjectives describe the deep tan acquired by a shepherdess practising her 'vocation'. The infusion of the Virgin Mary's clear rays brings Joan closer to the Elizabethan conception of aristocratic beauty. Hall depicts Joan as ugly (Bullough, 56); Holinshed as fair (Bullough, 75).

85 **With** by virtue of
infused poured, shed

87 **thou canst possible** you possibly can (Abbott §419)

88 **unpremeditated** extempore

89 **My ... combat** An invention of the dramatist which allows for an element of sexual horseplay in modern productions.

91 **Resolve** be assured

92 **mate** (a) companion (b) (possibly) lover. The play's occasionally equivocal language in the presentation of Joan helps to undermine her dignity, but Charles's astonishment at her 'high terms' (l. 93) suggests how subdued (b) is. Joan's athletic beauty in these early scenes attracts the language of the bawdy pun, though she herself seems above the sexual fray at this stage. Both the French and English nobility—the English in particular—see her in crudely sexual terms. Her (sexual) degeneration in the fifth act plays into their hands, and brings to a climax the play's schizophrenic view of her. (See Introduction pp. 44–50.) Arguably, Shakespeare's (or the play's) grasp of her is incoherent.

93 **high terms** elevated language

95 **buckle** grapple at close quarters (with an inevitable sexual connotation)

97 **confidence** confidential intimacy (*OED* 6)

99 **Decked** decorated
fine The ease with which the compositor could confuse 'n' and 'u' makes Steevens's emendation to 'five' attractive in the light of Holinshed's description of Joan's sword as having 'fiue floure delices' (163). By the same token F's 'n' is just as likely.
flower-de-luces fleurs-de-lis (in the arms of France)

(*Aside*) The which at Touraine, in Saint Katherine's
    churchyard,   100
Out of a great deal of old iron I chose forth.

CHARLES

Then come a God's name; I fear no woman.

JOAN

And while I live I'll ne'er fly from a man.
    Here they fight and Joan la Pucelle overcomes

CHARLES

Stay, stay thy hands. Thou art an Amazon,
And fightest with the sword of Deborah.   105

JOAN

Christ's mother helps me, else I were too weak.

CHARLES

Whoe'er helps thee, 'tis thou that must help me.
Impatiently I burn with thy desire;
My heart and hands thou hast at once subdued.
Excellent Pucelle, if thy name be so,   110

---

100 churchyard] F; Church POPE   101 great deal] F; deal DYCE   102 come a] F; come, o'
CAIRNCROSS   God's name] F; ~ great ~ CAIRNCROSS *conj.*   I fear] F; ~ do ~ WALKER   103 fly
from a] F1; flye no F2   103.1 *Joan la Pucelle*] ROWE; *Ioane de Puzel* F; *Joan Puzel* BURNS

100–1 **The which . . . forth** There are next
to no asides marked in Shakespeare's
quartos and folios. All asides therefore are
at the discretion of later editors and at
times entail, as in this instance, significant decisions of interpretation. As an
aside these lines underscore Joan's sardonic self-awareness; she perceives herself at least in part as something of a
mountebank. There is no need as yet,
however, to question her sincerity or her
sanctity. Hattaway suggests that the tone
of these lines and the unmetrical l. 100
indicate a prose aside (as in the 1983 BBC
production). This incident is scornfully
recorded in both Hall and Holinshed as an
indication of French credulity.
100 **Touraine** Region of central France.
   churchyard The line could be made more
metrical by removing 'yard' as some editions, following the sources, have done.
Still, it is more likely that an old sword
would be found in a churchyard than in a
church, and its location helps to establish
Joan's sardonic tone.
102 **a** in

103 **And . . . man** A probably irresistible
temptation for the actors playing Reignier
and Alençon to respond with a snigger.
105 **Deborah** The story of Deborah, the
Hebrew prophet and military genius
behind Barak's campaign against Sisera,
can be found in Judges 4 and 5. She is one
of a number of active women in public
affairs celebrated in the Book of Judges.
Holinshed compares Joan to Deborah
(605).
106 **Christ's . . . weak** Contrast Talbot's
assessment of who is Joan's mentor in a
parallel encounter with her: 'Blood will I
draw on thee . . . And straightway give
thy soul to him [the devil] thou serv'st'
(1.6.6–7).
108 **thy desire** (a) desire for you (b) desire (for
a victory over the English) that you have
instilled in me
110 **Excellent** exalted
   if . . . so Her name has yet to be mentioned, which may account for Charles's
hesitancy; or he may be (maybe pretending to be) loath to use such a loaded
term.

Let me thy servant and not sovereign be.
'Tis the French Dauphin sueth to thee thus.

JOAN

I must not yield to any rites of love,
For my profession's sacred from above.
When I have chasèd all thy foes from hence,   115
Then will I think upon a recompense.

CHARLES

Meantime look gracious on thy prostrate thrall.

REIGNIER ⌈*to the other lords apart*⌉

My lord, methinks, is very long in talk.

ALENÇON

Doubtless he shrives this woman to her smock,
Else ne'er could he so long protract his speech.   120

REIGNIER

Shall we disturb him since he keeps no mean?

ALENÇON

He may mean more than we poor men do know;
These women are shrewd tempters with their tongues.

REIGNIER (*to Charles*)

My lord, where are you? What devise you on?
Shall we give over Orléans or no?   125

---

113 rites] POPE; rights F   125 over] ROWE; o'er F

---

111 **servant** (a) follower (b) lover. This
second meaning seems to animate Joan's
reply.

112 **'Tis . . . thus** A line that seems in its self-
advertisement to contradict Charles's
claim that he is not addressing Joan as her
sovereign liege.

114 **profession** Burns suggests that the word
is used here to mean the fact of being professed in a religious order (*OED* 1a). If this
is so, Joan's vocation as a nun will be a
temporary condition as she indicates in
the next two lines. The word more likely
means the 'solemn declaration' (*OED* 1b)
she has made to chase the English out of
France.
  sacred consecrated

117 **prostrate** 'Charles may still be on the
ground after the fight' (Hattaway). With

Joan, Burns impishly suggests, standing
or sitting on him.

119 **shrives . . . smock** thoroughly hears her
confession and grants absolution. White
robes (smocks) were worn as a sign of pen-
itence. Alençon's expression is a playful
way of saying that Charles attends closely
to what she is saying to him, with the
added provocative sense that he's stripping
her to her undergarments (with his eyes?)

121 **Shall . . . mean** i.e. Charles's indecor-
ously lengthy interview with Joan invites
their own indecorous interruption
  keeps no mean uses no moderation

122 **poor** humble, insignificant (*OED a.* B 5d)

123 **shrewd** cunning, artful

124 **where are you** what do you plan to do
  devise you on have you decided (lit. what
do you decide on)

JOAN

Why, no, I say. Distrustful recreants!
Fight till the last gasp; I'll be your guard.

CHARLES

What she says I'll confirm. We'll fight it out.

JOAN

Assigned am I to be the English scourge.
This night the siege assurèdly I'll raise.   130
Expect Saint Martin's summer, halcyon days,
Since I have enterèd into these wars.
Glory is like a circle in the water,
Which never ceaseth to enlarge itself
Till, by broad spreading, it disperse to naught.   135
With Henry's death the English circle ends;
Dispersèd are the glories it included.
Now am I like that proud insulting ship
Which Caesar and his fortune bore at once.

CHARLES

Was Mahomet inspirèd with a dove?   140

127 I'll] F; I will CAPELL   131 halcyon] F3 (Halcyon); *Halcyons* F1; halcyons' RIVERSIDE
132 entered] F1; entred thus F3   139 bore] F (bare)

126–7 **Why . . . guard** Significantly, it is Joan
who replies, although the questions were
directed at Charles.
126 **Distrustful recreants** faithless cowards
131 **Saint Martin's summer** The feast of St
Martin is celebrated on 11 November.
Fine weather at this time would be a
rather unexpected pleasure, an Indian
summer, and would be in contrast to the
normal bleak November climate.
halcyon idyllic. A halcyon is a mythical bird
(sometimes identified with a kingfisher)
that ancient writers claimed to breed in a
nest floating at sea at the winter solstice,
charming wind and waves into calm.
Cairncross notes that this etymology
leads us into the calm water of glory's
circle.
134 **enlarge** broaden
135 **naught** (a) nought (as a mathematical
term) (b) nothing (in terms of worth)
138–9 **Now . . . once** The story—probably
unhistorical—is told in Plutarch's *Life of
Julius Caesar*. During the war with Pom-
pey, Caesar boarded a boat alone and
incognito to sail to Brundisium to rejoin
his army. In the ensuing rough weather

Caesar reassured the fearful sea-captain
that nothing would happen to them
because the boat was carrying Caesar and
his destiny. Presumably Joan is envisag-
ing the Dauphin as Caesar, his fortune as
the fortunes of France, and herself as the
boat carrying them. But it is a strained
analogy as it is Caesar who is the magical
talisman, not the boat, and it might be
considered bathetic after the 'Shakespearian' image of glory spreading in the
water. Ominously for Joan perhaps (and
perhaps also for the captain) in Plutarch
the captain's ship is forced to turn back.
139 **at once** once
140–1 **Was . . . then** Shakespeare was fond of
this comparison of the eagle with lesser
birds. He contrasts the eagle with a raven
in *A Midsummer Night's Dream*, a puttock
(kite) in *Cymbeline*, a fly in *Antony and
Cleopatra*, a wren in *Richard III*, a crow in
Coriolanus, and a sparrow in *Macbeth*. The
contrast here is between the bird of peace
and the bird of war.
140 **Mahomet** The prophet Muhammad or
Mohammed (*c*.570–632). This form of the
name is retained for metrical reasons: the

Thou with an eagle art inspirèd then.
Helen, the mother of great Constantine,
Nor yet Saint Philip's daughters were like thee.
Bright star of Venus, fallen down on the earth,
How may I reverently worship thee enough?   145

ALENÇON
Leave off delays, and let us raise the siege.

REIGNIER
Woman, do what thou canst to save our honours;
Drive them from Orléans and be immortalized.

CHARLES
Presently we'll try. Come, let's away about it.
No prophet will I trust if she prove false.   *Exeunt*   150

I.3   *Enter the Duke of Gloucester, with his Servingmen in*
           blue coats

GLOUCESTER
I am come to survey the Tower this day;

143 Saint] F (S.)   145 reverently] F; reverent DYCE 1864–7   148 Orléans] F (Orleance);
hence CAPELL   and be] F; be MARSHALL   149 Presently we'll] F; Presently POPE
    I.3] CAPELL; *not in* F   o.1 *the Duke of*] OXFORD (*so throughout play*); *not in* F   o.2 *in blue
coats*] CAPELL; *not in* F   3.1 *The . . . gates*] CAPELL (*subs.*); *not in* F

accents are on the first and final syllables.
Reputedly, Muhammad trained a dove to
take corn from his ear, and then claimed
that the bird was a manifestation of the
Holy Ghost whispering divine revelation
to him.

141 **Thou . . . then** As was the apostle John.
Joan's holiness is not only made more
militant by this comparison but also
Christian as the Christian eagle is opposed
to the Islamic dove.

142 **Helen . . . Constantine** Helen was the
mother of the Emperor Constantine
whom she converted to Christianity. A
Joan-like vision led her to the discovery of
the true cross buried on Mount Calvary.

142 **Constantine** (*c.*274–337) Roman emper-
or. In 324 he made Christianity a state
religion.

143 **Saint Philip's daughters** Acts 21: 8–9
talks of the daughters as virginal
prophets.

144 **Bright . . . Venus** This pagan climax to
Charles's list of Joan's spiritual ancestors
jars with the saintly Christian ones.

147 **Woman** Reignier's bluff mode of address

to Joan is in striking contrast to the
Dauphin's. See note to 1.2.72. Saluta-
tions in this play calibrate (changing)
social relations as when Burgundy, having been 'turned' by Joan, writes a letter
to Henry scandalously addressing him
'No more but plain and bluntly "To the
King" ' (4.1.50–1).

148 **Drive . . . immortalized** With the accent
over the 'e' in 'Orléans' this makes the
line an appropriately ceremonial alexan-
drine stretching out in response to Joan's
immortality.

149 **Presently** at once

1.3.0.2 **blue** The traditional colour for the liv-
ery of servingmen. The contrast between
the blue of Gloucester's retainers, the
tawny of Winchester's, and the scarlet of
the 'scarlet hypocrite' Winchester (l. 56)
makes for a colourful spectacle, especially
when the colours merge and break away
in the scene's frequent skirmishes.

1 **survey** inspect. Gloucester is concerned
to see what weapons may have been
appropriated by Winchester (1.3.60–1);
Winchester has the same suspicions
about Gloucester (1.3.67–8).

Since Henry's death I fear there is conveyance.
Where be these warders that they wait not here?
   ⌈*The servingmen knock at the gates*⌉
Open the gates; 'tis Gloucester that calls.

FIRST WARDER ⌈*within the Tower*⌉

Who's there that knocks so imperiously?   5

FIRST SERVINGMAN

It is the noble Duke of Gloucester.

SECOND WARDER ⌈*within the Tower*⌉

Whoe'er he be, you may not be let in.

FIRST SERVINGMAN

Villains, answer you so the Lord Protector?

FIRST WARDER ⌈*within the Tower*⌉

The Lord protect him, so we answer him.
We do no otherwise than we are willed.   10

GLOUCESTER

Who willèd you? Or whose will stands but mine?
There's none Protector of the realm but I.
(*To Servingmen*) Break up the gates; I'll be your
   warrantize.
Shall I be flouted thus by dunghill grooms?
   Gloucester's men rush at the Tower gates, and
   Woodville, the Lieutenant, speaks within

WOODVILLE

What noise is this? What traitors have we here?   15

5, 7, 9 *within the Tower*] OXFORD; *not in* F; *within* MALONE; *Enter two Warders on the walls*] BURNS (*after line* 4)   5 knocks] F; knocketh THEOBALD   6 FIRST SERVINGMAN] HATTAWAY (*subs.*); *Glost. I. Man* F; *Gloucester's First Man* OXFORD   7 you] F; he CAPELL

2 **conveyance** 'Furtive or light-fingered carrying off' (*OED* 4).
3 **warders** guards
4 **Gloucester** Trisyllabic here (and at ll. 6, 62, and 81).
5 *within the Tower* Burns has the two warders enter on the walls in his edition (i.e. on the tiring-house gallery) rather than speak from within the tiring-house as F indicates. (The tiring-house = the part of the theatre behind the stage where the actors dress and from which they come on stage.) Burns's sophistication of the F direction would be more persuasive if he had extended it to Woodville whom he keeps 'within' even though Woodville

speaks more lines than do the warders. Oxford suggests that such an extended use of voices within indicates that both warders and Woodville might have appeared at a barred window on the tiring-house façade, or 'above', or even from behind an on-stage structure (see *Textual Companion*, 220).
10 **willed** commanded
11 **stands** prevails
13 **Break up** batter down
   warrantize pledge, guarantee
14 **dunghill grooms** And so Pistol in *2 Henry IV*: 'Shall dunghill curs confront the Helicons?' (5.3.105).

GLOUCESTER

Lieutenant, is it you whose voice I hear?

Open the gates; here's Gloucester that would enter.

WOODVILLE

Have patience, noble duke, I may not open;

The Cardinal of Winchester forbids.

From him I have express commandment   20

That thou, nor none of thine, shall be let in.

GLOUCESTER

Faint-hearted Woodville, prizest him fore me?

Arrogant Winchester, that haughty prelate,

Whom Henry, our late sovereign, ne'er could brook?

Thou art no friend to God or to the King.   25

Open the gates or I'll shut thee out shortly.

SERVINGMEN

Open the gates unto the Lord Protector,

Or we'll burst them open, if that you come not quickly.

> *Enter, to the Protector at the Tower gates, the Bishop of*
> *Winchester and his men in tawny coats*

WINCHESTER

How now, ambitious Humphrey, what means this?

GLOUCESTER

Peeled priest, dost thou command me to be shut out?   30

19 The Cardinal] F; My lord OXFORD   20 commandment] F4; commandement F1; com-
mandëment OXFORD   28 Or we'll] F; We'll POPE   28.1 *the Bishop of*] OXFORD (*so throughout
play*); *not in* F   29 Humphrey] THEOBALD; Vmpheir F1; Vmpire F2; vizier OXFORD
30 Peeled] F (Piel'd)   to be] F; be POPE

19 **Cardinal of Winchester** Oxford goes to
considerable lengths to regularize the
chronology of the Cardinal's career as it is
presented in the play, expunging references to him as Cardinal in this scene, and
replacing them with Bishop, his proper
title at this time. But there is simply too
much dramatic fall-out here from the Cardinal appearing as a Cardinal—his scarlet
hat and his robes for instance—to allow
us to correct F's contradictory chronology at the expense of the scene's colour
and flair. (Cairncross notes that at this
time Winchester was Bishop of Winchester and Cardinal of St Eusebius.)

20 **commandment** Pronounced as four syllables (commandement), as indicated in F1,
2 and 3.

21 **thine** your followers

22 **prizest** do you respect

24 **Whom . . . brook** Hall has a passage
describing Henry V's refusal to confirm
Winchester as cardinal (Bullough, 51–2).

26 **shut thee out** dismiss you from your post.
'The metre suggests a stress on *thee*' (Burns).

28 **Or . . . quickly** Does this line's irregular
length enact the meaning, 'bursting' free
from the constraint of the decasyllabic?

28.2 *tawny coats* Worn by the summoners of
the ecclesiastical courts who attended on
a bishop.

29 **Humphrey** Theobald's emendation of F's
'Vmpheir' still seems the most plausible
correction of a word resulting from the
compositor's 'working from a chaos of
minims' (Burns). Contemporary spellings
of Humphrey as Vmfray or Vmfrey (i.e.
Umfray, Umfrey) go some way to explain-
ing F's reading.

30 **Peeled** tonsured, shaven

WINCHESTER

    I do, thou most usurping proditor—

    And not Protector—of the King or realm.

GLOUCESTER

    Stand back thou manifest conspirator.

    Thou that contrived'st to murder our dead lord,

    Thou that giv'st whores indulgences to sin,   35

    I'll canvas thee in thy broad cardinal's hat

    If thou proceed in this thy insolence.

WINCHESTER

    Nay, stand thou back! I will not budge a foot.

    This be Damascus, be thou cursèd Cain,

    To slay thy brother Abel, if thou wilt.   40

GLOUCESTER

    I will not slay thee but I'll drive thee back.

    Thy scarlet robes, as a child's bearing-cloth,

    I'll use to carry thee out of this place.

WINCHESTER

    Do what thou dar'st; I beard thee to thy face.

GLOUCESTER

    What, am I dared and bearded to my face?   45

---

34 dead] F1; dread F2   36 I'll . . . hat] F; *not in* OXFORD   42 scarlet] F; purple OXFORD

31 **proditor** traitor. The choice of this unusual word—its only occurrence in Shakespeare—was determined by its resemblance to 'protector'. It doesn't appear in Shakespeare's sources.

34 **Thou . . . lord** In Hall Gloucester recounts how Henry V once told him that Winchester had suborned a man to kill him while he was still Prince of Wales (Bullough, 50). This is a much more damaging accusation than that of praying against Henry V (1.1.33–4).

    contrived'st schemed, plotted

35 **Thou . . . sin** This is an accusation that, unlike the previous one, has historical evidence to justify it. The see of Winchester owned land in Southwark—a district later infamous for its places of pleasure (brothels, taverns, theatres—including the Rose—and the like)—on which brothels licensed by the bishops operated. One of the brothels had the sign of a cardinal's hat. (See Stow, ii. 54–5.)

    indulgences i.e. remission of sins in the form of a papal document procured by acts of charity by the sinners (usually in the form of cash payments to the church). Here, the act of charity takes the form of payments to the Bishop by pimp or madam for their licence to operate on his land.

36 **canvas** (a) entangle in a net (b) toss in a blanket

    cardinal's hat An exotic piece of headgear, broad-brimmed, scarlet, carrying a burden of signification in this colourful, irascible encounter. See note at l. 19 for a discussion of its anachronistic presence.

38 **thou** This word would be stressed by an actor.

39 **This be** let this be

    Damascus A city in present-day Syria said to be built on the site of the murder of Abel by Cain. Not surprisingly, Winchester thinks of himself as Abel, and Gloucester as Cain. (Winchester was actually Gloucester's half-uncle not his brother.)

42 **bearing-cloth** christening robe (*OED*, *bearing*, 17). 'Gloucester is still thinking perhaps of the canvassing process' (Hart).

44 **beard** defy, challenge

Draw, men, for all this privilegèd place.
    All draw their swords
Blue coats to tawny coats! Priest, beware your beard.
I mean to tug it and to cuff you soundly.
Under my feet I'll stamp thy cardinal's hat.
In spite of Pope or dignities of church,   50
Here by the cheeks I'll drag thee up and down.

WINCHESTER

Gloucester, thou wilt answer this before the Pope.

GLOUCESTER

Winchester goose! I cry, 'A rope, a rope!'
(To his servingmen)
Now beat them hence; why do you let them stay?
(To Winchester)
Thee I'll chase hence, thou wolf in sheep's array.   55
Out, tawny coats! Out, scarlet hypocrite!
    Here Gloucester's men beat out the Bishop's men.
    Enter in the hurly-burly the Mayor of London and his
    Officers

46.1 *All . . . swords*] OXFORD; *not in* F   47 tawny coats] F; tawny POPE   49 I'll] F2 (Ile); I F1
cardinal's hat] F; bishop's mitre OXFORD   52 thou wilt] F; thou'lt POPE   56 scarlet] F;
cloaked OXFORD   56.1 *Bishop's*] OXFORD; *Cardinalls* F   56.2 *Enter*] OXFORD; *and enter* F

---

46 **for all** despite
    privilegèd place Because the Tower came
    directly under royal jurisdiction the
    drawing of weapons there was strictly
    forbidden.

49 **I'll** Some editors retain F's 'I' as the use on
    Gloucester's part of the dramatic present
    (not, that is, implying an accompanying
    action).
    cardinal's hat Oxford replaces this phrase
    with 'bishop's mitre' which is not only
    more awkward in terms of scansion but
    would be a positive hazard for the feet of
    the stamper.

50 **dignities** dignitaries (*OED sb.* 3b)

52 **answer** pay for

53 **Winchester goose** A swelling in the groin
    caused by venereal disease, but by exten-
    sion a (Southwark) prostitute, and by fur-
    ther extension Winchester himself who
    may be suffering from a disease brought
    on by one of his licensed whores.
    A rope (a) a hangman's halter (b) a

parrot's cry (hence a term of abuse).
Hattaway also suggests a third meaning:
Winchester's pox-ridden penis. This
seems unlikely though Anne Lancashire
doesn't think so, arguing in her article
'Lily and Shakespeare on the Ropes', *JEGP*
68 (1969), 237–44, that Gloucester's
'rope' 'insultingly emphasizes the sexual
organ that brought the disease to him'
(243).

56.2 **hurly-burly** uproar. 'Formerly a more
    dignified word than now' (Hart, 30).

56.2 **Mayor of London** The chief magistrate
    for the City of London, the Mayor would
    have juridical authority over the Tower
    and its grounds. His powers were limited
    to a small area in the centre of London,
    however—'the square mile whose bound-
    aries were still marked by walls the
    Romans partly built, by eight gates and by
    the Tower' (Rutter, 10)—and did not
    extend to Winchester's Southwark or to
    Westminster.

MAYOR

Fie, lords, that you, being supreme magistrates,
Thus contumeliously should break the peace.

GLOUCESTER

Peace, mayor, thou know'st little of my wrongs.
Here's Beaufort—that regards nor God nor king—   60
Hath here distrained the Tower to his use.

WINCHESTER (*to Mayor*)

Here's Gloucester, a foe to citizens,
One that still motions war and never peace,
O'ercharging your free purses with large fines—
That seeks to overthrow religion,   65
Because he is Protector of the realm,
And would have armour here out of the Tower
To crown himself king and suppress the Prince.

GLOUCESTER

I will not answer thee with words but blows.

Here the factions skirmish again

MAYOR

Naught rests for me, in this tumultuous strife,   70
But to make open proclamation.
Come, officer, as loud as thou canst cry.

⌈*He hands the Officer a paper*⌉

---

60 Beaufort] CAPELL; Beauford F   nor God] F1; not ~ F3   69.1 *the factions*] OXFORD; *they* F
72 as loud . . . canst cry.] This edition; as lowd as e're thou canst, cry: F; as loud as e'er thou
canst. | Cry. CAIRNCROSS; as loud as e'er thou canst. | [*The Officer gives the*] *cry*: BURNS
72.1 *He hands . . . paper*] HATTAWAY (*subs.*); *not in* F

57–8 **Fie . . . peace** Keeping the peace was an
     important function of the Lord Mayor and
     his Court of Aldermen. If they failed to do
     so they gave the Privy Council reason to
     intervene in their affairs.
57 **Fie** A strong rebuke.
   supreme Accented on the first syllable.
   magistrates members of the executive
   government
58 **contumeliously** insolently
59 **Peace** A sarcastic echo of the Mayor's
   word.
60 **Beaufort** (Winchester's family name)
   regards nor has respect for neither
61 **distrained** seized, confiscated. 'A loose use
   of the legal term' (Hart).
63 **still motions** always advocates

64 **O'ercharging . . . fines** taking advantage
   of your generosity by imposing heavy
   taxes
65 **religion** Pronounced as four syllables.
66 **Because . . . realm** (heavily sarcastic)
68 **suppress** make powerless
   Prince Henry VI (i.e. the term is not used
   generically here)
70 **rests** remains
71 **proclamation** Pronounced as five
   syllables.
72 **cry** F has a comma before this word making it a separate command. Some editors
   have 'Cry' as part of a stage direction or
   as one in its entirety. F's 'e're' (= 'ever') is
   oddly superfluous.

OFFICER All manner of men, assembled here in arms this
    day against God's peace and the King's, we charge and
    command you in his highness' name to repair to your   75
    several dwelling places, and not to wear, handle, or use
    any sword, weapon, or dagger henceforward, upon pain
    of death.
        The skirmishes cease

GLOUCESTER
    Cardinal, I'll be no breaker of the law;
    But we shall meet and break our minds at large.   80

WINCHESTER
    Gloucester, we'll meet to thy cost, be sure.
    Thy heart-blood I will have for this day's work.

MAYOR
    I'll call for clubs if you will not away.
    (*To the audience*) This Cardinal's more haughty than the
        devil.

GLOUCESTER
    Mayor, farewell. Thou dost but what thou mayst.   85

WINCHESTER
    Abominable Gloucester, guard thy head,
    For I intend to have it ere long.
        Exeunt ⌈all but the Mayor and his Officers⌉

MAYOR
    See the coast cleared, and then we will depart.
    Good God, these nobles should such stomachs bear!
    I myself fight not once in forty year.   *Exeunt*   90

---

73 OFFICER] HANMER (*subs.*); *not in* F   76.1 *The . . . cease*] OXFORD; *not in* F   77 Cardinal] F;
Bishop OXFORD   79 we'll] F; we will WILSON (*conj.* Walker)   cost] F1; dear cost F2   87 it ere
long] F1; it e're be long F3; it, ere't be long CAPELL   89 these] F; that ROWE

75 **several** separate
80 **break our minds** (a) reveal, express our
    thoughts (b) crack heads
    at large at length
83 **clubs** Originally, 'clubs' was the call
    designed to bring out London's appren-
    tices (armed with clubs and staves) to
    put down riots (though they often con-
    tributed to them). Here, the reference is
    most likely to peace officers armed with
    clubs, an early version of riot gear.
84 *To the audience* Burns's direction
    acknowledges this aside as an example of

the kind of audience involvement characteristic of Shakespeare's dramatic tradition and exploited by him throughout his
career.
86 **Abominable** unnatural
88 **coast cleared** 'The Mayor's language is
characterized as rich in cliche and semi-
proverbial phrasing' (Burns).
89 **stomachs** ill-temper, aggressiveness. The
stomach was thought to be the seat of
strong emotion, especially of a belligerent
nature.
90 **I . . . year** i.e. never in his lifetime

1.4   *Enter the Master Gunner of Orléans and his Boy*

MASTER GUNNER

Sirrah, thou know'st how Orléans is besieged,

And how the English have the suburbs won.

BOY

Father, I know, and oft have shot at them;

Howe'er, unfortunate, I missed my aim.

MASTER GUNNER

But now thou shalt not. Be thou ruled by me.   5

Chief Master Gunner am I of this town;

Something I must do to procure me grace.

The Prince's spials have informèd me

How the English, in the suburbs close entrenched,

Went through a secret grate of iron bars   10

In yonder tower, to overpeer the city,

1.4] CAPELL; *not in* F   8 Prince's spials] POPE (*subs.*); Princes espyals F; Prince' espials CAIRNCROSS   10 Went] F; Wont STEEVENS (*conj.* Tyrrwhitt)

1.4 The staging of this scene and the following ones is not straightforward. Some modern editions meld some or all of them into one continuous scene. I have chosen to follow the conventional separation of scenes between 1.4 and 1.5 as the fourth scene in all likelihood would be played on the main stage and the fifth one (at least in part) 'aloft' on the gallery at the back of the stage (but we should note the explicit reference at 1.5.4 to 'this turret's top' which, as Burns notes, in its very explicitness suggests the possibility that a new location for the main stage was being identified for the audience). When the Master Gunner talks of 'yonder tower' (l. 11) he would gesture to the back of the stage where the English would appear in the next scene '*on the turrets*', i.e. on the rear-stage gallery or some higher point in the theatre. As Burns helpfully points out the position of this tower would in fact be on the other side of the Loire from where the gunners—on ground inside Orléans—are speaking. Where then is the Master Gunner's 'piece of ordnance' (1.4.15)? In all likelihood—especially in the absence of any indication in the spoken lines of a gestural confirmation—off-stage somewhere. David Riggs points out that 'it is only the French who employ such modern implements of war as artillery and fortified siege walls'

(*Shakespeare's Heroical Histories: Henry VI and Its Literary Tradition* (Cambridge, Mass., 1971), 21).

1 **Sirrah** An affectionate use of a term usually reserved for servants and the like.
Orléans Pronounced as two syllables here; see note on 1.1.157.

2 **suburbs** i.e. the outer parts of Orléans on the other side of the Loire. Holinshed tells us that the English won the tower that guards the bridge over the Loire.

4 **Howe'er** although
Howe'er . . . aim The history of the Boy's ineptness as an apprentice gunner emphasizes how lucky he was to hit Salisbury and Gargrave. But was it entirely luck? E. I. Berry in *Patterns of Decay: Shakespeare's Early Histories* (Charlottesville, Va., 1975) suggests that we're meant to see the 'mystique' of Joan at work here (13).

5 **But . . . not** What does the Master Gunner mean? That his Boy will have better luck with this piece of ordnance? Or that he won't be using the gun at all as he has to run to get his father?

7 **grace** honour

8 **Prince's spials** Dauphin's spies

9 **close entrenched** fortified nearby

10 **Went** were accustomed to go (*OED*, *go*, v. 32)

11 **overpeer** look down on

And thence discover how with most advantage
They may us vex with shot or with assault.
To intercept this inconvenience,
A piece of ordnance 'gainst it I have placed,   15
And even these three days have I watched if I could see
  them.
Now do thou watch, for I can stay no longer.
If thou spiest any, run and bring me word,
And thou shalt find me at the Governor's.

BOY

Father, I warrant you, take you no care—   20
                    Exit ⌈Master Gunner at one door⌉
I'll never trouble you, if I may spy them.
                                   Exit ⌈at the other door⌉

1.5   *Enter the Earl of Salisbury and Lord Talbot above on the*
           turrets with others, among them Sir Thomas Gargrave
           and Sir William Glasdale

SALISBURY

Talbot, my life, my joy, again returned?
How wert thou handled, being prisoner?
Or by what means got'st thou to be released?
Discourse, I prithee, on this turret's top.

TALBOT

The Duke of Bedford had a prisoner   5

13 They may us vex] OXFORD *conj.*; They may vex vs F; Vex us they may CAIRNCROSS   16 And
. . . them.] BURNS; And . . . watcht, | If . . .them. F   have I watched] F; watched CAIRNCROSS
(*conj.* Vaughan)   17 Now . . . longer] BURNS; Now . . .watch, | For . . . longer F   20 *Exit*
⌈*Master Gunner at one door*⌉] OXFORD; *Exit (at line* 19 *in* F)

   1.5] *scene-break* OXFORD (1.6); *not in* F   0.1 *the Earl of*] OXFORD (*so throughout play*); *not in* F
Lord] OXFORD (*so throughout play*); *not in* F   0.3 *among . . . Glasdale*] CAPELL (*subs.*); *not in* F
Glasdale] OXFORD; *Glansdale* F   3 got'st] F (got's)   5 Duke] THEOBALD; Earle F

13 **vex** harass
14 **intercept** prevent, hinder (*OED* v. 2)
   inconvenience harm
15 **piece of ordnance** small cannon
   'gainst aimed at
20 **take . . . care** don't worry
21 **I'll . . . them** 'It is important that the Boy
   say these lines after his father has gone—
   it shows him set on claiming the glory for
   himself, in implicit contrast to the Talbots
   father and son, in 4.5' (Burns).
1.5.0.2 *turrets* See note at the beginning of
   1.4.
0.2 *others* Burns suggests that the 'others'

are Gargrave and Glasdale. But, as he also
mentions, 'others' would be useful in this
scene to carry away the bodies.
2 **being** while you were
4 **this turret's top** Presumably the gallery at
   the back of the stage, but Christine Eccles
   suggests that the 'top' may be higher still,
   closer to the roof, where the trumpeter
   advertises the beginning of the play's
   performance (143). But would there be
   room up there for more than one person,
   and could they all be seen?
5 **Duke** Shakespeare demotes him to an
   earl, but he was made a duke in 1415.

Called the brave Lord Poton de Saintrailles;
For him was I exchanged and ransomèd.
But with a baser man-of-arms by far,
Once in contempt they would have bartered me—
Which I, disdaining, scorned, and cravèd death   10
Rather than I would be so vile-esteemed.
In fine, redeemed I was as I desired.
But O, the treacherous Fastolf wounds my heart,
Whom with my bare fists I would execute
If I now had him brought into my power.   15

SALISBURY

Yet tell'st thou not how thou wert entertained.

TALBOT

With scoffs and scorns and contumelious taunts.
In open market place produced they me
To be a public spectacle to all.
'Here', said they, 'is the terror of the French,   20
The scarecrow that affrights our children so.'
Then broke I from the officers that led me,
And with my nails digged stones out of the ground
To hurl at the beholders of my shame.
My grisly countenance made others fly.   25
None durst come near for fear of sudden death.
In iron walls they deemed me not secure;
So great fear of my name 'mongst them were spread
That they supposed I could rend bars of steel
And spurn in pieces posts of adamant.   30

---

6 Poton] This edition; *Ponton* F   Saintrailles] F (*Santrayle*)   7 ransomèd] F (ransom'd)
11 vile] THEOBALD (*subs.*); pil'd F; pilled CAPELL; peeled BURNS   28 were] F; was ROWE

6 **Poton de Saintrailles** Hall mentions that
  he is a captain not a lord.
8 **baser man-of-arms** soldier of lower
  rank
11 **vile-esteemed** Sonnet 121 begins: ' 'Tis
  better to be vile than vile esteemed',
  which gives some plausibility to Pope's
  emendation of an awkward sounding
  combination.
12 **In fine** in short
  redeemed ransomed
14 **fists** hands
  execute kill (*OED* v. 6b)
16 **entertained** treated
17 **contumelious** insolent

21 **The scarecrow . . . so** This contemptuous
  attitude looks forward to the Countess of
  Auvergne's derision in the second act.
25 **grisly** grim; 'also with a sense of
  "grizzly", grey, ageing, grey-haired'
  (Burns, 152). (But see my discussion of
  Shakespeare's puns on pp. 66–8 in the
  Introduction.)
28 **were** was. The plural form may have been
  suggested by the preceding word, 'them'.
  But agreement at this time was notably
  erratic (see note to l. 44).
30 **spurn** kick
  adamant A legendary mineral of supreme
  durability.

Wherefore a guard of chosen shot I had
That walked about me every minute while;
And if I did but stir out of my bed
Ready they were to shoot me to the heart.

> *The Boy ⌈passes over the stage⌉ with a linstock ⌈lit and*
> *burning⌉*

SALISBURY

I grieve to hear what torments you endured;   35
But we will be revenged sufficiently.
Now it is supper time in Orléans.
Here, through this iron grate, I count each one,
And view the Frenchmen how they fortify.
Let us look in: the sight will much delight thee.   40
Sir Thomas Gargrave and Sir William Glasdale,
Let me have your express opinions
Where is best place to make our battery next.

> ⌈*They look through the grate*⌉

GARGRAVE

I think at the north gate, for there stands lords.

34.1–2 *The . . . burning*] BURNS; *Enter the Boy with a Linstock* F   38 iron grate] This edition;
Grate F; secret grate DYCE   count each one] F1; can count every one F2   41 Glasdale]
OXFORD; *Glansdale* F

31 **chosen shot** handpicked expert
marksmen
32 **every minute while** all the time
34.1 *The Boy . . . burning* F's '*Enter the Boy
with a Linstock*' is cryptic. He clearly cannot remain on stage during the ensuing
conversation between the English lords,
even though they are 'above' and he
'below'. He has to attend to the piece of
ordnance off stage provided by his father.
Burns's addition of '*lit and burning*' builds
on Wilson who argues that the Boy's
crossing the stage with a lighted linstock
warns 'the spectators what to expect'.
Even in an open-air theatre a lighted linstock would be more ominous than one
unlit. Burns notes that in the interests of
safety the explosion had to take place off
stage.
34.1 **linstock** A stick with a cleft in one end
for holding the gunner's match to light
the fuse of a cannon.
38 **iron** In F the line lacks a foot. In his article
on corruptions in the text of *1 Henry VI*,
'The siege of Orléans and the cursing of
Joan: corruptions in the text of *Henry VI
Part 1*', *English Language Notes*, 33.3

(1996), 1–6, R. J. C. Watt suggests that
more than likely the word 'iron' got left
out due to 'eye-skip from the *yr* of *yron* to
the similar-looking *gr* of *grate*' (2) and I
have adopted his suggestion.
grate This would probably be one of the
windows at one of the gallery's ends.
each one i.e. each French soldier
39 **fortify** establish their defensive positions
40 **in** i.e. into the city
42 **express** considered
43 **make our battery** direct our line of fire
44 **stands lords** This not very satisfactory
locution has aroused debate. Oxford's
Textual Companion suggests replacing
lords with Lou, referring to the Bastille
of Saint Lou found in Holinshed. But
the Bastille is quite some distance from
Orléans and in any case Lou standing on
its own would probably be incomprehen-
sible to an Elizabethan audience, and
certainly—comically so—to a modern-
day one. Killing French lords—lords
especially—would have been a laudable
ambition for the English army. Watt (and
before him, McKerrow) suggests Loire,
though it is odd to see the name of a river

GLASDALE

And I, here, at the bulwark of the bridge.   45

TALBOT

For aught I see this city must be famished,

Or with light skirmishes be enfeeblèd.

> *Here* ⌈*within*⌉ *they shoot off chambers and Salisbury*
> *and Gargrave fall down*

SALISBURY

O Lord, have mercy on us, wretched sinners!

GARGRAVE

O Lord, have mercy on me, woeful man!

TALBOT

What chance is this that suddenly hath crossed us?   50

Speak, Salisbury—at least, if thou canst, speak.

How far'st thou, mirror of all martial men?

One of thy eyes and thy cheek's side struck off?

Accursèd tower! Accursèd fatal hand

That hath contrived this woeful tragedy!   55

In thirteen battles Salisbury o'ercame.

Henry the Fifth he first trained to the wars.

Whilst any trump did sound or drum struck up

His sword did ne'er leave striking in the field.

Yet liv'st thou, Salisbury? Though thy speech doth fail,   60

---

43 battery] F (batt'ry)   43.1 *They . . . grate*] OXFORD; *not in* F   44 stands lords] F1; stand ~
F2; stands Lou OXFORD   46 aught] F (ought)   47 be enfeebled] This edition; enfeebled F
47.1 *within*] OXFORD   *shoot off chambers*] OXFORD; *shot*, F   47.2 *and Gargrave*] OXFORD; *not in*
F   *fall*] OXFORD; *falls* F   51 canst,] F; ~∧ POPE

without the definite article and the object
of 'stands'. The singular verb with a
plural subject is commonplace at this
time. The BBC production of the play
gets round this debate by having the actor
gesture one way to the North Gate and
another to lords as though the lords were
English ones and the North Gate French.

45 **bulwark** fortification (manned with
soldiers)

46 **must be** will have to be
famished 'reduced to famine (here as a
deliberate military strategy), expressing
what the English must do, not a description of the current state of the town. The
besieged town is better supplied than
its besiegers, whose hunger has been
described at 1.2.7' (Burns).

47 **be enfeeblèd** F lacks 'be' and thereby is
missing a foot. The stage direction that
follows this line is in the margin in F,
crowding the line. Possibly the 'be' was
dropped to help accommodate a lengthy
stage direction.

47.1 *they* The Master Gunner's Boy in fact
(but perhaps an indication that it took
more than one stagehand to '*shoot off
chambers*').

48 **O . . . us** Frequently to be found in the
liturgy.

50 **chance** mischance
crossed thwarted

52 **mirror** model
martial men soldiers

58 **trump** trumpet

59 **leave** cease from

One eye thou hast to look to heaven for grace.
The sun with one eye vieweth all the world.
Heaven, be thou gracious to none alive
If Salisbury wants mercy at thy hands.
Sir Thomas Gargrave, hast thou any life?   65
Speak unto Talbot. Nay, look up to him.—
Bear hence his body; I will help to bury it.
　　⌈*Exit one with Gargrave's body*⌉
Salisbury, cheer thy spirit with this comfort:
Thou shalt not die whiles—
He beckons with his hand and smiles on me   70
As who should say, 'When I am dead and gone,
Remember to avenge me on the French.'
Plantagenet, I will—and like thee, Nero,
Play on the lute, beholding the towns burn.
Wretched shall France be only in my name.   75
　　Here an alarum, and it thunders and lightens
What stir is this? What tumult's in the heavens?

64 wants] F; want CAIRNCROSS   67 Bear . . . it] *as here* CAIRNCROSS; *after l.* 64 *in* F   I will] F;
I'll CAIRNCROSS   *Exit . . . body*] OXFORD; *not in* F   73 like thee, Nero] MALONE; like thee, F1;
Nero-like will F2; Nero-like POPE; like the Roman WALKER *conj.*

62 **The sun . . . world** Not much of a
comfort, one would think. Hattaway
refers us to Polyphemus' wooing of
Galatea in Ovid's *Metamorphoses* for a
comparable usage; but in Polyphemus'
case he is a monster with one eye in the
middle of his forehead 'as big as a good-
sized shield' (13.856), so that Ovid's comparison with the single eye of the sun
'who can see everything here on earth'
(857) has a certain tenuous integrity.
64 **wants** lacks
67 **Bear . . . it** In F this line follows l. 64
and must refer to the yet (barely) living
Salisbury. On a suggestion by Harold
Brooks, Cairncross repositions the line so
that it refers to the dead Gargrave. Burns
retains the F position arguing that failure
to act immediately on Talbot's command
is an indication of 'the bathetic collapse of
his control'. It seems more likely that it
was Compositor A who was confused
rather than Talbot.
69 **whiles** until. Until what or when? Perhaps
until the French are defeated.
70 **and smiles on me** No mean feat with his
'cheek's side struck off' (l. 53).

73 **Plantagenet** Thomas de Montague, 4th
Earl of Salisbury, was a descendant of
Edward III's friend William de Montague.
The first Neville Earl of Salisbury,
Thomas's son-in-law and successor,
was the son of Joan Beaufort and thus a
Plantagenet.
Nero An addition by later editors who
rearrange F2's 'Nero-like will'. Tucker
Brooke stays with F's version describing
the modern blending of F2 as 'a perver-
sion which nearly all modern editors have
unfortunately accepted'. Nero's fiddling
while Rome burned is catchpenny history. Burns questions the appropriateness
of Talbot's description of himself as a
Nero-like figure given the differences
between the English hero and the Roman
megalomaniac. (Although there is a hint
of megalomania in Talbot's desire to
behold the French towns burn.)
75 **only in** at the mere sound of
75.1 ***thunders and lightens*** Presaging news
of the 'holy prophetess' brought by the
Messenger.

Whence cometh this alarum and the noise?
> *Enter a Messenger*

MESSENGER

My lord, my lord, the French have gathered head.
The Dauphin, with one Joan la Pucelle joined,
A holy prophetess new risen up,   80
Is come with a great power to raise the siege.
> *Here Salisbury lifteth himself up and groans*

TALBOT

Hear, hear, how dying Salisbury doth groan;
It irks his heart he cannot be revenged.
Frenchmen, I'll be a Salisbury to you.
Puzzel or pucelle, dolphin or dogfish,   85
Your hearts I'll stamp out with my horse's heels
And make a quagmire of your mingled brains.
Convey me Salisbury into his tent,
And then we'll try what these dastard Frenchmen dare.
> *Alarum. Exeunt carrying Salisbury*

1.6   *Here an alarum again, and Lord Talbot pursueth the*
           Dauphin and driveth him. Then enter Joan la Pucelle
           driving Englishmen before her ⌈and exeunt⌉. Then enter
           Lord Talbot

TALBOT

Where is my strength, my valour, and my force?

77 the] F; this POPE   79 la Pucelle] WILSON; *de Puzel* F   85 Puzzel or pucelle] F (*Puzel or Pussel*); *Pucelle* or Pucelle OXFORD; Puzel or Pussel BURNS   88 me] F; we CAIRNCROSS (*conj.* Vaughan)   89 then we'll] F; then CAIRNCROSS   what these] F; what POPE   89.1 *carrying Salisbury*] OXFORD; *not in* F

1.6] CAPELL (1.5); *not in* F   0.2 *Joan la Pucelle*] THEOBALD; *Ioane de Puzel* F; *Joan Puzel* BURNS   0.2–3 *and exeunt*] OXFORD; *not in* F; *and exit after them* DYCE

78 **gathered head** rallied their forces
81 **power** army
81.1 **groans** 'The groan is probably intended to signify prescience of what will follow Joan's appearance' (Wilson).
85 **Puzzel**, slut
   pucelle virgin, girl, maid
   dolphin or dogfish Spelling Dauphin with the lower-case 'd' and the F 'ol' brings out the intent of Talbot's dismissive comparison of the French prince to two kinds of fish, one princely, the other scavenging (dogfish = a small shark). Hart notes: '"Dolphin" of the folio is considerably allowed to stand in the text here for the

sake of the quibbling'. The pairing of the fish mirrors the equally dismissive pairing of 'puzzel' and 'pucelle'.
88 **me** for me (the ethical dative)
1.6 A swashbuckling scene, vivid and exciting, with the stage a location for combat between groups of soldiers and individuals. The whirling of Talbot's thoughts (l. 19) is an appropriate response to the scene's kinetic, gymnastic quality.
0.2 **driveth him** i.e. drives the Dauphin before him as Joan does the English soldiers in the next line
1 **Where . . . force** We are meant to understand that they have been drained away

Our English troops retire; I cannot stay them.
A woman clad in armour chaseth them.
    Enter Joan la Pucelle
Here, here she comes. I'll have a bout with thee.
Devil or devil's dam, I'll conjure thee. 5
Blood will I draw on thee—thou art a witch—
And straightway give thy soul to him thou serv'st.

JOAN

Come, come, 'tis only I that must disgrace thee.
    Here they fight

TALBOT

Heavens, can you suffer hell so to prevail?
My breast I'll burst with straining of my courage 10
And from my shoulders crack my arms asunder
But I will chastise this high-minded strumpet.
    They fight again

JOAN

Talbot, farewell. Thy hour is not yet come.

---

3 them] F; men OXFORD (*conj.* Vaughan)   3.1 *Enter . . . Pucelle*] F (*Enter Puzel.*); *not in* BURNS
4 a bout] F1; about F2   6 thou art a] F; arrant CAIRNCROSS *conj.*

from him magically. Alan C. Dessen suggests that 'a mere touch from Joan's sword should have the effect of a sledgehammer blow' ('The Logic of Elizabethan Stage Violence: Some Alarums and Excursions for Modern Critics, Editors, and Directors', *Renaissance Drama*, 9 (1978), 52). In Michael Bogdanov's production *The Wars of the Roses: the House of Lancaster* she 'bewitches' him with a wave of her sword. Charles Edelman, however, thinks no witchcraft is necessary (see p. 58).

2 **stay** stop
4 **bout** a military (and perhaps sexual) encounter. In 4.7 Talbot's son disdains to fight Joan, refusing 'To be the pillage of a giglot wench' (4.7.41).
5 **dam** mother
  conjure (a) send back to hell (b) engage in sexual intercourse (perhaps)
6 **Blood . . . witch** Drawing a witch's blood was supposed to be a protection from her power. So Talbot will counter Joan's evil supernatural magic with his own soldierly form of good magic: shedding Joan's

blood in honest combat. 'It was believed . . . that to scratch a witch cancelled her power, in the same way as one could avert the black magic with the name of Jesus or with holy water. Letting the blood of a witch flow could place her in your power, could break the spell of her wholeness: her flow restored her to the normal world, where the blood of menstruation is a badge of lowliness and weakness' (Warner, 109).

7 **him** i.e. the devil
9 **Heavens . . . prevail** See Matthew 16: 18: 'And the gates of hell shall not prevail against it'.
  suffer permit
10 **courage** vigour, vital force (*OED sb.* 3)
12 **But I will** if I do not
  high-minded arrogant (*OED a.* 1)
13 **Talbot . . . come** The text leaves it open as to what has happened in the second bout between Joan and Talbot to make Joan withdraw. Should Talbot—despite Joan's magical prowess—start to get the upper hand? Should Joan be distracted by some kind of off-stage commotion as is perhaps indicated in the next line?

I must go victual Orléans forthwith.

> *A short alarum, then ⌈the French pass over the stage*
> *and⌉ enter the town with soldiers*

O'ertake me if thou canst. I scorn thy strength.   15

Go, go, cheer up thy hunger-starvèd men.

Help Salisbury to make his testament.

This day is ours, as many more shall be.   *Exit*

TALBOT

My thoughts are whirlèd like a potter's wheel.

I know not where I am nor what I do.   20

A witch by fear, not force, like Hannibal,

Drives back our troops and conquers as she lists.

So bees with smoke and doves with noisome stench

Are from their hives and houses driven away.

They called us, for our fierceness, English dogs;   25

Now like to whelps we crying run away.

> *A short alarum. ⌈Enter English soldiers⌉*

Hark, countrymen: either renew the fight

14.1–2 then . . . soldiers] OXFORD; *not in* F   16 hunger-starved] ROWE (*subs.*); hungry-starued
F   26 like to] F1; like the F2   26.1 *Enter . . . soldiers*] OXFORD; *not in* F

14 **victual** provision
    forthwith at once
14.1–2 *A . . . soldiers* The French soldiers
    presumably rush by Joan and Talbot as
    she is extricating herself from her strug-
    gle with him. The soldiers then enter the
    'town' through the doors at the rear of
    the stage, leaving Joan to address Talbot
    before she too exits. What does he do
    during her four lines of speech to him?
    Perhaps he should give some physical
    sign of his 'whirlèd' state, staggering,
    unable to move after her.
15 **O'ertake** strike (*OED*, *overtake*, *v.* 2)
16 **hunger-starved** dying of hunger
19 **potter's wheel** There are a number of ref-
    erences in the Old Testament to the idea of
    God as a potter making (and breaking) his
    peoples out of clay. But Talbot focuses on
    the wheel rather than the potter which
    suggests something closer to 'the giddy
    round of fortune's wheel' (*The Rape of
    Lucrece*, 952).
21 **not . . . Hannibal** F's comma after 'force'
    suggests that we take Hannibal and Joan

as both working by fear rather than by
force, even though Hannibal might be
considered the exemplar of force in his
extraordinary career as a general against
the Romans. For Hannibal's exploitation
of 'fear', the play's commentators refer to
Plutarch's and Livy's accounts of the
incident where Hannibal ordered his men
to tie lit torches to the horns of two thousand oxen to make the Romans think
they were outnumbered. Hart suggests
that this reference in the text—however
submerged—leads on to the thoughts of
smoke and stench in the next lines.
21 **Hannibal**   (247–182   BCE)   Famous
    Carthaginian general.
22 **lists** pleases
23–4 **So . . . away** The analogy is not perfect
    as these stratagems are forceful enough.
23 **noisome** noxious
24 **driven** Pronounced as one syllable.
25 **English dogs** 'A particular type of hound
    or hunting dog, the Talbot, is associated
    with the Talbot family' (Burns).
26 **whelps** puppies

Or tear the lions out of England's coat.
Renounce your soil; give sheep in lions' stead.
Sheep run not half so treacherous from the wolf,   30
Or horse or oxen from the leopard,
As you fly from your oft-subduèd slaves.

> *Alarum. Here another skirmish ⌈in which the English*
> *attempt to enter Orléans and are forced back⌉*

It will not be; retire into your trenches.
You all consented unto Salisbury's death,
For none would strike a stroke in his revenge.   35
Pucelle is entered into Orléans
In spite of us or aught that we could do.

> ⌈*The English sound a⌉ retreat ⌈and exeunt soldiers⌉*

O would I were to die with Salisbury.
The shame hereof will make me hide my head.   *Exit.*

I.7   *Flourish. Enter on the walls Joan la Pucelle, Charles the*
       Dauphin, Reignier Duke of Anjou, the Duke of Alençon
       and French Soldiers ⌈with colours⌉

JOAN
   Advance our waving colours on the walls;

29 soil] F; style MARSHALL (*conj.* Dyce); shield VAUGHAN *conj.*   30 treacherous] F; timorous
POPE   32.1–2 *in . . . back*] BURNS (*subs.*); *not in* F   37.1 *The . . . soldiers*] This edition; F *has*
'Exit Talbot. Alarum, Retreat, Flourish.' *at the end of the scene.*
   I.7] CAPELL (I.6); *not in* F   0.1 *Joan la Pucelle*] THEOBALD; *Puzel* F   *Charles the Dauphin*]
OXFORD; *Dolphin* F   0.2 *Reignier Duke of Anjou*] OXFORD (*subs.*); *Reigneir* F   0.2–3 *with
colours*] OXFORD; *not in* F   2 English] F1; English wolves F2; ~ dogs STAUNTON

28 **lions** In the English coat of arms three
   lions passant (i.e. standing, one foot
   raised) guardant (i.e. with heads turned
   to look at the viewer) were quartered with
   the fleur-de-lis.
29 **soil** country
   give . . . stead 'in place of heraldic lions,
   display sheep (as a symbol of cowardice)'
   (Sanders).
30–2 **Sheep . . . slaves** Another imperfect
   analogy. For soldiers to flee from oft-
   subdued slaves may indeed be treacherous; for sheep, horse and oxen to flee from
   their natural predators clearly isn't.
   Burns suggests that the word 'treacherous' is 'purposefully absurd' but the
   absurdity may be unintended.
31 **leopard** Pronounced as three syllables.
32 **oft-subduèd** frequently defeated

33 **It . . . be** it's hopeless
34 **consented unto** acquiesced in (*OED* v. 6)
35 **his revenge** in revenge of his death
37.1 *Retreat* F has 'Alarum. Retreat. Flourish'
   after Talbot's exit. It's clear that in the
   staging Talbot's soldiers exeunt after l. 37
   and it seems appropriate to sound the
   retreat at this time on their behalf, leaving
   Talbot alone on stage for his bitter self-
   recriminations. The retreat would nor-
   mally be played on a single trumpet and
   drum.
1.7.0.1 *Flourish* See note at 1.2.0.1. It is
   a triumphant riposte to the English
   'Retreat'.
0.1 *on the walls* i.e. on the tiring-house
   gallery
1 **Advance** raise aloft
   colours standards

Rescued is Orléans from the English.
Thus Joan la Pucelle hath performed her word.
CHARLES
Divinest creature, Astraea's daughter,
How shall I honour thee for this success?   5
Thy promises are like Adonis' garden
That one day bloomed and fruitful were the next.
France, triumph in thy glorious prophetess.
Recovered is the town of Orléans;
More blessèd hap did ne'er befall our state.   10
REIGNIER
Why ring not out the bells aloud throughout the town?
Dauphin, command the citizens make bonfires,
And feast and banquet in the open streets
To celebrate the joy that God hath given us.
ALENÇON
All France will be replete with mirth and joy   15
When they shall hear how we have played the men.
CHARLES
'Tis Joan, not we, by whom the day is won—
For which I will divide my crown with her,
And all the priests and friars in my realm
Shall in procession sing her endless praise.   20
A statelier pyramis to her I'll rear

---

3 Joan la Pucelle] ROWE; *Ioane de Puzel* F   4 Astraea's] F1; bright ~ F2   6 garden] F; gardens HANMER   11 Why . . . town?] POPE; Why . . . alowd, | Throughout . . . Towne? F   out the bells] F; bells CAIRNCROSS (*conj.* Steevens)

---

4 **Astraea** The goddess of justice, and the daughter of Jupiter. She lived on earth during the golden age but, at the advent of the iron age, repelled by men's wickedness, she carried her divine scales off to the constellation of Libra. Her return to earth would signal a new age of justice. Charles continues to combine the Christian with the pagan in his celebrations of Joan (see 1.2.140–5).

6 **Adonis' garden** Mythical gardens of miraculous fecundity famously celebrated as a 'joyous Paradise' in Spenser's *Faerie Queene* (3.6.29), a poem roughly contemporary with this play and perhaps an influence on it. Charles emphasizes the celerity of Joan's achievement.

10 **hap** accident

15 **replete with** full of

16 **played the men** acted courageously

19 **priests and friars** A reminder that we are dealing with Catholic France. (Though see notes on Bishop of Winchester in 'Persons of the Play' and 5.1.14.)

21 **pyramis** pyramid

Than Rhodope's of Memphis ever was.
In memory of her, when she is dead,
Her ashes, in an urn more precious
Than the rich-jewelled coffer of Darius, 25
Transported shall be at high festivals
Before the kings and queens of France.
No longer on Saint Denis will we cry,
But Joan la Pucelle shall be France's saint.
Come in, and let us banquet royally 30
After this golden day of victory.   *Flourish. Exeunt*

22 of] DYCE (*conj.* Capell); or F   25 rich-jewelled coffer] F; rich jewel-coffer CAIRNCROSS; rich jewel'd coffer POPE   27 Before] F; Ever before HANMER   kings] F; royal kings CAIRNCROSS *conj.* France] F; France up-borne CAPELL *conj.*   29 Joan la Pucelle] THEOBALD; *Ioane de Puzel* F

22 **Rhodope's of Memphis** All editions, except Burns's, agree with Capell's emendations of F and Tucker Brooke's explanation of it. 'One of the most beautiful pyramids was said to have been built by Rhodope, a Greek courtesan who married the king of Memphis. The reading of the text is a conjecture of Capell for "Rhodophes or Memphis" of the folios'. Burns, however, accepts the F reading that Rhodope (a mistake, he argues from Herodotus, for Rhodopis) and Memphis refer to different pyramids. If Rhodope's involvement with the building of a pyramid at Memphis was a mistake it was one that was widely held. In Robert Greene's *Mamillia*, for instance, published in 1583, Mamillia writes to the Lady Modesta comparing the phenomenal beauty of Sylvia as a tourist attraction to the 'Pyramids built by Rhodope' in Memphis (2.270). Johnson notices the *frisson* of her profession: 'I think he means to call her strumpet all the while he is making this loud praise of her' (Arthur Sherbo, ed., *Johnson on Shakespeare*, Yale Edition of the Works of Samuel Johnson, viii (New Haven, 1968), 569–70).

23–7 **In . . . France** An unfortunate prediction. Joan's ashes remain uncollected and unvenerated as Richard indicates: 'Break thou in pieces, and consume to ashes, | Thou foul accursèd minister of hell' (5.5.92–3).

25 **rich-jewelled . . . Darius** 'Coffer' here either means: (a) a chest (which leads to Cairncross's emendation) or more likely (b) a coffin (*OED* sb. 3) which the context suggests. Burns notes that though the death of Darius is recorded in Herodotus (at the beginning of Book 7) no mention is made of his coffin. On the other hand, in North, Nashe, and Puttenham, mention is made of Darius's jewel-coffer (as opposed to his jewelled coffer), used by Alexander after his victory over Darius to contain the works of Homer, Alexander's most precious possession. Shakespeare uses 'coffer' to mean 'coffin' only once more, in *Pericles*, Scene 14, line 2.

28 **Saint Denis** First bishop of Paris and patron saint of France.

29 **France's saint** Joan was beatified in 1909 and canonized in 1920. How quickly things can change is exemplified in the following scene where Joan becomes for Charles a 'deceitful dame' (2.1.51).

2.1   *Enter ⌈on the walls⌉ a French Sergeant of a band, with*
          two Sentinels

SERGEANT

Sirs, take your places and be vigilant.

If any noise or soldier you perceive

Near to the walls, by some apparent sign

Let us have knowledge at the court of guard.

A SENTINEL

Sergeant, you shall.   *Exit Sergeant*

          Thus are poor servitors,   5

When others sleep upon their quiet beds,

Constrained to watch in darkness, rain, and cold.

          Enter Lord Talbot, the Dukes of Bedford and Burgundy,
          and soldiers with scaling ladders

2.1] F (*Actus Secundus. Scena Prima.*)   *on the walls*] CAIRNCROSS;   *aloft* HATTAWAY;   *to the Gate*
CAPELL   *French*] CAPELL;   *not in* F   5   A SENTINEL] CAPELL;   *Sent.* F   *Exit Sergeant*] CAPELL;   *not*
in F   7.1   *the Dukes of*] OXFORD (*so throughout play*);   *not in* F   7.2   *scaling ladders*] CAIRNCROSS
(*subs.*);   *scaling Ladders: their Drummes beating a Dead March.* F

2.1 The retaking of Orléans by Talbot is
Shakespeare's invention, although some
of the details seem to be taken from the
recapture of Le Mans in 1428 (Holinshed,
160, and Hall, 143). An addition of this
kind to the already complicated network
of gains and reversals dramatized by
the play's military action illustrates
Shakespeare's delight in making his early
plots even more labyrinthine than they
were in his sources, in order in this
instance to stress fortune's turbulent
changes of favour. Bullough writes: 'The
play is quite cleverly built up as a series of
see-saw movements in place and mood:
from England to France and vice versa,
between the French and English armies in
France, between discord and harmony at
home, between defeat and victory in
France' (39). In his early comedies Shakespeare likewise complicates already complicated situations; in *The Comedy of
Errors*, for example, he adds an extra set
of twins to his source from Plautus to
increase the comedy of bewilderment.

0.1 *Sergeant* A higher rank than in the
modern military (*OED sb.* 9).

0.1 *band* company of soldiers (guarding the
town)

3 **apparent** obvious

4 **court of guard** guard-room

5 **servitors** common soldiers

6 **upon . . . beds** peacefully in their beds

7 **watch** (a) keep guard (b) stay awake

7.2 *soldiers . . . ladders* F tacks on to this
direction '*Their Drummes beating a Dead
March*' but has no such direction (or any
other) in 2.2 when Talbot orders the body
of Salisbury to be brought on to the stage
(2.2.4–6). Hattaway—following Wilson's
suggestion—conjectures that Salisbury
might be carried in here in a funeral procession from which Talbot and others
break away to attack the French. This
hardly seems likely. More plausibly, Gary
Taylor suggests that a dead march here
would be appropriate for a sneak attack at
night and need not necessarily signify a
funeral procession (*Textual Companion*,
221). Although it isn't clear as to how the
confusion arose, it seems to me most
likely that the direction was intended for
the later occasion when Salisbury's body
is ceremoniously brought on to the stage.
Burns omits '*and soldiers*' arguing that the
scaling ladders—three of them—could be
brought in by the named characters. But
his suggestion that Orléans is—even if

TALBOT

  Lord Regent, and redoubted Burgundy—

  By whose approach the regions of Artois,

  Wallon, and Picardy are friends to us—   10

  This happy night the Frenchmen are secure,

  Having all day caroused and banqueted.

  Embrace we then this opportunity,

  As fitting best to quittance their deceit,

  Contrived by art and baleful sorcery.   15

BEDFORD

  Coward of France! How much he wrongs his fame,

  Despairing of his own arms' fortitude,

  To join with witches and the help of hell.

BURGUNDY

  Traitors have never other company.

  But what's that Pucelle whom they term so pure?   20

TALBOT

  A maid, they say.

BEDFORD   A maid? And be so martial?

BURGUNDY

  Pray God she prove not masculine ere long.

---

only symbolically—taken by the three men alone on stage strains credulity. What then happens to the scaling ladders? Presumably they could be pushed off-stage by soldiers in the ensuing hurly-burly. Burns's suggestion that the ladders remain on the walls ignored by the panic-stricken French soldiers leaping over the walls is attractive. The walls that the ladders scale would be represented by the tiring-house gallery. 'This gallery, which probably was on a level with the audience's first-storey gallery, would have involved a small climb' (Eccles, 144).

8 **redoubted** (a) feared, dreaded (b) distinguished

8–10 **Burgundy . . . us** The alliance with Burgundy during the reign of Henry V brought both the Duchy of Burgundy (south-east of Paris) and territories in the Low Countries friendly to him into an accord with England.

8 **Burgundy** It was customary to refer to rulers of countries by the name of the country standing alone. See note to 3.2.35.

9 **approach** arrival
  Artois Region of north-east France.

10 **Wallon** See note at 1.1.137.
   Picardy Region of northern France.

11 **secure** free from care; overconfident (*OED* a. 1)

14 **quittance** repay

15 **art** black magic
   baleful pernicious

16 **Coward of France** i.e. the Dauphin
   fame reputation

17 **fortitude** strength

19 **Traitors . . . company** An ironic remark considering Burgundy's past and future.

22 **prove not masculine** doesn't (a) turn out to be a man (b) turn out to be pregnant with a male child
   ere long before long, soon

If underneath the standard of the French
She carry armour as she hath begun—

TALBOT

Well, let them practise and converse with spirits.   25
God is our fortress, in whose conquering name
Let us resolve to scale their flinty bulwarks.

BEDFORD

Ascend, brave Talbot. We will follow thee.

TALBOT

Not all together. Better far, I guess,
That we do make our entrance several ways,   30
That, if it chance the one of us do fail,
The other yet may rise against their force.

BEDFORD

Agreed. I'll to yon corner.

BURGUNDY   And I to this.

TALBOT

And here will Talbot mount, or make his grave.
Now, Salisbury, for thee, and for the right   35
Of English Henry, shall this night appear
How much in duty I am bound to both.

> ⌈*Talbot, Bedford, Burgundy and their soldiers scale the
> walls*⌉

SENTINELS

Arm! Arm! The enemy doth make assault!

⌈*Exeunt above*⌉

24 begun—] OXFORD; ~. F 29 all together] F (altogether) 31 fail] F; fall CAIRNCROSS
33 yon] F (yond) 37.1 *Talbot . . . walls*] This edition; *not in* F; *The English, having scaled the
Walls, Cry, St. George!, A Talbot!* HATTAWAY; *Cry, 'Saint George!' 'A Talbot!' The English scale the
walls, and exeunt* CAIRNCROSS; *Talbot and his soldiers scale the walls* OXFORD 38 SENTINELS] F
(*Sent.*) *Exeunt above*] OXFORD; *not in* F

23–4 **If . . . begun**—It's hard to make sense of
these lines as completing a statement begun
by 'Pray God she prove not masculine ere
long'. Oxford's suggestion that the lines
comprise the beginnings of a new sentence
interrupted by Talbot's 'Well' is persuasive.

23 **standard** ensign

24 **carry armour** (a) wear armour (b) bear
the weight in the sexual act of a soldier in
armour

25 **practise and converse** Both terms suggest
having transactions with the spirits on a
literal and sexual level.

26 **God . . . fortress** Shaheen notes that only

the Geneva Bible uses the term 'fortress'
(the other Bibles have 'castle') and offers
this as evidence of Shakespeare's reliance
on it. Of course, the phrase could just
as easily have come from the general
culture.

29 **Not all together** not all up one ladder
guess judge (*OED v.* 4)

30 **several** separate

31 **That** so that
one of us We have to imagine that 'and
our company of soldiers' is understood.

32 **rise** scale the walls

36 **shall** it shall

ENGLISH SOLDIERS Saint George! À Talbot!

> *Exeunt above* ⌈*in pursuit*⌉
> ⌈*Alarum.*⌉ *The French* ⌈*soldiers*⌉ *leap o'er the walls in*
> *their shirts* ⌈*and exeunt*⌉. *Enter several ways the Bas-*
> *tard of Orléans, the Duke of Alençon, and Reignier Duke*
> *of Anjou, half ready and half unready*

ALENÇON

How now, my lords? What, all unready so?   40

BASTARD

Unready? Ay, and glad we scaped so well.

REIGNIER

'Twas time, I trow, to wake and leave our beds,
Hearing alarums at our chamber doors.

ALENÇON

Of all exploits since first I followed arms
Ne'er heard I of a warlike enterprise   45
More venturous or desperate than this.

BASTARD

I think this Talbot be a fiend of hell.

REIGNIER

If not of hell, the heavens sure favour him.

ALENÇON

Here cometh Charles. I marvel how he sped.

> *Enter Charles the Dauphin and Joan la Pucelle*

BASTARD

Tut, holy Joan was his defensive guard.   50

---

39 Saint . . . Talbot!] OXFORD; *Cry, S. George, A Talbot* F *(as stage direction)*   *in pursuit*] This
edition; *not in* F   39.1–2 *Alarum . . . exeunt*] OXFORD; *The French leape . . . shirts* F   39.2
ways] F; *ways below* HATTAWAY   *the Bastard of*] OXFORD *(so throughout play)*; *not in* F   39.3
and] OXFORD; *not in* F   49.1 *Joan la Pucelle*] THEOBALD; *Ioane* F

39.1 ***The . . . shirts*** This quasi-comic episode
is taken from Hall's account of the
retaking of Le Mans in May 1428, in
the adjacent province of Maine. The
French soldiers, 'suddenly taken, were so
amazed, in so much that some of them,
being not out of their beds, got up in their
shirts, and leapt over the walls' (160).
Orléans was not in fact retaken by the
English, but its fall here serves to
emphasize the remorselessly repetitive
nature of the clashes between the English
and French forces. 'Lost and recovered in
a day again!' (3.2.113) marvels Talbot at a
later repetition.

39.1 ***o'er the walls*** i.e. they leap down from
the rear-stage gallery onto the main stage.
39.2 ***several*** separate
39.4 ***half . . . unready*** half dressed. All the
French soldiers are in a dishevelled, half-
dressed state.
46 **venturous** daring
49 **marvel** wonder
   sped fared
50 **Tut** An exclamation of mild impatience or
contempt (*OED sb.* 3). The form 'tut, tut'
is common, as in its only other appearance in the play, from Richard Plantagenet at 2.4.19.
   defensive protecting

CHARLES

Is this thy cunning, thou deceitful dame?
Didst thou at first, to flatter us withal,
Make us partakers of a little gain
That now our loss might be ten times so much?

JOAN

Wherefore is Charles impatient with his friend?   55
At all times will you have my power alike?
Sleeping or waking must I still prevail,
Or will you blame and lay the fault on me?
Improvident soldiers, had your watch been good,
This sudden mischief never could have fallen.   60

CHARLES

Duke of Alençon, this was your default,
That, being captain of the watch tonight,
Did look no better to that weighty charge.

ALENÇON

Had all your quarters been as safely kept
As that whereof I had the government,   65
We had not been thus shamefully surprised.

BASTARD

Mine was secure.

REIGNIER   And so was mine, my lord.

CHARLES

And for myself, most part of all this night
Within her quarter and my own precinct

---

58 me?] F; ~?—OXFORD   64 your] F1; our F2

51 **cunning** skill in magic (*OED sb.* 4)
52 **flatter** encourage, inspire (*OED v.* 7)
55 **Wherefore** why
   impatient angry
   friend (a) companion (b) lover
57 **still** always
58 **me**? Oxford's dash following the question mark indicates that Joan turns away from the commanders of the army to reprimand the sentinels on duty. It makes more sense, and is more powerful theatre, to have Joan continue to lambast the French leaders.
59 **Improvident** negligent
60 **mischief** catastrophe
   fallen happened

61 **default** fault
62 **tonight** last night
63 **weighty charge** important duty
64 **your** Not specifically directed at Charles.
   quarters apartments
   kept guarded
69 **her** i.e. Joan's
   quarter There is the possibility of a pun here on (hind)-quarter, but many of these sexual possibilities are elusive in these exchanges and to insist on them smacks of an editorial ingenuity of a rather desperate kind. *Pace* Burns, for instance, 'precinct', 'passing', 'relieving' and 'shift' are probably innocent of sexual equivocation.

I was employed in passing to and fro
About relieving of the sentinels.
Then how or which way should they first break in?

JOAN

Question, my lords, no further of the case,
How or which way; 'tis sure they found some place
But weakly guarded where the breach was made.   75
And now there rests no other shift but this—
To gather our soldiers, scattered and dispersed,
And lay new platforms to endamage them.

Alarum. Enter an English Soldier

ENGLISH SOLDIER À Talbot! À Talbot!

The French fly, leaving their clothes behind

ENGLISH SOLDIER

I'll be so bold to take what they have left.   80
The cry of 'Talbot' serves me for a sword,
For I have loaden me with many spoils,
Using no other weapon but his name.   *Exit*

2.2   *Enter Lord Talbot, the Dukes of Bedford and Burgundy,
a Captain and soldiers*

BEDFORD

The day begins to break and night is fled,
Whose pitchy mantle overveiled the earth.
Here sound retreat and cease our hot pursuit.

Retreat is sounded

---

78 them] CAPELL; them. *Exeunt* F   78.1 *an English Soldier*] CAPELL; *a Souldier* F   79 ENGLISH
... Talbot!] OXFORD; *crying, a Talbot, a Talbot:* F (*as stage direction*)   79.1 *The French*] OXFORD;
not in F   80 ENGLISH] OXFORD; *not in* F
    2.2] CAPELL; *not in* F   0.1–2 *and soldiers*] OXFORD; *not in* F   3.1 *is sounded*] OXFORD;
not in F

75 **But** only
76 **rests** remains
   shift stratagem
78 **lay new platforms** make fresh plans (*OED*,
   platform, sb. 3a)
   them the English
2.2 'This scene creates a parallel to the start
   of the play, and so represents the English
   once again attempting to recoup loss in
   heroic ceremony' (Burns).

1–2 **The day ... earth** Bedford supplies the
   necessary information that dawn is
   breaking to an audience attending the
   performance, in all likelihood, in the
   afternoon.
2 **pitchy** black
   mantle i.e. a covering (not necessarily a
   cloak), as in 'So we, well covered with the
   night's black mantle' (*Richard Duke of
   York* (*3 Henry VI*) 4.2.22).
   overveiled covered (as with a veil)

TALBOT

Bring forth the body of old Salisbury,
And here advance it in the market place,   5
The middle centre of this cursèd town.
⌜Enter soldiers with the body of Salisbury, their drums
    beating a dead march⌝
Now have I paid my vow unto his soul.
For every drop of blood was drawn from him
There hath at least five Frenchmen died tonight.
And that hereafter ages may behold   10
What ruin happened in revenge of him,
Within their chiefest temple I'll erect
A tomb wherein his corpse shall be interred,
Upon the which, that everyone may read,
Shall be engraved the sack of Orléans,   15
The treacherous manner of his mournful death,
And what a terror he had been to France.   ⌜Exit Funeral⌝
But, lords, in all our bloody massacre
I muse we met not with the Dauphin's grace,
His new-come champion, virtuous Joan of Arc,   20
Nor any of his false confederates.

6 centre] F (Centure); cincture HATTAWAY   6.1 Enter . . . march] CAIRNCROSS (subs.); not in F
17.1 Exit Funeral] CAIRNCROSS; not in F   20 Arc] ROWE (subs.); Acre F; Aire CAIRNCROSS

5 **advance** raise aloft (on a bier)
6 **The . . . town** The scene has now moved
    from outside Orléans to the centre of the
    town.
6.1–2 **their . . . march** See note to 2.1.7.1–2.
8 **was** that was
10 **hereafter** future
12–13 **Within . . . interred** Hall tells us that
    Salisbury's body was brought home to
    England and buried in Bisham (Bullough,
    56).
15 **sack** i.e. the story of the sack
16 **mournful** causing sorrow
17.1 **Exit Funeral** Burns suggests that the
    body should remain on stage until the
    end of the scene as part of a pattern of
    'interrupted obsequies'.
19 **muse** wonder
    Dauphin's grace A phrase that can't be
    pinned down as qualifying exclusively
    either Charles or Joan. If it refers to
    Charles it is a sarcastic honorific (his
    grace the dauphin); if to Joan, as is a little

more likely, it is an equally sarcastic
metonym for 'graceful woman' (see The
Two Gentlemen of Verona 5.4.164).
20 **virtuous** (here used ironically)
    Arc F reads 'Acre' which is doubtless an
    error for 'Aire' as its later appearance
    (5.5.49) in F indicates. Both of these are
    versions of Holinshed's 'Are' (Bullough,
    75) which in turn is a mistake for 'Arc' (in
    all likelihood). Burns, however, retains
    'Air' ('Aire') in both instances largely
    for its 'connotations . . . in a relation to
    virtue and innocence'. Interestingly, Joan
    herself in history never used Arc or 'of
    Arc'; instead it 'is a fascinating even dis-
    turbing example of how culture works
    on history to recreate its protagonists in
    familiar forms. Arc, with its multiple
    meanings of "bow," "arch" and "curve,"
    places Joan at the centre of a web of
    imagery associated with the power of
    women since antiquity' (Warner, 198–
    9).

BEDFORD

'Tis thought, Lord Talbot, when the fight began,
Roused on the sudden from their drowsy beds,
They did amongst the troops of armèd men
Leap o'er the walls for refuge in the field.   25

BURGUNDY

Myself, as far as I could well discern
For smoke and dusky vapours of the night,
Am sure I scared the Dauphin and his trull,
When arm-in-arm they both came swiftly running,
Like to a pair of loving turtle-doves   30
That could not live asunder day or night.
After that things are set in order here
We'll follow them with all the power we have.

    Enter a Messenger

MESSENGER

All hail, my lords. Which of this princely train
Call ye the warlike Talbot, for his acts   35
So much applauded through the realm of France?

TALBOT

Here is the Talbot. Who would speak with him?

---

27 dusky] F; dusty ROWE

23 **drowsy** A transferred epithet: = bed on which they were drowsing.
27 **For** despite
28 **trull** whore
30 **turtle-doves** Emblematic of constancy in love (Tilley T624).
33 **power** armed forces (*OED sb.* 9).
34 **All hail** 'Often used in Shakespeare . . . to introduce an episode of treachery' (Hattaway).
34–6 **Which . . . France** Unlike Joan with the Dauphin the French Messenger has trouble picking out the leader of the English. His inability to do so anticipates Shakespeare's presentation of Talbot as the Countess of Auvergne's 'writhled shrimp' (2.3.22) in the scene that follows. Hattaway suggests that the Messenger's theatrical metaphor is intentionally reductive and insulting, as is, perhaps, his (pretended) inability to recognize Talbot.
36 **applauded** praised (*OED sb.* 4). It's an odd thought that the 'scourge of France' should be praised by (presumably) the French—but this is the language of feudal courtesy. Jones suggests that the theatrical metaphor 'marks a complete break in tone from what has gone before' (144), introducing a more relaxed atmosphere.
37 **the Talbot** Talbot is one of the few characters in the history plays who describes himself or is described by others in this way (see 2.3.15, 3.3.20, 3.3.31, and 3.4.13). The effect of the use of the definite article and the third person is to turn Talbot into a superior 'thing', a manifestation perhaps of warriordom, chivalry, reified feudalism. (The actor has to be careful, however, not to raise a laugh.) The Countess's use of the phrase at 2.3.15 is mocking. The closest the play comes again to this usage is when Burgundy refers to himself as 'the Burgundy' at 3.3.37, but Burgundy is not a name like Talbot. Abbott claims that the 'the' expresses notoriety (Abbott §92). See also *OED, the, dem. adj.* B. 10, especially c.
would wishes to

MESSENGER

The virtuous lady, Countess of Auvergne,
With modesty admiring thy renown,
By me entreats, great lord, thou wouldst vouchsafe   40
To visit her poor castle where she lies,
That she may boast she hath beheld the man
Whose glory fills the world with loud report.

BURGUNDY

Is it even so? Nay, then I see our wars
Will turn unto a peaceful comic sport,   45
When ladies crave to be encountered with.
You may not, my lord, despise her gentle suit.

TALBOT

Ne'er trust me then, for when a world of men
Could not prevail with all their oratory,
Yet hath a woman's kindness overruled.   50
And therefore tell her I return great thanks,
And in submission will attend on her.—
Will not your honours bear me company?

BEDFORD

No, truly, 'tis more than manners will.
And I have heard it said, unbidden guests   55
Are often welcomest when they are gone.

TALBOT

Well then, alone—since there's no remedy—
I mean to prove this lady's courtesy.
Come hither, captain.
          He whispers

                    You perceive my mind?

38 Auvergne] F (Ouergne)   54 'tis] F; it is MALONE   59 captain. *He whispers*] JOHNSON; minde. *Whispers.* F   mind?] DYCE; minde. F

41 **lies** dwells
43 **loud report** (a) of acclamation (b) of the cannon
44–6 **our . . . with** A not inaccurate description of Shakespeare's other major dramatic interest at this time: romantic comedy.
46 **crave . . . encountered** Both these terms suggest the importunity of sexual as well as social desire (see Partridge, 'encounter').
47 **gentle suit** courteous request
48 **Ne'er . . . then** then don't trust me when I

do (i.e. despise her suit)
48 **world** large number
49 **oratory** eloquence
50 **overruled** prevailed (*OED v.* 3)
52 **in submission** with due (courtly) deference
    attend on visit
55–6 **And I . . . gone** Proverbial: 'Welcome when you go' (Dent W259).
57 **remedy** alternative
58 **prove** test
59 **perceive my mind** understand me

CAPTAIN

I do, my lord, and mean accordingly.   *Exeunt*   60

2.3   *Enter the Countess of Auvergne and her Porter*

COUNTESS

Porter, remember what I gave in charge;

And when you have done so, bring the keys to me.

PORTER Madam, I will.   *Exit*

COUNTESS

The plot is laid. If all things fall out right

I shall as famous be by this exploit   5

As Scythian Tomyris by Cyrus' death.

Great is the rumour of this dreadful knight,

And his achievements of no less account.

Fain would mine eyes be witness with mine ears,

To give their censure of these rare reports.   10

    Enter Messenger and Lord Talbot

MESSENGER

Madam, according as your ladyship desired,

By message craved, so is Lord Talbot come.

COUNTESS

And he is welcome. What, is this the man?

MESSENGER

Madam, it is.

2.3] CAPELL; *not in* F 0.1 *of Auvergne*] OXFORD; *not in* F *and her Porter*] POPE; *not in* F 11 Madam] F; *not in* CAIRNCROSS desired] F; *not in* POPE

60 **mean** intend to act (*OED v.* 1f)

2.3 This scene, like the one following, has no basis in the Chronicles.

0.1 *Porter* In charge of the castle gate.

1 **gave in charge** ordered

6 **Tomyris** Herodotus recounts the story of Tomyris, Queen of the Messagetae, who avenged the suicide of Spargapises, her son, captured by Cyrus, King of Persia, by having Cyrus' head cut off after he had been killed by her forces. Herodotus writes: 'Tomyris filled a wineskin with human blood and searched among the Persian corpses for Cyrus' body. When she found it, she shoved his head into the wineskin, and in her rage addressed his body as follows . . .' (93). Tomyris' bloodthirsty revenge perhaps anticipates the severity of the Countess's plans for the 'scourge of France' (2.3.14), but Wilson asks a pertinent question about the refer-

ence: 'how many spectators understood it?' Emrys Jones notes: 'The mention of Tomyris here may have contributed to the theatrical or pageant-like associations of this scene' (145).

7–10 **Great . . . reports** Shaheen believes these lines to be patterned on the words of the Queen of Sheba at 2 Chronicles 9: 6: 'Howbeit I believed not their report, until I came, and mine eyes had seen it'.

7 **rumour** fame
   dreadful rousing dread

10 **censure** judgement
   rare remarkable

14–71 **Is . . . art** These exchanges seem to be based on a commonplace from an emblem book of the period, 'Praesentia minuit fama' = 'Fame grows less in presence'. (See Geoffrey Whitney, *A Choice of Emblems*, ed. H. Green (1866), p. 20.)

COUNTESS   Is this the scourge of France?
Is this the Talbot, so much feared abroad   15
That with his name the mothers still their babes?
I see report is fabulous and false.
I thought I should have seen some Hercules,
A second Hector, for his grim aspect
And large proportion of his strong-knit limbs.   20
Alas, this is a child, a silly dwarf.
It cannot be this weak and writhled shrimp
Should strike such terror to his enemies.

TALBOT

Madam, I have been bold to trouble you.
But, since your ladyship is not at leisure,   25
I'll sort some other time to visit you.

COUNTESS (*to Messenger*)

What means he now? Go ask him whither he goes.

MESSENGER

Stay my lord Talbot, for my lady craves
To know the cause of your abrupt departure.

TALBOT

Marry, for that she's in a wrong belief,   30
I go to certify her Talbot's here.
          Enter Porter with keys

21 silly] F; seely OXFORD   26 you.] F; you. *Going.* CAPELL   27 What . . . goes.] POPE; What
. . . now? | Goe . . . goes? F

15 **abroad** everywhere
16 **still** quieten
17 **fabulous** fictitious, a fable
18–19 **Hercules . . . Hector** Chosen by the
    Countess for their physical prowess and
    fabled size: their *large proportion of strong-
    knit limbs*. Burns notes that they also came
    to grief through women, but it is impossi-
    ble to know from the context whether
    Shakespeare had this fact in mind.
19 **for** because of
    grim aspect threatening appearance
    (aspect is accented on the second syllable)
20 **proportion** form (*OED sb.* 7)
21 **this . . . dwarf** 'The countess exaggerates
    greatly. Talbot was 80 years of age when
    he fell in battle, an examination of his
    bones, when they were exhumed in 1874,
    showed that he could not have been
    undersized' (Tucker Brooke). If Alleyn
    played Talbot he would in fact have
    loomed over the (boy) Countess because,

according to Stanley Wells, he was over
six feet tall (*Shakespeare For All Time*
(2002), p. 71). No doubt an Elizabethan
audience would have appreciated the
joke.
    silly feeble, helpless
22 **writhled** wrinkled. Burns notes that in the
    1977 **RSC** production of the play the
    Countess—played by an actress appre-
    ciably taller than Talbot—at this point
    glanced significantly down at Talbot's
    crotch.
25 **since . . . leisure** A courtly rebuke worthy
    of a romantic comedy.
26 **sort** arrange
30 **Marry** A mild oath, suitable in a lady's
    presence (originally an oath on the name
    of the Virgin Mary).
    in . . . belief under a misapprehension
31 **I . . . here** As the essential Talbot is defined
    by his freedom, his ability to move freely
    proves that he is really there; hence the

COUNTESS

If thou be he, then art thou prisoner.

TALBOT

Prisoner? To whom?

COUNTESS   To me, bloodthirsty lord;

And for that cause I trained thee to my house.

Long time thy shadow hath been thrall to me,   35

For in my gallery thy picture hangs.

But now the substance shall endure the like,

And I will chain these legs and arms of thine

That hast by tyranny these many years

Wasted our country, slain our citizens   40

And sent our sons and husbands captivate.

TALBOT Ha, ha, ha!

COUNTESS

Laughest thou, wretch? Thy mirth shall turn to moan.

TALBOT

I laugh to see your ladyship so fond

To think that you have aught but Talbot's shadow   45

Whereon to practise your severity.

COUNTESS

Why? Art not thou the man?

TALBOT

I am indeed.

COUNTESS   Then have I substance too.

TALBOT

No, no, I am but shadow of myself.

You are deceived, my substance is not here;   50

43 Laughest . . . moan.] POPE; Laughest thou Wretch? | Thy . . . moane. F

Countess is mistaken to think that he has departed.

31.1 **with keys** The ones the Duchess had asked him to bring her at the scene's opening. Presumably the Porter has locked the castle gate which is then broken down by the English soldiers at l. 59.

34 **trained** lured

35 **shadow** portrait, image
thrall slave. 'Does she not mean she has been torturing his waxen representation, according to the received custom in witchcraft of the time?' (Hart).

37 **the like** to be hanged

39 **tyranny** cruelty (*OED sb.* 3)

41 **captivate** into captivity

43 **moan** lamentation

44 **fond** foolish

49 **shadow** (a) delusive semblance or image (*OED sb.* 6a) (b) actor (*sb.* 6b). When Suffolk hands over Margaret to Henry in the opening scene of Part Two he produces another variation of this common topos: 'To your most gracious hands, that are the substance | Of that great shadow I did represent' (1.1.13–14).

For what you see is but the smallest part
And least proportion of humanity.
I tell you, madam, were the whole frame here,
It is of such a spacious lofty pitch
Your roof were not sufficient to contain't.   55
COUNTESS
This is a riddling merchant for the nonce.
He will be here, and yet he is not here.
How can these contrarieties agree?
TALBOT
That will I show you presently.

> *He winds his horn. Within, drums strike up; a peal of*
> *ordnance. Enter English soldiers*

How say you, madam? Are you now persuaded   60
That Talbot is but shadow of himself?
These are his substance, sinews, arms, and strength,
With which he yoketh your rebellious necks,
Razeth your cities and subverts your towns,
And in a moment makes them desolate.   65
COUNTESS
Victorious Talbot, pardon my abuse.
I find thou art no less than fame hath bruited,
And more than may be gathered by thy shape.
Let my presumption not provoke thy wrath,

---

59 That] F; That, madam, STEEVENS *conj.*; Lady, that KEIGHTLEY   59.1 *He*] OXFORD; *not in* F
Within] OXFORD; *not in* F   59.2 *English*] OXFORD; *not in* F

---

52 **humanity** humankind (here represented by the English army)

53 **the whole frame** (a) my entire body (b) the body of the army

54–5 **It . . . contain't** Talbot's hyperbole involving height responds to the Countess's 'Alas, this is a child, a silly dwarf' (l. 21).

54 **pitch** height

56 **riddling merchant** trader in riddles (but 'merchant' also meant 'fellow')
for the nonce as the occasion requires (a dismissive tag)

58 **contrarieties** contradictions (*OED* 2b). In '"Contrarieties Agree": an Aspect of Dramatic Technique in *Henry VI*', *SS* 37

(1984), 75–83, Roger Warren argues that exploiting contradictions is a structural principle in the *Henry VI* trilogy as Shakespeare 'dramatizes the expectations and disappointments, the switchback reversals, of the Wars of the Roses' (83).

59 **presently** immediately

59.1 **winds** sounds

59.1–2 **peal of ordnance** burst of cannon-fire, which 'probably suggests the gates are blown in' (Wilson).

62 **sinews** strength, energy, force (*OED sb.* 3)

64 **subverts** destroys

66 **abuse** ill-usage

67 **fame hath bruited** rumour has reported

68 **by** from

For I am sorry that with reverence   70
I did not entertain thee as thou art.

TALBOT

Be not dismayed, fair lady, nor misconster
The mind of Talbot, as you did mistake
The outward composition of his body.
What you have done hath not offended me;   75
Nor other satisfaction do I crave
But only, with your patience, that we may
Taste of your wine and see what cates you have;
For soldiers' stomachs always serve them well.

COUNTESS

With all my heart—and think me honourèd   80
To feast so great a warrior in my house.   *Exeunt*

2.4   *Enter Richard Platagenet, the Earl of Warwick, the*
           Duke of Somerset, the Earl of Suffolk, Vernon, and a
           Lawyer

RICHARD PLANTAGENET

Great lords and gentlemen, what means this silence?
Dare no man answer in a case of truth?

77 your] F1; our F2
  2.4] CAPELL; *not in* F   0.2 *Suffolk . . . Lawyer*] CAPELL (*subs.*); *Poole, and others.* F   1
RICHARD PLANTAGENET] OXFORD (*so throughout play*); *Yorke* F; Plantagenet ROWE   Great . . .
silence?] POPE; Great . . . Gentlemen, | What . . . silence? F

71 **entertain** receive
  as thou art as the great man you really are
72 **misconster** misinterpret. F's normal
  sixteenth-century form is retained for
  the metre: the accent is on the second
  syllable.
77 **patience** permission
78 **cates** delicacies
79 **stomachs** (a) appetites (b) courage
80–1 **With . . . house** Jones notes: 'The
  Countess episode brings to an end the
  long first sequence of *1 Henry VI*.
  Shakespeare's company may well have
  arranged an interval after it' (155).
2.4 This scene has no basis in the Chronicles
  and is an instance of what John
  W. Blanpied in *Time and the Artist in
  Shakespeare's English Histories* (London
  and Toronto, 1983) describes as one of
  those imaginatively conceived 'subhistori-
  cal hollows nonexistent for the chroni-

clers' (34). It probably takes place in the
garden—clearly marked in Prockter and
Taylor—of the Inner Temple, one of the
four Inns of Court in Fleet Street that
make up the 'official legal university of
England' (Ringrose, 1). The Inner Temple
and the Middle Temple were leased to students of the Common Law from the early
fourteenth century onwards. In 'Manuscript evidence for an earliest date of
Henry VI Part One', B. J. Sokol suggests
that the garden would have induced 'a
thrill of familiarity' in the London audience of the 1590s as it had just been created in 1591. He argues from this for a
date of 1591 for the play's composition
(*Notes and Queries*, 47 (2000), 58–63). The
scene dramatizes the beginnings of the
Wars of the Roses, the struggle between
the Houses of York and Lancaster, over an
obscure point of law, the 'case of truth' of

SUFFOLK

Within the Temple hall we were too loud;
The garden here is more convenient.

RICHARD PLANTAGENET

Then say at once if I maintained the truth;   5
Or else was wrangling Somerset in th'error?

SUFFOLK

Faith, I have been a truant in the law,

6 th'error] F;   error HUDSON (*conj.* Dyce);   right JOHNSON *conj.*

l. 2, and is crucial for understanding the
development of *The First Part of the Contention* [*2 Henry VI*] and *The True Tragedy
of Richard Duke of York* [*3 Henry VI*], as are
the events of Shakespeare's second historical tetralogy, from *Richard II* to *Henry
V*. The Wars of the Roses developed out of
the instability caused when Bolingbroke
seized the throne. Warwick solemnly
insists: 'And here I prophesy: this brawl
today, . . . Shall send between the red rose
and the white | A thousand souls to death
and deadly night' (2.4.124–7). Given the
importance of the white and red roses as
props in this scene, Oxford adds '*A rose
brier*' to the introductory direction.
Appropriately for the setting, the scene's
vocabulary is noticeably legal. This scene
tears away the veneer of courtly civility
that dominated the exchanges between
Talbot and the Countess in the previous
scene. It is a scene that most commentators most confidently ascribe to Shakespeare (see Gary Taylor, 'Shakespeare and
Others: The Authorship of *Henry the
Sixth, Part One*', *Medieval and Renaissance
Drama in England*, 7 (1995), 145–205;
167).

0.2 *Vernon* An invention of the dramatist,
he is a follower of York. It is he who
suggests—naively as it turns out—that
the dumb significants (the roses) be con-
strued as ballots in a vote as to who is in
the right in the case of truth.
    a Lawyer F's 'and others' is clearly impre-
cise. Presumably, the 'great lords and
gentlemen' are students of the law not
lawyers themselves, though perhaps
Vernon is.

2 **case of truth** 'While this is . . . left undefined, it is clear that the question at issue
was one affecting Plantagenet's reinstate-
ment or the succession to the crown, or
both combined' (Cairncross). Or perhaps

neither: we never do find out what the
particular 'case' is, and later remarks
stress its triviality (e.g. 4.1.145) or its
inconsequentiality (e.g. 2.5.45). The
scene might glancingly (because of contemporary sensitivities) allude to a
major cause of the Wars of the Roses: the
accumulation of land and thus power by
a few magnates. If, as Somerset later
claims, York was attainted, he cannot
hold land.

3–4 **Within . . . convenient** A slightly comic
non-sequitur considering Richard complains about 'this silence'. Perhaps the
actor playing Suffolk should convey an
embarrassed evasion of Richard's
question.

3 **Temple hall** The Middle Temple Hall of the
Inns of Court in Fleet Street, erected in
1572, and the location for the performance of numerous plays and masques at
this time including Shakespeare's *Twelfth
Night* (1602). 'Temple' refers to the
Knights Templar, owners of the site
1184–1313.
  were would be

4 **convenient** suitable

6 **Or . . . th'error** A difficult line that seems
to say the opposite of what it means.
Cairncross suggests that 'Or else' = 'in
other words', Hattaway that the line is
'jocular', Burns that 'wrangling' may =
'wrangling with'. Perhaps we should
simply emend 'error' to 'right' as Johnson
conjectured.
  wrangling (a) quarrelsome (b) disputing.
The young lords' rancorous exchanges
echo the insults traded between
Winchester and Gloucester. Henry's
politically blind attempts to resolve ani-
mosity by royal fiat, rather than by tough
leadership, lead inevitably to disaster.

7 **truant** poor student

And never yet could frame my will to it,
And therefore frame the law unto my will.

SOMERSET

Judge you, my lord of Warwick, then, between us.   10

WARWICK

Between two hawks, which flies the higher pitch,
Between two dogs, which hath the deeper mouth,
Between two blades, which bears the better temper,
Between two horses, which doth bear him best,
Between two girls, which hath the merriest eye,   15
I have perhaps some shallow spirit of judgement;
But in these nice sharp quillets of the law,
Good faith, I am no wiser than a daw.

RICHARD PLANTAGENET

Tut, tut, here is a mannerly forbearance.
The truth appears so naked on my side   20
That any purblind eye may find it out.

SOMERSET

And on my side it is so well apparelled,
So clear, so shining, and so evident,
That it will glimmer through a blind man's eye.

RICHARD PLANTAGENET

Since you are tongue-tied and so loath to speak,   25

8, 9 **frame** shape, bend

8 **will** intention, purpose (*OED sb.*[1] 5b)

9 **And . . . will** An ominous boast. Suffolk's disdain for authority emerges strongly at the end of the play; justice becomes an inevitable casualty of the civil war, prefigured by his disregard for law.
will desire, wish (*OED sb.*[1] 1a)

11 **pitch** altitude

12 **deeper mouth** more resonant bark. Gervase Markham in *Country Contents* (1615) writes: 'If you would have your kennel for sweetness of cry, then you must compound it of some large dogs, that have deep, solemn mouths and are swift in spending, which must (as it were) bear the bass in the consort; then a double number of roaring and loud ringing mouths, which must bear the counter-tenor; then some hollow, plain, sweet mouths, which must bear the mean or middle part; and so with these three parts of music you shall make your cry perfect' (7).

13 **temper** i.e. the capacity of a sword's metal to hold an edge

14 **bear him** carry itself

16 **spirit** Pronounced as one syllable.

17 **nice** fine, subtle
quillets verbal niceties, subtle distinctions

18 **daw** jackdaw, proverbial for its stupidity (Tilley D50)

19 **mannerly forbearance** polite unwilling-ness to get involved (said sarcastically)

21 **purblind** Although Shakespeare usually uses this word to mean 'thoroughly blind', it probably means 'weak-sighted' here as in *Venus and Adonis* 679. Somerset then goes one better in his reply when he argues that the truth, his truth, is so bright it would penetrate 'a blind man's eye'.

22 **apparelled** As opposed to being 'naked' for Richard.

24 **glimmer through** shine brightly into (*OED v.* 1)

25 **you** i.e. Warwick, Suffolk, Vernon and the Lawyer

In dumb significants proclaim your thoughts.
Let him that is a true-born gentleman
And stands upon the honour of his birth,
If he suppose that I have pleaded truth,
From off this brier pluck a white rose with me.   30
    He plucks a white rose
SOMERSET

Let him that is no coward nor no flatterer,
But dare maintain the party of the truth,
Pluck a red rose from off this thorn with me.
    He plucks a red rose
WARWICK

I love no colours, and without all colour
Of base insinuating flattery   35
I pluck this white rose with Plantagenet.
SUFFOLK

I pluck this red rose with young Somerset,
And say withal I think he held the right.
VERNON

Stay, lords and gentlemen, and pluck no more
Till you conclude that he upon whose side   40
The fewest roses from the tree are cropped
Shall yield the other in the right opinion.
SOMERSET

Good Master Vernon, it is well objected.

26 significants] F; significance MALONE *conj.*   30.1 *He . . . rose*] OXFORD; *not in* F   33.1 *He
. . . rose*] OXFORD; *not in* F   41 from . . . cropped] CAIRNCROSS; are cropt from the Tree F

26 **dumb significants** wordless symbols
28 **stands upon** sets store by
29 **suppose** judge
   pleaded put the (legal) case for
30 **white rose** Previously the badge of the
   Mortimers.
32 **party** side (*OED sb.* 5)
33 **red rose** Since the thirteenth century the
   red rose had been the badge of the House
   of Lancaster. The unified red and white
   rose became the Tudor emblem.
34 **colours** Warwick's use of the word combines two of a number of possible meanings: (a) deceptions (*OED sb.* 11) and,
   in view of what he says in the next line,
   (b) rhetorical embellishments (*OED sb.*
   13). He therefore seems to have decided,
   despite his earlier intention to remain
   neutral, that Richard's case is the case of

truth. Strictly speaking, white is not a
colour, so by picking the white rose he is,
in fact, avoiding 'colours'.
   colour semblance (*OED sb.* 11)
35 **insinuating** ingratiating
38 **withal** at the same time
   held was in
40 **conclude** decide (*OED v.* 12)
41 **cropped** plucked
42 **yield . . . opinion** concede the rightness of
   the other's opinion
43-4 **Good . . . silence** Somerset's forceful
   approval of Vernon's scheme suggests
   that he expects Vernon to be on his side,
   which helps to account for his threat
   against Vernon in ll. 49–51 when Vernon
   chooses a white rose.
43 **objected** brought forward, offered (*OED v.*
   3)

If I have fewest I subscribe in silence.
RICHARD PLANTAGENET And I.   45
VERNON

Then, for the truth and plainness of the case,
I pluck this pale and maiden blossom here,
Giving my verdict on the white rose side.

SOMERSET

Prick not your finger as you pluck it off,
Lest, bleeding, you do paint the white rose red,   50
And fall on my side so against your will.

VERNON

If I, my lord, for my opinion bleed,
Opinion shall be surgeon to my hurt,
And keep me on the side where still I am.

SOMERSET   Well, well, come on, who else?   55

LAWYER

Unless my study and my books be false,
The argument you held was wrong in law,
In sign whereof I pluck a white rose too.

RICHARD PLANTAGENET

Now, Somerset, where is your argument?

SOMERSET

Here in my scabbard, meditating that   60
Shall dye your white rose in a bloody red.

RICHARD PLANTAGENET

Meantime your cheeks do counterfeit our roses,
For pale they look with fear, as witnessing
The truth on our side.

SOMERSET   No, Plantagenet,
'Tis not for fear, but anger, that thy cheeks   65

---

57 law] CAIRNCROSS; you F   65 thy] F1; my F3

44 **subscribe** concede (lit. = sign at the foot of a document)
51 **fall . . . side** find yourself in agreement with me (i.e. by staining the white rose with the red of your blood)
53 **Opinion** public opinion, my reputation
55 **Well . . . else** 'The short line could emphasize Somerset's undignified, almost comic impatience' (Burns).
57 **law** Everything the lawyer says in these lines, as well as his profession, supports the justice of Cairncross's emendation of

F's 'you'. (Though at the expense of one of those clinching couplets—'you/too'—common in this play.)
59 **Now . . . argument** Somerset has lost the count of the roses but clearly has no intention of subscribing in silence.
60 **meditating that** contemplating that which
61 **a bloody red** The colour of Richard's spilled blood.
62 **counterfeit** imitate

Blush for pure shame to counterfeit our roses,
And yet thy tongue will not confess thy error.

RICHARD PLANTAGENET

Hath not thy rose a canker, Somerset?

SOMERSET

Hath not thy rose a thorn, Plantagenet?

RICHARD PLANTAGENET

Ay, sharp and piercing, to maintain his truth,   70
Whiles thy consuming canker eats his falsehood.

SOMERSET

Well, I'll find friends to wear my bleeding roses
That shall maintain what I have said is true,
Where false Plantagenet dare not be seen.

RICHARD PLANTAGENET

Now, by this maiden blossom in my hand,   75
I scorn thee and thy fashion, peevish boy.

SUFFOLK

Turn not thy scorns this way, Plantagenet.

RICHARD PLANTAGENET

Proud Pole, I will, and scorn both him and thee.

SUFFOLK

I'll turn my part thereof into thy throat.

SOMERSET

Away, away, good William de la Pole.   80
We grace the yeoman by conversing with him.

WARWICK

Now, by God's will, thou wrong'st him, Somerset.
His grandfather was Lionel, Duke of Clarence,
Third son to the third Edward, King of England.
Spring crestless yeomen from so deep a root?   85

---

72 roses] F; rose' DYCE 1864–7   76 fashion] F; passion POPE; faction THEOBALD   78 Pole] F (Poole)

68 **canker** blight, disease (caused by the caterpillar that feeds on rosebuds)
70, 71 **his** its
75 **maiden** White is the colour of virginity.
76 **fashion** i.e. of wearing red roses
    peevish obstinate, headstrong (*OED a.* 4)
79 **turn . . . throat** 'throw back (the slanders) into the throat from whence they came' (Sanders).
81 **yeoman** A man under the rank of gentle-

man who owns a small estate (*OED sb.* 4a). The jibe harks back to the forfeiture of Plantagenet's lands after Richard's father, the Earl of Cambridge, had been convicted of treason.
83 **grandfather** ancestor (*OED sb.* 3). The Duke of Clarence was actually Richard's great-great-grandfather.
85 **crestless** without a heraldic crest and therefore ignoble, cowardly

RICHARD PLANTAGENET

He bears him on the place's privilege,

Or durst not for his craven heart say thus.

SOMERSET

By him that made me, I'll maintain my words

On any plot of ground in Christendom.

Was not thy father Richard, Earl of Cambridge,   90

For treason executed in our late king's days?

And by his treason stand'st not thou attainted,

Corrupted, and exempt from ancient gentry?

His trespass yet lives guilty in thy blood,

And till thou be restored thou art a yeoman.   95

RICHARD PLANTAGENET

My father was attachèd, not attainted,

Condemned to die for treason, but no traitor;

And that I'll prove on better men than Somerset

Were growing time once ripened to my will.

For your partaker Pole, and you yourself,   100

I'll note you in my book of memory,

To scourge you for this apprehension.

Look to it well, and say you are well warned.

SOMERSET

Ah, thou shalt find us ready for thee still,

91 executed] F; headed POPE   102 this apprehension] F; misapprehension VAUGHAN *conj.*;
this reprehension THEOBALD

86 **bears him on** relies upon
place's privilege The use of weapons was
forbidden on the Temple grounds.
87 **craven** cowardly
88 **maintain** stand by
89 **Christendom** the countries professing
Christianity
91 **our late king's days** the reign of Henry V
92 **attainted** (a) subject to attainder (*OED*
ppl. a. 2) (b) tainted. Someone subject to
attainder was not permitted to inherit
lands or title, and Richard would be in this
category, according to Somerset, because
his father had been condemned by the
judicial process.
93 **Corrupted** The essence of the legal definition of 'attainder' = 'corruption' or the
stain of the blood of the criminal (*OED*,
attainder, 1).
exempt excluded
gentry rank of gentleman

96 **attachèd, not attainted** arrested but not
subject to attainder. As the next line
makes clear, Richard is splitting hairs.
Nonetheless, it may be that, as Richard
insists, his father was actually arrested
and executed summarily for treason by
order of Henry V, and not by a full bill of
attainder in Parliament. Richard implies
that perfect justice was not done. To
Mortimer he later describes his father's
execution as 'bloody tyranny' (2.5.100).
98 **prove on** demonstrate to
99 **Were . . . will** if events unfold the way I want
them to (which they do in *The First Part of the
Contention* [*2 Henry VI*] and *Richard Duke of
York* [*3 Henry VI*] until his death at the end of
Act 1 in *Richard Duke of York*)
100 **partaker** supporter
102 **apprehension** (pronounced as five syllables) opinion
104 **still** at all times

And know us by these colours for thy foes; 105
For these my friends, in spite of thee, shall wear.

RICHARD PLANTAGENET

And, by my soul, this pale and angry rose,
As cognizance of my blood-drinking hate,
Will I forever, and my faction, wear
Until it wither with me to my grave, 110
Or flourish to the height of my degree.

SUFFOLK

Go forward, and be choked with thy ambition.
And so farewell until I meet thee next. *Exit*

SOMERSET

Have with thee, Pole.—Farewell, ambitious Richard. *Exit*

RICHARD PLANTAGENET

How I am braved, and must perforce endure it. 115

WARWICK

This blot that they object against your house
Shall be wiped out in the next parliament,
Called for the truce of Winchester and Gloucester.
An if thou be not then created York
I will not live to be accounted Warwick. 120
Meantime, in signal of my love to thee,
Against proud Somerset and William Pole
Will I upon thy party wear this rose.
And here I prophesy: this brawl today,
Grown to this faction in the Temple garden, 125
Shall send between the red rose and the white
A thousand souls to death and deadly night.

RICHARD PLANTAGENET

Good Master Vernon, I am bound to you,
That you on my behalf would pluck a flower.

---

109 forever] OXFORD; for ever F   117 wiped] F2 (wip't); whipt F1; whipped BURNS   127 A]
F; Ten CAIRNCROSS *conj.*

---

105 **colours** i.e. the red roses
108 **cognizance** token, badge
111 **degree** noble rank
114 **Have with thee** I'll go along with you
115 **braved** scorned
  perforce of necessity
116 **object** bring forward as an objection
  against

117 **wiped** F's 'whipt' sits oddly with 'blot'
  but is just possible.
118 **Called . . . of** summoned to make peace
  between
121 **signal** token
124 **brawl** quarrel
125 **faction** splitting into factions
127 **deadly** death-like (*OED a.* 7c)

VERNON

In your behalf still will I wear the same.   130

LAWYER And so will I.

RICHARD PLANTAGENET Thanks, gentle sirs.

Come, let us four to dinner. I dare say

This quarrel will drink blood another day.   *Exeunt*

2.5   *Enter Edmund Mortimer, brought in a chair, and*
          Jailers

MORTIMER

Kind keepers of my weak decaying age,

Let dying Mortimer here rest himself.

Even like a man new-halèd from the rack,

So fare my limbs with long imprisonment;

And these grey locks, the pursuivants of death,   5

Argue the end of Edmund Mortimer,

Nestor-like agèd in an age of care.

These eyes, like lamps whose wasting oil is spent,

Wax dim, as drawing to their exigent;

Weak shoulders, overborne with burdening grief,   10

And pithless arms, like to a withered vine

---

132 gentle sirs] This edition; gentle F; gentle Sir F2; gentleman SISSON; gentlemen CAIRN-CROSS; gentles OXFORD

2.5] CAPELL; *not in* F   0.1 *Edmund*] OXFORD; *not in* F   3 rack] POPE; Wrack F   5 death] F; Death CAIRNCROSS   6–7 Argue ... Mortimer, | Nestor-like ... care.] OXFORD; *Nestor-like* ... Care, | Argue ... *Mortimer*. F   11 like to] F; look like VAUGHAN *conj.*; are like CAIRNCROSS

---

132 **gentle sirs** Richard is responding to both Vernon and the Lawyer so F2's 'sir' should be made plural.

132 **dinner** The main meal of the day, eaten at midday.

2.5 The scene takes place in a room in the Tower of London where Edmund Mortimer is imprisoned. It is Shakespeare's invention.

3 **new-halèd** recently dragged

5 **pursuivants** heralds

6–7 **Argue ... care** I have followed Oxford's reversal of these lines: 'Mortimer is more plausibly compared to Nestor than are his "locks" or "death"' (*Textual Companion*, 222).

6 **Argue** give evidence of

7 **Nestor** The oldest and wisest of the Greeks who fought at Troy. In Shakespeare's *Troilus and Cressida* he is treated with

much less reverence than he deserves, especially by Thersites who describes him as 'that stale old mouse-eaten dry cheese Nestor' (5.4.9–10).

age (a) my old age (b) a time

care sorrow, trouble (*OED sb.* 1)

8 **These ... spent** See 'My wasting lamps some fading glimmer left', *Comedy of Errors* 5.1.317.

wasting i.e. becoming less

9 **Wax** grow

exigent end, extremity (*OED sb.*[1] 1b)

10–12 **Weak ... ground** 'The lack of a principal verb in this sentence suggests that a line has been lost' (Hattaway). Perhaps so; but the very lack of an active main verb dramatizes Mortimer's weariness. See note to 1.3.28.

10 **overborne** oppressed

11 **pithless** without marrow, feeble

That droops his sapless branches to the ground.
Yet are these feet—whose strengthless stay is numb,
Unable to support this lump of clay—
Swift-wingèd with desire to get a grave,   15
As witting I no other comfort have.
But tell me, keeper, will my nephew come?

KEEPER
Richard Plantagenet, my lord, will come.
We sent unto the Temple, to his chamber,
And answer was returned that he will come.   20

MORTIMER
Enough. My soul shall then be satisfied.
Poor gentleman, his wrong doth equal mine.
Since Henry Monmouth first began to reign—
Before whose glory I was great in arms—
This loathsome sequestration have I had;   25
And even since then hath Richard been obscured,
Deprived of honour and inheritance.
But now the arbitrator of despairs,
Just Death, kind umpire of men's miseries,
With sweet enlargement doth dismiss me hence.   30
I would his troubles likewise were expired,
That so he might recover what was lost.
          Enter Richard Plantagenet

KEEPER
My lord, your loving nephew now is come.

MORTIMER
Richard Plantagenet, my friend, is he come?

---

19 to his] ROWE; unto his F1; his F2   32.1 *Plantagenet*] OXFORD; *not in* F   34 is he] F; is
CAIRNCROSS

12 **his** its
13–16 **Yet . . . have** 'None but Shakespeare
    could write elaborate verse like this in the
    early nineties' (Wilson).
13 **stay is numb** support is paralysed
    (Mortimer is lame)
16 **As witting** as if they knew
17 **nephew** See notes on Richard Plantagenet
    and Mortimer in 'Persons of the Play',
    pp. 91 and 92.
22 **his wrong** the wrong done to him

23 **Henry Monmouth** Henry V, who was
    born at Monmouth in 1387.
24 **glory** rise to power
25 **sequestration** imprisonment
30 **enlargement** release, freedom
31 **his** Richard's
34 **my friend** Probably directed at the Jailer
    even though Richard answers. (Reinforc-
    ing the sense of Mortimer's feebleness in
    old age.)

RICHARD PLANTAGENET
  Ay, noble uncle, thus ignobly used: 35
  Your nephew, late despisèd Richard, comes.
MORTIMER (*to Keepers*)
  Direct mine arms I may embrace his neck
  And in his bosom spend my latter gasp.
  O tell me when my lips do touch his cheeks,
  That I may kindly give one fainting kiss.   40
    He embraces Richard
  And now declare, sweet stem from York's great stock,
  Why didst thou say of late thou wert despised?
RICHARD PLANTAGENET
  First lean thine agèd back against mine arm,
  And in that ease I'll tell thee my disease.
  This day in argument upon a case,   45
  Some words there grew 'twixt Somerset and me,
  Among which terms he used his lavish tongue,
  And did upbraid me with my father's death;
  Which obloquy set bars before my tongue,
  Else with the like I had requited him.   50
  Therefore, good uncle, for my father's sake,
  In honour of a true Plantagenet,
  And for alliance' sake, declare the cause
  My father, Earl of Cambridge, lost his head.
MORTIMER
  That cause, fair nephew, that imprisoned me,   55
  And hath detained me all my flow'ring youth
  Within a loathsome dungeon, there to pine,
  Was cursèd instrument of his decease.
RICHARD PLANTAGENET
  Discover more at large what cause that was,
  For I am ignorant and cannot guess.   60

37 arms I] F; ~—~ BURNS   40.1 *He . . . Richard*] HATTAWAY; *not in* F   47 used] F; loos'd WARBURTON *conj.*

36 **late despisèd** recently treated with contempt
37 **I may** i.e. so that I may
38 **latter** last (*OED adj.* 3)
40 **kindly** (a) lovingly (b) as a kinsman
44 **disease** dis-ease, discomfort
47 **lavish** unrestrained, immoderate
49 **obloquy** slander

49 **set . . . tongue** made me speechless. But this is hardly the case; Richard spoke as volubly and vehemently as Somerset.
53 **alliance'** kinship's
55 **That cause** the same
59 **Discover . . . large** reveal more fully
60 **For . . . guess** A conventionally incredible admission of ignorance on Richard's part

MORTIMER
　I will, if that my fading breath permit,
　And death approach not ere my tale be done.
　Henry the Fourth, grandfather to this king,
　Deposed his nephew Richard, Edward's son,
　The first begotten and the lawful heir   65
　Of Edward, king, the third of that descent,
　During whose reign the Percies of the north,
　Finding his usurpation most unjust,
　Endeavoured my advancement to the throne.
　The reason moved these warlike lords to this   70
　Was for that—young Richard thus removed,
　Leaving no heir begotten of his body—
　I was the next by birth and parentage;
　For by my mother I derivèd am
　From Lionel Duke of Clarence, the third son   75
　To King Edward the Third—whereas the King

61 fading] F; failing HUDSON (*conj.* Walker)　71 Richard] F1; King Richard F2　75 the
third] F2; third F1　76 To . . . Third] F; Unto the third King Edward CAIRNCROSS　the King]
OXFORD; hee F; Bolingbroke POPE; he, Bolingbroke CAPELL

designed with the audience rather than
Richard in mind.

64 **nephew** (here) first cousin
　Edward's son Richard was the son of
　Edward, the Black Prince, eldest son of
　Edward III.
66 **of that descent** 'Edward's father was
　Edward II, his father Edward I; so Edward
　III is both the third Edward and the third
　king in that line of descent' (Burns).
67 **whose reign** i.e. Henry IV's
67 **Percies . . . north** Earls of Northumber-
　land. In the third scene of *1 Henry IV* Hot-
　spur, Sir Henry Percy, eldest son of the
　Earl of Northumberland, vividly describes
　the deposition of Richard, 'that sweet
　lovely rose' (1.3.173) by the canker,
　Bolingbroke, later Henry IV. In the play,
　the Percy family gives their support to
　Richard's heir, Mortimer. Historically,
　Sir Edmund's sister was married to
　Hotspur.
70 **moved** that moved
71 **for that** that
　young Richard was thirty-three when he
　was murdered.
73 **next** next in line to the throne
74–92 **For . . . suppressed** Mortimer's eluci-
　dation of the entwined genealogies of

his and Richard's families is made (even
more) confusing by wayward pronouns
and the fact that he is a composite character. Shakespeare's history plays often
indulge these lengthy genealogical justifi-
cations, the most notorious being
the Archbishop of Canterbury's mind-
numbing defence of Henry's claim to the
French throne in the second scene of
Henry V. In *The First Part of the Contention*
[*2 Henry VI*], following an even more
convoluted explanation by Richard of
his claim to the throne than this one,
Warwick asks: 'What plain proceedings is
more plain than this?' (2.2.53)
74 **mother** Historically, the mother of Sir
　Edmund, and grandmother of the 5th
　Earl of March. The Chronicles and
　Shakespeare again confuse two
　Mortimers.
　derivèd descended
76–8 **whereas . . . line** Henry IV was the son
　of John of Gaunt, fourth son of Edward
　III.
76 **the King** To whom does F's 'hee' belong in
　its unmetrical line? The only two plausi-
　ble candidates are Henry IV and Henry
　VI. Earlier editors (Pope and Capell)
　plump for Henry IV (Bolingbroke) and
　emend accordingly. Does l. 77's 'doth',

From John of Gaunt doth bring his pedigree,
Being but fourth of that heroic line.
But mark: as in this haughty great attempt
They laboùred to plant the rightful heir,   80
I lost my liberty and they their lives.
Long after this, when Henry the Fifth,
Succeeding his father Bolingbroke, did reign,
Thy father, Earl of Cambridge then—derived
From famous Edmund Langley, Duke of York—   85
Marrying my sister that thy mother was,
Again, in pity of my hard distress,
Levied an army, weening to redeem
And have installed me in the diadem;
But, as the rest, so fell that noble earl,   90
And was beheaded. Thus the Mortimers,
In whom the title rested, were suppressed.

RICHARD PLANTAGENET
Of which, my lord, your honour is the last.

MORTIMER
True, and thou seest that I no issue have,
And that my fainting words do warrant death.   95
Thou art my heir. The rest I wish thee gather—
But yet be wary in thy studious care.

RICHARD PLANTAGENET
Thy grave admonishments prevail with me.

84 Cambridge then—] BURNS; ~ , ~ F

however, indicate by its return to the
present that Mortimer has moved on to
Henry VI, the present-day king? If it does
it goes against the sense of 'Long after
this' (l. 82) which consigns the preceding
lines to the past. Oxford's 'the King'
fleshes out the line but retains the ambi-
guity. Burns's suggestion that Mortimer's
'doth' slips into the dramatic present and
is still about Henry IV is attractive.

79 **But mark** Perhaps a necessary admoni-
tion after the confusion of the preceding
lines.
   haughty exalted, noble (*OED adj.* 3)
84 **Earl of Cambridge** See note on Richard
Plantagenet in 'Persons of the Play',
p. 91.
   derived descended

86 **my sister** i.e. Anne Mortimer
88 **Levied an army** Hattaway notes that this
is not one of the charges brought against
the Earl of Cambridge in *Henry V* 2.2, but
his association with others is mentioned
in Holinshed.
   weening to redeem intending to reclaim
89 **diadem** crown
90 **the rest** i.e. the Percies
94 **issue** offspring
95 **warrant** assure
96 **The rest . . . gather** (a) I hope you gather
in the rest of your inheritance (b) I want
you to work out the further implications
of what I'm saying (namely, how to
achieve the crown)
97 **studious** diligent
98 **admonishments** warnings

But yet, methinks, my father's execution
Was nothing less than bloody tyranny.   100
MORTIMER
With silence, nephew, be thou politic.
Strong fixèd is the house of Lancaster,
And, like a mountain, not to be removed.
But now thy uncle is removing hence,
As princes do their courts, when they are cloyed   105
With long continuance in a settled place.
RICHARD PLANTAGENET
O uncle, would some part of my young years
Might but redeem the passage of your age.
MORTIMER
Thou dost then wrong me, as that slaughterer doth
Which giveth many wounds when one will kill.   110
Mourn not except thou sorrow for my good;
Only give order for my funeral.
And so farewell, and fair be all thy hopes,
And prosperous be thy life in peace and war.   *Dies*
RICHARD PLANTAGENET
And peace, no war, befall thy parting soul.   115
In prison hast thou spent a pilgrimage,
And like a hermit overpassed thy days.
Well, I will lock his counsel in my breast,
And what I do imagine—let that rest.
Keepers, convey him hence, and I myself   120

---

108 passage] F; passing CAIRNCROSS   113 be all] F; befall THEOBALD

---

101 **politic** prudent
104 **removing hence** i.e. dying
105 **cloyed** bored
106 **settled** firmly established
108 **redeem** buy back
111 **Mourn ... good** 'Mourn only for what
was good in me; but there is a possible
meaning of "Don't mourn unless you can
turn it to my advantage—posthumously,
that is, in revenge"' (Burns). And possibly: 'Do not mourn because you would
only be mourning for my good' (where
good = the peace that death brings).
except unless

112 **give order** make arrangements
115–29 **And peace ... good** John Blanpied
argues that these lines are part of the presentation of Richard as 'the first character in the histories to have an interior
life—a life, that is, separable not only
from the public view of him, but from the
prevailing rhetorical texture of the play's
nearly uniform surface' (*Time and the
Artist*, 36).
117 **overpassed** spent
119 **imagine** plan (*OED v.* 3)
let that rest leave that alone

Will see his burial better than his life.

                     Exeunt Keepers with Mortimer's body

Here dies the dusky torch of Mortimer,
Choked with ambition of the meaner sort.
And for those wrongs, those bitter injuries,
Which Somerset hath offered to my house,   125
I doubt not but with honour to redress.
And therefore haste I to the Parliament,
Either to be restorèd to my blood,
Or make mine ill th'advantage of my good.   *Exit*

3.1   *Flourish. Enter King Henry, the Dukes of Exeter and*
        Gloucester, the Bishop of Winchester; the Duke of
        Somerset and the Earl of Suffolk ⌈with red roses⌉; the
        Earl of Warwick and Richard Plantagenet ⌈with white
        roses⌉. Gloucester offers to put up a bill; Winchester
        snatches it, tears it

WINCHESTER

Com'st thou with deep premeditated lines?
With written pamphlets studiously devised?
Humphrey of Gloucester, if thou canst accuse,
Or aught intend'st to lay unto my charge,
Do it without invention, suddenly,   5

121.1 *Exeunt . . . body*] CAPELL (*subs.*); *Exit.* F 122 dies] F; lies WARBURTON 129 mine ill]
CAIRNCROSS; my will F; my ill THEOBALD

    3.1] F (*Actus Tertius. Scena Prima.*) 0.1 *Henry*] OXFORD; *not in* F *and*] OXFORD; *not in* F
0.2–3 *with red roses*] OXFORD; *not in* F 0.3–4 *with white roses*] OXFORD; *not in* F 1 deep pre-
meditated] F; deep-premeditated DYCE

121 **better . . . life** i.e. Mortimer's funeral will
    be more fitting for his rank than his
    imprisonment, but the phrase also picks
    up the notion of death as a comfort.
122 **dusky** extinguished
123 **meaner sort** i.e. the followers of Henry
    IV
124 **for** as for
128 **blood** hereditary rights
129 **ill** The either/or format of these lines
    makes Theobald's original emendation,
    as Tucker Brooke argues, one of his more
    convincing ones.
3.1 This scene takes place in Parliament in
    London, though historically at Leicester
    where the parliament of 1426 met (three

years before the relief of Orléans). Unhistorically, Henry VI plays the unavailing
peacemaker here, despite, as he puts it,
his 'tender years' (l. 71): tender, indeed,
as in real life he was five when this parliament met.
0.3 **with red roses** Oxford's helpful addition
    to the opening direction takes its cue from
    the lords' promise in the second act to
    wear their roses 'forever'.
0.5 **offers . . . bill** attempts to present a list of
    accusations (presumably to the King)
1 **lines** written statements (*OED sb.* 23a)
2 **pamphlets** documents
5 **invention** rhetorical composition
  suddenly extemporaneously

As I with sudden and extemporal speeech
Purpose to answer what thou canst object.

GLOUCESTER

Presumptuous priest, this place commands my patience,
Or thou shouldst find thou hast dishonoured me.
Think not, although in writing I preferred   10
The manner of thy vile outrageous crimes,
That therefore I have forged or am not able
Verbatim to rehearse the method of my pen.
No, prelate, such is thy audacious wickedness,
Thy lewd, pestiferous, and dissentious pranks,   15
As very infants prattle of thy pride.
Thou art a most pernicious usurer,
Froward by nature, enemy to peace,
Lascivious, wanton—more than well beseems
A man of thy profession and degree.   20
And for thy treachery, what's more manifest
In that thou laid'st a trap to take my life,
As well at London Bridge as at the Tower?
Beside, I fear me, if thy thoughts were sifted,
The King, thy sovereign, is not quite exempt   25
From envious malice of thy swelling heart.

---

13 the method . . . pen] F; my method penn'd CAIRNCROSS

---

7 **object** bring forward (against me)
8 **this place** parliament
10 **preferred** put forward
11 **The manner . . . crimes** Southworth suggests that this line echoes Marlowe's *1 Tamburlaine*: 'The country swarms with vile outrageous men' (2.2.22).
12 **forged** concocted lies
13 **Verbatim** orally, without a written document
   rehearse repeat
   method order and arrangement (of a composition) (*OED sb.* 6)
15 **lewd** wicked
   pestiferous deadly
   dissentious pranks quarrelsome, malicious acts
16 **As very** that even
17 **pernicious** wicked (*OED adj.*[1] b)
   usurer The Chronicles accuse Winchester of amassing a large fortune through embezzlement and through his activity as

a Southwark land- and brothel-owner. See note to 1.3.35. Of course, lending money at interest (usury) was officially forbidden by Christianity, but that did not prevent Winchester from lending vast sums, at high interest rates, to Henry V and the Council of Henry VI to support the French wars.

18 **Froward** perverse
20 **profession and degree** religious calling and rank
23 **London Bridge** Hall tells us that Gloucester accused Winchester of setting an ambush for him with armed soldiers at the Southwark end of London Bridge if he attempted to join the King at Eltham (Bullough, 50).
   Tower See Act 1, Scene 3.
25 **exempt** immune
26 **envious** evil (*OED adj.* 2)
   swelling proud (*OED ppl. a.* 7a)

WINCHESTER

    Gloucester, I do defy thee. Lords, vouchsafe

    To give me hearing what I shall reply.

    If I were covetous, ambitious, or perverse—

    As he will have me—how am I so poor?   30

    Or how haps it I seek not to advance

    Or raise myself but keep my wonted calling?

    And for dissension, who preferreth peace

    More than I do?—except I be provoked.

    No, my good lords, it is not that offends;   35

    It is not that that hath incensed the Duke.

    It is because no one should sway but he,

    No one but he should be about the King;

    And that engenders thunder in his breast

    And makes him roar these accusations forth.   40

    But he shall know I am as good—

GLOUCESTER   As good?

    Thou bastard of my grandfather!

WINCHESTER

    Ay, lordly sir; for what are you, I pray,

    But one imperious in another's throne?

GLOUCESTER

    Am I not Protector, saucy priest?   45

WINCHESTER

    And am not I a prelate of the church?

GLOUCESTER

    Yes—as an outlaw in a castle keeps,

    And useth it to patronage his theft.

WINCHESTER

    Unreverent Gloucester!

29 If I were] F; If CAIRNCROSS   31 it] F; that CAIRNCROSS   41 good—] F2; good. F1   45 Am I not] F1; Am not I F3   Protector] F; Lord Protector KEIGHTLEY (*conj.* Walker)

30 **how . . . poor** A laughable claim if the Chronicles are to be believed.
31–2 **Or . . . calling** Another disingenuous question: Winchester begins the play as a Bishop and ends it as a Cardinal.
31 **haps it** does it happen that
33 **preferreth** urges
35 **that** that which (Abbott §244)
37 **because** i.e. because he thinks that
   sway govern
42 **bastard . . . grandfather** Winchester was

born the illegitimate son of John of Ghent (pronounced 'Gaunt') by his mistress Catherine Swynford who later became his third wife.
44 **imperious** ruling (*OED adj.* 2)
45 **saucy** insolent
47 **keeps** lives (using the castle as a defence)
48 **to patronage** to give patronage to; to countenance, uphold, protect, defend (*OED*)
49 **Unreverent** irreverent

GLOUCESTER   Thou art reverend
  Touching thy spiritual function, not thy life.   50
WINCHESTER
  Rome shall remedy this.
⌈GLOUCESTER⌉   Roam thither then.
⌈WARWICK⌉ (*to Winchester*)
  My lord, it were your duty to forbear.
SOMERSET
  Ay, so the bishop be not overborne:
  Methinks my lord should be religious,
  And know the office that belongs to such.   55
WARWICK
  Methinks his lordship should be humbler.
  It fitteth not a prelate so to plead.
SOMERSET
  Yes, when his holy state is touched so near.
WARWICK
  State holy or unhallowed, what of that?
  Is not his grace Protector to the King?   60
RICHARD PLANTAGENET (*aside*)
  Plantagenet, I see, must hold his tongue,

---

49 reverend] F (reuerent)   51 Rome . . . this] F; This Rome shall remedy HANMER GLOUCESTER]
HANMER; *Warw<icke>*. F   Rome thither] F; Go thither HANMER   52 WARWICK] HANMER; *not
in* F   53 SOMERSET] F (*Som.*); *War<wick>*. THEOBALD   Ay, so] SISSON (*conj.* McKerrow); I, see
F; I'll see HANMER   56 Methinks] F; *To Winchester* Methinks HATTAWAY

49 **reverend** deserving of respect
50 **Touching . . . function** with regard to
  your role as priest (the implication being
  that he is scrupulous in name only)
51–2 **Roam . . . forbear** F assigns this line
  and a half to Warwick but it is clear that
  the half-line is part of the rancorous
  exchange between Gloucester and
  Winchester. F does not indicate to whom
  Warwick's 'My lord' is directed. Most
  editors conclude that it must be aimed
  at Winchester as Warwick is of
  Gloucester's party.
53 **so** so long as. F's 'see' would only make
  sense if Warwick in the previous line were
  addressing Gloucester, and could easily
  be a misreading of 'soe'. Somerset agrees
  with Warwick that Winchester's duty is
  to forbear, but only if he is not bullied into
  submission.
  overborne oppressed, subdued (*OED*)
54–5 **Methinks . . . such** Most editors con-

tend that Somerset's 'my lord' is aimed at
Gloucester. But why should Gloucester be
particularly religious (i.e. pious)? It seems
more likely that Somerset is continuing
to defend Winchester so that 'should
be' = is quite rightly.
55 **office** duty
  such i.e. prelates
56 **his lordship** Winchester
57 **plead** wrangle (*OED v.* 1b)
58 **when . . . near** 'when his status as a
  senior churchman is under such intense
  attack' (Burns).
60 **his grace** the Duke of Gloucester
61 **Plantagenet . . . tongue** Richard is following Mortimer's advice to be politic with
  silence (2.5.101). He plays this role in *The
  First Part of the Contention* [*2 Henry VI*]:
  'Then, York, be still a while till time do
  serve. | Watch thou, and wake when
  others be asleep, | To pry into the secrets
  of the state—' (1.1.248–50).

Lest it be said, 'Speak, sirrah, when you should;
Must your bold verdict enter talk with lords?'
Else would I have a fling at Winchester.

KING HENRY

Uncles of Gloucester and of Winchester,   65
The special watchmen of our English weal,
I would prevail—if prayers might prevail—
To join your hearts in love and amity.
O what a scandal is it to our crown
That two such noble peers as ye should jar!   70
Believe me, lords, my tender years can tell
Civil dissension is a viperous worm
That gnaws the bowels of the commonwealth.
  A noise within
⌈SERVINGMEN⌉ (*within*) Down with the tawny coats!

KING HENRY

What tumult's this?

WARWICK   An uproar, I dare warrant,   75
Begun through malice of the Bishop's men.
  A noise again
⌈SERVINGMEN⌉ (*within*) Stones, stones!
  Enter the Mayor of London

63 enter talk] F; entertalke HART; intertalk OXFORD 70 jar!] F (jar?); ~? BURNS 73.1–74 *A noise . . . coats!*] OXFORD; *A noise within* [*Gloucester's Men shout:*] . . . coats. BURNS; *A noyse within, Downe with the Tawny-Coats.* F 76.1–77 *A noise . . . stones!*] OXFORD; *A noise again* [*Gloucester's and Winchester's Men shout:*] . . . stones. BURNS; *A noyse againe, Stones, Stones.* F 77.1 *of London*] OXFORD; *not in* F

62 **sirrah** A patronizing form of address to an inferior or a child.
63 **verdict** opinion (*OED sb.* 3)
 enter talk converse
64 **have a fling at** speak aggressively to
65–8 **Uncles . . . amity** Henry's first words, religious, full of sweetness and light, and expressed ominously in the weak optative mood.
66 **watchmen** guardians
 weal (a) well-being (b) state
68 **love and amity** Hattaway notes that the phrase, recalling (anachronistically) the Book of Common Prayer, is appropriate for Henry.
70 **jar** quarrel
71 **tender years** Just how tender were they? Historically, Henry was nine months old when his father died, and would have

been five at the time of the quarrel between Gloucester and Winchester; it was Bedford, as Hall tells us, who rebuked the fractious lords (Hall, 130). We are to imagine Henry here as someone in his teens.
72 **viperous worm** venomous snake. Jones (124) suggests an echo here of Lydgate's prose tract *The Serpent of Division*, written during the first year of Henry's reign and printed in 1559, the first year of Elizabeth's, and warning England of the perils of division.
73 **gnaws . . . commonwealth** Pliny records the myth of the female viper killed by her young as they eat their way out of her womb at birth (Pliny, 10.82).
74 SERVINGMEN (belonging to Gloucester)
75 **uproar** insurrection (*OED sb.* 1)

MAYOR

O my good lords, and virtuous Henry,
Pity the city of London, pity us;
The Bishop and the Duke of Gloucester's men,   80
Forbidden late to carry any weapon,
Have filled their pockets full of pebble stones,
And, banding themselves in contrary parts,
Do pelt so fast at one another's pate
That many have their giddy brains knocked out.   85
Our windows are broke down in every street,
And we for fear compelled to shut our shops.

> *Enter in skirmish, with bloody pates, Winchester's*
> *Servingmen in tawny coats and Gloucester's in blue*
> *coats*

KING HENRY

We charge you, on allegiance to ourself,
To hold your slaught'ring hands and keep the peace.
Pray, Uncle Gloucester, mitigate this strife.   90

> ⌈*The skirmish ceases*⌉

FIRST SERVINGMAN Nay, if we be forbidden stones, we'll fall
to it with our teeth.

SECOND SERVINGMAN

Do what ye dare, we are as resolute.

> *Skirmish again*

---

82 pebble] F (peeble)   84 pate] F; pates POPE   *and Gloucester's in blue coats*] OXFORD; *not in* F *mish ceases*] OXFORD; *not in* F

87.1–2 *Winchester's Servingmen in tawny coats*
88 ourself] F1; ourselves F2   90.1 *The skir-*

78 **O . . . Henry** A significant word order
   indicating where the true authority lies.
80 **Bishop** i.e. Bishop's
81 **late** recently
83 **contrary** (accented on the second syllable)
   opposing
   parts gangs, factions
84 **pate** head
85 **giddy** mad with anger (*OED adj.* 1b)
86 **windows** shutters (*OED sb.* 1). The
   Mayor's use of 'broke down' suggests that
   'windows' = 'shutters'. Not all windows
   at this time were glassed, but all would
   be shuttered, especially in riot-prone
   London.
87 **shops** workshops; or perhaps as Stanley
   Wells suggests (privately communicated)
   the window-boards on which the wares
   were displayed.
87.1–3 *Enter . . . coats* A trickle-down effect

frequently found in Shakespeare's plays,
most famously in *Romeo and Juliet* with
the fighting between the servants of the
Montagues and Capulets.
90 **mitigate** calm down
90.1 *The skirmish ceases* The placing of this
   inserted direction is not insignificant. F
   has '*Skirmish again*' after l. 92 so at some
   point the skirmishing has had to stop.
   Some editors, following the example of F,
   do not insert a direction at all (e.g.
   Burns); some insert it after l. 89. This has
   the skirmishers stopping at the behest of
   the King. If they stop after l. 90 they do so
   at the behest of 'Uncle Gloucester' whom
   the King has called in to help. A performance that wishes to stress the King's
   weakness will follow the latter direction.
91–3 **Nay . . . resolute** In 'The only Shake-
   Scene', *Philological Quarterly*, 54 (1975),

GLOUCESTER

    You of my household, leave this peevish broil,

    And set this unaccustomed fight aside. 95

THIRD SERVINGMAN

    My lord, we know your grace to be a man

    Just and upright and, for your royal birth,

    Inferior to none but to his majesty;

    And ere that we will suffer such a prince,

    So kind a father of the commonweal, 100

    To be disgracèd by an inkhorn mate,

    We and our wives and children all will fight

    And have our bodies slaughtered by thy foes.

FIRST SERVINGMAN

    Ay, and the very parings of our nails

    Shall pitch a field when we are dead.

        They begin to skirmish again

GLOUCESTER   Stay, stay, I say! 105

    And if you love me, as you say you do,

    Let me persuade you to forbear a while.

KING HENRY

    O how this discord doth afflict my soul.

    Can you, my lord of Winchester, behold

    My sighs and tears, and will not once relent? 110

    Who should be pitiful if you be not?

    Or who should suffer to prefer a peace

    If holy churchmen take delight in broils?

WARWICK

    Yield, my lord Protector; yield, Winchester—

95 fight] F; sight VAUGHAN *conj.* 105 *They . . . again*] OXFORD; *Begin againe.* F 114 Yield, my lord Protector] F; My Lord Protector, yield POPE

47–67, Ronald Watkins remarks of these lines: 'One speaks unruly prose, the other steadfast verse: the difference is a subtle distinction of character' (51).

94 **peevish** senseless

95 **unaccustomed** (a) unusual (b) disorderly

96–103 **My . . . foes** An eloquent intervention of a Servant, unusual in this play, but not in later ones. See note to 4.7.17 and 5.6.25.

99 **ere that** before
    prince i.e. Gloucester

101 **disgracèd** insulted
    inkhorn mate scribbling fellow (ink-horn = portable container for ink)

104–5 **parings . . . field** nail-clippings will provide the defensive stakes for a battle-field. Perhaps, as Burns notes, an allusion to the myth of Cadmus and the dragon's teeth where 'nail clippings will spring up as new soldiers' (Ovid, *Metamorphoses*, 3.97).

105 **Stay** cease

110 **once** at once

111 **pitiful** merciful

112 **prefer** promote

Except you mean with obstinate repulse   115
To slay your sovereign and destroy the realm.
You see what mischief—and what murder too—
Hath been enacted through your enmity.
Then be at peace—except ye thirst for blood.

WINCHESTER
He shall submit, or I will never yield.   120

GLOUCESTER
Compassion on the King commands me stoop,
Or I would see his heart out ere the priest
Should ever get that privilege of me.

WARWICK
Behold, my lord of Winchester, the Duke
Hath banished moody discontented fury,   125
As by his smoothèd brows it doth appear.
Why look you still so stern and tragical?

GLOUCESTER
Here, Winchester, I offer thee my hand.
⌈*Winchester spurns Gloucester's hand*⌉

KING HENRY
Fie, Uncle Beaufort! I have heard you preach
That malice was a great and grievous sin;   130
And will not you maintain the thing you teach,
But prove a chief offender in the same?

WARWICK
Sweet King! The Bishop hath a kindly gird.
For shame, my lord of Winchester, relent.
What, shall a child instruct you what to do?   135

WINCHESTER
Well, Duke of Gloucester, I will yield to thee
Love for thy love, and hand for hand I give.
⌈*He takes Gloucester's hand*⌉

128.1 *Winchester . . . hand*] BURNS (*subs.*); *not in* F; *Winchester turns away* HATTAWAY
137.1 *He . . . hand*] OXFORD; *not in* F

115 **Except** unless
   repulse refusal (*OED sb.* 2)
117 **mischief** evil, harm
119 **except** unless
122 **his** Winchester's
123 **privilege** advantage (*OED sb.* 2d)
125 **moody** arrogant (*OED adj.* 2)

126 **it** i.e. the fact that he has banished
   anger
133 **kindly gird** well-intentioned, appropriate
   rebuke
135 **child** Perhaps, as Hattaway suggests, an
   indication that Henry was played by a
   boy-player.

GLOUCESTER (*aside*)

  Ay, but I fear me with a hollow heart.

  (*To the others*) See here, my friends and loving

    countrymen,

  This token serveth for a flag of truce   140

  Betwixt ourselves and all our followers.

  So help me God, as I dissemble not.

WINCHESTER

  So help me God. (*Aside*) As I intend it not.

KING HENRY

  O loving uncle, kind Duke of Gloucester,

  How joyful am I made by this contract.   145

  (*To Servingmen*) Away, my masters, trouble us no more,

  But join in friendship as your lords have done.

FIRST SERVINGMAN Content. I'll to the surgeon's.

SECOND SERVINGMAN And so will I.

THIRD SERVINGMAN And I will see what physic the tavern   150

  affords.

            Exeunt the Mayor and Servingmen

WARWICK

  Accept this scroll, most gracious sovereign,

  Which in the right of Richard Plantagenet

  We do exhibit to your majesty.

GLOUCESTER

  Well urged, my lord of Warwick—for, sweet prince,   155

  An if your grace mark every circumstance,

  You have great reason to do Richard right,

---

144 kind] F; and kind COLLIER 1858; most kind STEEVENS; gentle POPE 150.1 *Exeunt . . .
Servingmen*] CAPELL (*subs.*); *Exeunt.* F 156 An] OXFORD; And F

138 *aside* See note to 1.2.100–1. Although
  Burns suggests that this line need not be
  an aside, and that any production should
  be given the freedom to make it one or
  not, what Gloucester then says (138–42)
  contradicts l. 138 and is obviously spoken
  more openly and loudly. It seems to me
  that no one, not even Winchester, is
  intended to hear this accusation of
  hypocrisy.
140 **token** i.e. the handshake
143 *Aside* A case can be made for omitting
  this direction if Winchester means that
  he too will not dissemble. Or the aside

could, as Pope suggests, follow the speech
prefix. More likely, this half-line fulfils
Gloucester's prediction that Winchester
(like Gloucester) is negotiating with a
hollow heart.
145 **contract** (accented on the second
  syllable)
146 **masters** A polite, if condescending, form
  of address to social inferiors.
150 **physic** medicine
152 **scroll** document
154 **exhibit** submit for consideration (*OED v.*
  5a)
156 **mark** heed

Especially for those occasions
At Eltham Place I told your majesty.

KING HENRY

And those occasions, uncle, were of force.   160
Therefore, my loving lords, our pleasure is
That Richard be restorèd to his blood.

WARWICK

Let Richard be restorèd to his blood:
So shall his father's wrongs be recompensed.

WINCHESTER

As will the rest, so willeth Winchester.   165

KING HENRY

If Richard will be true, not that alone
But all the whole inheritance I give
That doth belong unto the house of York,
From whence you spring by lineal descent.

RICHARD PLANTAGENET

Thy humble servant vows obedience   170
And humble service till the point of death.

KING HENRY

Stoop then and set your knee against my foot.
    Richard kneels
And in reguerdon of that duty done
I gird thee with the valiant sword of York.
Rise, Richard, like a true Plantagenet,   175
And rise created princely Duke of York.

RICHARD DUKE OF YORK (*rising*)

And so thrive Richard, as thy foes may fall,
And, as my duty springs, so perish they
That grudge one thought against your majesty.

---

166 alone] F2; all alone F1   171 humble] F; faithful POPE   172.1 *Richard kneels*] OXFORD; *not in* F   174 gird] F (gyrt)

158 **occasions** considerations (pronounced as four syllables)
160 **of force** weighty
162 **restorèd . . . blood** 'reinstated in his titles and hereditary rights (as heir to the Earl of Cambridge)' (Sanders).
165 **As . . . Winchester** And so the arch-enemies, Gloucester and Winchester (reluctantly?), are in agreement over the disastrous re-establishment of Richard Plantagenet's power.
166 **true** loyal
172 **Stoop** kneel
173 **reguerdon** reward
177 **RICHARD DUKE OF YORK** So titled for the remainder of the play.
179 **grudge one thought** have one hostile thought

ALL BUT RICHARD AND SOMERSET

  Welcome, high prince, the mighty Duke of York.   180

SOMERSET (*aside*)

  Perish, base prince, ignoble Duke of York.

GLOUCESTER

  Now will it best avail your majesty

  To cross the seas and to be crowned in France;

  The presence of a king engenders love

  Amongst his subjects and his loyal friends,   185

  As it disanimates his enemies.

KING HENRY

  When Gloucester says the word, King Henry goes,

  For friendly counsel cuts off many foes.

GLOUCESTER

  Your ships already are in readiness.

                Sennet. Flourish. Exeunt all but Exeter

EXETER

  Ay, we may march in England or in France   190

  Not seeing what is likely to ensue.

  This late dissension grown betwixt the peers

  Burns under feignèd ashes of forged love,

  And will at last break out into a flame.

  As festered members rot but by degree   195

  Till bones and flesh and sinews fall away,

  So will this base and envious discord breed.

  And now I fear that fatal prophecy

  Which, in the time of Henry named the Fifth,

  Was in the mouth of every sucking babe: 200

---

180 ALL . . . SOMERSET] OXFORD; *All.* F   189.1 *Flourish.*] F; *not in* OXFORD   *Exeunt all but Exeter*] OXFORD; *Exeunt. | Manet Exeter.* F   195 festered] F (festred)   degree] F; degrees ROWE

186 **disanimates** disheartens

189.1 *Sennet* Set of notes on a trumpet as a signal for the arrival or departure of a procession.

192 **late dissension** i.e. between Gloucester and Winchester. The dissension between Richard and Somerset continues into *The First Part of the Contention* [*2 Henry VI*] until Somerset's death but at first takes a back seat to Gloucester and Winchester's vendetta.

193 **feignèd . . . love** An odd metaphor that relies on the association of 'ashes' with repentance and humility (see *OED sb.* 7).

194 **at last** eventually

  break . . . flame As it does symbolically with Joan's burning torch in the next scene.

195 **festered** gangrenous

  by degree little by little

198 **prophecy** Recounted by Hall (Bullough, 42–3).

That Henry born at Monmouth should win all,
And Henry born at Windsor should lose all—
Which is so plain that Exeter doth wish
His days may finish ere that hapless time.   *Exit*

3.2   *Enter Joan la Pucelle, disguised ⌈as a poor peasant⌉,*
          with four French Soldiers with sacks upon their backs

JOAN
These are the city gates, the gates of Rouen,
Through which our policy must make a breach.
Take heed. Be wary how you place your words;
Talk like the vulgar sort of market men
That come to gather money for their corn.   5
If we have entrance, as I hope we shall,
And that we find the slothful watch but weak,
I'll by a sign give notice to our friends
That Charles the Dauphin may encounter them.

A SOLDIER
Our sacks shall be a mean to sack the city,   10
And we be lords and rulers over Rouen.
Therefore we'll knock.
          They knock
WATCH (*within*)
          Qui là?

202 should lose] F2; lose F1 (loose)
    3.2] F (*Scoena Secunda.*)   0.1 *Joan la Pucelle*] THEOBALD; *Pucell* F   *as . . . peasant*] BURNS; *not in* F   *French*] OXFORD; *not in* F   10 A SOLDIER] OXFORD; *Souldier* F; *1 Sold.* CAPELL   12.1 *They*] OXFORD; *not in* F   13 *Qui là?*] F (*Che*); *Qui est la?* MALONE   *Paysans . . . France*] BURNS; *Peasauns la pouure gens de Fraunce* F; *Paysans, pauvre gens de France* ROWE; *Paysans, la pauvre gent de France* SANDERS

201 **Henry . . . Monmouth** Henry V
202 **Henry . . . Windsor** Henry VI
204 **hapless** miserable
3.2 This scene is unhistorical—'Chronology and facts are utterly scorned' (Boswell-Stone, 224)—but a similar stratagem to Joan's can be found in Hall in the capture of Cornill Castle by the English in 1441 (197). Joan was in fact burnt at the stake in 1431 and Rouen wasn't lost until 1449. The location is outside the town walls of Rouen. (See note to 1.4.) As with 1.4 it is possible, as in the Oxford edition, to make the successive alarums and excursions separate scenes, but it is closer to the spirit and pace of these encounters to meld these short episodes into one scene.

0.2 *four* The number in Fabyan; six in the other Chronicles.
2 **policy** stratagem
3 **place** arrange (*OED v.* 1b)
4 **vulgar** ordinary (not disparaging)
5 **corn** grain
7 **that** if
9 **That . . . them** 'The Dauphin is rather awkwardly dragged in here, so the audience may be warned of his proximity in ambush' (Wilson).
    encounter attack
13 *Qui . . . France* 'Who is there?' 'Peasants, poor people of France.' This is the only occasion when the play slips into French and is perhaps intended—in some bizarre fashion—to illustrate that the infiltrators

JOAN   *Paysans, les pauvres gens de France*;

Poor market folks that come to sell their corn.

WATCH (*opening the gates*)

Enter, go in—the market bell is rung.   15

JOAN (*aside*)

Now, Rouen, I'll shake thy bulwarks to the ground.

            Exeunt

     Enter Charles the Dauphin, the Bastard of Orléans, the
     Duke of Alençon and Reignier Duke of Anjou ⌈and
     French soldiers⌉

CHARLES

Saint Denis bless this happy stratagem,

And once again we'll sleep secure in Rouen.

BASTARD

Here entered Pucelle and her practisants.

Now she is there, how will she specify   20

'Here is the best and safest passage in'?

REIGNIER

By thrusting out a torch from yonder tower,

Which, once discerned, shows that her meaning is:

No way to that—for weakness—which she entered.

     Enter Joan la Pucelle on the top, thrusting out a burning
     torch

JOAN

Behold, this is the happy wedding torch   25

That joineth Rouen unto her countrymen,

But burning fatal to the Talbonites.   ⌈*Exit*⌉

15 *opening the gates*] OXFORD; *not in* F   16.1 *of Orléans*] OXFORD (*so throughout play*); *not in* F
16.2 *and Reignier*] WILSON; *not in* F   *and French soldiers*] CAPELL; *not in* F   20 specify∧] ROWE;
specifie? F   21 Here] F; Where ROWE   24.1 *Joan la*] THEOBALD; *not in* F   27 Talbonites] F;
Talbotites THEOBALD   *Exit*] CAIRNCROSS; *not in* F

are now talking 'like the vulgar sort of
market men' (l. 4). There is the occasional
French word elsewhere in the play: e.g.
'*seigneur*' (3.2.66), '*Cœur de Lion*'
(3.2.81), '*maréchal*' (4.7.70).

15 **market bell** 'The market bell would be
rung just before dawn, to warn would-be
traders of the opening of the market and,
most probably here, of a last chance to
enter the town before the gates were shut
again. With an irony typical of the play,
the good-natured leniency of the English
watch allows the French into the town

when strictly he should not, and they
then kill him' (Burns).
17 **Saint Denis** See note at 1.7.28.
19 **practisants** conspirators. The only
instance in *OED*.
24 **No . . . that** no way to compare with that
24.1 *on the top* See note to 1.5.4.
27 **Talbonites** followers of Talbot
Exit There seems no reason to leave
Joan standing on the back-stage gallery (or
in a turret above it) while the others speak on
the main stage. The burning torch 'stands'
in 'yonder turret', according to the Bastard,
no doubt placed in a sconce there by Joan.

BASTARD

See, noble Charles, the beacon of our friend.
The burning torch in yonder turret stands.

CHARLES

Now shine it like a comet of revenge,   30
A prophet to the fall of all our foes!

REIGNIER

Defer no time; delays have dangerous ends.
Enter and cry, 'The Dauphin!', presently,
And then do execution on the watch.   *Alarum.* ⌈*Exeunt*⌉
        An alarum. Enter Lord Talbot in an excursion

TALBOT

France, thou shalt rue this treason with thy tears   35
If Talbot but survive thy treachery.
Pucelle, that witch, that damnèd sorceress,
Hath wrought this hellish mischief unawares,
That hardly we escaped the pride of France.   *Exit*
        An alarum. Excursions. The Duke of Bedford brought
        in sick in a chair. Enter Lord Talbot and the Duke of
        Burgundy, without; within, Joan la Pucelle, Charles
        the Dauphin, the Bastard of Orléans, ⌈*the Duke of*
        Alençon,⌉ *and Reignier Duke of Anjou on the walls*

---

30 shine] F1; shines F3   34 *Exeunt*] CAPELL (*subs.*); *not in* F   34.1 *Enter Lord*] OXFORD; *not in*
F   39 the pride] F; the prize THEOBALD; being prize HANMER   39.2 *Burgundy*] F (*Burgonie*)
39.2–3 *Joan la Pucelle*] THEOBALD; *Pucell* F   39.3–4 *the Duke of Alençon*] HANMER; *not in* F

---

30 **shine it** may it shine
   comet See note to 1.1.3.
31 **A prophet to** presaging
32 **Defer** put off
32 **delays . . . ends** Proverbial (Dent D195).
33 **presently** immediately
34 **do . . . watch** kill the guards
34.1 *excursion* 'entrance at a run . . . Talbot
   is escaping from the town' (Burns).
35 **France** i.e. the kingdom of France.
   Although it was customary to refer to
   rulers of countries by the name of the
   country standing alone, the Dauphin is
   not acknowledged to be King of France
   until (perhaps) 5.5.123 (see note). Also
   see note to 2.1.8. Countries in this play
   are frequently personified, as is France
   again, for instance at 3.3.50–1.
38 **unawares** by surprise

39 **hardly** with difficulty
39.1 *Excursions* Running skirmishes
   between small groups of soldiers.
39.2 *The Duke . . . chair* This is an emblematic moment for the meaning of this
   scene. After the excitement of the *excursions* and slightly before—perhaps—the
   entrance of Talbot and the Duke of
   Burgundy, two attendants carry in the
   dying Bedford. Slumped in his chair, he
   represents visually the nadir of English
   hopes.
39.4–5 *Duke of Alençon* In the F direction
   only Reignier (who doesn't speak in this
   scene) is mentioned, not Alençon (who
   does speak). 'It is not at all likely that
   Alençon and Reignier were both on the
   walls . . . in addition to Charles, Joan, and
   the Bastard' (Tucker Brooke).

JOAN

Good morrow, gallants. Want ye corn for bread?   40
I think the Duke of Burgundy will fast
Before he'll buy again at such a rate.
'Twas full of darnel. Do you like the taste?

BURGUNDY

Scoff on, vile fiend and shameless courtesan.
I trust ere long to choke thee with thine own,   45
And make thee curse the harvest of that corn.

CHARLES

Your grace may starve, perhaps, before that time.

BEDFORD

O let no words, but deeds, revenge this treason.

JOAN

What will you do, good greybeard? Break a lance
And run a-tilt at death within a chair?   50

TALBOT

Foul fiend of France, and hag of all despite,
Encompassed with thy lustful paramours,
Becomes it thee to taunt his valiant age
And twit with cowardice a man half dead?
Damsel, I'll have a bout with you again,   55
Or else let Talbot perish with this shame.

JOAN

Are ye so hot, sir? Yet, Pucelle, hold thy peace.
If Talbot do but thunder, rain will follow.
    The English whisper together in counsel
God speed the parliament; who shall be the Speaker?

49–50 What . . . lance | And . . . chair?] POPE; What . . . gray-beard? | Breake . . . Death, |
Within a Chayre. F   56 this] F; his ROWE   57 Are . . . sir?] F; Are . . . hot? POPE   58.1 *The
English*] CAPELL; *They* F

40 **gallants** gentlemen (said ironically, see
    OED sb. 2)
41–3 **I . . . taste** 'The lines imply that the
    French may have disdainfully pelted
    the English below with the corn from
    the sacks they had carried in' (Hattaway).
43 **darnel** A weed—wild rye grass—with
    narcotic properties.
45 **thine own** your own bread
46 **harvest . . . corn** final outcome of your
    trickery
49 **greybeard** Prematurely grey as Bedford
    was thirty-six at this time.
50 **run a-tilt** joust (using the chair as a horse)

50 **within** in
51 **hag . . . despite** totally malignant witch
52 **Encompassed with** surrounded by
55 **Damsel** girl, country lass (said slightingly;
    see *OED* 2)
    bout (a) fight (b) sexual encounter
57 **hot** This word responds to both meanings
    of 'bout'.
57–8 **Yet . . . follow** Some editions render
    this line and a half as an aside, but it's
    clear that Joan intends her remark to be
    derisive and insulting.
59 **Speaker** (a) spokesman (b) Speaker (of the
    House of Commons)

TALBOT

   Dare ye come forth and meet us in the field?   60

JOAN

   Belike your lordship takes us then for fools,

   To try if that our own be ours or no.

TALBOT

   I speak not to that railing Hecate,

   But unto thee, Alençon, and the rest.

   Will ye, like soldiers, come and fight it out?   65

ALENÇON

   Seigneur, no.

TALBOT   *Seigneur*, hang! Base muleteers of France,

   Like peasant footboys do they keep the walls,

   And dare not take up arms like gentlemen.

JOAN

   Away, captains, let's get us from the walls,

   For Talbot means no goodness by his looks.   70

   Goodbye, my lord. We came but to tell you

   That we are here.   *Exeunt French from walls*

TALBOT

   And there will we be, too, ere it be long,

   Or else reproach be Talbot's greatest fame.

   Vow, Burgundy, by honour of thy house,   75

   Pricked on by public wrongs sustained in France,

   Either to get the town again or die.

   And I, as sure as English Henry lives,

   And as his father here was conqueror,

   As sure as in this late betrayèd town   80

---

66 *Seigneur*] HATTAWAY; Seignior F; Signior CAIRNCROSS; Seignieur OXFORD   muleteers] F (Muleters) 69 Away, captains] F; Captains, away ROWE 71–2 We . . . you | That . . . here] F; We . . . here BURNS 71 Goodbye] F (God b'uy) came] F1; come sir F2 but to tell you] F; to tell you but CAIRNCROSS 72 *French*] OXFORD; *not in* F

---

63 **Hecate** (pronounced as three syllables) goddess of the moon, night, and the underworld
66 *Seigneur* lord
   muleteers peasant mule drivers
67 **footboys** servants
   keep stay within
70 **goodness** good

73 **ere it be** before
74 **reproach** disgrace (*OED sb.* 2)
   fame reputation
76 **Pricked** spurred
79 **his . . . conqueror** Henry V captured Rouen in 1419.
80 **late** recently

Great Cœur de Lion's heart was burièd,
So sure I swear to get the town or die.
BURGUNDY
My vows are equal partners with thy vows.
TALBOT
But ere we go, regard this dying prince,
The valiant Duke of Bedford. (*To Bedford*) Come, my lord,   85
We will bestow you in some better place,
Fitter for sickness and for crazy age.
BEDFORD
Lord Talbot, do not so dishonour me.
Here will I sit before the walls of Rouen,
And will be partner of your weal or woe.   90
BURGUNDY
Courageous Bedford, let us now persuade you.
BEDFORD
Not to be gone from hence; for once I read
That stout Pendragon, in his litter sick,
Came to the field and vanquishèd his foes.
Methinks I should revive the soldiers' hearts,   95
Because I ever found them as myself.
TALBOT
Undaunted spirit in a dying breast!
Then be it so; heavens keep old Bedford safe.
And now no more ado, brave Burgundy,

81 Cœur de Lion's] F (*Cordelions*)   97 Undaunted] F1 ; Undaunting F2

81 **Cœur de Lion** Holinshed says that in his
will Richard I requested that his heart
should be buried in Rouen in recognition
of his love for its citizens (ii. 270). Richard
was known as the Lionheart from his fight
with a lion in the court of Leopold,
Archduke of Austria. He thrust his hand
down the animal's throat and tore out its
heart.
84 **regard** look after
87 **crazy** decrepit
90 **weal** happiness (*OED sb.* 2)
93 **stout** resolute
Pendragon Geoffrey of Monmouth's
Historia Regum Britanniae tells the story of
Uther Pendragon, King Arthur's father,
who, sick and in a litter, led his army
against the Saxons and defeated them

(Bullough, 79–80). Holinshed's *History
of Scotland* tells the same story about
Pendragon's brother, Aurelius Ambrosius
(Bullough, 79). In the *Historia* Pendragon
'called out in a merry voice: "These
marauders called me the half-dead
king, for that I was lying sick of my
malady in the litter, and so in truth I
was. Yet would I rather conquer them
half-dead, than be conquered by them
safe and sound and have to go on living
thereafter. For better is death with honour than life with shame" ' (*History of the
Kings of Britain*, trans. Sebastian Evans,
rev. C. W. Dunn (1958), Book 8, Chap. 23,
p. 181).
96 **Because . . . myself** because I always
identified with them

But gather we our forces out of hand   100
And set upon our boasting enemy.
    Exeunt ⌈all but Bedford with two attendants⌉
   An alarum. Excursions. Enter Sir John Fastolf and a
   Captain

CAPTAIN
Whither away, Sir John Fastolf, in such haste?
FASTOLF
Whither away? To save myself by flight.
We are like to have the overthrow again.
CAPTAIN
What, will you fly, and leave Lord Talbot?   105
FASTOLF
Ay, all the Talbots in the world, to save my life. *Exit*
CAPTAIN
Cowardly knight, ill fortune follow thee.   *Exit*
   Retreat. Excursions. Joan, Alençon, and Charles ⌈enter
   and⌉ fly

BEDFORD
Now, quiet soul, depart when heaven please,
For I have seen our enemies' overthrow.
What is the trust or strength of foolish man?   110
They that of late were daring with their scoffs
Are glad and fain by flight to save themselves.
   Bedford dies, and is carried in by two in his chair
   An alarum. Enter Lord Talbot, the Duke of Burgundy,
   and the rest of the English soldiers

101.1 *Exeunt . . . attendants*] BURNS; *Exit.* F; *Exeunt Burgundy, Talbot, and Forces; leaving Bed-*
ford under the Guard of a Captain, and Others CAPELL; *Exit with Burgundy and Forces into the town*
DYCE; *Exit with Burgundy* OXFORD 102 Sir John] F; John CAIRNCROSS 106 Ay . . . life] F; Ay,
| All . . . life HANMER 107.1 *Joan*] OXFORD; *Pucell* F *enter and*] MALONE (*subs.*); *not in* F 112
glad] F; fled VAUGHAN *conj.* 112.2–3 *of the . . . soldiers*] OXFORD; *not in* F

100 **out of hand** immediately
101.2 *Excursions* See note to l. 39.1.
102 **Fastolf** 'The name may have been punningly pronounced "Fast-off" ' (Hattaway).
104 **have the overthrow** be defeated
 again Boswell-Stone (208) suggests that
 perhaps Fastolf is referring here to the
 Battle of Patay where his original act of
 cowardice occurred (see 1.1.130–5).
106 **Ay . . . life** Although there is no connection between Fastolf and the later
 Shakespeare's Falstaff, what they have in
 common is an overwhelming investment

in self-preservation. Falstaff, however,
manages to preserve himself with much
more élan and less cowardice than his
(approximate) namesake.
108–9 **Now . . . overthrow** These lines echo
 Luke 2: 29–30 underscoring Bedford's
 sanctity: 'Lord now lettest thou thy servant depart in peace, according to thy
 word. For mine eyes have seen thy
 salvation.'
112 **fain** eager
112.1 *in* i.e. into the town of Rouen (via the
 tiring-house)

TALBOT

Lost and recovered in a day again!

This is a double honour, Burgundy;

Yet heavens have glory for this victory.   115

BURGUNDY

Warlike and martial Talbot, Burgundy

Enshrines thee in his heart, and there erects

Thy noble deeds as valour's monuments.

TALBOT

Thanks, gentle Duke. But where is Pucelle now?

I think her old familiar is asleep.   120

Now where's the Bastard's braves, and Charles his
   gleeks?

What, all amort? Rouen hangs her head for grief

That such a valiant company are fled.

Now will we take some order in the town,

Placing therein some expert officers,   125

And then depart to Paris, to the King,

For there young Henry with his nobles lie.

BURGUNDY

What wills Lord Talbot pleases Burgundy.

TALBOT

But yet, before we go, let's not forget

The noble Duke of Bedford late deceased,   130

But see his exequies fulfilled in Rouen.

A braver soldier never couchèd lance;

A gentler heart did never sway in court.

But kings and mightiest potentates must die,

For that's the end of human misery.   *Exeunt*   135

---

115 Yet] F; Let DYCE 1864–7   121 gleeks] F (glikes)

114 **double honour** There can be no honour
   in being defeated so 'double' must be a
   mere intensive here emphasizing how
   honourable it is to come back from a
   defeat to win a victory on one and the
   same day.

120 **familiar** A witch's attendant spirit, often
   in the form of a small animal. Sanders
   suggests that Talbot may have the devil in
   mind.

121 **braves** boasts
   Charles his gleeks Charles's taunts. See

note to 1.2.1.

122 **amort** lifeless, dispirited

123 **That . . . fled** (heavily sarcastic)

124 **take some order** make arrangements for
   governing

125 **expert** experienced

127 **lie** reside

131 **exequies fulfilled** funeral rites performed

132 **couchèd lance** lowered a spear to the
   position of attack (*OED v.* 7)

133 **sway** exercise authority

3.3   *Enter Charles the Dauphin, the Bastard of Orléans, the*
           Duke of Alençon, Joan la Pucelle, ⌈and French soldiers⌉

JOAN

Dismay not, princes, at this accident,
Nor grieve that Rouen is so recovered;
Care is no cure, but rather corrosive,
For things that are not to be remedied.
Let frantic Talbot triumph for a while,   5
And like a peacock sweep along his tail;
We'll pull his plumes and take away his train,
If Dauphin and the rest will be but ruled.

CHARLES

We have been guided by thee hitherto,
And of thy cunning had no diffidence.   10
One sudden foil shall never breed distrust.

BASTARD (*to Joan*)

Search out thy wit for secret policies,
And we will make thee famous through the world.

ALENÇON (*to Joan*)

We'll set thy statue in some holy place
And have thee reverenced like a blessed saint.   15
Employ thee then, sweet virgin, for our good.

JOAN

Then thus it must be—this doth Joan devise:
By fair persuasions mixed with sugared words
We will entice the Duke of Burgundy
To leave the Talbot and to follow us.   20

CHARLES

Ay, marry, sweeting, if we could do that

3.3] F (*Scoena Tertia.*)   0.2 *Joan la*] OXFORD; *not in* F   *and French soldiers*] OXFORD; *not in* F
18 sugared] F (sugred)

3.3.1 **Dismay** do not be dismayed
  accident unforeseen event (*OED sb.* 1)
3 **Care . . . corrosive** 'worry solves nothing,
  it only eats away at things (like rust)'
  (Burns)
  corrosive (accented on the first syllable)
  aggravating
5 **frantic** (a) proud (b) mad
7 **train** (a) the peacock's feathers (b)
  Talbot's followers
8 **be but ruled** only follow instructions
10 **cunning** skill
  diffidence lack of confidence, doubt

11 **foil** setback
12 **Search . . . policies** use your intelligence
  to think up unexpected stratagems
16 **Employ thee** get to work
18 **fair persuasions** good arguments
19–20 **We . . . us** The actual seduction of
  Burgundy by the French took place over a
  number of years and his defection had
  numerous causes. It had nothing to do
  with Joan.
20 **the Talbot** See note to 2.2.37.
21 **sweeting** darling, sweetheart

France were no place for Henry's warriors,
Nor should that nation boast it so with us,
But be extirpèd from our provinces.
ALENÇON
For ever should they be expulsed from France,   25
And not have title of an earldom here.
JOAN
Your honours shall perceive how I will work
To bring this matter to the wishèd end.
          Drum sounds afar off
Hark—by the sound of drum you may perceive
Their powers are marching unto Paris-ward.   30
          Here sound an English march
There goes the Talbot with his colours spread,
And all the troops of English after him.
          Here sound a French march
Now in the rearward comes the Duke and his;
Fortune in favour makes him lag behind.
Summon a parley. We will talk with him.   35
          Trumpets sound a parley
CHARLES ⌈*calling*⌉
A parley with the Duke of Burgundy.
          ⌈*Enter the Duke of Burgundy*⌉
BURGUNDY
Who craves a parley with the Burgundy?
JOAN
The princely Charles of France, thy countryman.
BURGUNDY
What sayst thou, Charles?—for I am marching hence.

30.1 *Here . . . march*⌉ F; *Enter, and pass over at a distance, Talbot, and his forces* CAPELL; *Here . . . offstage* BURNS   32.1 *Here . . . march*⌉ OXFORD; *French March.* F; *Enter the Duke of Burgundy and Forces* CAPELL; *French march* [*sounds offstage*] BURNS   36 *calling*⌉ OXFORD; *not in* F   36.1 *Enter . . . Burgundy*⌉ CAIRNCROSS; *not in* F

24 **extirpèd** rooted out, thrown out
25 **expulsed** expelled
30 **unto Paris-ward** towards Paris
30.1 *Here . . . march* 'The dramatists here demand an identifiably English march, but perhaps the differentiation is largely in instrumentation, with the English using the trumpet and the French the fife, in improvised tunes over the basic beat' (Burns). Hart suggests that the French forces would be 'lagging' because the music would be very slow. Both English and French marches are played off stage and Joan's careful descriptions of Talbot's and the Duke of Burgundy's forces suggest that no representatives of either army parade across the stage.
31 **colours spread** banners unfurled
33 **rearward** rearguard
   his his forces
34 **in favour** i.e. in our favour
37 **the Burgundy** See note to 2.2.37.

CHARLES

    Speak, Pucelle, and enchant him with thy words.   40

JOAN

    Brave Burgundy, undoubted hope of France,

    Stay; let thy humble handmaid speak to thee.

BURGUNDY

    Speak on, but be not over-tedious.

JOAN

    Look on thy country, look on fertile France,

    As looks the mother on her lowly babe   45

    When death doth close his tender-dying eyes,

    And see the cities and the towns defaced

    By wasting ruin of the cruel foe.

    See, see the pining malady of France;

    Behold the wounds, the most unnatural wounds,   50

    Which thou thyself hast given her woeful breast.

    O turn thy edgèd sword another way,

    Strike those that hurt, and hurt not those that help.

    One drop of blood drawn from thy country's bosom

    Should grieve thee more than streams of foreign gore.   55

    Return thee therefore with a flood of tears,

    And wash away thy country's stainèd spots.

BURGUNDY ⌈*aside*⌉

    Either she hath bewitched me with her words,

    Or nature makes me suddenly relent.

JOAN

    Besides, all French and France exclaims on thee,   60

    Doubting thy birth and lawful progeny.

45–6 As . . . eyes] This edition; *after line* 48 *in* F   45 lowly] F; lovely WARBURTON   46 tender-dying] F; tender dying POPE   48 foe.] POPE; ~, F   55 foreign] F1; common F3

40 **enchant** (a loaded term)
41 **Brave** worthy, excellent (*OED adj.* 3)
   undoubted certain
42 **let . . . thee** Compare Abigail to David, 'let thine handmaid speak to thee' (1 Samuel 25: 24). Joan's 'humble' intensifies the (tactical) self-abasement.
43 **over-tedious** too tedious (*OED*'s first example)
44 **Look on** 'In biblical sense of "look with pity on"' (Wilson).
45–6 **As . . . eyes** I have adopted Hattaway's hesitant suggestion that these lines should qualify 'Look on thy country, look on fertile France' and not come awk-

wardly after l. 48 as in F. The repetition of 'look[s]' suggests that these lines follow on from l. 44. (See note to 2.5.6–7.)
46 **tender-dying** dying at a tender age
47 **defaced** disfigured
52 **edgèd** sharp
   another way i.e. against the English
59 **nature** natural feeling (*OED sb.* 9e)
60 **exclaims on** denounces
61 **Doubting . . . progeny** 'An impossible inference historically, since the cause of Burgundy's alliance with England was his father's murder by Charles VII's men' (Wilson).
   progeny ancestry, lineage

Who join'st thou with but with a lordly nation
That will not trust thee but for profit's sake?
When Talbot hath set footing once in France,
And fashioned thee that instrument of ill,   65
Who then but English Henry will be lord,
And thou be thrust out like a fugitive?
Call we to mind—and mark but this for proof—
Was not the Duke of Orléans thy foe?
And was he not in England prisoner?   70
But when they heard he was thine enemy
They set him free without his ransom paid,
In spite of Burgundy and all his friends.
See, then, thou fight'st against thy countrymen,
And join'st with them will be thy slaughtermen.   75
Come, come, return; return, thou wandering lord,
Charles and the rest will take thee in their arms.

BURGUNDY ⌈*aside*⌉

I am vanquishèd. These haughty words of hers
Have battered me like roaring cannon-shot
And made me almost yield upon my knees.   80
(*To the others*) Forgive me, country, and sweet
    countrymen;
And, lords, accept this hearty kind embrace.
My forces and my power of men are yours.
So farewell, Talbot. I'll no longer trust thee.

62 Who] F1; Whom F2   78 I . . . hers] ROWE; I . . . vanquished: | These . . . hers F

65 **fashioned . . . ill** shaped you into an agent
of destruction
67 **fugitive** deserter (*OED sb.* 1b)
68 **Call . . . mind** let us remember
69 **Duke of Orléans** Charles, Duke of
Orléans, father of the Bastard of
Orléans, captured by the English in 1415, but not
released until 1440. See note in 'Persons'
and l. 72 n.
72 **set him free** Hall tells us in fact that the
ransom for the Duke of Orléans was paid
by Burgundy and amounted 'as some
writers affirm [to] four hundred thousand
crowns' (Bullough, 67). In history, this
transaction was politically complicated,
and had nothing to do with Joan, occurring nine years after her death.
75 **will** who will
slaughtermen murderers
76 **wandering** (a) erring (b) straying

78 **I am vanquishèd** Abrupt changes of heart
are commonplace and conventional in
Shakespeare's drama (and in Elizabethan
drama generally). In *The First Part of the
Contention* [2 *Henry VI*], for instance,
Clifford provides a comic, though sinister,
variation in his ability to change the
hearts and minds of Cade's followers in
the space of a few lines (4.7.189–207).
'*They forsake Cade*' (4.7.207.1) is the off-
hand direction. Hall notes however: 'And
so . . . without long argument or pro-
longing of time, he [Burgundy] took a
determinate peace' (176). The character
anticipates history by several years since
Joan died in 1431 and the real-life
Burgundy began to change sides in
1435.
haughty lofty
83 **power** army

JOAN

    Done like a Frenchman—⌈*aside*⌉ turn and turn again.   85

CHARLES

    Welcome, brave Duke. Thy friendship makes us fresh.

BASTARD

    And doth beget new courage in our breasts.

ALENÇON   90

    Pucelle hath bravely played her part in this,

    And doth deserve a coronet of gold.

CHARLES

    Now let us on, my lords, and join our powers,

    And seek how we may prejudice the foe.   *Exeunt*

3.4   ⌈*Flourish.*⌉ *Enter King Henry, the Duke of Gloucester,*
       the Bishop of Winchester, the Duke of Exeter; Richard
       Duke of York, the Earl of Warwick, and Vernon ⌈*with*
       white roses⌉; *the Earl of Suffolk, the Duke of Somerset,*
       and Basset ⌈*with red roses*⌉. *To them, with his soldiers,*
       enter Lord Talbot

TALBOT

    My gracious prince and honourable peers,

    Hearing of your arrival in this realm

    I have a while given truce unto my wars

    To do my duty to my sovereign;

    In sign whereof, this arm—that hath reclaimed   5

    To your obedience fifty fortresses,

    Twelve cities, and seven walled towns of strength,

    Beside five hundred prisoners of esteem—

    Lets fall his sword before your highness' feet,

    And with submissive loyalty of heart   10

    Ascribes the glory of his conquest got

---

90 Now . . . powers,] POPE; Now . . . Lords, | And . . . Powers, F

   3.4] F (*Scoena Quarta.*) 0.1 *Flourish.*] OXFORD; *not in* F 0.1 *Henry*] OXFORD; *not in* F
0.2 *Richard Duke of*] OXFORD; *not in* F 0.3 *with white roses*] OXFORD; *not in* F 0.5 *with red
roses*] OXFORD; *not in* F 0.6 *enter Lord*] OXFORD; *not in* F

85 **Done . . . again** Should the 'aside' come in the middle of the line, or at the beginning, or, following F, be dispensed with? Dyce maximizes the line's function by inserting the stage direction in the middle. No matter where it is, or whether the line arouses controversy.

86 **makes us fresh** renews us

88 **bravely** (a) courageously (b) magnificently

91 **prejudice** harm

3.4 This scene has no basis in the Chronicles.

0.1 *Flourish* See note at 1.2.0.1.

0.5 *Basset* An invention of the dramatist, he is the Lancastrian counterpart of Vernon.

5 **reclaimed** subdued (*OED v.* 3)

9, 11 **his** its (i.e. his arm)

First to my God, and next unto your grace.
⌈*He kneels*⌉
KING HENRY

Is this the Lord Talbot, uncle Gloucester,
That hath so long been resident in France?
GLOUCESTER

Yes, if it please your majesty, my liege.   15
KING HENRY (*to Talbot*)

Welcome, brave captain and victorious lord.
When I was young—as yet I am not old—
I do remember how my father said
A stouter champion never handled sword.
Long since we were resolvèd of your truth,   20
Your faithful service and your toil in war,
Yet never have you tasted our reward,
Or been reguerdoned with so much as thanks,
Because till now we never saw your face.
Therefore stand up, and for these good deserts   25
We here create you Earl of Shrewsbury,
And in our coronation take your place.
            Sennet. Flourish. Exeunt all but Vernon and Basset
VERNON

Now sir, to you that were so hot at sea,
Disgracing of these colours that I wear
In honour of my noble lord of York—   30
Dar'st thou maintain the former words thou spak'st?

12.1 *He kneels*] WILSON (*subs.*); *not in* F; *after line* 9 *in* BURNS   13 the Lord Talbot] F; the Talbot
CAPELL; the fam'd Lord Talbot ROWE   20 were] F1; have F3   27.1 *Flourish.*] F; *not in* OXFORD
Exeunt all but] F (*Exeunt. Manet.*)

13–15 **Is . . . liege** Later Shakespeare would
    probably have dropped these lines and
    begun with l. 16 'Welcome, brave captain
    . . .'. After Talbot's lengthy description of
    his military feats Henry's question to
    Gloucester might well raise an unfortu-
    nate laugh from an audience.
18–19 **I . . . sword** As Henry VI was only nine
    months old when his father died it is
    impossible for him to remember anything
    that his father said to him.
19 **stouter** more valiant
20 **we** (the royal plural)
    resolvèd convinced, satisfied (*OED ppl. a.* 2)
    truth loyalty

23 **reguerdoned** rewarded
26 **We . . . Shrewsbury**   'Talbot   was . . .
    ennobled in 1442, eleven years after the
    coronation of Henry, to which the king
    invites him in the next line' (Tucker
    Brooke). Jones argues that an Elizabethan
    audience's awareness of Talbot's succes-
    sor 'would have given an extra force to
    the oddly brief scene in which Henry
    VI creates Talbot Earl of Shrewsbury'
    (120).
28 **hot** angry
29 **Disgracing of** insulting, mocking
    colours insignia, emblems (i.e. the white
    rose)

BASSET

Yes, sir, as well as you dare patronage
The envious barking of your saucy tongue
Against my lord the Duke of Somerset.

VERNON

Sirrah, thy lord I honour as he is.   35

BASSET

Why, what is he?—as good a man as York.

VERNON

Hark ye, not so; in witness, take ye that.
    Vernon strikes him

BASSET

Villain, thou know'st the law of arms is such
That whoso draws a sword 'tis present death,
Or else this blow should broach thy dearest blood.   40
But I'll unto his majesty, and crave
I may have liberty to venge this wrong,
When thou shalt see I'll meet thee to thy cost.

VERNON

Well, miscreant, I'll be there as soon as you,
And after meet you sooner than you would.   *Exeunt*   45

4.1   ⌜*Flourish.* ⌝ *Enter King Henry, the Duke of Gloucester,*
    the Bishop of Winchester, the Duke of Exeter; Richard
    Duke of York, and the Earl of Warwick ⌜*with white*
    roses⌝; *the Earl of Suffolk and the Duke of Somerset*
    ⌜*with red roses*⌝; *Lord Talbot, and the Governor of Paris*

GLOUCESTER

Lord Bishop, set the crown upon his head.

34 my lord] F1; *not in* F2   37 ye] F1; you F3   37.1 *Vernon*] OXFORD; *not in* F   38 know'st] F
(knowest)   39 'tis present] F; in th' presence 'tis WARBURTON

4.1] F (*Actus Quartus. Scena Prima.*)   0.1 *Flourish.*] OXFORD; *not in* F   0.1 *Henry*] OXFORD;
not in F   0.2 *Duke of York*] OXFORD; *not in* F   0.3 *with white roses*] OXFORD; *not in* F   0.5 *with
red roses*] OXFORD; *not in* F   0.5 *of Paris*] OXFORD; *not in* F

32 **patronage** uphold, defend. See note to
    3.1.48.
33 **envious** malicious
35 **Sirrah** (contemptuous usage)
    as for what
38 **law of arms** Yet another occasion ⌜see
    1.3.77, 2.4.86, 3.1.8, 4.1.137–8) when
    place or circumstances prevents an alter-
    cation from becoming physical. In this
    instance, the sanctity of a royal palace

and/or the restrictions in place at a time of
war stay Vernon's hand.
39 **present** immediate
40 **broach** tap (as of a barrel)
42 **liberty** permission
44 **miscreant** wrongdoer
45 **after** i.e. 'after the King's permission to
    duel has been granted' (Sanders).
4.1 Henry's coronation in Paris. Historically,
    the coronation was a sumptuous affair

WINCHESTER

God save King Henry of that name the sixth!
Winchester crowns the King

GLOUCESTER

Now, Governor of Paris, take your oath
That you elect no other king but him;
Esteem none friends but such as are his friends,   5
And none your foes but such as shall pretend
Malicious practices against his state.
This shall ye do, so help you righteous God.
Enter Sir John Fastolf with a letter

FASTOLF

My gracious sovereign, as I rode from Calais
To haste unto your coronation,   10
A letter was delivered to my hands,
⌈*He presents the letter*⌉
Writ to your grace from the Duke of Burgundy.

TALBOT

Shame to the Duke of Burgundy and thee!
I vowed, base knight, when I did meet thee next,

2.1 *Winchester . . . King*] OXFORD; *not in* F   3 oath] F; oath, *Governor kneels* CAPELL   8 God.]
F; ~ *Exeunt* Governor *and Train* CAPELL   8.1 *Sir John*] OXFORD; *not in* F   *with a letter*] OXFORD;
not in F   11.1 *He . . . letter*] OXFORD; *not in* F   12 the Duke] F (th'Duke)   13 thee] F (the)

---

belying its cursory treatment in the
scene's opening lines (though any production could linger on the visual spectacle). Commentators note that this
fourth act, like the first and third, begins
with a ceremony that is twice interrupted,
part of a pattern in the play of chaos and
disintegration. As usual, Shakespeare is
not constrained by historical fact: 'Historically Talbot, who had been captured at
the Battle of Patay, was still in French
hands; Exeter was dead; and Gloucester
was in England' (Sanders).

0.5 *Governor of Paris* A non-speaking
part, he accepts the dominion of an
English king over France on behalf of
France's most important city. (In the
BBC production he just avoids being
non-speaking by repeating Gloucester's
last line with the appropriate change of
pronouns.)

1 **Lord Bishop** If Winchester is by now a
Cardinal (as he was in history) then

Gloucester's mode of address is deliberately insulting, but it is more likely
that the confusion continues to be
inadvertent.

4 **elect** acknowledge
6 **pretend** intend
7 **practices** plots
8 **This . . . God** Many editions, beginning
with Capell, have the Governor exit at this
line. But there is no need to get rid of
him; Fastolf's interruption is more effective dramatically if the Governor stays,
especially if he is in the middle of repeating Gloucester's final line. See note to 0.5
above.

11.1 **He . . . letter** Appropriately enough
the letter from a turncoat is delivered by
a coward (not until 1435, however, in
history.)

To tear the Garter from thy craven's leg,   15
    ⌈*He tears it off*⌉
Which I have done because unworthily
Thou wast installèd in that high degree.—
Pardon me, princely Henry and the rest.
This dastard at the Battle of Patay
When but in all I was six thousand strong,   20
And that the French were almost ten to one,
Before we met, or that a stroke was given,
Like to a trusty squire did run away;
In which assault we lost twelve hundred men.
Myself and divers gentlemen beside   25
Were there surprised and taken prisoners.
Then judge, great lords, if I have done amiss,
Or whether that such cowards ought to wear
This ornament of knighthood: yea or no?
GLOUCESTER
To say the truth, this fact was infamous   30

15.1 *He . . . off*] CAPELL; *not in* F; *after line* 13 *in* BURNS   19 Patay] MALONE (*conj.* Capell); *Poictiers* F

---

15 **Garter** Part of the insignia of the Order of the Garter, the highest degree of English knighthood, worn just below the left knee. The same king who began the Hundred Years War against the French, Edward III, created the Order of the Knights of the Garter around 1348 (though Holinshed gives 1344), after Edward's return in late 1347 from his victorious campaign in France. (See Juliet Vale, *Edward III and Chivalry: Chivalric Society and its Context, 1270–1350* (1982), pp. 76–91, and D'A. J. Dacre Boulton, *The Knights of the Crown: The Monarchical Orders of Knighthood in Later Medieval Europe, 1325–1520* (1987), pp. 101–17).
   craven's coward's
15.1 *He . . . off* Historically, it was Bedford who stripped Fastolf of his Garter; in the play Bedford dies in Act 3. Burns suggests that Talbot's 'have done' in l. 16 might refer to his oath to remove the Garter rather than to the act of its removal. Were that the case, then the Garter could be removed after l. 45 at the King's instigation rather than at Talbot's. But Talbot's

apology in l. 18, and in l. 27, and the lack of any indication in l. 45 of an act of removal suggest that the action occurs here. Moreover it is appropriate that the play's symbolic hero should discipline the play's coward—appropriate too that the weak king should be denied any direct involvement in such a symbolic act of power.

17 **installèd** 'The knights of the garter were (and are) literally "installed", in that they are awarded the right to a "stall", or official seat' in St George's Chapel in Windsor Castle (Burns).

19 **dastard** contemptible coward
   Patay F's 'Poictiers' is an ironic error, Burns suggests, as it was the site of an English victory under Edward III. An account of the Battle of Patay (though unnamed) is given by the Messenger at 1.1.110–40. Talbot tells us his feelings about Fastolf at 1.5.13–15.

20 **but . . . was** I was in all only
23 **trusty squire** (said sarcastically)
25 **divers** various
30 **fact** crime (i.e. Fastolf's cowardice)

And ill beseeming any common man,
Much more a knight, a captain, and a leader.

TALBOT

When first this order was ordained, my lords,
Knights of the Garter were of noble birth,
Valiant and virtuous, full of haughty courage,   35
Such as were grown to credit by the wars;
Not fearing death nor shrinking for distress,
But always resolute in most extremes.
He then that is not furnished in this sort
Doth but usurp the sacred name of knight,   40
Profaning this most honourable order,
And should—if I were worthy to be judge—
Be quite degraded, like a hedge-born swain
That doth presume to boast of gentle blood.

KING HENRY (*to Fastolf*)

Stain to thy countrymen, thou hear'st thy doom.   45
Be packing, therefore, thou that wast a knight.
Henceforth we banish thee on pain of death.   *Exit Fastolf*
And now, my lord Protector, view the letter
Sent from our uncle, Duke of Burgundy.

GLOUCESTER

What means his grace that he has changed his style?   50
No more but plain and bluntly 'To the King'?
Hath he forgot he is his sovereign?
Or doth this churlish superscription
Pretend some alteration in good will?

38 most] F; worst HANMER   47 *Exit Fastolf*] WILSON (*subs.*); *not in* F1; *Exit* F2   48 my lord]
F2; Lord F1   51 bluntly . . . King'?] F (bluntly? (*To the King.*))   54 Pretend] F; Portend ROWE
1714

31 **common man** man without title
33 **ordained** An appropriate word to describe the formation of an order so strongly influenced by Christian language and ideals.
35 **haughty** See note to 2.5.79.
36 **were . . . credit** had achieved distinction
38 **most extremes** the greatest danger
39 **furnished . . . sort** accomplished in this way
43 **quite degraded** completely reduced in rank
   hedge-born swain person of very low birth, a peasant. In *The First Part of the*

Contention Jack Cade, the revolutionary swain, was born 'under a hedge' (4.2.52).
44 **gentle** noble
45 **Stain** blemish
   doom sentence
46 **Be packing** be off with you
49 **uncle** Henry's uncle, the Duke of Bedford, married Anne, the Duke of Burgundy's sister.
50 **style** form of greeting
53 **churlish superscription** ill-mannered mode of address (i.e. 'To the King')
54 **Pretend** signify

What's here? 'I have upon especial cause,   55
Moved with compassion of my country's wrack,
Together with the pitiful complaints
Of such as your oppression feeds upon,
Forsaken your pernicious faction
And joined with Charles, the rightful King of France.'   60
O monstrous treachery! Can this be so?
That in alliance, amity, and oaths
There should be found such false dissembling guile?

KING HENRY
What? Doth my uncle Burgundy revolt?

GLOUCESTER
He doth, my lord, and is become your foe.   65

KING HENRY
Is that the worst this letter doth contain?

GLOUCESTER
It is the worst—and all, my lord, he writes.

KING HENRY
Why then, Lord Talbot there shall talk with him,
And give him chastisement for this abuse.
How say you, my lord, are you not content?   70

TALBOT
Content, my liege? Yes. But that I am prevented,
I should have begged I might have been employed.

KING HENRY
Then gather strength and march unto him straight.
Let him perceive how ill we brook his treason,
And what offence it is to flout his friends.   75

TALBOT
I go, my lord, in heart desiring still
You may behold confusion of your foes.   ⌈Exit⌉
    Enter Vernon ⌈*wearing a white rose*⌉ *and Basset* ⌈*wear-
    ing a red rose*⌉

65 your] F1; my F2   70 How . . . lord,] F (*subs.*); My lord, how say you, POPE   77 *Exit*]
ROWE; *not in* F   77.1 *Enter . . . red rose*] OXFORD; *Enter Vernon and Bassit.* F

56 **wrack** ruin
58 **feeds** preys
59 **pernicious faction** 'evil gang' (Burns)
64 **revolt** change sides
69 **abuse** injury (*OED sb.* 5)
71 **prevented** anticipated (by the King's
    request)

73 **strength** soldiers
    straight immediately
74 **brook** tolerate
75 **flout** insult, mock
76 **still** always
77 **confusion** the defeat
    Exit 'to give the actor time to arm himself

VERNON

Grant me the combat, gracious sovereign.

BASSET

And me, my lord, grant me the combat too.

RICHARD DUKE OF YORK (*pointing to Vernon*)

This is my servant; hear him, noble prince.   80

SOMERSET (*pointing to Basset*)

And this is mine, sweet Henry; favour him.

KING HENRY

Be patient, lords, and give them leave to speak.

Say, gentlemen, what makes you thus exclaim,

And wherefore crave you combat, or with whom?

VERNON

With him, my lord, for he hath done me wrong.   85

BASSET

And I with him; for he hath done me wrong.

KING HENRY

What is that wrong whereof you both complain?

First let me know and then I'll answer you.

BASSET

Crossing the sea from England into France,

This fellow here with envious carping tongue   90

Upbraided me about the rose I wear,

Saying the sanguine colour of the leaves

Did represent my master's blushing cheeks

When stubbornly he did repugn the truth

About a certain question in the law   95

Argued betwixt the Duke of York and him,

With other vile and ignominious terms.

In confutation of which rude reproach,

And in defence of my lord's worthiness,

I crave the benefit of law of arms.   100

80 *pointing to Vernon*] OXFORD; *not in* F   81 *pointing to Basset*] OXFORD; *not in* F   87 whereof]
F1; whereon F2   90 envious] F1; *not in* F2   93 represent] F1; present F2

in preparation for the next scene (and in
obedience to a royal command)' (Burns).

78 **combat** permission to fight a duel
80 **servant** follower
84 **wherefore** why
90 **envious** malicious
92 **sanguine** blood-red
   leaves petals

94 **repugn** oppose
95 **certain . . . law** See note to 2.4.2.
98 **confutation** refutation
98 **rude** ignorant
100 **benefit . . . arms** privilege of trial by
   combat. 'The two men compete, somewhat farcically, to gain moral advantage,
   by having the King grant this *benefit* to
   each of them first' (Burns).

VERNON

And that is my petition, noble lord;
For though he seem with forgèd quaint conceit
To set a gloss upon his bold intent,
Yet know, my lord, I was provoked by him,
And he first took exceptions at this badge,   105
Pronouncing that the paleness of this flower
Bewrayed the faintness of my master's heart.

RICHARD DUKE OF YORK

Will not this malice, Somerset, be left?

SOMERSET

Your private grudge, my lord of York, will out,
Though ne'er so cunningly you smother it.   110

KING HENRY

Good Lord, what madness rules in brainsick men
When for so slight and frivolous a cause
Such factious emulations shall arise?
Good cousins both of York and Somerset,
Quiet yourselves, I pray, and be at peace.   115

RICHARD DUKE OF YORK

Let this dissension first be tried by fight,
And then your highness shall command a peace.

SOMERSET

The quarrel toucheth none but us alone;
Betwixt ourselves let us decide it then.

---

115 I pray] F1; *not in* F2

---

102 **quaint conceit** ingenious invention
103 **set . . . upon** give a fine appearance to
105 **took exceptions to** found fault with
107 **Bewrayed** revealed
  faintness pusillanimity
108 **left** put aside
109 **grudge** enmity
111 **brainsick** addle-headed, deluded
112 **so . . . cause** If the king is referring to the 'private grudge' between York and Somerset then 'the case in truth' (2.4.2), the cause of that grudge, may well be about a trivial matter, a 'toy, a thing of no regard' (4.1.145), a 'trifle' (4.1.150). (The

king's 'cause' may, however, refer to Vernon's and Basset's remarks about the roses.) At all events, the cause of York and Somerset's hatred remains mysterious. We should bear in mind Wilson's caveat, though Shakespeare may not have done: 'Henry of course would know nothing of the quarrel in the Temple Garden' (Wilson).
113 **factious emulations** divisive rivalries
114 **cousins** kinsmen
118–19 **The quarrel . . . then** A naive disclaimer when we consider the strife that follows.
118 **toucheth** involves

RICHARD DUKE OF YORK

 There is my pledge. Accept it, Somerset.   120
  ⌜*York throws down one of the white roses*⌝

VERNON

 Nay, let it rest where it began at first.

BASSET

 Confirm it so, mine honourable lord.

GLOUCESTER

 Confirm it so? Confounded be your strife,
 And perish ye with your audacious prate!
 Presumptuous vassals, are you not ashamed   125
 With this immodest clamorous outrage
 To trouble and disturb the King and us?
 And you, my lords, methinks you do not well
 To bear with their perverse objections,
 Much less to take occasion from their mouths   130
 To raise a mutiny betwixt yourselves.
 Let me persuade you take a better course.

EXETER

 It grieves his highness. Good my lords, be friends.

KING HENRY

 Come hither, you that would be combatants.   •
 Henceforth I charge you, as you love our favour,   135
 Quite to forget this quarrel and the cause.
 And you, my lords, remember where we are—
 In France, amongst a fickle wavering nation.
 If they perceive dissension in our looks,

120.1 *York . . . roses*] This edition; *not in* F; *York throws down his gauntlet* BURNS   133 It . . .
friends.] POPE; It . . . Highnesse, | Good . . . Friends. F

120 **pledge** gage of battle (*OED sb.* 2c). What
  form does it take here? It need not necessarily be a glove or gauntlet (though this is
  customary). A white rose would be effective theatre.
121 **let . . . first** i.e. in the quarrel between
  the 'servants', Basset and Vernon
124 **audacious** impudent (*OED adj.* 2)
  prate prattle
125 **vassals** slaves
126 **immodest** immoderate
129 **bear with** tolerate
  perverse objections wilful accusations
  ('objections' = four syllables)

130 **occasion** opportunity
131 **mutiny** broil
133 **It . . . friends** A typical intervention (see
  note on Exeter in 'Persons of the Play',
  p. 91).
134–73 **Come . . . rout** This, the longest
  speech in the play, is given to Henry, the
  play's least effective authority, as though
  to confirm the primacy of action over
  ratiocination.
134 **combatants** i.e. Vernon and Basset
135 **charge** order
138 **fickle** treacherous, deceitful (*OED sb.*
  1)

And that within ourselves we disagree,   140
How will their grudging stomachs be provoked
To wilful disobedience and rebel!
Beside, what infamy will there arise
When foreign princes shall be certified
That for a toy, a thing of no regard,   145
King Henry's peers and chief nobility
Destroyed themselves and lost the realm of France!
O think upon the conquest of my father,
My tender years, and let us not forgo
That for a trifle that was bought with blood.   150
Let me be umpire in this doubtful strife.
I see no reason, if I wear this rose,
        He takes a red rose
That anyone should therefore be suspicious
I more incline to Somerset than York;
Both are my kinsmen, and I love them both.   155
As well they may upbraid me with my crown
Because, forsooth, the King of Scots is crowned.
But your discretions better can persuade
Than I am able to instruct or teach:
And therefore, as we hither came in peace,   160
So let us still continue peace and love.

151 umpire] F (Vmper)   152.1 *He . . . rose*] OXFORD; *not in* F; *Putting on a red rose* JOHNSON;
Takes the red rose from Basset BURNS (*after line* 151)

140 **within** among
141 **grudging stomachs** resentful tempers
  provoked 'Quibbling on the medical
  sense, with "within", "stomachs",
  "rebel", and "disagree"' (Wilson). But
  this is debatable.
142 **rebel** rebellion (*OED sb.*[2])
144 **certified** informed
145 **a toy . . . regard** See note to l.112.
149 **forgo** surrender
151 **doubtful** (a) worrying (b) uncertain
152.1 *He . . . rose* From where? From whom?
  Burns's direction specifies from Basset,
  but Henry might well take it from
  Somerset himself, from Suffolk even. Better, perhaps, to leave open precisely who
  and where it comes from, but in the
  theatre it has to come from someone and
  from somewhere.
153 **suspicious** disposed to suspect (*OED a.* 2)
154 **incline to** favour
155 **Both . . . both** The King continues this

studied impartiality into the second play:
'For my part, noble lords, I care not
which: | Or Somerset or York, all's one to
me' (*The First Part of the Contention* [*2
Henry VI*] 1.3.104–5). But see note to lines
162–3.
156–7 **As . . . crowned** This is not a working
  analogy. Presumably, Henry means that
  it is as irrelevant to think that he favours
  Somerset by choosing to wear a red rose
  as it is to criticize his wearing his crown
  just because the Scots king is also
  crowned. The 'forsooth' in l. 157 signals
  that what follows is a deliberately silly non
  sequitur. It does, however, make more
  sense for Henry to choose a red rather
  than a white rose as he is de facto a
  Lancastrian, a descendant of John of
  Gaunt, Duke of Lancaster, like the
  Beauforts, which Richard is not.
158 **discretions** ability to make distinctions
161 **still** ever

Cousin of York, we institute your grace
To be our regent in these parts of France;
And, good my lord of Somerset, unite
Your troops of horsemen with his bands of foot,   165
And like true subjects, sons of your progenitors,
Go cheerfully together and digest
Your angry choler on your enemies.
Ourself, my lord Protector, and the rest,
After some respite, will return to Calais,   170
From thence to England, where I hope ere long
To be presented, by your victories,
With Charles, Alençon, and that traitorous rout.
                    Flourish. Exeunt all but York, Warwick,
                                    Vernon, and Exeter

WARWICK

My lord of York, I promise you, the King
Prettily, methought, did play the orator.   175

RICHARD DUKE OF YORK

And so he did; but yet I like it not
In that he wears the badge of Somerset.

WARWICK

Tush, that was but his fancy; blame him not.
I dare presume—sweet prince—he thought no harm.

---

163 these] F; the CAIRNCROSS   167 digest] F1; disgest F2   173.1 *Flourish.*] THEOBALD; *after*
line 181 in F   *Exeunt all but*] OXFORD; *Manet* F

162–3 **Cousin . . . France** It is curious that
   York, despite having been given this pres-
   tigious post by the King who, by so doing,
   seems to favour him over Somerset,
   should say nothing about his promotion
   and continue to brood on the insult given
   him by the King's wearing the red rose
   of Somerset. Just as curiously, nothing
   is said here about Somerset's attitude
   towards Henry's choice of regent. (Hart
   quotes from a contemporary document to
   illustrate the historical Somerset's disdain
   for York's promotion.) Perhaps these
   omissions are intended to emphasize the
   symbolic power of the rose. In *The First*
   Part of the Contention, following Hall,
   Gloucester persuades Henry to substitute
   Somerset for York as regent in France,
   after Peter Thump has accused his master
   Thomas Horner of promoting York as the

'rightful heir unto the English crown'
   (1.3.187). In this nervous climate this
   is all it takes to end York's career in
   France.

162 **institute** appoint
163 **these parts** the regions
164–5 **unite . . . foot** 'It was characteristic
   of Henry's lack of worldly wisdom to
   expect York to "unite" his forces with
   Somerset's' (Cairncross).
165 **bands of foot** infantry
167 **digest** dissipate (*OED v.* 1b)
168 **choler** bile
170 **respite** stay
173 **rout** rabble
173.1 *Vernon* Although he doesn't speak,
   Vernon stays on stage because he is
   York's follower. Basset leaves with
   Somerset.
174 **promise** assure (*OED v.* 5)

RICHARD DUKE OF YORK

An if I wist he did—but let it rest.   180
Other affairs must now be managèd.

                                        Exeunt all but Exeter

EXETER

Well didst thou, Richard, to suppress thy voice;
For had the passions of thy heart burst out
I fear we should have seen deciphered there
More rancorous spite, more furious raging broils,   185
Than yet can be imagined or supposed.
But howsoe'er, no simple man that sees
This jarring discord of nobility,
This shouldering of each other in the court,
This factious bandying of their favourites,   190
But that it doth presage some ill event.
'Tis much when sceptres are in children's hands,
But more when envy breeds unkind division—
There comes the ruin; there begins confusion.   *Exit*

4.2   *Enter Lord Talbot with a trumpeter and drummer and
          soldiers before Bordeaux*

TALBOT

Go to the gates of Bordeaux, trumpeter.
Summon their general unto the wall.

          *The trumpeter sounds a parley. Enter French General,
          aloft*

180 An] OXFORD; And F   wist] CAPELL; wish F; wis THEOBALD   181.1 *Exeunt all but*]
WILSON; *Exeunt.* | *Flourish. Manet* F   191 But] F1; By F3   that] F; sees CAIRNCROSS *(conj. H.
Brooks)*; at VAUGHAN *conj.*   194 There] F1; Then F2
    4.2] CAPELL; *not in* F   0.1–2 *Enter . . . Bordeaux*] OXFORD; *Enter Talbot with Trumpe and
Drumme, before Burdeaux.* F   2.1 *The . . . parley*] OXFORD; *not in* F   *French*] OXFORD; *not in* F
General] F; *Captain* BURNS; *General and others* MALONE

180 **wist** thought
181 **managèd** taken in hand
182 **Well . . . voice** Richard continues to fol-
     low Mortimer's advice (see 3.1.61).
184 **deciphered** revealed
187 **simple** ordinary
189 **shouldering** jostling
190 **factious bandying** contentious wrangling
     favourites supporters (*OED sb.* 4)
191 **But that** but sees that
     event outcome
192 **much** a serious matter
193 **envy** malice, hatred
     unkind unnatural

194 **confusion** destruction
4.2 Shakespeare continues to play fast and
     loose with history: Bordeaux welcomed
     Talbot in 1451. The events here corre-
     spond to the Chronicles' account of the
     Battle of Castillon where Talbot was killed
     in 1453, i.e. twenty-two years after the
     coronation in the previous scene, and in
     the middle of the events of *The First Part of
     the Contention* [*2 Henry VI*].
  2 **general** Burns's contention that *general*
     means representatives of the populace
     of Bordeaux has to ignore F's direction
     '*Enter Generall aloft*'. It seems unlikely

English John Talbot, captain, calls you forth,
Servant in arms to Harry, King of England.
And thus he would: open your city gates, 5
Be humble to us, call my sovereign yours,
And do him homage as obedient subjects,
And I'll withdraw me and my bloody power.
But if you frown upon this proffered peace
You tempt the fury of my three attendants— 10
Lean famine, quartering steel, and climbing fire—
Who, in a moment, even with the earth
Shall lay your stately and air-braving towers
If you forsake the offer of their love.

3 captain] OXFORD; Captaines F   calls] F2; call F1   6 humble] F1; humbled F2   7 And do]
F; Do HATTAWAY   14 their] F; our HANMER; his WILSON

that Talbot would call for more than one—the chief—representative of the town's forces (though, as Malone's direction indicates, he may well be accompanied by some of his followers). And while it may be true that in strict terms the French General would = the Dauphin, the word could be used more flexibly than in this restricted sense as Shakespeare himself illustrates in *All's Well That Ends Well* where the Duke of Florence describes Bertram as '[t]he general of our horse' (3.3.1).

3 **captain** F's '(Captaines)' is presumably wrong (though some editions accept it), but 'captain', the usual emendation, does not support Burns's suggestion that we are not dealing with a general. *OED* (*sb.* 3) gives one meaning of 'captain' as 'an able general or commander'.

4 **Harry** This is the first and only time in the play that the colloquial alternative of Henry's name is used and issues appropriately enough from the mouth of the play's straight-talking warrior-hero. It anticipates the number of occasions in the second tetralogy where 'Harry' humanizes 'Henry', most notably in Henry V's reassuring words to his brothers: 'Not Amurath an Amurath succeeds, | But Harry Harry' (*2 Henry IV* 5.2.48–9). Talbot's use of this sturdy English nickname follows nicely on the phrase he uses to describe himself: 'English John Talbot'

(4.2.3). In *Richard III* Margaret as grieving widow refers to Henry as 'holy Harry' (4.4.25). For a contemptuous variation, see Margaret's use of 'Dickie' for Richard in *Richard Duke of York* [*3 Henry VI*] 1.4.77. Gary Taylor believes 'Harry' to indicate Shakespeare's hand (see 'Shakespeare and Others', 168).

5 **he** i.e. Henry VI
   would desires

8 **bloody power** forces capable of bloodshed

10–11 **You . . . fire** Shakespeare reworks this magnificently in the opening Chorus in *Henry V*: 'and at his heels, | Leashed in like hounds, should famine, sword, and fire | Crouch for employment' (6–8). 'The figures are not identical, but each bears the Shakespearean stamp, and both . . . are reminiscent of the speech which the chroniclers report Henry V to have made to the besieged citizens of Rouen' (Tucker Brooke).

11 **Lean famine** War, like sleep, attracts Shakespeare's use of personification throughout his career. Also 'pale destruction' (l. 27).
   quartering dismembering (lit. = cutting the body into four pieces)

12 **even** level

13 **air-braving** i.e. very high

14 **forsake** refuse
   their Presumably Talbot's three attendants—famine, steel, fire—though it's difficult to imagine them having anything but fury to offer.

GENERAL

> Thou ominous and fearful owl of death,   15
> Our nation's terror and their bloody scourge,
> The period of thy tyranny approacheth.
> On us thou canst not enter but by death,
> For I protest we are well fortified
> And strong enough to issue out and fight.   20
> If you retire, the Dauphin, well appointed,
> Stands with the snares of war to tangle thee.
> On either hand thee there are squadrons pitched
> To wall thee from the liberty of flight;
> And no way canst thou turn thee for redress   25
> But death doth front thee with apparent spoil,
> And pale destruction meets thee in the face.
> Ten thousand French have ta'en the sacrament
> To rive their dangerous artillery
> Upon no Christian soul but English Talbot.   30
> Lo, there thou stand'st, a breathing valiant man
> Of an invincible unconquered spirit.
> This is the latest glory of thy praise,
> That I thy enemy due thee withal;
> For ere the glass that now begins to run   35
> Finish the process of his sandy hour,
> These eyes that see thee now well colourèd
> Shall see thee withered, bloody, pale, and dead.
>   *Drum afar off*

---

29 rive] F (ryue); drive JOHNSON *conj.*; fire OXFORD   31 stand'st] F (standst)   34 due] F (dew)

15 **owl of death** The shrieking owl presages death in many cultures.
17 **period** end
   tyranny cruelty (*OED sb.* 3)
21 **appointed** equipped, prepared
22 **snares** traps for small animals, and hence a deprecatory term
   tangle entrap
23 **hand** side of
   pitched set in battle order
24 **wall** hem in
26 **front** confront
   apparent spoil 'visible ruin' (Burns)
28 **ta'en the sacrament** sworn an oath
29 **rive** A much disputed term. *OED* (*v.* B3)

gives 'thrust' (i.e. as from a knife), but perhaps (4) is closer: 'to rend or split by means of shock'.
   dangerous artillery See headnote to 1.4.
30 **English Talbot** A mocking echo of Talbot's 'English John Talbot' (l. 3).
31 **breathing** living
33 **latest** final
34 **due thee withal** pay you as your due
35 **glass** hourglass
36 **his** its
   sandy hour hour measured by the sand of the hourglass
37 **well colourèd** And therefore in good health.

Hark, hark, the Dauphin's drum, a warning bell,
Sings heavy music to thy timorous soul,   40
And mine shall ring thy dire departure out.   *Exit*
TALBOT
He fables not. I hear the enemy.
Out, some light horsemen, and peruse their wings.
                                    ⌈*Exit one or more*⌉
O negligent and heedless discipline,
How are we parked and bounded in a pale,   45
A little herd of England's timorous deer
Mazed with a yelping kennel of French curs.
If we be English deer, be then in blood;
Not rascal-like to fall down with a pinch,
But rather, moody-mad and desperate stags,   50
Turn on the bloody hounds with heads of steel
And make the cowards stand aloof at bay.
Sell every man his life as dear as mine
And they shall find dear deer of us, my friends.
God and Saint George, Talbot and England's right,   55
Prosper our colours in this dangerous fight.   *Exeunt*

43.1 *Exit . . . more*] OXFORD; *not in* F   50 moody-mad and] CAPELL; moodie mad: And F
56 *Exeunt*] F2; *not in* F1; *Exit* BURNS

39 **the Dauphin's drum** (beating out a particular tattoo)
   warning bell foretelling death
40 **heavy** doleful
41 **mine** i.e. his drumbeat for Talbot's
   funeral (as opposed to the Dauphin's)
   dire departure horrible death
43 **light** lightly armed (for surveillance
   purposes)
   peruse their wings reconnoitre their
   flanks
44 **discipline** military training or skill (*OED*
   sb. 3b)
45 **parked** enclosed (as in a deer park)
   pale fenced-in area
46–7 **A little . . . curs** This is in vivid contrast
   to Talbot's triumphant production of the
   English army (or its representatives) when
   the Countess of Auvergne believes she has
   him captured: then they were 'his sub-
   stance, sinews, arms, and strength, |

With which he yoketh your rebellious
necks' (2.3.62–3).
47 **Mazed** bewildered by
   kennel pack
48 **in blood** (a) in prime condition (b) in
   nobility (c) in battle
49 **rascal-like** (a) like an inferior deer (b) like
   a scoundrel
   pinch 'slight nip (of hounds)' (Sanders).
50 **moody-mad** mad with rage
51 **heads of steel** A combination of the
   soldiers' helmets and the stags'
   antlers.
54 **my friends** To whom is this addressed? In
   the absence of any obvious on-stage candidates—only the drummer and trumpeter may remain—Burns's suggestion
   that Talbot is turning to the audience here
   in the spirit of patriotic camaraderie is
   attractive.
56 **colours** banners

4.3   *Enter a Messenger that meets the Duke of York. Enter*
         Richard Duke of York with a trumpet and many soldiers

RICHARD DUKE OF YORK

Are not the speedy scouts returned again

That dogged the mighty army of the Dauphin?

MESSENGER

They are returned, my lord, and give it out

That he is marched to Bordeaux with his power

To fight with Talbot; as he marched along,   5

By your espials were discoverèd

Two mightier troops than that the Dauphin led,

Which joined with him and made their march for
     Bordeaux.

RICHARD DUKE OF YORK

A plague upon that villain Somerset

That thus delays my promisèd supply   10

Of horsemen that were levied for this siege.

Renownèd Talbot doth expect my aid,

And I am louted by a traitor villain,

And cannot help the noble chevalier.

God comfort him in this necessity;   15

If he miscarry, farewell wars in France.

     Enter another messenger ⌈*Sir William Lucy*⌉

4.3] CAPELL; *not in* F   0.1 *Richard Duke of*] OXFORD; *not in* F   0.2 *a*] OXFORD; *not in* F
5 Talbot; . . . along,] This edition; ~_∧_ . . . along. F; ~: . . . along, F2; ~. . . . ~, OXFORD   8
Bordeaux.] F (Burdeaux _∧_); Bourdeaux. *Exit* CAIRNCROSS   13 louted] F; flouted JOHNSON *conj.*
16.1 *Sir William Lucy*] THEOBALD; *not in* F

4.3 This scene and the one that follows
record a fictitious moment in the dispute
between York and Somerset. Historically,
they were in England during this time,
though York's troops were on the plains of
Gascony where this scene takes place.

0.1–2 *Enter . . . soldiers* York and the Messenger—one of York's officers—would
enter from opposite sides of the stage. The
direction's phrasing suggests a pause
before York enters.

0.2 *trumpet* trumpeter
many soldiers 'To emphasize by contrast
the isolation of Talbot in the previous
scene, F's direction specifies *many
Soldiers*' (Burns). Cairncross argues
that the indefinite 'many' suggests the
author's hand.

2 **dogged** tracked

3 **give it out** report

6 **espials** spies, scouts

9–11 **A plague . . . siege** In immediate con-
tradistinction to news of the Dauphin's
forces linking up with 'two mightier
troops' (l. 7). (Henry had asked Somerset
to unite 'Your troops of horsemen with
his [York's] bands of foot' (4.1.165).)

10 **supply** reinforcements (*OED sb.* 5)

12 **expect** await (*OED v.* 2)

13 **louted** mocked

14 **chevalier** knight (pronounced as three
syllables with the accent on first and
third)

16 **miscarry** come to harm

16.1 **Sir William Lucy** By no means just
another Messenger as F's direction here
implies. Giving him a name emphasizes
his distinction from other messengers,
borne out by his short soliloquy in Exeter-
like vein that ends this scene. He returns

LUCY

Thou princely leader of our English strength—
Never so needful on the earth of France—
Spur to the rescue of the noble Talbot,
Who now is girdled with a waste of iron   20
And hemmed about with grim destruction.
To Bordeaux, warlike Duke, to Bordeaux, York,
Else farewell Talbot, France, and England's honour.

RICHARD DUKE OF YORK

O God, that Somerset, who in proud heart
Doth stop my cornets, were in Talbot's place!   25
So should we save a valiant gentleman
By forfeiting a traitor and a coward.
Mad ire and wrathful fury makes me weep,
That thus we die while remiss traitors sleep.

LUCY

O send some succour to the distressed lord.   30

RICHARD DUKE OF YORK

He dies, we lose; I break my warlike word;
We mourn, France smiles; we lose, they daily get,
All 'long of this vile traitor Somerset.

LUCY

Then God take mercy on brave Talbot's soul,
And on his son, young John, who two hours since   35
I met in travel toward his warlike father.
This seven years did not Talbot see his son,
And now they meet where both their lives are done.

---

17 LUCY] THEOBALD; 2. *Mes.* F   20 waste] F; waist STEEVENS   23 France, . . . honour.] F; ~∧
. . . ~. BURNS   30, 34, 47 LUCY] THEOBALD; *Mes.* F   36 travel] F3; trauaile F1

in Scene 4 (or stays on stage if the scenes are combined) to deal with Somerset, and does so in no uncertain terms.

20 **waste** (a) vast expanse (b) belt. A favourite pun with Shakespeare, occurring most famously in reference to Falstaff's girth and extravagance in *2 Henry IV* and in Sonnet 129, 'Th'expense of spirit in a waste of shame'.

21 **destruction** (pronounced as four syllables)

25 **stop** prevent the departure of (*OED v.* 15)

25 **cornets** cavalry companies (so called because of the curved pennants attached to their lances)

29 **we** i.e. the men on our side
   remiss (accented on the first syllable) (a) idle (b) negligent

30 **distressed** in difficulties

32 **get** derive profit (*OED v.* . 3b; *OED*'s first example of this usage)

33 **'long of** because of

37 **This seven years** for a long time (a proverbial phrase, Dent Y25)

RICHARD DUKE OF YORK

Alas, what joy shall noble Talbot have,
To bid his young son welcome to his grave?   40
Away—vexation almost stops my breath,
That sundered friends greet in the hour of death.
Lucy, farewell; no more my fortune can
But curse the cause I cannot aid the man.
Maine, Blois, Poitiers, and Tours are won away   45
'Long all of Somerset and his delay.

                     Exeunt all but Lucy

LUCY

Thus, while the vulture of sedition
Feeds in the bosom of such great commanders,
Sleeping neglection doth betray to loss
The conquest of our scarce-cold conqueror,   50
That ever-living man of memory,
Henry the Fifth. Whiles they each other cross,
Lives, honours, lands, and all, hurry to loss.   ⌈*Exit*⌉

46.1 *Exeunt . . . Lucy*] COLLIER (*subs.*); *Exit* F   53 *Exit*] F2; *not in* F1

40 **his grave** Whose exactly? Talbot's or his
son's?
41 **vexation** affliction (*OED sb.* 4)
42 **sundered** separated
    friends kinsmen (*OED sb.* 3)
    greet should greet
43 **no . . . can** the only thing I can do in the
present circumstances
44 **the cause** i.e. Somerset
46 **'Long all** all because
47–8 **vulture . . . bosom** An allusion to the
story of Prometheus who was chained to
a rock by Zeus as a punishment for steal-
ing the gods' fire. Each day an eagle came
and ate his liver, which grew back at
night, until he was released from his
torment by Heracles. A subsidiary possibility is the story of Tityus, a son of Gaia,
who in the underworld had two vultures
eating his liver (the seat of passion) as a
punishment for assaulting Leto (or
Latona) who was a Titaness and mother
of Apollo and Artemis (Diana). The tales
are related in *Aeneid*, 6.595–600 and
Metamorphoses, 4.457–8.

47 **sedition** Hattaway, following *OED*'s first
definition, glosses this as 'factious con-
test'. But the context suggests *OED*'s second definition, 'revolt, mutiny'.
49 **Sleeping neglection** drowsy negligence
50 **scarce-cold conqueror** 'Historically Henry
V had been dead for 31 years; but Shakespeare throughout the play contrasts the
glories of his reign (as if they were very
recent) with the immediate disorders of
his son's reign' (Sanders).
51 **ever-living . . . memory** a man who will
live ever in our memory. A felicitous
transposition in that in this play Henry
V—his spirit anyway—is a dominating
presence. See note to 1.1.0.1. Henry V
continues his talismanic career in the
other plays of the cycle. In *The First Part of
the Contention* (*2 Henry VI*), for example,
Cade complains that 'The name of Henry
the Fifth hales them [his erstwhile
followers] to an hundred mischiefs'
(4.7.211–12).
52 **they** i.e. York and Somerset
    cross thwart

4.4   *Enter Somerset and Forces; a Captain of Talbot's with him*

SOMERSET (*to the Captain*)

It is too late; I cannot send them now.
This expedition was by York and Talbot
Too rashly plotted. All our general force
Might with a sally of the very town
Be buckled with. The over-daring Talbot   5
Hath sullied all his gloss of former honour
By this unheedful, desperate, wild adventure.
York set him on to fight and die in shame,
That, Talbot dead, great York might bear the name.
          ⌈*Enter Lucy*⌉

CAPTAIN

Here is Sir William Lucy, who, with me,   10
Set from our o'ermatched forces forth for aid.

SOMERSET

How now, Sir William, whither were you sent?

4.4] CAPELL; *not in* F   0.1 *Enter . . . him*] CAPELL; *Enter Somerset with his Armie.* F
9.1 *Enter Lucy*] CAPELL; *not in* F   12, 13 whither] F (whether)

4.4 Most editors, following F2's lead, provide Lucy with an exit, and begin a new scene. Some, however, choose to follow F, leaving Lucy on stage to keep the action continuous. But F mostly ignores scene division, anyway, and it is clear that Somerset must be in some other location than York's, and the manner in which the Captain and Somerset greet Lucy (ll. 10–12) intimates that Lucy enters. (Lucy's couplet at 4.3.52–3 also suggests the end of a scene. Also see the beginning of 4.7.)

1 **them** i.e. the troops of horsemen

2 **This expedition** i.e. against Bordeaux
Talbot Unlike York, Somerset includes Talbot in his condemnation. He goes on to amplify it in the following lines.

3–5 **All . . . with** just the town's garrison (without any other reinforcements) might successfully come forth to engage our entire army (i.e. without Somerset's and York's soldiers Talbot's army is no larger than the town's garrison)

5 **buckled** grappled, engaged

7 **unheedful** careless, rash

8–9 **York . . . name** Somerset's accusations get wilder and wilder. Is he imagining here that York will inherit Talbot's honours, or that, with Talbot dead, York thinks he might become England's most illustrious soldier?

8 **set him on** encouraged him

9 **bear the name** claim superiority

11 **o'ermatched** outnumbered

12 **whither** Burns notes that this is an odd question. Lucy replies as though 'whither' = 'from where' which *OED* does not support. In any case, the Captain has just told Somerset that Lucy has come, as has the Captain himself, from Talbot's forces. Perhaps, as Burns suggests, Somerset is eager to know whether Lucy has gone to York first and Lucy tactfully deflects the question. And yet later Lucy feels free to tell Somerset that York accuses Somerset of the same offence Somerset has just levelled at York (ll. 30–2) thereby revealing that Lucy had had an earlier meeting with York.

LUCY

Whither, my lord? From bought and sold Lord Talbot,
Who, ringed about with bold adversity,
Cries out for noble York and Somerset   15
To beat assailing death from his weak legions;
And whiles the honourable captain there
Drops bloody sweat from his war-wearièd limbs,
And, in advantage ling'ring, looks for rescue,
You his false hopes, the trust of England's honour,   20
Keep off aloof with worthless emulation.
Let not your private discord keep away
The levied succours that should lend him aid,
While he, renownèd noble gentleman,
Yield up his life unto a world of odds.   25
Orléans the Bastard, Charles, Burgundy,
Alençon, Reignier, compass him about,
And Talbot perisheth by your default.

SOMERSET

York set him on; York should have sent him aid.

LUCY

And York as fast upon your grace exclaims,   30
Swearing that you withhold his levied horse
Collected for this expedition.

16 legions] ROWE; Regions F   19 in advantage ling'ring] F; unadvantaged, ling'ring OXFORD
25 Yield] F1; Yeelds F2   26 Charles,] F1; ~, and F2   27 Reignier] ROWE; *Reignard* F
31 horse] HANMER (*conj*. Theobald); hoast F

13 **bought and sold** betrayed (as Christ was by Judas)
16 **legions** Rowe's emendation marginally improves the sense. *OED*'s '[v]aguely used for: a host of armed men' (2) would fit the bill here, especially if the definition's vagueness allowed 'host' to mean 'an armed company of men' (*OED sb*. 1) rather than a multitude.
18 **bloody sweat** See Luke 22: 44 describing Christ on the eve of his death: 'his sweat were like drops of blood'.
19 **in advantage ling'ring** clinging on to his superior battlefield position. The point here is that Talbot's exceptional generalship is vitiated by the 'world of odds' (l. 25) facing him.
20 **trust** guardian, trustee

21 **worthless emulation** dishonourable jealousy
22 **private** personal
23 **levied succours** recruited reinforcements
25 **a world of** i.e. overwhelming
26–7 **Orléans . . . Reignier** Spelling out the names of the leaders of the united French forces underlines the disunity of the fractured English army, the absence of their leaders from the field.
27 **compass** encircle
28 **default** failure (*OED sb*. 5)
29 **set him on** incited him
30 **as . . . exclaims** just as vigorously accuses your grace
31 **horse** F's 'host' makes sense, but it is specifically cavalry that Somerset has been asked to contribute to the battle (see 4.3.9–11).

SOMERSET

York lies. He might have sent and had the horse.
I owe him little duty and less love,
And take foul scorn to fawn on him by sending.   35

LUCY

The fraud of England, not the force of France,
Hath now entrapped the noble-minded Talbot.
Never to England shall he bear his life,
But dies betrayed to fortune by your strife.

SOMERSET

Come, go. I will dispatch the horsemen straight;   40
Within six hours they will be at his side.

LUCY

Too late comes rescue. He is ta'en or slain,
For fly he could not if he would have fled,
And fly would Talbot never, though he might.

SOMERSET

If he be dead—brave Talbot, then adieu.   45

LUCY

His fame lives in the world; his shame in you.   *Exeunt*

4.5   *Enter Lord Talbot and his son John*

TALBOT

O young John Talbot, I did send for thee
To tutor thee in stratagems of war,
That Talbot's name might be in thee revived
When sapless age and weak unable limbs
Should bring thy father to his drooping chair.   5
But—O malignant and ill-boding stars—
Now thou art come unto a feast of death,
A terrible and unavoided danger.

---

41 side] CAIRNCROSS; ayde F
  4.5] CAPELL; *not in* F   0.1 *John*] OXFORD; *not in* F

33 **sent** sent for
35 **take foul scorn** would think myself foully
    disgraced
    by sending Somerset seems to mean that it
    would be a disgrace to send the cavalry
    without first having been requested by
    York to do so (despite Henry's command at
    4.1.164–5). This absurd insistence on the
    niceties of a specious protocol is another
    indication of the perversion of the stan-
    dards of noble conduct in this play.

36 **fraud** faithlessness (*OED sb.* 1)
42 **ta'en** captured
4.5 Historically, this scene takes place in
    1453 at Castillon not Bordeaux.
5 **drooping chair** chair for an old, feeble per-
    son (transferred epithet)
6 **malignant** having an evil influence
    ill-boding presaging evil
8 **unavoided** unavoidable (*OED ppl. a.* 2a)

Therefore, dear boy, mount on my swiftest horse,
And I'll direct thee how thou shalt escape   10
By sudden flight. Come—dally not, be gone.

JOHN

Is my name Talbot? and am I your son?
And shall I fly? O, if you love my mother,
Dishonour not her honourable name
To make a bastard and a slave of me.   15
The world will say, 'He is not Talbot's blood
That basely fled when noble Talbot stood.'

TALBOT

Fly to revenge my death if I be slain.

JOHN

He that flies so will ne'er return again.

TALBOT

If we both stay we both are sure to die.   20

JOHN

Then let me stay and, father, do you fly.
Your loss is great; so your regard should be.
My worth unknown, no loss is known in me.
Upon my death the French can little boast;
In yours they will, in you all hopes are lost.   25
Flight cannot stain the honour you have won;

---

11 **sudden** immediate

13–15 **O . . . me** This line of argument would not have been possible had Shakespeare included Talbot's bastard son at the battle as he was in history. See note on John Talbot in 'Persons'.

16–55 **blood . . . fly** From here to the end of the scene (and into the following two scenes) the Talbots' extended and repetitive leave-taking is expressed in couplets so banal, according to Roger Warren in 'Comedies and Histories at Two Stratfords, 1977', *SS* 31 (1978), 145–55, that the passages in question must be 'non-Shakespearian' (148). Just how banal these heroic couplets are is open to debate (for another view, see Alexander Leggatt, 'The Death of John Talbot', in *Shakespeare's English Histories: A Quest for Form and Genre*, ed. J. W. L. Velz (Binghamton, NY, 1996), 11–30, and Marco Mincoff, 'The Composition of *Henry VI, Part 1*', *SQ* 16 (1965), 199–207).

In no other play does Shakespeare use them in a tragic passage.

16–17 **blood . . . stood** In Shakespeare's time *blood* was pronounced as today's 'good'. See *OED*, *blood*, *sb*.

19 **He . . . again** A deceptively simple-sounding reply. Young John Talbot presumably means that anyone who flies from the battle in order to return to avenge his father's death cannot in fact do so as the cowardice involved in the flight will make him too ashamed to return. But the precise meaning is elusive.

22 **Your loss** the loss of you
   regard 'care for your own safety' (Johnson).

23 **known** revealed, manifested (*OED*, *know*, *v*. 13)

24–5 **boast . . . lost** *OED* lists an alternative spelling *bost* that probably indicates the pronunciation of *boast*.

26 **Flight . . . won** Forced to retreat and fly before Joan, Talbot has already experi-

But mine it will, that no exploit have done.
You fled for vantage, everyone will swear,
But if I bow, they'll say it was for fear.
There is no hope that ever I will stay   30
If the first hour I shrink and run away.
Here on my knee I beg mortality,
Rather than life preserved with infamy.
⌈*He kneels*⌉

TALBOT
Shall all thy mother's hopes lie in one tomb?

JOHN
Ay, rather than I'll shame my mother's womb.   35

TALBOT
Upon my blessing I command thee go.
⌈*John rises*⌉

JOHN
To fight I will, but not to fly the foe.

TALBOT
Part of thy father may be saved in thee.

JOHN
No part of him, but will be shamed in me.

TALBOT
Thou never hadst renown, nor canst not lose it.   40

JOHN
Yes, your renownèd name—shall flight abuse it?

TALBOT
Thy father's charge shall clear thee from that stain.

33.1 *He kneels*] BURNS; *not in* F   36.1 *John rises*] BURNS; *not in* F   37 to fly] F1; flye F3
39 shamed] HUDSON (*conj.* Walker); shame F

enced shame: 'O would I were to die with Salisbury. | The shame hereof will make me hide my head' (1.6.38–9). But in that case the whole army, 'like to whelps' (1.6.26), was in retreat, whereas what Talbot's son is advocating here reminds us of Sir John Fastolf, the play's archetypal coward, when he replies to the Captain 'Whither away? To save myself by flight' (3.2.103). Abandoning the army and retreating with it are different propositions. This is made clear later by Talbot when his son suggests that they both fly: 'And leave my followers here to fight and die? | My age was never tainted with such shame' (4.5.45–6).

28 **for vantage** as a strategic necessity
29 **bow** yield
30 **ever** at any other time
31 **shrink** retreat
32 **mortality** death
37 **will,** Retaining F's comma in this instance conveys the actor's slight pause before the revelation of the line's second half. See l. 39 and l. 51.
42 **charge** order
   stain moral blemish

209

JOHN

You cannot witness for me, being slain.

If death be so apparent, then both fly.

TALBOT

And leave my followers here to fight and die?   45

My age was never tainted with such shame.

JOHN

And shall my youth be guilty of such blame?

No more can I be severed from your side

Than can yourself your self in twain divide.

Stay, go, do what you will: the like do I,   50

For live I will not, if my father die.

TALBOT

Then here I take my leave of thee, fair son,

Born to eclipse thy life this afternoon.

Come, side by side, together live and die,   55

And soul with soul from France to heaven fly.   *Exeunt*

4.6   *Alarum. Enter Alençon, Bastard, Burgundy and other*
        French and English soldiers in excursions, wherein Lord
        Talbot's son John is hemmed about and Talbot ⌐re-enters
        and⌐ rescues him. ⌐The English then drive off the
        French⌐

TALBOT

Saint George and victory! Fight, soldiers, fight!

The Regent hath with Talbot broke his word,

55 *Exeunt*] ROWE; *Exit.* F

   4.6] CAPELL (*subs.*); *not in* F   0.1–2 *Enter . . . in*] This edition; *not in* F; *Enter Alençon, Bastard and Burgundy in* BURNS   0.3 *about*] F; *about [by the three Frenchmen, as he goes after his father]* BURNS   *re-enters and*] BURNS; *not in* F   0.3–4 *The . . . French*] OXFORD (*subs.*); *not in* F

44 **apparent** inevitable, certain
46 **My age** (a) my whole life (b) the age in which I live
52–3 **son . . . afternoon** Rhyming on a vowel like the 'u' in 'educated'.
53 **eclipse** extinguish. The word is inspired by 'son' (sun) on the previous line.
4.6 There are two concerns about this scene: (a) whether or not it should be a separate scene; (b) whether it should be in the play at all. (a) F's *Exit* at the end of Scene 5 may be intentionally in the singular leaving Talbot's son alone on stage to face the French soldiers in a continuous action (as in Burns). Or it may = *exeunt* so that Tal-

bot and his son leave the stage together, 'side by side' (4.5.54) as Talbot says. (F's *Exit* may have been used to save space; the extra letters in *Exeunt* would have required another line. See 4.6.57.) Leaving his son alone on stage strikes me as odd both psychologically and in view of what Talbot says. If they go off together (as I think they do) we have to imagine the *Excursions* beginning off stage and spilling over on to the stage at the beginning of Scene 6 with Talbot's son having been separated temporarily by them from his father. (The *Textual Companion* reminds us that in this play

And left us to the rage of France his sword.
Where is John Talbot? Pause, and take thy breath.
I gave thee life, and rescued thee from death.   5
JOHN
O twice my father, twice am I thy son:
The life thou gav'st me first was lost and done
Till with thy warlike sword, despite of fate,
To my determined time thou gav'st new date.
TALBOT
When from the Dauphin's crest thy sword struck fire   10
It warmed thy father's heart with proud desire
Of bold-faced victory. Then leaden age,
Quickened with youthful spleen and warlike rage,
Beat down Alençon, Orléans, Burgundy,
And from the pride of Gallia rescued thee.   15
The ireful bastard Orléans, that drew blood
From thee, my boy, and had the maidenhood
Of thy first fight, I soon encounterèd,
And, interchanging blows, I quickly shed
Some of his bastard blood, and in disgrace   20
Bespoke him thus: 'Contaminated, base,
And misbegotten blood I spill of thine,
Mean and right poor, for that pure blood of mine

21 him thus: 'Contaminated] F; him: 'This contaminated VAUGHAN

especially act and scene divisions were later 'literary' additions having no theatrical significance. They are 'incoherent' (p. 218). See 4.7 n.) (b) A complicated argument beginning in John Dover Wilson's edition of *1 Henry VI* in 1952 and culminating in E. Pearlman's 'Shakespeare at Work: The Two Talbots', *Philological Quarterly*, 75 (1996), 1–20, argues that 4.6 is a redundant scene superseded by 4.5 which is in essence Shakespeare's revision. It is an intriguing theory but not sufficiently compelling to warrant abandoning 4.6 or relegating it to an Appendix.

2–3 word . . . sword Rhyming as in 'ward'.

2 Regent York (see 4.1.162–3)

3 France his i.e. the King of France's (probably)

4 Where . . . Talbot Although Talbot has just rescued his son, as the stage direction at the beginning of the scene tells us, we are to imagine that in the continuing mêlée the Talbots get separated again.

6 O . . . son As 4.6 repeats in some measure what happens in 4.5 John's line has an added resonance.

9 determined appointed, fated. Strictly speaking John's claim is illogical, as something that is determined cannot, by definition, be changed.
   date limit

10 crest helmet

13 Quickened . . . spleen invigorated with youthful anger (either Talbot's or John's)

15 pride of Gallia best of France. 'Talbot gives his enemies more of their due than usual, in celebrating his son's achievement' (Burns).

16–17 blood . . . maidenhood See note at 4.5.16–17.

20 in disgrace as an insult

21 Bespoke him spoke out against him

23 Mean inferior

Which thou didst force from Talbot, my brave boy.'
Here, purposing the Bastard to destroy,   25
Came in strong rescue. Speak, thy father's care,
Art thou not weary, John? How dost thou fare?
Wilt thou yet leave the battle, boy, and fly,
Now thou art sealed the son of chivalry?
Fly, to revenge my death when I am dead;   30
The help of one stands me in little stead.
O, too much folly is it, well I wot,
To hazard all our lives in one small boat.
If I today die not with Frenchmen's rage,
Tomorrow I shall die with mickle age.   35
By me they nothing gain and, if I stay,
'Tis but the short'ning of my life one day.
In thee thy mother dies, our household's name,
My death's revenge, thy youth, and England's fame.
All these and more we hazard by thy stay;   40
All these are saved if thou wilt fly away.
JOHN
  The sword of Orléans hath not made me smart;
  These words of yours draw life-blood from my heart.
  On that advantage, bought with such a shame,
  To save a paltry life and slay bright fame,   45
  Before young Talbot from old Talbot fly,
  The coward horse that bears me fall and die!
  And like me to the peasant boys of France,
  To be shame's scorn and subject of mischance.
  Surely, by all the glory you have won,   50

44 On that] F; Out on that THEOBALD; Oh! what HANMER   45 fame,] F; ~? BURNS

25 **purposing** while I was intending
28–9 **Wilt . . . chivalry** This repetition of Tal-
     bot's urging in 4.5 has suggested to some
     commentators that this scene is an
     earlier, less successful, dispensable ver-
     sion of 4.5. See the opening note to this
     scene.
29 **sealed** confirmed, certified
31 **stands . . . stead** does not help me very
     much
32 **wot** know
35 **mickle** great
38 **In . . . name** 'Actually John was a
     younger son by a second wife' (Hatt-
     away). See note in 'Persons'.

42 **smart** feel pain, suffer
44 **On that advantage** in order to gain those
     benefits (i.e. Talbot's revenge and so on in
     l. 39)
45 **slay bright fame** i.e. Talbot's (as opposed
     to England's future fame through Talbot's
     son in l. 39)
47 **fall** may it fall
48 **like** liken
49 **shame's scorn** the object of shameful
     derision
   subject of mischance victim of
     misfortune

And if I fly, I am not Talbot's son.
Then talk no more of flight, it is no boot;
If son to Talbot, die at Talbot's foot.

TALBOT

Then follow thou thy desperate sire of Crete,
Thou Icarus; thy life to me is sweet.   55
If thou wilt fight, fight by thy father's side,
And, commendable proved, let's die in pride.   *Exeunt*

4.7   *Alarum. Excursions. Enter old Lord Talbot led by a*
          Servant

TALBOT

Where is my other life? Mine own is gone.
O where's young Talbot, where is valiant John?
Triumphant death, smeared with captivity,
Young Talbot's valour makes me smile at thee.

---

54 desperate] F (desp'rate)   57 *Exeunt*] ROWE; *Exit* F
  4.7] CAPELL (*subs.*); *not in* F   0.1 *by a Servant*] WILSON; *not in* F

---

51 **And if** if
52 **boot** use
53 **If . . . Talbot** if I am Talbot's son
55 **Icarus** In Greek mythology, the son of the
   mythical inventor, Daedalus. He was
   warned by his father not to fly too close to
   the sun when the two were escaping from
   Crete with the wings Daedalus had contrived. But Icarus flew too high, the heat
   of the sun melted the wax which held the
   wings together, and he fell to his death in
   the Icarian Sea, called so after him.
   Although he was very popular with the
   Elizabethans as a warning against over-
   weening ambition, Shakespeare refers to
   him only in *1 Henry VI* (twice) and once in
   Richard Duke of York (*3 Henry VI*). Talbot
   seems to be using him here as an example
   of filial devotion rather than as an example of ambition to be shunned.
57 **commendable** (accented on the first
   syllable)
   pride glory
4.7 This edition's 5.1 is oddly designated
   '*Scena Secunda*' in F which would make all
   the scenes up to and including this one
   one long scene. (F's fifth act is extremely
   short beginning at 5.6 in this edition; it
   makes more sense to begin Act 5 when the

play returns to London.) Burns argues
that F's '*Scena Secunda*' might indicate
that 4.7 could well begin Act 5 (i.e. as its
'*Scena Prima*') but he chooses instead not
only to keep it in Act 4 but to make it continuous with and part of 4.6. (It would
indeed be odd to begin Act 5 before the
episode of the Talbots is concluded.) I
have followed the traditional separation of
4.7 from 4.6 as the more likely alternative, however, as, once again, the Talbots
exeunt together, and, once again, in the
fracas off stage, get separated. This time
Talbot's son is killed and Talbot himself
led back on to the stage in a condition of
dismal weakness. (In the argument about
the desirability of continuous action we
might note that scene division is purely a
convenience for the reader and is in no
way a prescription as to how the play
should be presented in the theatre.) The
details of this scene are fictitious.
0.1 *old* F's mode of differentiation from the
   son is poignant here.
3 **Triumphant** 'riding in a triumph and
   leading captives after him' (Hattaway).
   smeared with captivity daubed with the
   blood of those captured and killed in battle (not just with the blood of the Talbots)

When he perceived me shrink and on my knee,   5
His bloody sword he brandished over me,
And like a hungry lion did commence
Rough deeds of rage and stern impatience.
But when my angry guardant stood alone,
Tend'ring my ruin and assailed of none,   10
Dizzy-eyed fury and great rage of heart
Suddenly made him from my side to start
Into the clust'ring battle of the French,
And in that sea of blood my boy did drench
His over-mounting spirit; and there died   15
My Icarus, my blossom, in his pride.
    Enter English soldiers with John Talbot's body, borne

SERVANT

O my dear lord, lo where your son is borne.

TALBOT

Thou antic death, which laugh'st us here to scorn,
Anon from thy insulting tyranny,
Coupled in bonds of perpetuity,   20
Two Talbots, wingèd, through the lither sky
In thy despite shall scape mortality.
  (*To John*) O thou, whose wounds become hard-favoured
    death,
Speak to thy father ere thou yield thy breath.
Brave death by speaking, whether he will or no;   25

16.1 *English soldiers*] OXFORD; *not in* F   *Talbot's body*] OXFORD; *Talbot* F   18 antic] F (antique)
25 whether] F (whither)

5 **shrink** yield
8 **impatience** (pronounced as four syllables)
   anger
9 **guardant** protector, guardian (a heraldic
   term). See 1.6.28 n.
10 **Tend'ring my ruin** solicitous of my fall
11 **Dizzy-eyed** wild-eyed
13 **clust'ring battle** swarming army
14 **drench** drown
15 **over-mounting** aspiring too high (as did
   Icarus)
16 **Icarus** 'This further reference to the Icarus
   story presents the blood of the battle as
   the sea in which John/Icarus drowns, and
   so transforms the story from a tale of rash
   accident to one of heroic resolve' (Burns).
   pride glory
17 **O . . . borne** Cited by M. M. Mahood in *Bit
   Parts in Shakespeare's Plays* (Cambridge,

1992) as a line that brings a bit part, the
Servant's, to life (4), and by Alexander
Leggatt in 'The Death of John Talbot' as
the final pun on 'born' indicating the way
the play 'allows parents to live on through
their children' (16).
18 **antic** grotesque jester
   here in this world
19 **Anon** soon
   insulting tyranny scornful cruelty
20 **Coupled . . . perpetuity** bound together
   for ever
21 **Two . . . sky** (like Icarus and his father)
   lither pliant, supple
22 **In thy despite** in spite of you
23 **become** (a) suit, are appropriate for (b)
   make beautiful
   hard-favoured ugly
25 **Brave** defy, challenge

Imagine him a Frenchman and thy foe.
Poor boy, he smiles, methinks, as who should say
'Had death been French, then death had died today.'
Come, come, and lay him in his father's arms.
    Soldiers lay John in Talbot's arms
My spirit can no longer bear these harms.   30
Soldiers, adieu. I have what I would have,
Now my old arms are young John Talbot's grave.
      He dies. ⌈*Alarum. Exeunt soldiers leaving the bodies*⌉
      Enter Charles the Dauphin, the Dukes of Alençon and
      Burgundy, the Bastard of Orléans, and Joan la Pucelle

CHARLES

Had York and Somerset brought rescue in,
We should have found a bloody day of this.

BASTARD

How the young whelp of Talbot's, raging wood,   35
Did flesh his puny sword in Frenchmen's blood.

JOAN

Once I encountered him, and thus I said:
'Thou maiden youth, be vanquished by a maid.'
But with a proud, majestical high scorn
He answered thus: 'Young Talbot was not born   40
To be the pillage of a giglot wench.'

29.1 *Soldiers . . . arms*] OXFORD; *not in* F   32.1 *He dies.*] F1 (*subs.*); *Dies. Actus Quintus. Scoena
Prima.* F2   *Alarum . . . bodies*] CAPELL; *not in* F   32.3 *Joan la Pucelle*] THEOBALD; *Pucell* F

27 **methinks** it seems to me
   as who as one who
28 **had** would have
30 **My . . . harms** Talbot, then, like Bedford,
does not die by the sword, but of a broken
heart over the death of his son (emphasized by Talbot's warrior-prowess in the
previous scene). This brings to a climax
the play's unrelenting focus on the suici-
dal unreliability of the English nobles
first denounced by the Messenger in the
opening scene: 'whilst a field should be
dispatched and fought, | You are disput-
ing of your generals' (1.1.72–3).
   harms wounds
32.1 *Alarum . . . bodies* Capell's direction
is necessary here otherwise there would
be an awkward presence on stage of
English soldiers who do nothing when
Charles and the others enter. Talbot's

'Soldiers, adieu' (31) thus serves a double
purpose.
33–4 **Had . . . this** A reminder of the real
cause of the French victory.
35 **whelp** 'young dog (with a quibble on
"talbot" meaning "hound")' (Sanders).
   wood mad
36 **puny** inexperienced (*OED adj.* 3)
37–43 **Once . . . fight** Joan's admiring description at her own expense of Young
Talbot's scorn of her as a 'giglot wench' is
conventional enough in the drama of the
time. But it nonetheless contributes to her
unsteadiness as a character.
38 **maiden** untried in battle
   by The actor would probably emphasize
this preposition to bring out the paral-
lelism between 'maiden' and 'maid'.
41 **pillage** plunder, spoil
   giglot (a) giddy (b) wanton

So, rushing in the bowels of the French,
He left me proudly, as unworthy fight.
BURGUNDY
Doubtless he would have made a noble knight.
See where he lies inhearsèd in the arms   45
Of the most bloody nurser of his harms.
BASTARD
Hew them to pieces, hack their bones asunder,
Whose life was England's glory, Gallia's wonder.
CHARLES
O no, forbear; for that which we have fled
During the life, let us not wrong it dead.   50
        Enter Sir William Lucy ⌈with a French herald⌉
LUCY
Herald, conduct me to the Dauphin's tent
To know who hath obtained the glory of the day.
CHARLES
On what submissive message art thou sent?
LUCY
Submission, Dauphin? 'Tis a mere French word.
We English warriors wot not what it means.   55
I come to know what prisoners thou hast ta'en,
And to survey the bodies of the dead.
CHARLES
For prisoners ask'st thou? Hell our prison is.
But tell me whom thou seek'st.

50.1 *with . . . herald*] CAPELL; *not in* F   51 Herald] F; *not in* POPE   52 To . . . day] F; To know
| Who . . . day POPE   To know who] F; Who HANMER

42 **bowels** midst
45 **inhearsèd** contained as in a coffin (in the
    'grave' of l. 32)
46 **bloody . . . harms** Talbot, himself covered
    in blood and critically wounded, seems to
    be nursing his dead son's wounds. But
    'his harms' could also = the wounds doled
    out by Talbot's son 'raging wood' among
    the French, so that Burgundy could be
    thinking of Talbot as his son's instructor
    ('nurser') in warfare. (A more far-fetched
    possibility has Talbot as the cause of his
    own son's death, the French not hav-
    ing witnessed, as we have, Talbot's
    attempts to persuade his son to fly from
    the battle.)
48 **Gallia's** France's

51–2 'Lucy's lines suggest that he expected
    an English victory' (Hattaway).
54 **mere** exclusively
55 **wot** know
58 **Hell . . . is** The French have killed the Eng-
    lish soldiers rather than captured them,
    so, as there's no question of their going to
    heaven as far as the French are con-
    cerned, hell is their only prison. (There is
    also the suggestion that the French have
    killed any prisoners they did take.)
59–60 **But . . . field** Hattaway notices the
    awkwardness of these lines with their
    chiming 'Buts' and suggests a number of
    reasons for it, the most interesting of
    which (and the most likely) proffers a
    bewildered pause on Lucy's part as he

LUCY

> But where's the great Alcides of the field,   60
> Valiant Lord Talbot, Earl of Shrewsbury,
> Created for his rare success in arms
> Great Earl of Wexford, Waterford, and Valence,
> Lord Talbot of Goodrich and Archenfield,
> Lord Strange of Blackmere, Lord Verdun of Alton,   65
> Lord Cromwell of Wingfield, Lord Furnival of Sheffield,
> The thrice victorious Lord of Falconbridge,
> Knight of the noble order of Saint George,
> Worthy Saint Michael, and the Golden Fleece,

60 But where's] F; Where is ROWE   63 Wexford] F (*Washford*)   64 Goodrich] F (*Goodrig*)   Archenfield] F (*Vrchinfield*)   66 Lord Cromwell . . . Lord Furnival] F (*Furniuall*); Cromwell . . . Furnival CAIRNCROSS (*conj.* Capell)   70 Maréchal] OXFORD; Marshall F

gazes anxiously around for a glimpse of England's foremost warrior. Charles's short line (58) also suggests that Lucy pauses before launching into his encomium's 'stately style'.

60 **Alcides** Hercules
61 **Lord Talbot** Lucy never gets beyond Talbot to ask after the other prisoners. Talbot's titles seem to have diverted him from pursuing their fates.
63–71 **Great . . . France** There is a complicated paper trail leading to the origins of Talbot's epitaph on a tomb erected to him in Falaise and since destroyed. (See G. Lambin's 'Here Lyeth John Talbot', *Études Anglaises*, 24 (1971), 361–76, for an account of this and J. Pearce's 'An Earlier Talbot Epitaph', *Modern Language Notes*, 59 (1944), 327–9, for possible literary sources.) Emrys Jones, however, claims the epitaph was taken from Rouen cathedral (see p. 143).
63 **Wexford** The modern name for the Irish town known in Shakespeare's time as Washford. Talbot succeeded to this title 'on the death of his niece Ankaret in 1421' (Hattaway).
    Waterford Another town in Ireland. Talbot was created Earl of Waterford when he was Governor of Ireland in 1446.
    Valence Joan of Valence, sister of Aymer de Valence, last Earl of Pembroke of that line, was an ancestor of Talbot's.
64 **Goodrich** Talbot's father was Richard, fourth Baron Talbot, of Goodrich Castle in the Welsh marches.
    Archenfield A district in south-east Herefordshire.

65 **Lord . . . Blackmere** 'Through his mother, Talbot was the sole heir of the last Lord Strange of Blackmere, a place close to Whitchurch in Shropshire' (Hattaway). It may be no coincidence that the current Lord Strange (Ferdinando Stanley) was patron of actors who performed in 'harey the vj' at the Rose in 1592— including Alleyn, who perhaps played Talbot.
    Lord . . . Alton Talbot held this title through Joan Furnival (see l. 66 n.), a descendant of Theobald de Verdun (d. 1316). Alton or Arelton Castle is in Staffordshire.
66 **Wingfield** An estate in Derbyshire, bought by John, 2nd Earl of Shrewsbury, sometime between 1440 and 1445. It might have been known as a Talbot/Shrewsbury property because Mary Queen of Scots was held there while in the custody of the sixth Earl.
    Lord . . . Sheffield 'Talbot held this title in the right of his first wife, Maud, only daughter of Thomas Neville, who held the title in the right of his wife, Joan Furnival' (Hattaway).
67 **Falconbridge** It is not known where Shakespeare derived this title. (It may be a misreading based on the fact that in 1447 the Earl of Shrewsbury and Lord Fauconberg were taken prisoner together by the French.)
68 **Knight** Talbot was knighted in 1413, and made a member of the Order of the Garter in 1424.
69 **Worthy . . . Fleece** The play continues to mingle Christian and pagan honours.
    Worthy as valuable as

Great *Maréchal* to Henry the Sixth   70
Of all his wars within the realm of France?

JOAN

Here's a silly stately style indeed.
The Turk, that two-and-fifty kingdoms hath,
Writes not so tedious a style as this.
Him that thou magnifiest with all these titles   75
Stinking and flyblown lies here at our feet.

LUCY

Is Talbot slain, the Frenchmen's only scourge,
Your kingdom's terror and black Nemesis?
O, were mine eye-balls into bullets turned,
That I in rage might shoot them at your faces!   80
O, that I could but call these dead to life
It were enough to fright the realm of France.
Were but his picture left amongst you here
It would amaze the proudest of you all.

75 magnifiest] F (magnifi'st)

69 **Saint Michael** The French royal Order of
Saint-Michel was established in 1469 in
imitation of the Golden Fleece (see next
note). Michael was the warrior archangel
of the Bible and protector of souls.
Golden Fleece The Burgundian chivalric
order, created on the model of the Garter
in 1430. Although a Christian order with
Saint Andrew as patron, it was named
after the famous fleece in Greek mythology sought by Jason and the Argonauts,
evoking Jason's selection of the foremost
heroes of his time as companions on his
quest; it possibly also referred to the wool
trade, the source of Burgundy's wealth. It
is unlikely that Talbot was ever a member.
In fact, much of this list of honours has a
dubious veracity.

70 *Maréchal* commander-in-chief. I have
adopted Oxford's modernized French version of F's 'Marshall' on the grounds that
it was at this time a French title with a
French syllabification. The extra syllable
in *Maréchal* and the possibility of pronouncing Henry as three syllables regularizes the line rhythmically. It is wittily
insulting for Lucy to climax his oration in
front of Joan and Charles with a French
word and Talbot's position in France,
which helps to account for Joan's scornful
response.

72 **silly stately** simple-mindedly ornate
73 **Turk** The Sultan of Turkey, a favourite
symbol for the Elizabethans of a spurious
magniloquence, grandiosity, and tyran-
nical behaviour.
73 **two-and-fifty kingdoms** Bajazeth, the
Turkish Sultan in Marlowe's *Tamburlaine*,
has 130 kingdoms (*2 Tamburlaine* 3.1.1
–7).
75 **magnifiest** F's two-syllable 'magnifi'st'
does not quite do justice to the word's
scornful contrast to *Stinking* and *flyblown*
in Joan's reply.
76 **flyblown** crawling with maggots (a minor
instance of Shakespeare's carefree han-
dling of time: the putrefaction process
has been greatly accelerated as Talbot has
only just been killed)
77 **only** supreme
78 **black** malignant, baneful (*OED a.* 8)
Nemesis goddess of retributive justice
81 **these dead** i.e. (presumably) both Talbots.
Yet Lucy moves so rapidly from (and yet
still within) the encomium to Talbot, the
father, that the plural form here suggests
that he is thinking of Talbot as the persons of his titles, great Earl of Wexford,
Waterford, Valence, etc.
83 **picture** portrait (*OED sb.* 1c). Contrast the
fate of Talbot's 'shadow' at the hands of
the Countess of Auvergne (2.3.35).
84 **amaze** terrify

218

Give me their bodies, that I may bear them hence   85
And give them burial as beseems their worth.
JOAN (*to Charles*)
I think this upstart is old Talbot's ghost,
He speaks with such a proud commanding spirit.
For God's sake let him have them. To keep them here
They would but stink and putrefy the air.   90
CHARLES
Go, take their bodies hence.
LUCY   I'll bear them hence;
But from their ashes shall be reared
A phoenix that shall make all France afeard.
CHARLES
So we be rid of them, do with them what thou wilt.
                    ⌈*Exeunt Lucy and herald with the bodies*⌉
And now to Paris in this conquering vein.   95
All will be ours now bloody Talbot's slain.   *Exeunt*

5.1   *Sennet. Enter King Henry, the Dukes of Gloucester and*
            Exeter, ⌈*and others*⌉
KING HENRY (*to Gloucester*)
Have you perused the letters from the Pope,
The Emperor, and the Earl of Armagnac?

85 may bear] F; bear CAIRNCROSS   89 have them] THEOBALD (*subs.*); haue him F   91–2 Go
...them hence; | But...reared] POPE; Go...bodies hence. | *Lucy.* Ile...reard F   92
ashes] F; ashes, Dauphin, POPE; noble ashes CAIRNCROSS   94 rid of them] F; rid CAPELL
with them] F2; with him F1   thou] F2; you F1   94.1 *Exeunt...bodies*] CAPELL (*subs.*); *not in*
F   96 *Exeunt*] ROWE; *Exit.* F

5.1] CAPELL; *Scena secunda* F   0.1 *Henry*] OXFORD; *not in* F   0.1–2 *and others*] CAPELL; *not*
in F   2 Armagnac] F (Arminack)

86 **beseems** suits
87 **upstart** insolent fellow
93 **phoenix** A mythical bird of which there is
   only one alive at any given time. Every
   500 years, in the deserts of Arabia, it
   regenerates itself from the ashes of its
   funeral pyre upon which it had immol-
   ated itself. It is therefore 'an emblem of
   the survival of individual worth in defi-
   ance of the logic of natural survival'
   (Burns). However, as Leggatt points out,
   this prophecy—'unusually for the *Henry*
   VI plays' ('The Death of John Talbot',
   19)—comes to nothing.
5.1 Yet another conflation of separate
   events. In 1435 attempts at peace-making
   at Arras (by the Pope and the Emperor);
   in 1442 proposals for the marriage of

Henry and Armagnac's daughter; in
1427 Winchester's installation as
Cardinal.
0.1 *Sennet* See note at 3.1.187.
1 **the letters** All three letters urge the King
   to make peace with France. The Pope's in
   addition confirms Winchester's elevation
   to Cardinal, and the Earl of Armagnac's
   may well treat of the marriage proposal
   between his daughter and Henry, bro-
   kered originally by Gloucester. Henry's
   question here intimates that he himself
   has not (yet) read the letters. Gloucester
   interprets them for him.
   Pope Eugenius IV (1431–47)
2 **Emperor** Sigismund of Luxemburg, Holy
   Roman Emperor and King of Hungary
   and Bohemia (1368–1437)

GLOUCESTER

I have, my lord, and their intent is this:
They humbly sue unto your excellence
To have a godly peace concluded of   5
Between the realms of England and of France.

KING HENRY

How doth your grace affect their motion?

GLOUCESTER

Well, my good lord, and as the only means
To stop effusion of our Christian blood,
And 'stablish quietness on every side.   10

KING HENRY

Ay, marry, uncle, for I always thought
It was both impious and unnatural
That such immanity and bloody strife
Should reign among professors of one faith.

GLOUCESTER

Beside, my lord, the sooner to effect   15
And surer bind this knot of amity,
The Earl of Armagnac—near knit to Charles—
A man of great authority in France,
Proffers his only daughter to your grace
In marriage with a large and sumptuous dowry.   20

KING HENRY

Marriage, uncle? Alas, my years are young,
And fitter is my study and my books
Than wanton dalliance with a paramour.

7 their] F1; this F4   16 this] F1; his F4   17 Armagnac] F (Arminacke)   knit] F; kin POPE

3 **intent** import (*OED sb.* 5)
7 **affect** incline towards
  motion proposal
9 **effusion** spilling
10 **'stablish quietness** establish peace
  every each (*OED a.* 7c)
11 **marry** See note at 2.3.30. This is an appropriate oath from the saintly Henry.
13 **immanity** monstrous cruelty, ferocity
  (*OED* 2)
14 **professors . . . faith** Perhaps a necessary
  reminder in the 1590s that both the
  French and English sides professed Roman
  Catholicism, though Henry, following
  Gloucester, might simply mean 'Christian'. See note on Winchester in 'Persons'.
17 **near knit** closely tied

20 **sumptuous dowry** Its sumptuousness,
  according to the Chronicles, consisted of
  immense sums of money, castles, and
  towns. Contrast Margaret's penury.
21 **my . . . young** Henry was twenty-one at
  this time.
23 **wanton . . . paramour** Henry's immediate
  response to Gloucester's urging of a politically advantageous marriage suggests a
  callow sexuality and anticipates his surrender to Suffolk's incendiary description
  in 5.6 of the delights awaiting him in
  a union with Margaret of Anjou. Hart
  notes that 'paramour' in these early plays
  is always used 'with a repugnant sense'—
  though see note to 5.4.38. (In ll. 26–7
  Henry retreats into his customary piety.)

Yet call th'ambassadors, *⌈Exit one or more⌉*
          and, as you please,
So let them have their answers every one. 25
I shall be well content with any choice
Tends to God's glory and my country's weal.
    Enter the Bishop of Winchester, now in Cardinal's
    habit, and three ambassadors, one a Papal Legate, ⌈an-
    other from the Earl of Armagnac⌉
EXETER (*aside*)
  What, is my lord of Winchester installed
  And called unto a cardinal's degree?
  Then, I perceive, that will be verified 30
  Henry the Fifth did sometime prophesy:
  'If once he come to be a cardinal,
  He'll make his cap co-equal with the crown.'
KING HENRY
  My lords ambassadors, your several suits
  Have been considered and debated on. 35
  Your purpose is both good and reasonable,
  And therefore are we certainly resolved
  To draw conditions of a friendly peace,
  Which by my lord of Winchester we mean
  Shall be transported presently to France. 40
GLOUCESTER *⌈to the ambassador of the Earl of Armagnac⌉*
  And for the proffer of my lord your master,
  I have informed his highness so at large

---

24 *Exit . . . more*] OXFORD; *not in* F 27.1 *now . . . habit*] CAPELL (*subs.*); *not in* F 27.2 *one . . . Legate*] OXFORD; *not in* F *another . . . Armagnac*] This edition (*after* BURNS); *not in* F

27 **Tends** that tends
  weal welfare, good government
27.1–2 ***Cardinal's habit*** Winchester has now the right officially to wear his scarlet hat and robes. See note to 1.3.19.
27.2 ***three ambassadors*** One the Pope's Legate, another an ambassador from the Emperor, a third representing the interests of the Earl of Armagnac.
28 *aside* Exeter's role in the play as choric observer justifies Munro's reading of this speech as an aside.
29 **degree** rank
31 **sometime** once
33 **cap** A disparaging reference to the Cardinal's red hat.

34 **several suits** individual requests
37 **certainly** fixedly, so as not to be altered (*OED adv.* 2b)
38 **draw** frame, compose (*OED v. v* 63)
39 **mean** intend (*OED v.* 1d)
40 **presently** at once
42–5 **I . . . queen** This, Gloucester's, is the first report of two wooings of Henry by proxy. The second is by Suffolk in the play's final scene. In both cases what is actually said on behalf of the two women occurs off stage, so we are not privy to Suffolk's seductive blandishments that changed Henry's mind. Suffolk doesn't anticipate much difficulty: 'Henry is youthful, and will quickly yield' (5.4.55).

As, liking of the lady's virtuous gifts,
Her beauty, and the value of her dower,
He doth intend she shall be England's queen.   45
KING HENRY
In argument and proof of which contract
Bear her this jewel, pledge of my affection.
⌈_He gives the Ambassador a ring_⌉
(_To Gloucester_) And so, my lord Protector, see them
    guarded
And safely brought to Dover, wherein shipped,
Commit them to the fortune of the sea.   50
    Exeunt ⌈_severally_⌉ _all but Winchester and Legate_
WINCHESTER
Stay, my lord legate; you shall first receive
The sum of money which I promisèd
Should be delivered to his holiness
For clothing me in these grave ornaments.
    ⌈_He hands him money_⌉
LEGATE
I will attend upon your lordship's leisure.   _Exit_   55
WINCHESTER
Now Winchester will not submit, I trow,
Or be inferior to the proudest peer.
Humphrey of Gloucester, thou shalt well perceive
That neither in birth or for authority
The Bishop will be overborne by thee.   60
I'll either make thee stoop and bend thy knee,
Or sack this country with a mutiny.   _Exit_

47.1 _He gives . . . ring_] BURNS (_subs._); _not in_ F   49 wherein shipped] F1; _where_ inshipp'd F4
50.1 _all . . . legate_] CAPELL (_subs._); _not in_ F   54.1 _He hands him money_] This edition; _not in_ F
55 _Exit_] DYCE; _not in_ F   59 neither] F; _nor_ POPE   62 _Exit_] DYCE; _Exeunt_ F

43 **virtuous   gifts** estimable   natural
    endowments
46 **In argument** as demonstration
    contract (accented on second syllable)
48 **them** i.e. the three ambassadors
49 **shipped** embarked
51 **legate** ecclesiastic deputed to represent
    the Pope and armed with his authority

54 **grave ornaments** dignified robes
60 **Bishop** By which Winchester means
    the 'chief priest' (_OED sb._ 2), though he
    might well have taken the opportunity to
    refer to himself by his new title.
62 **mutiny** rebellion

5.2   *Enter Charles the Dauphin* ⌈*reading a letter*⌉, *the Dukes*
        of Burgundy and Alençon, the Bastard of Orléans,
        Reignier Duke of Anjou, and Joan la Pucelle

CHARLES

    These news, my lords, may cheer our drooping spirits;
    'Tis said the stout Parisians do revolt
    And turn again unto the warlike French.

ALENÇON

    Then march to Paris, royal Charles of France,
    And keep not back your powers in dalliance.   5

JOAN

    Peace be amongst them if they turn to us;
    Else ruin combat with their palaces.
       Enter a Scout

SCOUT

    Success unto our valiant general,
    And happiness to his accomplices.

CHARLES

    What tidings send our scouts? I prithee, speak.   10

SCOUT

    The English army, that divided was
    Into two parties, is now conjoined in one,
    And means to give you battle presently.

CHARLES

    Somewhat too sudden, sirs, the warning is;
    But we will presently provide for them.   15

BURGUNDY

    I trust the ghost of Talbot is not there.

5.2] CAPELL; *Scoena Tertia* F   0.1 *reading a letter*] OXFORD; *not in* F   0.2 *Duke of Anjou*]
OXFORD; *not in* F   0.2–3 *Joan la Pucelle*] THEOBALD; *Ione* F   5 powers] F1; power F2   7 combat with] F; come within CAIRNCROSS   7.1 *a*] OXFORD; *not in* F   12 is now conjoined] F; now
conjoins CAIRNCROSS

5.2.0.1 *reading a letter* The opening of this
   scene parallels that of the previous one;
   both begin with the perusal of a letter.
   Letters will be a staple feature of Shakespearian drama—*King Lear*, for example,
   is full of them.
2 **stout** resolute
   Parisians do revolt 'But, technically, in
   this play at least, the oath of allegiance to
   Henry has not been explicitly sworn—

unless one takes this line in itself as evidence that it was' (Burns).
3 **turn again** The Messenger had brought
   news to the English lords of England's loss
   of Paris to the French at 1.1.61.
5 **dalliance** idleness
9 **accomplices** allies
12 **conjoined** united
13, 15 **presently** immediately

⌈JOAN⌉

   Now he is gone, my lord, you need not fear.

   Of all base passions fear is most accursed.

   Command the conquest, Charles, it shall be thine;

   Let Henry fret and all the world repine.   20

CHARLES

   Then on, my lords, and France be fortunate.   *Exeunt*

5.3   *Alarum. Excursions. Enter Joan la Pucelle*

JOAN

   The Regent conquers and the Frenchmen fly.

   Now help, ye charming spells and periapts,

   And ye choice spirits that admonish me

   And give me signs of future accidents.

       Thunder

   You speedy helpers, that are substitutes   5

   Under the lordly monarch of the north,

   Appear, and aid me in this enterprise.

       Enter Fiends

   This speedy and quick appearance argues proof

---

17 JOAN Now . . . fear. | Of] OXFORD; Now . . . fear. | *Pucel.* Of F

5.3] CAPELL; *not in* F   0.1 *Joan la Pucelle*] ROWE (*le*); *Ione de Pucell* F   8 speedy and quick] F; speed ~ ~ DYCE; speedy quick POPE

---

17 **Now . . . fear** F gives this line to Burgundy, but it is odd that he should express a concern for the possible presence of Talbot's ghost and then immediately reassure Charles (presumably) that 'he [Talbot] is gone'. More than likely the line has strayed from Joan's attempt to stiffen Burgundy's resolve. Her rejection of Burgundy's superstitiousness hardly prepares us for her successful invocation of her fiends in the next scene, but it is in keeping with the play's schizophrenic treatment of her character and personality. An alternative emendation can be found in Sanders who gives l. 16 to Charles and l. 17 to Burgundy. But again, it is odd—though not impossible—for Charles to move from the confidence of l. 15, 'But we will presently provide for them' (the English army), to a fear that the presence of Talbot's ghost may in fact make providing for them problematic.

18 **passions** emotions

20 **repine** complain

5.3.1 The Regent Richard, Duke of York.

Historically, Bedford was Regent when Joan was captured in 1430.

2 **charming** magic

  periapts 'written charms, inscribed on a bandage and wrapped around a part of the body which they were deemed to protect' (Burns).

3 **choice** of special excellence

  admonish forewarn

4 **accidents** events (*OED sb.* 1)

4.1 **Thunder** 'Thunder generally disguised the clatter of stage traps as spirits rose from below' (Wilson).

5 **substitutes** deputies

6 **lordly . . . north** Lucifer. See Isaiah 14: 13: 'I will climb up into heaven, and exalt my throne above beside the stars of God. I will sit also upon the mount of the congregation toward the north.' The mount is Mount Moriah. In *Paradise Lost* Satan assembles his rebel angels in the 'Quarters of the North' (5.689). In his plays Shakespeare links trouble with winter.

8 **argues proof** gives evidence

Of your accustomed diligence to me.
Now, ye familiar spirits, that are culled   10
Out of the powerful regions under earth,
Help me this once, that France may get the field.
　　They walk and speak not
O hold me not with silence overlong!
Where I was wont to feed you with my blood,
I'll lop a member off and give it you   15
In earnest of a further benefit,
So you do condescend to help me now.
　　They hang their heads
No hope to have redress? My body shall
Pay recompense if you will grant my suit.
　　They shake their heads
Cannot my body nor blood-sacrifice   20
Entreat you to your wonted furtherance?
Then take my soul—my body, soul, and all—
Before that England give the French the foil.

　　　　　　　　　　　　　　　They depart

See, they forsake me. Now the time is come
That France must vail her lofty-plumèd crest   25
And let her head fall into England's lap.
My ancient incantations are too weak,
And hell too strong for me to buckle with.

10 culled] F (cull'd); call'd COLLIER 11 regions] F; legions SINGER (*conj.* Warburton)

9 **accustomed** customary
10 **familiar spirits** See note at 3.2.120. Perhaps Joan's fiends would appear in the likeness of animals as in the case of the devils that Prospero and Ariel set on Stefano and Trinculo in the fourth act of *The Tempest*. David Daniell in 'Opening up the Text: Shakespeare's *Henry VI* Plays in Performance', in *Themes in Drama*, 1 (1979), 247–77, notes that in the Terry Hands production in 1977 the fiends appeared 'looking like gas-masked soldiers from the French trenches of the First World War' (257). In Michael Boyd's 2000 production at the Swan in Stratford-upon-Avon the fiends were women (prefiguring the Witches in *Macbeth*).
culled chosen
12 **get the field** win the battle
12.1 ***They . . . not*** Traditionally spirits were loath to answer questions or to speak at

all. In *The First Part of the Contention* the spirit Asnath only grudgingly talks with the witch, Margery Jordan, 'Ask what thou wilt, that I had said and done' (1.4.29).
13 **hold** keep
14 **Where** whereas
15 **member** limb
16 **In earnest** as a token
17 **condescend** agree (*OED v.* 5)
18 **redress** help
21 **wonted furtherance** customary assistance
22 **soul** Repetition of this word suggests that this is the offer the fiends should not be able to refuse, Joan's last throw of the dice, the 'further benefit' of l. 16.
23 **give . . . foil** defeat
25 **vail** lower
crest helmet
27 **ancient** (a) former (b) time-honoured
28 **buckle** grapple, fight

225

Now, France, thy glory droopeth to the dust.   *Exit*
          Excursions. The Dukes of Burgundy and York fight hand
          to hand. The French enter with Joan la Pucelle and fly.
          Joan is taken by York

RICHARD DUKE OF YORK

Damsel of France, I think I have you fast.   30
Unchain your spirits now with spelling charms,
And try if they can gain your liberty.
A goodly prize, fit for the devil's grace.
See how the ugly witch doth bend her brows
As if with Circe she would change my shape.   35

JOAN

Changed to a worser shape thou canst not be.

RICHARD DUKE OF YORK

O, Charles the Dauphin is a proper man.
No shape but his can please your dainty eye.

JOAN

A plaguing mischief light on Charles and thee!
And may ye both be suddenly surprised   40
By bloody hands, in sleeping on your beds.

RICHARD DUKE OF YORK

Fell banning hag! Enchantress, hold thy tongue!

JOAN

I prithee, give me leave to curse awhile.

29.2 *The . . . fly*] BURNS (*subs.*); *French fly* F   *Joan . . . York*] HATTAWAY (*subs.*); *not in* F; *Joan la Pucelle is taken* OXFORD   33 devil's] F (diuels)

29 *Exit* Joan's exit here, leaving the stage momentarily empty, is a cue for some editions to begin a new scene (e.g. the Oxford). But again the pace of events suggests continuous action. See headnote to 3.2.

29.1 *Burgundy* Some editors have suggested that F's Burgundy is a mistake for Joan but, bearing in mind Burgundy's defection to the English in Act 3, his defeat (and death?) by York, and York's capture of Joan (after a presumably listless defence on her part, perhaps made more pointed by a spirited combat between the men) emphasize the comprehensiveness of the French defeat. Historically, Burgundy survived long enough to support Edward Earl of March and to see him become Edward IV.

31 **spelling** bewitching

33 **grace** favour

34 **bend her brows** frown, scowl

35 **with** like
     Circe In Greek mythology an enchantress who lived on the island of Aeaea with her wild animals. Odysseus' companions were changed into pigs by her potions (*Odyssey*, trans. A. T. Murray, rev. George E. Dimock, Loeb edn., 2 vols. (1995) i. 10, ll. 133–574).

37 **proper** handsome

38 **dainty** fastidious

40–1 **And . . . beds** For York's dismal fate see the note on Richard Plantagenet in 'Persons'. Charles died peacefully in 1461 after having recovered most of the land seized by the English. He modernized the army and laid the foundations of French power in the last decades of the century.

41 **in** while

42 **Fell banning** ugly cursing

RICHARD DUKE OF YORK

Curse, miscreant, when thou com'st to the stake. *Exeunt*

5.4   *Alarum. Enter the Earl of Suffolk with Margaret in his*
        hand

SUFFOLK

Be what thou wilt, thou art my prisoner.
    He gazes on her
O fairest beauty, do not fear nor fly,
For I will touch thee but with reverent hands,
And lay them gently on thy tender side.
I kiss these fingers for eternal peace.   5
Who art thou? Say, that I may honour thee.

MARGARET

Margaret my name, and daughter to a king,
The King of Naples—whosoe'er thou art.

---

44 com'st] F (comest)

5.4] OXFORD; *not in* F   3 reverent] HANMER; reuerend F   4–5 And . . . side. | I . . . peace.]
CAPELL; I . . . peace | And . . . side. F (*subs.*)   6 thou? Say,] OXFORD; ~, ~? F; ~, ~, CAIRN-
CROSS

---

44 **miscreant** heretic
5.4 The centre of attention shifts for the
moment from Joan to the beginnings of
the love affair between Suffolk and Margaret of Anjou and, for this reason, if for
no other, justifies a new scene. As well, at
l. 86 Reignier's appearance on his castle
walls indicates that the scene has shifted
from the unlocalized 5.3 (somewhere
before Angiers). Margaret's capture
coincides with Joan's by York. 'It is
no accident that, as one captured
French "enchantress" is led off prisoner,
another, her direct successor, is led
on, "prisoner"' (Cairncross). Suffolk's
romantic involvement with Margaret is
pursued in *The First Part of the Contention*
(*2 Henry VI*) and is unhistorical, though
there are faint hints of it in Hall.

0.1 **in** led by the
1 **Be . . . prisoner** because you are my prisoner, you are free to do whatever you
wish (a gallant untruth)
1.1 *He . . . her* An explicitly provocative invitation to the actor. How Margaret
responds would depend upon how the
actress interprets her behaviour at this
stage of the proceedings. She is later

clearly complicit with Suffolk's flirtatious-
ness, but here she could be annoyed or
frightened.
4–5 **And . . . peace** F's reversal of these lines
is followed by many editions despite the
awkwardness of Suffolk's straying fingers, prompting Hattaway indeed to
suggest that Suffolk may place them on
Margaret's crotch, which hardly seems in
the spirit of touching her with 'reverent
hands' (l. 3). It's hard to imagine the
hands being reverent but the fingers not. I
follow Capell here in his assumption that
the lines were somehow reversed in the
printing process, a fairly commonplace
occurrence. Although we should be wary
of emending Shakespeare simply to make
him more pleasing to our aesthetic judgement we might note that Hart calls these
lines as they stand in F 'utterly puerile'.
He does not, however, think Capell's
emendation much of an improvement.
5 **fingers** Capell's emendation of the order of
ll. 4–5 requires that the fingers in question here be Margaret's. F's line order
allows them to belong either to Margaret
or to Suffolk.
for in token of

SUFFOLK

An earl I am, and Suffolk am I called.
Be not offended, nature's miracle,   10
Thou art allotted to be ta'en by me.
So doth the swan her downy cygnets save,
Keeping them prisoner underneath her wings.
Yet if this servile usage once offend,
Go, and be free again, as Suffolk's friend.   15
        She is going
O stay! (*To himself*) I have no power to let her pass.
My hand would free her, but my heart says no.
As plays the sun upon the glassy streams,
Twinkling another counterfeited beam,
So seems this gorgeous beauty to mine eyes.   20
Fain would I woo her, yet I dare not speak.
I'll call for pen and ink and write my mind.
Fie, de la Pole, disable not thyself!
Hast not a tongue? Is she not here?
Wilt thou be daunted at a woman's sight?   25
Ay; beauty's princely majesty is such
Confounds the tongue, and makes the senses rough.

MARGARET

Say, Earl of Suffolk—if thy name be so—
What ransom must I pay before I pass?
For I perceive I am thy prisoner.   30

---

12 her] F; his OXFORD   13 her] F2; his F1   24 here?] F1; heere thy prisoner? F2; prisoner
here? CAIRNCROSS; here to hear? OXFORD   27 Confounds] F ('Confounds)   makes . . . rough]
F; mocks the sense of touch COLLIER; Makes the senses nought VAUGHAN

---

11 **allotted** destined (*OED v.* 4)
12 **cygnets save** young swans protect
14 **servile usage** slavelike treatment
16–27 **I . . . rough** Suffolk debates with himself for eleven lines, a lengthy period for Margaret to be neglected. The actress playing her role must register some kind of response—boredom, impatience, irritation—for, as Suffolk himself points out, 'Is she not here?' (l. 24).
18–20 **As . . . eyes** 'i.e., she seems as gorgeous as the sun's reflection twinkling upon the water's surface' (Montgomery)
18 **glassy** like a mirror

23 **disable** disparage
24 **Is . . . here?** Editorial attempts—following the example of F2—to flesh out and regularize this line seem to me unnecessary. This question neatly balances the one in the first half of the line and in their abruptness both convey Suffolk's turbulent feelings.
25 **Wilt . . . sight** This parallels (with some significant differences) the daunting of Talbot by Joan.
    a woman's sight the sight of a woman
27 **Confounds** i.e. that it confounds
    makes . . . rough blunts the senses

SUFFOLK (*to himself*)

  How canst thou tell she will deny thy suit

  Before thou make a trial of her love?

MARGARET

  Why speak'st thou not? What ransom must I pay?

SUFFOLK (*to himself*)

  She's beautiful, and therefore to be wooed;

  She is a woman, therefore to be won.   35

MARGARET

  Wilt thou accept of ransom, yea or no?

SUFFOLK (*to himself*)

  Fond man, remember that thou hast a wife;

  Then how can Margaret be thy paramour?

MARGARET (*to herself*)

  I were best to leave him, for he will not hear.

SUFFOLK (*to himself*)

  There all is marred; there lies a cooling card.   40

MARGARET

  He talks at random; sure the man is mad.

SUFFOLK (*to himself*)

  And yet a dispensation may be had.

MARGARET

  And yet I would that you would answer me.

SUFFOLK (*to himself*)

  I'll win this Lady Margaret. For whom?

  Why, for my king—tush, that's a wooden thing.   45

39 I were] F; 'Twere POPE   41 random] F (randon)

32 **make . . . of** attempt to win

34–5 **She's . . . won** Proverbial: 'All women may be won' (Tilley W681). There is a strikingly similar expression of the same sentiment by Demetrius in *Titus Andronicus*: 'She is a woman, therefore may be wooed; | She is a woman, therefore may be won' (2.1.82–3).

37 **Fond** foolish

  thou . . . wife Suffolk was married to Alice . . . the Earl of Salisbury's widow.

38 **paramour** See note to 5.1.23. If Hart is right then this is precisely what Margaret can become, i.e. the illicit lover of Suffolk (*OED* B *sb.* 3). Clearly Suffolk is using the word unpejoratively as 'beloved person', 'sweetheart' (*OED* B *sb.* 2).

40 **There . . . card** Nearly all of these 'exchanges' could be self-directed. One or two of them, however (such as this one), suggest that the other person at least half-hears what is being said or hears lines that do not make any sense out of context.

  There for that reason (i.e. the fact that he's married)

  a cooling card In the card game an opponent's card that dashes one's hopes.

42 **And . . . had** See first note to l. 40. Margaret's parallel 'And yet' in the next line suggests she half-hears this line but without comprehending its meaning or significance.

  dispensation a dissolution of the marriage granted by the Pope

45 **tush . . . thing** Again, Margaret's line that follows confirms that she hears this half of Suffolk's line.

MARGARET (*to herself*)

  He talks of wood. It is some carpenter.

SUFFOLK (*to himself*)

  Yet so my fancy may be satisfied,

  And peace establishèd between these realms,

  But there remains a scruple in that too,

  For though her father be the King of Naples,   50

  Duke of Anjou and Maine, yet is he poor,

  And our nobility will scorn the match.

MARGARET

  Hear ye, captain? Are you not at leisure?

SUFFOLK (*to himself*)

  It shall be so, disdain they ne'er so much.

  Henry is youthful, and will quickly yield.   55

  (*To Margaret*) Madam, I have a secret to reveal.

MARGARET (*to herself*)

  What though I be enthralled, he seems a knight,

  And will not any way dishonour me.

SUFFOLK

  Lady, vouchsafe to listen what I say.

MARGARET (*to herself*)

  Perhaps I shall be rescued by the French,   60

  And then I need not crave his courtesy.

SUFFOLK

  Sweet madam, give me hearing in a cause.

MARGARET (*to herself*)

  Tush, women have been captivate ere now.

SUFFOLK

  Lady, wherefore talk you so?

---

64 Lady] F; Lady, sweet lady WALKER; Nay, hear me, lady CAPELL

---

45 **wooden thing** dull, lifeless, referring either to (a) the king or (b) the enterprise or to both. See the pun at 1.1.19.

47 **fancy** amorous inclination

49 **scruple** objection

53 **captain** 'Margaret is addressing Suffolk by a provocatively unflattering title; this is his rank within the army, but one might expect her to acknowledge his aristocratic status' (Burns). Especially as Suffolk has been at pains to point it out to her: 'An earl I am, and Suffolk am I called' (l. 9).

53 **Are . . . leisure** Cf. Talbot: 'since your ladyship is not at leisure, | I'll sort some other time to visit you' (2.3.25–6).

54 **disdain** disapprove

57 **enthralled** enslaved

62 **cause** serious proposal

63 **captivate** (a) made prisoner (b) strongly attracted

64 **wherefore** why

MARGARET

  I cry you mercy, 'tis but *quid* for *quo*.   65

SUFFOLK

  Say, gentle princess, would you not suppose

  Your bondage happy, to be made a queen?

MARGARET

  To be a queen in bondage is more vile

  Than is a slave in base servility,

  For princes should be free.

SUFFOLK   And so shall you,   70

  If happy England's royal king be free.

MARGARET

  Why, what concerns his freedom unto me?

SUFFOLK

  I'll undertake to make thee Henry's queen,

  To put a golden sceptre in thy hand,

  And set a precious crown upon thy head,   75

  If thou wilt condescend to be my—

MARGARET   What?

SUFFOLK His love.

MARGARET

  I am unworthy to be Henry's wife.

SUFFOLK

  No, gentle madam, I unworthy am

  To woo so fair a dame to be his wife   80

  (*Aside*) And have no portion in the choice myself.—

  How say you, madam; are ye so content?

MARGARET

  An if my father please, I am content.

83 An] F (And)

---

65 **cry you mercy** beg your pardon
   quid **for** *quo* tit for tat
67 **to be** if you were to be
68 **vile** worthless
69 **servility** slavery
70 **princes** Applicable to both men and women of royal blood.
71 **If . . . free** A compound irony. England (particularly its nobility) is not happy with Henry, who is not behaving in a sufficiently 'royal' manner, and is most certainly not 'free' in his subservience to his advisers.
76 **condescend** agree
77 **His love** The extra-metrical awkwardness of this line (noticeable even in performance) underscores Suffolk's (intended?) blunder.
81 **portion** share
   choice (a) the choosing (b) the thing chosen
83 **An if** if

SUFFOLK

    Then call our captains and our colours forth,

    And, madam, at your father's castle walls   85

    We'll crave a parley to confer with him.

       ⌈*Enter captains, colours, and trumpeters.*⌉ *Sound a par-*

       ley. Enter Reignier Duke of Anjou on the walls

    See, Reignier, see thy daughter prisoner.

REIGNIER

    To whom?

SUFFOLK   To me.

REIGNIER   Suffolk, what remedy?

    I am a soldier, and unapt to weep,

    Or to exclaim on fortune's fickleness.   90

SUFFOLK

    Yes, there is remedy enough, my lord.

    Consent—and for thy honour give consent—

    Thy daughter shall be wedded to my king,

    Whom I with pain have wooed and won thereto;

    And this, her easy-held imprisonment,   95

    Hath gained thy daughter princely liberty.

REIGNIER

    Speaks Suffolk as he thinks?

SUFFOLK   Fair Margaret knows

    That Suffolk doth not flatter, face, or feign.

REIGNIER

    Upon thy princely warrant I descend

    To give thee answer of thy just demand.   100

86.1 *Enter . . . trumpeters*] HATTAWAY; *not in* F   86.2 *a parley*] OXFORD; *not in* F *Duke of Anjou*] OXFORD; *not in* F   92 Consent] F; Assent OXFORD

84 **colours** standard bearers
86 **confer with** speak to
89 **unapt** disinclined
90 **exclaim on** complain of
92 **Consent . . . consent** A particularly uninspired line perhaps, not helped very much by Oxford's emendation of 'Consent' to 'Assent'. Separating off the clause 'and for thy honour give consent' underlines Suffolk's appeal to Reignier's self-interest. If Reignier consents to his daughter's

marriage to Henry he will also be consenting to something that will be well worth his while.
94 **Whom** As he is yet to break the news to Henry, this 'whom' must refer to Margaret. The line has therefore an obvious irony.
   pain considerable effort
95 **easy-held** comfortable
98 **face** deceive (*OED sb.* 4b)
99 **warrant** assurance

SUFFOLK

And here I will expect thy coming.

[*Exit Reignier above*]

Trumpets sound. Enter Reignier

REIGNIER

Welcome, brave Earl, into our territories.

Command in Anjou what your honour pleases.

SUFFOLK

Thanks, Reignier, happy for so sweet a child,

Fit to be made companion with a king.   105

What answer makes your grace unto my suit?

REIGNIER

Since thou dost deign to woo her little worth

To be the princely bride of such a lord—

Upon condition I may quietly

Enjoy mine own, the country Maine and Anjou,   110

Free from oppression or the stroke of war—

My daughter shall be Henry's, if he please.

SUFFOLK

That is her ransom. I deliver her,

And those two counties I will undertake

Your grace shall well and quietly enjoy.   115

REIGNIER

And I—again in Henry's royal name,

As deputy unto that gracious king—

Give thee her hand for sign of plighted faith.

---

101 coming.] F; ~ , Reignier. CAPELL   101.1 *Exit Reignier above*] OXFORD (*subs.*); *not in* F   110 country] F; countries CAPELL; county MALONE

101 **expect** await

103 **Anjou** 'From the English point of view, Anjou is not his at all; so his use of *our* could be heard as provocative' (Burns).

104 **happy for** fortunate in

107 **little worth** lowly state. Although this is a conventional expression of courtly modesty it is precisely Margaret's exiguous expectations that infuriates the English nobles (other than Suffolk), particularly Gloucester.

109 **quietly** in peace

110 **country** *OED's* first definition—'a tract or expanse of land of undefined extent; a region, district'—makes emendation unnecessary.

113 **That . . . ransom** i.e. her marriage to Henry. But wedged between Reignier's line and Suffolk's agreement over the 'two counties', Margaret's 'ransom' could ironically be considered the English abandonment of Maine and Anjou.
deliver free

114 **counties** domains of a count

117 **deputy** i.e. Suffolk

118 **plighted** pledged

SUFFOLK

    Reignier of France, I give thee kingly thanks,

    Because this is in traffic of a king.   120

    (*Aside*) And yet methinks I could be well content

    To be mine own attorney in this case.

    (*To Reignier*) I'll over then to England with this news,

    And make this marriage to be solemnized.

    So farewell, Reignier; set this diamond safe   125

    In golden palaces, as it becomes.

REIGNIER

    I do embrace thee as I would embrace

    The Christian prince King Henry, were he here.

                       ⌈*Exit Reignier*⌉

MARGARET

    Farewell, my lord. Good wishes, praise, and prayers

    Shall Suffolk ever have of Margaret.   130

       She is going

SUFFOLK

    Farewell, sweet madam; but hark you, Margaret—

    No princely commendations to my king?

MARGARET

    Such commendations as becomes a maid,

    A virgin, and his servant, say to him.

SUFFOLK

    Words sweetly placed, and modestly directed.   135

       ⌈*She is going*⌉

    But madam, I must trouble you again—

    No loving token to his majesty?

MARGARET

    Yes, my good lord: a pure unspotted heart,

    Never yet taint with love, I send the King.

128.1 *Exit Reignier*] This edition; *not in* F   131 madam] F; maid CAIRNCROSS   135 modestly]
F2; modestie FI   135.1 *She is going*] OXFORD; *not in* F

120 **traffic** the business
122 **To . . . case** to represent myself (rather than the King) as suitor
125 **this diamond** i.e. Margaret
126 **as it becomes** as is fitting for her
128.1 *Exit Reignier* Reignier might well exit after l. 130 with Margaret in tow. But it is not unlikely that, the marriage having been satisfactorily arranged, Reignier should leave Margaret alone with her future husband's representative.
132 **commendations** greetings
135 **placed** arranged
139 **taint** tainted, stained. An odd word to qualify 'love', but this is courtly hyperbole.

SUFFOLK And this withal.   140
  He kisses her
MARGARET
  That for thyself; I will not so presume
  To send such peevish tokens to a king.   ⌜*Exit*⌝
SUFFOLK
  O wert thou for myself!—but Suffolk, stay.
  Thou mayst not wander in that labyrinth:
  There Minotaurs and ugly treasons lurk.   145
  Solicit Henry with her wondrous praise;
  Bethink thee on her virtues that surmount,
  Natural graces that extinguish art.
  Repeat their semblance often on the seas,
  That when thou com'st to kneel at Henry's feet   150
  Thou mayst bereave him of his wits with wonder.
                                                             Exit

5.5   *Enter Richard Duke of York, the Earl of Warwick,*
        and a Shepherd
RICHARD DUKE OF YORK
  Bring forth that sorceress condemned to burn.
    Enter Joan la Pucelle guarded

140.1 *He kisses*] OXFORD; *Kisse* F   142 *Exit*] BURNS; *Exeunt Reignier and Margaret* CAPELL   148 Natural] This edition; Mad ~ F; And ~ CAPELL; 'Mid ~ COLLIER 1858; Maid ~ WILSON (*conj.* Perring)
 5.5] OXFORD; *not in* F   0.1 *Enter . . . Shepherd*] OXFORD; *Enter . . . Shepheard, Pucell* F; *Enter York, Warwick, and Others* CAPELL; *Enter York, Warwick, a Shepherd, La Pucelle guarded, and others* HATTAWAY   *Duke of York*] OXFORD; *not in* F   *the Earl of*] OXFORD; *not in* F   1.1 *Enter . . . guarded*] OXFORD; *not in* F; *Enter La Pucelle guarded and a Shepherd* CAPELL (*subs.*)

140 **withal** also
142 **peevish** trifling
144 **labyrinth** In Greek mythology, built by Daedalus at the command of Minos, King of Crete, to contain the Minotaur, a monster with a bull's head and a male human body. 'He' was the offspring of the union between Minos' wife Pasiphae and a bull. Suffolk is clearly thinking of any union between himself and Margaret as nightmarishly unnatural.
146 **Solicit** move, excite
  her wondrous praise mesmerizing praise of her
147 **surmount** excel
148 **Natural** F's qualifying 'Mad' is oddly superfluous both in terms of the line's meaning and metre (though 'natural' could at a pinch be dissyllabic). Editorial

attempts at emending 'mad' to something more appropriate are unconvincing. Burns's suggestion that 'Mad' is a printing error is persuasive and I have emended accordingly.
  extinguish eclipse
149 **Repeat their semblance** 'recall repeatedly the image of her virtues by rehearsing descriptions of them' (Sanders).
151 **bereave** deprive
5.5.0.2 *Shepherd* Joan's father who appears in Hall as 'a simple man and a silly soul' (Bullough, 63). Joan's repudiation of him and his outrage over it are an invention of Shakespeare's. The scene reveals a Joan shorn of her earlier spiritual and moral (and human) authority.

SHEPHERD

    Ah, Joan, this kills thy father's heart outright.

    Have I sought every country far and near,

    And—now it is my chance to find thee out—

    Must I behold thy timeless cruel death?   5

    Ah Joan, sweet daughter Joan, I'll die with thee.

JOAN

    Decrepit miser, base ignoble wretch,

    I am descended of a gentler blood.

    Thou art no father, nor no friend of mine.

SHEPHERD

    Out, out!—My lords, an't please you, 'tis not so.   10

    I did beget her, all the parish knows.

    Her mother liveth yet, can testify

    She was the first fruit of my bachelorship.

WARWICK (*to Joan*)

    Graceless, wilt thou deny thy parentage?

RICHARD DUKE OF YORK

    This argues what her kind of life hath been—   15

    Wicked and vile; and so her death concludes.

SHEPHERD

    Fie, Joan, that thou wilt be so obstacle.

    God knows thou art a collop of my flesh,

---

10 an't] F (and)   13 bachelorship] F (bach'lorship)

2 **kills . . . heart** 'Shakespeare generally uses this common expression with a humorous touch of irony. His shepherds never talk like this one' (Wilson).
   kills breaks

3 **sought every country** searched every region

4 **it is my chance** I have happened
   find thee out discover you

5 **timeless** untimely, premature

6 **I'll . . . thee** As Talbot's son decided to die with his father.

7 **Decrepit** worn with age
   miser wretch

8 **gentler** more noble

9 **friend** (a) friend (b) relation

10 **Out** An expression of indignant reproach (*OED int.* 2).
   an't if it

13 **bachelorship** (a) apprenticeship (as a shepherd; *OED* 4) (b) the state of being

unmarried (*OED* 1). It is not very likely that the Shepherd, however simple and silly, would be bragging about Joan as his illegitimate child, though 'bachelor' has a range of meanings including that of 'unmarried man (of marriageable age)' going back to medieval times. The naivety of his expression might well raise a laugh from York and Warwick (and the audience).

14 **Graceless** unfeeling wretch (*OED adj.* 3)

16 **concludes** settles the matter

17 **obstacle** obstinate, stubborn (*OED a.*). This is a dialect form of the word, no doubt to impersonate the Shepherd's rusticity. Many editions, however, gloss it as a malapropism for 'obstinate'.

18 **collop** A bit of meat, hence a piece of the Shepherd's flesh; used of offspring (*OED* 3b).

And for thy sake have I shed many a tear.
Deny me not, I prithee, gentle Joan.

JOAN

Peasant, avaunt! (*To the English*) You have suborned this man
Of purpose to obscure my noble birth.

SHEPHERD (*to the English*)

'Tis true I gave a noble to the priest
The morn that I was wedded to her mother.
(*To Joan*) Kneel down and take my blessing, good my girl.　　25
Wilt thou not stoop? Now cursèd be the time
Of thy nativity. I would the milk
Thy mother gave thee when thou suck'st her breast
Had been a little ratsbane for thy sake.
Or else, when thou didst keep my lambs afield,　　30
I wish some ravenous wolf had eaten thee.
Dost thou deny thy father, cursèd drab?
O burn her, burn her! Hanging is too good.　　*Exit*

RICHARD DUKE OF YORK (*to guards*)

Take her away, for she hath lived too long,
To fill the world with vicious qualities.　　35

JOAN

First let me tell you whom you have condemned:
Not one begotten of a shepherd swain,
But issued from the progeny of kings;
Virtuous and holy, chosen from above
By inspiration of celestial grace　　40
To work exceeding miracles on earth.

---

37 one] COLLIER (*conj.* Malone); me F

21 **avaunt** go away
　　suborned this man got this man to lie
23 **noble** a gold coin worth about a third of a pound. 'It would represent a significant sum to the Shepherd. He may have misunderstood what Joan has said, or he may be mocking her' (Burns). Simple and silly as he plainly is, it is unlikely that he would be mocking her.
29 **ratsbane** rat poison (usually a preparation of arsenic)
30 **keep** tend, guard
32 **drab** whore
33 **O . . . good** The Shepherd's extreme

response to his daughter's refusal to accept his blessing is appropriately melodramatic in this most melodramatic of Shakespeare's plays; but it does look forward to Lear's confrontation with his daughters. The authorities do, in fact, burn Joan.
37 **one** Malone's conjecture is persuasive as in secretary hand 'one' and 'me' were easy to confuse.
　　swain See note to 4.1.43.
38 **issued** descended
　　progeny of kings royal ancestors
41 **exceeding** extraordinary

I never had to do with wicked spirits;
But you, that are polluted with your lusts,
Stained with the guiltless blood of innocents,
Corrupt and tainted with a thousand vices—   45
Because you want the grace that others have,
You judge it straight a thing impossible
To compass wonders but by help of devils.
No, misconceivèd, Joan of Arc hath been
A virgin from her tender infancy,   50
Chaste and immaculate in very thought,
Whose maiden-blood, thus rigorously effused,
Will cry for vengeance at the gates of heaven.

RICHARD DUKE OF YORK

Ay, ay, (*to guards*) away with her to execution.

WARWICK (*to guards*)

And hark ye, sirs: because she is a maid,   55
Spare for no faggots; let there be enough.
Place barrels of pitch upon the fatal stake,
That so her torture may be shortened.

JOAN

Will nothing turn your unrelenting hearts?
Then, Joan, discover thine infirmity,   60

49 No, misconceivèd,] This edition; ~ˏ ~, F1; ~, ~ˏ F4; ~. ~! STEEVENS; ~, misconceivers ˏ
CAPELL   Arc] ROWE; Aire F   56 enough] F (enow)

42 **do with** 'With a sexual innuendo'
   (Hattaway).
46 **want** lack
47 **straight** immediately
48 **compass wonders** accomplish miracles
49 **misconceivèd** (a) you are mistaken (b)
   bastard. F's punctuation has generated
   consternation among editors.
49 **Joan of Arc** See note to 2.2.20.
51 **in very thought** even in her thoughts
52 **maiden-blood** Burns argues that the
   hyphen (especially) makes this compound
   'suggestive both of the breaking of the
   hymen and of menstrual blood'. Com-
   pounds like this one are, however, commonplace in Shakespeare—maiden pride,
   truth, modesty, honour, pilgrimage,
   shame, etc.—and in *Titus Andronicus*
   'maiden blood' (2.3.232). Whether the
   term comes with or without a hyphen,
   Burns's suggestion strains credibility.
   Joan's claim to virgin status is presumably
   a bare-faced lie, whether or not her later

claim to be pregnant is itself a desperate
lie designed to save herself from the
flames. We know that she has already lied
in this speech—'I never had to do with
wicked spirits' (l. 42)—so more than
likely she is lying about being chaste and
immaculate, and she may well be lying
about being pregnant. It is difficult, however, to maintain a coherent character for
Joan at this stage.
   rigorously effused cruelly spilled
55–8 **because . . . shortened**   'Warwick
   wishes Joan to feel the minimum pain and
   so bids the soldiers to employ the practice
   of making the fire smoke so that the
   victim died of asphyxiation rather than
   burned to death' (Sanders). Such a
   command is in keeping with the general
   presentation of Warwick in this play. (See
   note on Warwick in 'Persons'.)
58 **That so** so that by this means
59 **turn** change
60 **discover** reveal

That warranteth by law to be thy privilege:
I am with child, ye bloody homicides.
Murder not then the fruit within my womb,
Although ye hale me to a violent death.

RICHARD DUKE OF YORK

Now heaven forfend—the holy maid with child?   65

WARWICK (*to Joan*)

The greatest miracle that e'er ye wrought.
Is all your strict preciseness come to this?

RICHARD DUKE OF YORK

She and the Dauphin have been juggling.
I did imagine what would be her refuge.

WARWICK

Well, go to, we'll have no bastards live,   70
Especially since Charles must father it.

JOAN

You are deceived, my child is none of his.
It was Alençon that enjoyed my love.

RICHARD DUKE OF YORK

Alençon, that notorious Machiavel?
It dies an if it had a thousand lives.   75

61 to be thy] F; thy HANMER   68 juggling] F (iugling); ingling OXFORD (*conj.* McKerrow)
70 we'll] F1; we will F2   74 Machiavel] F (Macheuile)   75 an] F (and)

61 **That . . . privilege** that guarantees you by
law to be exempt from the death penalty.
Joan's pregnant condition at least would
allow her first to have the child before
being executed.
62 **homicides** murderers
64 **hale** drag
65 **forfend** forbid
67 **preciseness** morality
68 **juggling** Some editions change 'juggling'
('iugling' in F) to 'ingling' (fondling, caress-
ing; see *OED*, *ingle*, *v.* 1) because *OED*
records no explicitly sexual sense for 'juggling'. York's use of the word, however, clearly implies a sexual extension to
the meaning 'trickery', 'deception', and
that in itself justifies retention of F's word
(i.e. we don't need to emend in order to pick
up the implication). We should also bear in
mind: (a) *OED* is not exhaustive (b) other
reference works, e.g. Partridge, give sexual
connotations for both 'juggling' and 'jug-
gler' citing their appearances in other plays
by Shakespeare. Burns also justifies his
preference for 'ingling' for its homosexual

overtones but these seem to me in this context merely to confuse the issue.
69 **imagine** wonder
refuge final defence
70 **go to** Expressing derisive incredulity, see
'come, come' (*OED v.* 91b).
73 **It . . . love** Joan switches paternity to try
to save the child—if there is one—and
herself. She has the impossible task of
finding one whom the English will find
acceptable. Whether or not she is pregnant is hard to determine. Historically, of
course, Joan was imprisoned long enough
to determine that she was not pregnant.
See note at l. 68.
74 **Machiavel** A nonchalant anachronism
on Shakespeare's part as Niccolò
Machiavelli (1469–1527) was a famous
political writer in the sixteenth century.
The Prince (1513–15) established his name
as a byword for an unscrupulous and
cynical realpolitik. In *Stages of History:
Shakespeare's English Chronicles* (Ithaca,
NY, 1990), Phyllis Rackin argues that the
world of *1 Henry VI* is Machiavellian as

JOAN

  O give me leave, I have deluded you.

  'Twas neither Charles nor yet the Duke I named,

  But Reignier, King of Naples, that prevailed.

WARWICK

  A married man?—That's most intolerable.

RICHARD DUKE OF YORK

  Why, here's a girl; I think she knows not well—   80

  There were so many—whom she may accuse.

WARWICK

  It's sign she hath been liberal and free.

RICHARD DUKE OF YORK

  And yet, forsooth, she is a virgin pure!

  (*To Joan*) Strumpet, thy words condemn thy brat and

    thee.

  Use no entreaty, for it is in vain.   85

JOAN

  Then lead me hence—with whom I leave my curse.

  May never glorious sun reflex his beams

  Upon the country where you make abode,

  But darkness and the gloomy shade of death

  Environ you till mischief and despair   90

  Drive you to break your necks or hang yourselves.

RICHARD DUKE OF YORK

  Break thou in pieces, and consume to ashes,

  Thou foul accursèd minister of hell.

                  ⌈*Exit Joan, guarded*⌉

    Enter the Bishop of Winchester, now Cardinal

91 yourselves.] OXFORD; your selues. *Exit* F 93.1 *Exit . . . guarded*] OXFORD; *not in* F 93.2 *Enter . . . Cardinal*] CAPELL; *Enter Cardinall* F (*after line 91*)

opposed to that of *Richard III* which is providential (see p. 28). In terms of a more precise topicality, '[i]t is very likely that in coupling Alençon with Machiavel the author intended a by-reference to the notorious Duke of Alençon who came a-wooing to Queen Elizabeth in 1579 and aroused the violent antipathy of her subjects' (Tucker Brooke).

78 **prevailed** persuaded me to have sex
80 **here's a girl** This dismissive phrase echoes the only other use of 'girl' in the play, her father's 'good my girl' (5.5.25).
82 **liberal and free** licentious

87–8 **May . . . abode** An echo Southworth argues of lines from Marlowe's 1 *Tamburlaine*: 'For neither rain can fall upon the earth, | Nor sun reflex his virtuous beams thereon' (3.1.51–2).
87 **reflex** shed, throw
88 **make abode** dwell, live
90 **mischief** misfortune
92 **consume** burn up
93 **minister** servant
93.2 *Enter . . . Cardinal* By now any audience would be fully aware that Winchester was a Cardinal so Capell's explanatory direction is not strictly necessary. (See notes to 1.3.19, 4.1.1, 5.1.1.)

WINCHESTER

Lord Regent, I do greet your excellence
With letters of commission from the King.   95
For know, my lords, the states of Christendom,
Moved with remorse of these outrageous broils,
Have earnestly implored a general peace
Betwixt our nation and the aspiring French;
And here at hand the Dauphin and his train   100
Approacheth to confer about some matter.

RICHARD DUKE OF YORK

Is all our travail turned to this effect?
After the slaughter of so many peers,
So many captains, gentlemen, and soldiers
That in this quarrel have been overthrown   105
And sold their bodies for their country's benefit,
Shall we at last conclude effeminate peace?
Have we not lost most part of all the towns
By treason, falsehood, and by treachery,
Our great progenitors had conquerèd?   110
O Warwick, Warwick, I foresee with grief
The utter loss of all the realm of France.

WARWICK

Be patient, York. If we conclude a peace
It shall be with such strict and severe covenants
As little shall the Frenchmen gain thereby.   115

> *Enter Charles the Dauphin, the Duke of Alençon, the*
> *Bastard of Orléans, and Reignier Duke of Anjou*

CHARLES

Since, lords of England, it is thus agreed
That peaceful truce shall be proclaimed in France,
We come to be informèd by yourselves
What the conditions of that league must be.

---

99 aspiring] F; respiring WARBURTON   101 some matter] F; the same CAIRNCROSS   102 travail] F (trauell)   114 severe] F; several CAIRNCROSS (*conj.* Vaughan)   115.2 *Duke of Anjou*] OXFORD; *not in* F

95 **commission** instruction
96 **states** rulers
97 **remorse** pity
  outrageous violent, furious (*OED a.* 2)
100 **train** courtly followers
101 **some matter** i.e. the details of the 'general peace'

102 **travail** toil
  effect outcome
114 **severe** (accented on the first syllable)
  covenants articles of agreement
115 **As** that

RICHARD DUKE OF YORK
> Speak, Winchester, for boiling choler chokes   120
> The hollow passage of my poisoned voice
> By sight of these our baleful enemies.

WINCHESTER
> Charles and the rest, it is enacted thus:
> That, in regard King Henry gives consent,
> Of mere compassion and of lenity,   125
> To ease your country of distressful war
> And suffer you to breathe in fruitful peace,
> You shall become true liegemen to his crown.
> And, Charles, upon condition thou wilt swear
> To pay him tribute and submit thyself,   130
> Thou shalt be placed as viceroy under him,
> And still enjoy thy regal dignity.

ALENÇON
> Must he be then as shadow of himself—
> Adorn his temples with a coronet,
> And yet in substance and authority   135
> Retain but privilege of a private man?
> This proffer is absurd and reasonless.

CHARLES
> 'Tis known already that I am possessed
> With more than half the Gallian territories,
> And therein reverenced for their lawful king.   140
> Shall I, for lucre of the rest unvanquished,

---

121 poisoned] F (poyson'd); prison'd THEOBALD

120 **choler** In Renaissance humoral theory
= bile, the humour that caused anger.
122 **By** at the
  baleful deadly, mortal
123 **Charles** This is the first time in the play
  that the Dauphin is called by his Christian
  name by one of the English characters,
  which might suggest that at this stage the
  English (or Winchester at least) accepts
  Charles as the king of France. Or it might,
  more rewardingly, suggest the opposite.
  That is, Winchester, by not calling Charles
  the Dauphin, is denying him his status as
  heir to the French throne. Strictly speaking, the Dauphin should have been
  regarded as Charles VII all along since
  Charles VI died only two months after
  Henry V, but the English refused to recog-

nize his son as king (until now perhaps).
124 **in regard** in so far as
125 **Of** from (Abbott §109)
  mere pure
  lenity mercy
128 **true liegemen** loyal subjects
132 **still** continue to
134 **coronet** 'Worn by mere nobles and not
  by monarchs' (Hattaway).
136 **privilege** legal status
139 **Gallian** French
140 **reverenced for** honoured as
141–3 **Shall . . . whole** shall I, in order to gain
  possession of those territories I haven't
  already vanquished, give up being lawful
  king of half of France in order to be the
  subordinate ruler of all of France?
141 **lucre** profit

Detract so much from that prerogative
As to be called but viceroy of the whole?
No, lord ambassador, I'll rather keep
That which I have, than, coveting for more,   145
Be cast from possibility of all.

RICHARD DUKE OF YORK

Insulting Charles, hast thou by secret means
Used intercession to obtain a league,
And, now the matter grows to compromise,
Stand'st thou aloof upon comparison?   150
Either accept the title thou usurp'st—
Of benefit proceeding from our king
And not of any challenge of desert—
Or we will plague thee with incessant wars.

REIGNIER (*aside to Charles*)

My lord, you do not well in obstinacy   155
To cavil in the course of this contract.
If once it be neglected, ten to one
We shall not find like opportunity.

ALENÇON (*aside to Charles*)

To say the truth, it is your policy
To save your subjects from such massacre   160
And ruthless slaughters as are daily seen
By our proceeding in hostility;
And therefore take this compact of a truce—
Although you break it when your pleasure serves.

164 serves.] F; ~ . *Aside to the Dauphin* POPE

142 **Detract** take away
143 **but** merely
146 **cast . . . all** excluded from the possibility
of getting anything at all
148 **a league** With whom? Burns suggests
with the Emperor and/or the Pope, but
notes that the accusation is typically vague.
149–50 **And . . . comparison** This is not
clear. The 'matter' is presumably the
terms of the agreement between the
English and the French, though it could
refer to the arrangement between Charles
and his partners in their league. Incited
by his partners to make invidious compar-
isons, Charles may be reluctant now to
agree to the English terms.

151 **the title** i.e. viceroy
usurp'st A strong term here considering
that the title has been granted Charles by
Henry. Nevertheless, as far as the English
are concerned Charles's new (and old)
title is essentially illegitimate as Henry is
France's true king.
152 **Of . . . from** by the kindness of
153 **challenge of desert** claim to the title as by
right or merit
155 **in obstinacy** in being obstinate
156 **To . . . course** to bargain over minutiae
during the negotiating sessions
156 **contract** (accented on second syllable)
162 **proceeding** continuing
163 **compact** agreement

WARWICK

How say'st thou, Charles? Shall our condition stand?   165

CHARLES It shall:

Only reserved you claim no interest

In any of our towns of garrison.

RICHARD DUKE OF YORK

Then swear allegiance to his majesty,

As thou art knight, never to disobey   170

Nor be rebellious to the crown of England,

Thou nor thy nobles, to the crown of England.

     ⌈*They swear*⌉

So, now dismiss your army when ye please.

Hang up your ensigns, let your drums be still;

For here we entertain a solemn peace.   *Exeunt*   175

5.6   *Enter the Earl of Suffolk, in conference with King*
        Henry, and the Dukes of Gloucester and Exeter

KING HENRY (*to Suffolk*)

Your wondrous rare description, noble Earl,

Of beauteous Margaret hath astonished me.

Her virtues, gracèd with external gifts,

Do breed love's settled passions in my heart;

And like as rigour of tempestuous gusts   5

Provokes the mightiest hulk against the tide,

So am I driven by breath of her renown

Either to suffer shipwreck or arrive

Where I may have fruition of her love.

---

165 How ... stand?] POPE; How ... *Charles?* | Shall ... stand? F   172 England.] F; ~.
Charles and the rest give tokens of fealty. JOHNSON   172.1 *They swear*] OXFORD; *not in* F
    5.6] OXFORD; *Actus Quintus.* F   0.1 *King Henry*] OXFORD; *the King* F   *and ... of*] OXFORD;
not in F

165 **condition** arrangement of the treaty
167 **Only reserved** the only reservation
     being
168 **towns of garrison** fortified towns
175 **entertain** accept
5.6.0.1 *conference* conversation
  1 **rare** excellent (*OED a.* 6)
  2 **astonished me** filled me with wonder
  3 **virtues** accomplishments (*OED sb.* 5b)
    external gifts beauty of appearance
  4 **settled** rooted

5–6 **as ... tide** as the strength of stormy
    winds drives the largest ship against the
    tide
  5 **rigour** strength
  6 **hulk** ship
  7 **breath** report. Henry becomes the ship in
    this continuation of the metaphor and
    Margaret love's harbour. But the exten-
    sion of the metaphor is not perfect as
    there is no corresponding term in it for
    'tide'.

SUFFOLK

Tush, my good lord, this superficial tale   10
Is but a preface of her worthy praise.
The chief perfections of that lovely dame—
Had I sufficient skill to utter them—
Would make a volume of enticing lines,
Able to ravish any dull conceit;   15
And, which is more, she is not so divine,
So full replete with choice of all delights,
But with as humble lowliness of mind
She is content to be at your command—
Command, I mean, of virtuous chaste intents—   20
To love and honour Henry as her lord.

KING HENRY

And otherwise will Henry ne'er presume.
(*To Gloucester*) Therefore, my lord Protector, give consent
That Margaret may be England's royal queen.

GLOUCESTER

So should I give consent to flatter sin.   25
You know, my lord, your highness is betrothed
Unto another lady of esteem.
How shall we then dispense with that contract
And not deface your honour with reproach?

SUFFOLK

As doth a ruler with unlawful oaths,   30
Or one that, at a triumph having vowed

---

24 Margaret] F (*Marg'ret*)

10 **superficial** lacking depth or thoroughness
   (*OED a.* 5c)
11 **worthy praise** praise of her real worth
15 **ravish** enchant. But the meaning 'sexual
   violation' is more than elusively present.
   any dull conceit the most unimaginative
   person
17 **full** fully
20 **Command . . . intents** Suffolk's qualifying
   phrase counters (and at the same time
   inflames) the lubricity of his description
   of Margaret's 'choice of all delights'.
   Shakespeare's understanding of the
   erotic attraction of 'virtuous chaste
   intents' is magnificently demonstrated in
   his conception of Angelo's psychology in
   Measure for Measure.

25 **So . . . sin** Gloucester is the first of a line of
   royal counsellors in Shakespeare who tell
   their masters unflattering truths. Their
   apotheosis is Kent in *King Lear*.
   flatter gloss over, extenuate
27 **another lady** i.e. the Earl of Armagnac's
   daughter
28 **dispense with** set aside
   contract (accented on the second syllable)
29 **deface** soil
30 **As . . . oaths** There is nothing of course
   unlawful about Henry's promise of marriage to the Earl of Armagnac's daughter.
   On the contrary, then, as now, were
   Henry a commoner, he would be liable to
   a suit of breach of promise.
31 **triumph** chivalric tournament

To try his strength, forsaketh yet the lists
By reason of his adversary's odds.
A poor earl's daughter is unequal odds,
And therefore may be broke without offence.   35
GLOUCESTER
Why, what, I pray, is Margaret more than that?
Her father is no better than an earl,
Although in glorious titles he excel.
SUFFOLK
Yes, my lord, her father is a king,
The King of Naples and Jerusalem,   40
And of such great authority in France
As his alliance will confirm our peace,
And keep the Frenchmen in allegiance.
GLOUCESTER
And so the Earl of Armagnac may do,
Because he is near kinsman unto Charles.   45
EXETER
Beside, his wealth doth warrant a liberal dower,
Where Reignier sooner will receive than give.
SUFFOLK
A dower, my lords? Disgrace not so your King
That he should be so abject, base, and poor
To choose for wealth and not for perfect love.   50
Henry is able to enrich his queen,
And not to seek a queen to make him rich;
So worthless peasants bargain for their wives,
As market men for oxen, sheep, or horse.
Marriage is a matter of more worth   55
Than to be dealt in by attorneyship.

39 my] F1; ~ good F2   44 Armagnac] F (Arminacke)   46 warrant a] F1; warrant F2
55 Marriage] F1; But marriage F2

32 **lists** tilting area at a tournament
33 **By . . . odds** This analogy only makes
some kind of sense if Suffolk means that
the knight at the tournament should not
engage with an opponent manifestly inferior to him. But I'm not sure that 'his
adversary's odds' can be understood in
this way.
35 **may be broke** (the contract with her) may
be repudiated
38 **glorious titles** (said sarcastically)

40 **King . . . Jerusalem** Empty titles. See note
on Reignier in 'Persons'.
46 **warrant** guarantee
47 **Where** whereas
50 **perfect love** love alone
53 **worthless** extremely poor
56 **by attorneyship** by proxy, by a
go-between. Presumably, Suffolk means
either Gloucester or Exeter and the charge
is obviously ironic considering Suffolk's
role in Henry's infatuation with

Not whom we will, but whom his grace affects,
Must be companion of his nuptial bed.
And therefore, lords, since he affects her most,
Most of all these reasons bindeth us: 60
In our opinions she should be preferred.
For what is wedlock forcèd but a hell,
An age of discord and continual strife?
Whereas the contrary bringeth bliss,
And is a pattern of celestial peace. 65
Whom should we match with Henry, being a king,
But Margaret, that is daughter to a king?
Her peerless feature, joinèd with her birth,
Approves her fit for none but for a king.
Her valiant courage and undaunted spirit, 70
More than in women commonly is seen,
Will answer our hope in issue of a king.
For Henry, son unto a conqueror,
Is likely to beget more conquerors
If with a lady of so high resolve 75
As is fair Margaret he be linked in love.
Then yield, my lords, and here conclude with me
That Margaret shall be queen, and none but she.

60 Most] F; It most ROWE; Which most WILSON; That most CAIRNCROSS   64 bringeth] F;
ybringeth OXFORD *conj.*   72 Will . . . our] F; Answer our POPE; Will answer HUDSON (*conj.*
Steevens)

Margaret, continued in 'Not whom we
will, but whom his grace affects' (l. 57).
But 'attorneyship' as 'legal haggling'
(Sanders) also obtains.

57 **affects** desires
59–60 **since . . . us** the fact that he loves
her outweighs any other reason for our
obedience
62–3 **For . . . strife** As we see in *The First Part
of the Contention* (*2 Henry VI*) and *The True
Tragedy of Richard Duke of York* (*3 Henry
VI*) Henry's wedlock is close to the hell
Suffolk describes. It's arguable, of course,
that Henry's wedlock has been forced on
him by Suffolk—as Henry half intimates
in 'Whether it be through force of your
report' (5.6.79).
62 **wedlock forcèd** enforced marriage
63 **age** lifetime
64 **contrary** 'Pronounced as if written "con-
terary"' (Wilson).

65 **pattern . . . peace** 'image of heavenly harmony' (Sanders). A line of argument that
would appeal to the pious Henry.
68 **feature** figure
69 **Approves** proves
70–2 **Her . . . king** Prophetic words. Margaret
becomes a termagant in *The First Part of
the Contention* (*2 Henry VI*) and *The True
Tragedy* (*3 Henry VI*). (See notes on
Margaret in 'Persons' and to 5.6.62–3.)
Suffolk's lines anticipate the denser praise
of Macbeth for his wife: 'Bring forth men-
children only, | For thy undaunted mettle
should compose | Nothing but males'
(1.7.72–4). Burns notes that, after the
eventual birth of Margaret's son, Yorkist
gossip spread the rumour that Margaret's
undaunted mettle had chosen Suffolk as
the father rather than Henry.
72 **will . . . king** will satisfy our hopes for the
births of royal children
75 **resolve** courage, resolution

KING HENRY

    Whether it be through force of your report,

    My noble lord of Suffolk, or for that   80

    My tender youth was never yet attaint

    With any passion of inflaming love,

    I cannot tell; but this I am assured:

    I feel such sharp dissension in my breast,

    Such fierce alarums both of hope and fear,   85

    As I am sick with working of my thoughts.

    Take therefore shipping; post, my lord, to France;

    Agree to any covenants, and procure

    That Lady Margaret do vouchsafe to come

    To cross the seas to England and be crowned   90

    King Henry's faithful and anointed queen.

    For your expenses and sufficient charge,

    Among the people gather up a tenth.

    Be gone, I say, for till you do return

    I rest perplexèd with a thousand cares.   95

    (*To Gloucester*) And you, good uncle, banish all offence.

    If you do censure me by what you were,

    Not what you are, I know it will excuse

    This sudden execution of my will.

    And so conduct me where, from company,   100

    I may revolve and ruminate my grief.

                               Exit ⌈*with Exeter*⌉

---

82 love] F2; Ioue F1   87 shipping] OXFORD; ~, F; ~ʌ BURNS   90 To cross] F; Across HUDSON (*conj.* Walker)   101.1 *Exit* ⌈*with Exeter*⌉] OXFORD; *Exit.* F

80 **for that** because
81 **attaint** touched, corrupted
84 **such sharp dissension** 'such painful conflict—ironically, given the *dissension* depicted in *The First Part of the Contention* [*2 Henry VI*] and *The True Tragedy* [*3 Henry VI*]. It is as if the King is giving painful birth to future events—which in a sense he is' (Burns)
87 **post** hurry
88 **covenants** terms
    procure contrive
89 **vouchsafe** promise
91 **anointed** i.e. with oil at coronation

92 **charge** money for expenses
93 **a tenth** A tax that amounted to a tenth of income, property, or produce. A tax, Burns notes, that was much resented by taxpayers despite its biblical authority.
95 **rest** remain
96 **offence** objection, hostility
97–8 **If . . . are** judge me as though you were my age not as you are now
97 **censure** judge
99 **sudden** hasty
100 **from company** alone
101 **revolve** turn over in my mind

GLOUCESTER

  Ay, grief, I fear me, both at first and last.   *Exit*

SUFFOLK

  Thus Suffolk hath prevailed, and thus he goes,

  As did the youthful Paris once to Greece,

  With hope to find the like event in love—   105

  But prosper better than the Trojan did.

  Margaret shall now be queen, and rule the King;

  But I will rule both her, the King, and realm.   *Exit*

102 *Exit*] F (*Exit Glocester.*); *Exeunt Gloucester and Exeter* CAPELL

102 **grief** Gloucester uses the word in its more intensified sense as opposed to Henry's conventional expression of the melancholy of love.

104 **Paris . . . Greece** The Trojan Paris abducted Helen, wife of Menelaus, King of Sparta. This act precipitated the war between the Trojans and the Greeks.

105–6 **With . . . did** Suffolk hopes to enjoy Margaret as Paris did Helen but without Paris' tragic fate. In this, of course, he is wrong.

107–8 **Margaret . . . realm** 'The lines act as a kind of commercial for the second part of the play' (Hattaway).

INDEX

This selective index is in the main a guide to words and expressions explained in the Commentary and to names and original works in the Introduction. It excludes the names of modern critics, proverbial and biblical allusions, characters in *1 Henry VI*, and material in the section headings of the Introduction.

Women's Writing 1778–1838

WILLIAM BECKFORD	**Vathek**
JAMES BOSWELL	**Life of Johnson**
FRANCES BURNEY	**Camilla**
	Cecilia
	Evelina
	The Wanderer
LORD CHESTERFIELD	**Lord Chesterfield's Letters**
JOHN CLELAND	**Memoirs of a Woman of Pleasure**
DANIEL DEFOE	**A Journal of the Plague Year**
	Moll Flanders
	Robinson Crusoe
	Roxana
HENRY FIELDING	**Joseph Andrews** and **Shamela**
	A Journey from This World to the Next and **The Journal of a Voyage to Lisbon**
	Tom Jones
WILLIAM GODWIN	**Caleb Williams**
OLIVER GOLDSMITH	**The Vicar of Wakefield**
MARY HAYS	**Memoirs of Emma Courtney**
ELIZABETH HAYWOOD	**The History of Miss Betsy Thoughtless**
ELIZABETH INCHBALD	**A Simple Story**
SAMUEL JOHNSON	**The History of Rasselas**
	The Major Works
CHARLOTTE LENNOX	**The Female Quixote**
MATTHEW LEWIS	**Journal of a West India Proprietor**
	The Monk
HENRY MACKENZIE	**The Man of Feeling**
ALEXANDER POPE	**Selected Poetry**

The Anglo-Saxon World

Beowulf

Lancelot of the Lake

The Paston Letters

Sir Gawain and the Green Knight

Tales of the Elders of Ireland

York Mystery Plays

GEOFFREY CHAUCER **The Canterbury Tales**
Troilus and Criseyde

HENRY OF HUNTINGDON **The History of the English People**
1000–1154

JOCELIN OF BRAKELOND **Chronicle of the Abbey of Bury**
St Edmunds

GUILLAUME DE LORRIS **The Romance of the Rose**
and JEAN DE MEUN

WILLIAM LANGLAND **Piers Plowman**

SIR THOMAS MALORY **Le Morte Darthur**

The Oxford World's Classics Website

www.worldsclassics.co.uk

- Information about new titles
- Explore the full range of Oxford World's Classics
- Links to other literary sites and the main OUP webpage
- Imaginative competitions, with bookish prizes
- Peruse the Oxford World's Classics Magazine
- Articles by editors
- Extracts from Introductions
- A forum for discussion and feedback on the series
- Special information for teachers and lecturers

www.worldsclassics.co.uk

American Literature

British and Irish Literature

Children's Literature

Classics and Ancient Literature

Colonial Literature

Eastern Literature

European Literature

History

Medieval Literature

32014 Oxford English Drama

Poetry

Philosophy

Politics

Religion

The Oxford Shakespeare

A complete list of Oxford Paperbacks, including Oxford World's Classics, Oxford Shakespeare, Oxford Drama, and Oxford Paperback Reference, is available in the UK from the Academic Division Publicity Department, Oxford University Press, Great Clarendon Street, Oxford OX2 6DP.

In the USA, complete lists are available from the Paperbacks Marketing Manager, Oxford University Press, 198 Madison Avenue, New York, NY 10016.

Oxford Paperbacks are available from all good bookshops. In case of difficulty, customers in the UK can order direct from Oxford University Press Bookshop, Freepost, 116 High Street, Oxford OX1 4BR, enclosing full payment. Please add 10 per cent of published price for postage and packing.